Lecture Notes of the Institute for Computer Sciences, Social Informatics and Telecommunications Engineering 275

More information about this series at http://www.springer.com/series/8197

Gervais Mendy · Samuel Ouya ·
Ibra Dioum · Ousmane Thiaré (Eds.)

e-Infrastructure
and e-Services
for Developing Countries

10th EAI International Conference, AFRICOMM 2018
Dakar, Senegal, November 29–30, 2019
Proceedings

 Springer

Editors
Gervais Mendy
LIRT, ESP
Cheikh Anta Diop University
Dakar, Senegal

Samuel Ouya
LIRT, ESP
Cheikh Anta Diop University
Dakar, Senegal

Ibra Dioum
Lab d'Informatique Réseaux
Dakar, Senegal

Ousmane Thiaré
LIRT, ESP
Sanar, Senegal

ISSN 1867-8211   ISSN 1867-822X (electronic)
Lecture Notes of the Institute for Computer Sciences, Social Informatics
and Telecommunications Engineering
ISBN 978-3-030-16041-8   ISBN 978-3-030-16042-5 (eBook)
https://doi.org/10.1007/978-3-030-16042-5

Library of Congress Control Number: 2019934947

This Springer imprint is published by the registered company Springer Nature Switzerland AG
The registered company address is: Gewerbestrasse 11, 6330 Cham, Switzerland

Preface

It is our pleasure to welcome you to the proceedings of the 10th European Alliance for Innovation (EAI) International Conference on e-Infrastructure and e-Services for Developing Countries (AFRICOMM 2018). The conference was held in the city of Dakar, Senegal, during November 29–30, 2018, following up on the success of past editions. The conference constitutes a forum for the presentation and discussion of the latest results in the field of e-infrastructure and e-services for developing countries and aims at providing research directions and fostering collaborations among the participants. Scientists, practitioners, students, and professionals met to discuss research and development of efficient and effective infrastructures and solutions in situations of limited resources.

This year, the technical program of AFRICOMM 2018 drew from a number of submissions: 49 papers submitted from 14 countries representing three regions—West Africa, Europe, and South America. In the first stage, all papers submitted were screened for their relevance and general submission requirements. These manuscripts then underwent a rigorous peer-review process with at least two or three reviewers, coordinated by the international Program Committee. The Program Committee accepted 36 papers out of 49 submissions. The accepted papers provide research contributions in a wide range of research topics including e-health, environment, cloud, VPN and overlays, networks, services, e-learning, agriculture, Iot, social media, mobile communication, and security. We believe that this volume not only presents novel and interesting ideas but also that it will stimulate future research in the area of infrastructures and services. In addition to the high-quality technical paper presentations, the technical program also featured two keynote speeches. The invited speakers were Georgia Bullen from the Open Technology Institute, USA, Stephen Soltesz from Google, USA, and Prof. Yves Le Traon from the University of Luxembourg, Luxembourg. The IMRA (Internet Measurements Research in Africa) workshop at the conference aimed to address various aspects of mechanisms and challenges in measuring Africa's Internet topology.

Coordination with the conference manager, Andrea Piekova, was essential for the success of the conference. It was also a great pleasure to work with such an excellent organizing team, all of who did their parts in organizing and supporting the conference. We wish to express our deepest gratitude to all the Technical Program Committee, led by our TPC co-chairs, Dr. Ibra Dioum and Prof. Ousmane Thiaré, the publication chair, Dr. Tegawendé Bissyandé, and the external reviewers for their excellent job in the paper review process. Without their help, this program would not have been possible. We take this opportunity to thank all the presenters, session chairs, and participants for their presence at the conference, many of whom travelled long distances to attend this conference and make their valuable contributions.

We strongly believe that the AFRICOMM conference provides a good platform for all researchers, students, developers, and practitioners to discuss all scientific and technological aspects relevant to e-infrastructure and e-services for developing countries. We also expect that future AFRICOMM conferences will be as successful and stimulating as indicated by the contributions presented in this volume.

November 2018

Gervais Mendy
Samuel Ouya
Ibra Dioum
Ousmane Thiaré

Organization

Steering Committee

Imrich Chlamtac
Bruno Kessler — University of Trento, Italy

Organizing Committee

General Chair

Gervais Mendy — Université Cheikh Anta Diop de Dakar/Ecole Supérieure Polytechnique, Senegal

General Co-chairs

Yannis Manoussakis — Université Paris Sud 11/Laboratoire de Recherche en Informatique (LRI), France
Samuel Ouya — Université Cheikh Anta Diop de Dakar/Ecole Supérieure Polytechnique, Senegal

TPC Co-chairs

Ousmane Thiaré — Université Gaston Berger de Saint-Louis, Sénégal
Ibra Dioum — Université Cheikh Anta Diop de Dakar/Ecole Supérieure Polytechnique, Senegal

Sponsorship and Exhibit Chair

Alex Corenthin — Université Cheikh Anta Diop de Dakar/Ecole Supérieure Polytechnique, Senegal

Local Chair

Ahmath Bamba Mbacké — Université Cheikh Anta Diop de Dakar/Ecole Supérieure Polytechnique, Senegal

Workshops Chair

Tegawendé F. Bissyandé — University of Ouagadougou/University of Luxembourg, Burkina Faso/Luxembourg

Publicity and Social Media Co-chairs

Mirna Dzamonja — University of East England, UK
Jeanne Roux Ngo Bilong — Université Cheikh Anta Diop de Dakar/Ecole Supérieure Polytechnique, Senegal

Publications Chair

Tegawendé F. Bissyandé   University of Ouagadougou/University
                                of Luxembourg, Burkina Faso/Luxembourg

Web Chair

Ibrahima Gaye   Université Cheikh Anta Diop de Dakar/Ecole
                                Supérieure Polytechnique, Senegal

Posters and PhD Track Chair

Ahmath Bamba Mbacké   Université Cheikh Anta Diop de Dakar/Ecole
                                Supérieure Polytechnique, Senegal

Panels Chair

Bi Tra Gooré   Institut National Polytechnique FélixHouphouet
                                Boigny, INPHB, Ivory Coast

Demos Chair

Meissa Mbaye   Université Gaston Berger de Saint-Louis, Sénégal

Tutorials Chair

David Edgar Moussavou   Institut National de la Poste et des Technologies de
                                l'Information et de la Communication INPTIC,
                                Gabon

Technical Program Committee

Ousmane Thiaré   Université Gaston Berger de Saint-Louis, Sénégal
Ibra Dioum   Université Cheikh Anta Diop de Dakar/Ecole
                                Supérieure Polytechnique, Senegal
Tiguiane Yélémou   Université Nazi Boni, Burkina Faso
Moussa Lo   Université Virtuelle du Senegal, Senegal
Ahmed Kora   Ecole Supérieure Multinationale des
                                Télécommunications, Senegal
Bernard Pottier   Université de Brest, France
Maissa Mbaye   Université Gaston Berger de Saint Louis, Senegal
Cheikh Ba   Université Gaston Berger de Saint Louis, Senegal
Ndeye Massata Ndiaye   Université Virtuelle du Senegal, Senegal
Idy Diop   Université Cheikh Anta Diop de Dakar, Senegal
Gaoussou Camara   Université Alioune Diop de Bambey, Senegal
Waldir Moreira   AICOS, Fraunhofer, Portugal
Davy Edgard Moussavou   INPTIC, Gabon
Gayo Diallo   Université de Bordeaux, France
Idrissa Sarr   Université Cheikh Anta Diop de Dakar, Senegal

Contents

Main Tracks

A Superdirective and Reconfigurable Array Antennas for Internet of Vehicles (IoV)

Mamadou Mansour Khouma[1(✉)], Ibra Dioum[1], Idy Diop[2], Lamine Sane[2], Kadidiatou Diallo[1], and Samuel Ouya[1]

[1] Laboratoire d'Informatique, Réseaux et Télécoms (LIRT),
Ecole Supérieure Polytechnique (ESP), Dakar, Senegal
`mansourkhouma@gmail.com`
[2] Laboratoire d'Imagerie Médical et Bio-Informatique (LIMBI),
Ecole Supérieure Polytechnique (ESP), Dakar, Senegal
`http://www.esp.sn`

Abstract. This paper presents a prototype design of antenna for Internet of Vehicle (IoV). Presented antennas is an array of 4 quarter-wavelength monopoles set in form of lozenge and on an infinite ground plan confused to vehicle's roof. Monopoles are 2 by 2 linearly associated and are excited properly in magnitude and phase. Uzkov's theory is first used to calculated appropriate excitation coefficients and after that Non-Foster circuit theory for determining an impedance-matched with a Z_{load}. Ansys HFSS is used for simulations and results show a good bandwidth and particulary a superdirectivity in order of 8.2 dB reconfigurable in a desired and useful direction.

Keywords: Superdirectivity · End-fire · Impedance active · IoV

1 Introduction

Internet of Things (loT) is a world-wide network connecting all the smart objects together. It is the way in which all things are enabled to talk with each other. Whenever those smart things being connected over internet are restricted to only vehicles, then it is called as Internet of Vehicles (loV). According to recent predictions, 25 billion things will be connected to the Internet by 2020, of which vehicles will constitute a significant portion. In other words, IoV is the largest communication network between vehicles, vehicles owners and some third parties like servers ect. So we establish:

- A communication between the vehicles and the vehicle owners for:
  - security alert about the vehicle,
  - damage alert about the vehicle,
  - the attributes like proximity, tyre pressure and vehicle lock ect.

© ICST Institute for Computer Sciences, Social Informatics and Telecommunications Engineering 2019
Published by Springer Nature Switzerland AG 2019. All Rights Reserved
G. Mendy et al. (Eds.): AFRICOMM 2018, LNICST 275, pp. 3–11, 2019.
https://doi.org/10.1007/978-3-030-16042-5_1

- A communication between vehicles defining
  - Proximity between the vehicles,
  - The immediate surroundings of a vehicle through onboard cameras,
  - Speed of vehicles within a particular radius of the vehicle under consideration,
  - Tyre burst related accidental information.
- A communication between vehicles and a centralized server which stores and analyzes datas for the suitable solution
- A communication between server and third parties like police patrol, ambulance, fire-engine, etc.

By that way, detected and been capable to react either to a security inside and outside the vehicle or a human proximity or a thief in a seconde need absolutely an array antennas able to respond to that high need of permanent and directive connectivity.

In that paper, we present an array of 4 quater-wavelength monopoles antennas superdirective with radiation pattern reconfigurable in a desired direction. This array antenna maximize directivity as never obtained before for the least latence but allow to cover all 360 deg azimutal plane with radiation pattern reconfigurability in a desired direction.

2   Antenna Design

Our design is a 4 quarter-wavelength monopoles 0.1λ spaced. Antennas are made cooper and set on an electrically perfect ground plane considered as infinite as a vehicle's roof; we consider for that case a circular ground plane with a radius of 250 mm. We work it in a test simulation at 5.9 GHz resonant frequency with simulator Ansys HFSS.

2.1   Theorical Study

Theorical works on the design of materials giving a high directivity with moderate dimensions has since ever undergo a lot of research. Osseen has been the first most prolific one to state in his old works that it is theorically possible to have a directivity as high as desired with an antenna of arbitrarily small dimensions. Later, Harrington showed so far that a directivity in order of $N^2 + N$ can be obtained with a single antenna, with N representing the highest mode [1]. However, the most significant works for a large number of associating radiators is from Uzkov [2], who states in 1946 the possibility to make a superdirectivity, meaning a directivity in order of N^2, by linearly associating a larger number N of closely spaced radiating elements. Then, he showed from Eqs. (1) and (2) defined below that this directivity can be in a desired direction (θ, ϕ) when radiating elements are properly excited.

$$a_{0n} = H_{mn}^{*}{}^{-1}.e^{-jkr_0.r_m}.f_m^{*}(\theta_0, \phi_0).f_n(\theta_0, \phi_0) \tag{1}$$

$$H_{mn} = \langle \tfrac{1}{4\pi} \rangle \frac{\int_0^{2\pi} \int_0^{\pi} f_m(\theta, \phi) . f_n^*(\theta, \phi) e^{jk\vec{r} . (r_m - r_n)}}{\sin \theta \partial \theta \partial \phi} \qquad (2)$$

where

$f(\theta, \phi)$ is the far field in the (θ, ϕ) direction.
$f(\theta_0, \phi_0)$ is the far field in the (θ_0, ϕ_0) direction.
$\vec{r}$ is the far field vector in the (θ, ϕ) direction.
$\vec{r_0}$ is the far field vector in the (θ_0, ϕ_0) direction.
(θ_0, ϕ_0) is the direction (θ, ϕ) where the maximum directivity of the system can be attained.

Matrix a_{0n} are so far currents excitation coefficients which allow to properly excite antennas in magnitude and phase in order to maximize directivity in a desired direction (θ_0, ϕ_0).

Since ever then multiples works have been done theorically and in practice, proving that properly excited in magnitude and phase array antennas closely spaced can provide superdirectivity.

Altshuler et al. show in multiples and significants works with two quarter-wavelength monopoles 0.5λ spaced and excited by currents equal in magnitude but specifically different in phase, that a directivity of about 7.5 dB in the end-fire direction can be reached. This directivity slowly increases as the spacing is decreased and approach values of 9.8 dB and 10.5 dB for respectively distance of 0.2λ and 0.1λ between monopoles [3–5]. In an other way, in some others works, Donnell et al. shows that a similar gain of about 10 dB can be approximately reached when one of two elements 0.145λ spaced is excited and the other one shorted as a "parasitic" element [4]. Best et al. confirm this late possibility in 2 straight-wire monopoles by matching one of his this by an impedance [7].

However, since we state in our previous works that it is more benefit in term of mutual coupling for a two linearly associated monopoles to match antenna with Non-Foster circuit [11], we calculated appropriate Z_{load} (R, L and C) as defined below by Eqs. (3) and (4) to charge one antenna and to excite the other one by unity. For that, first is calculated the impedance matrix H_{mn} used it secondly to determine the current excitation coefficients a_{0n}. All calculations and simulations are done with Ansys HFSS, mostly for far fields determination in all values of (θ, ϕ).

$$Z_{active} = \frac{V(n)}{I(n)} = Z_{nn} + \sum_{\substack{m=1 \\ m \neq n}}^{N} Z_{mn} I_m \qquad (3)$$

$$Z_{load} = -Z_{active} \qquad (4)$$

Matrix Z_{mn} calculated give a Z_{load} with 37.191Ω resistance and $13.4485nF$ capacitor in a parallel circuit. So, as shown in Fig. 1, a design of 4 monopoles 2 by 2 linear is proposed. Monopoles are each others 0.1λ spaced in form of lozenge. The ones in the x-axis are 0.245λ length and excited by a unit power but the others in y-axis are 0.24λ length and charged with Z_{load}. So the principle

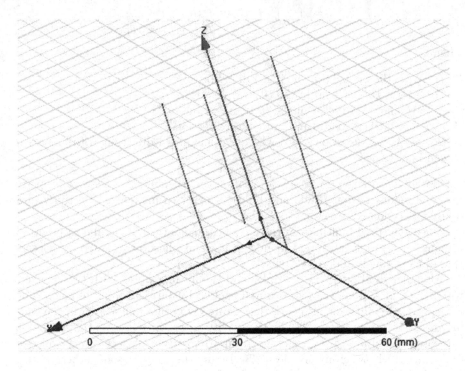

Fig. 1. Antennas geometry

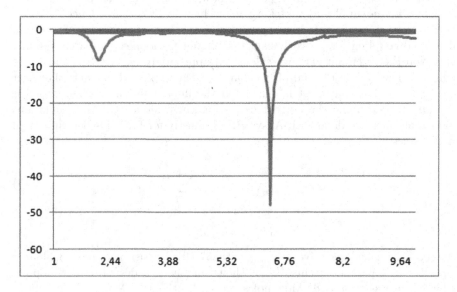

Fig. 2. S-Parameters

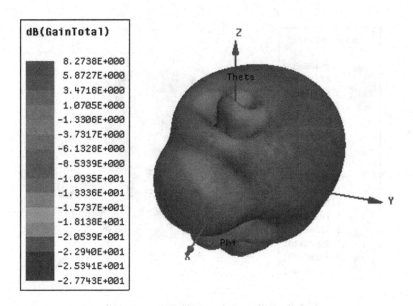

Fig. 3. Situation 1: 3D radiation pattern

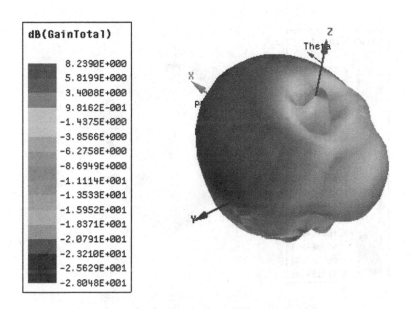

Fig. 4. Situation 2: 3D radiation pattern

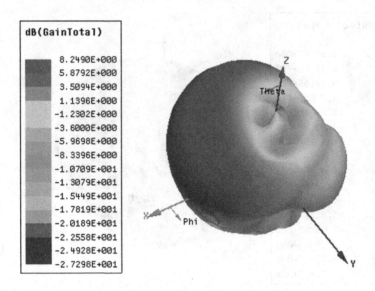

Fig. 5. Situation 3: 3D radiation pattern

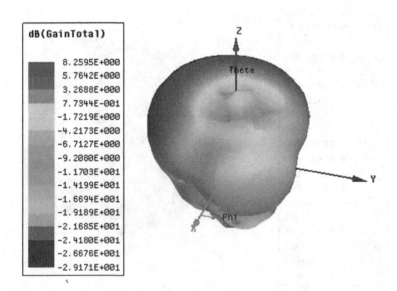

Fig. 6. Situation 4: 3D radiation pattern

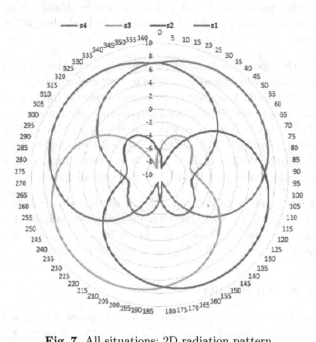

Fig. 7. All situations: 2D radiation pattern

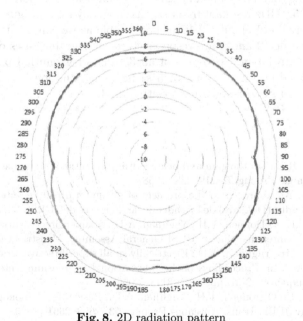

Fig. 8. 2D radiation pattern

is at any cases the monopoles 1 and 3 in x-axis are both excited at same time
and at any cases the monopoles 2 and 4 in y-axis are both charged at same time.
So situations are:

- Situation 1: Monopole 1 is excited by a unit power, Monopole 2 is charged
  by Z_{load} and monopoles 3 and 4 act like parasitic elements.
- Situation 2: Monopole 1 is excited by a unit power, Monopole 4 is charged
  by Z_{load} and monopoles 2 and 3 act like parasitic elements.
- Situation 3: Monopole 3 is excited by a unit power, Monopole 2 is charged
  by Z_{load} and monopoles 1 and 4 act like parasitic elements.
- Situation 4: Monopole 3 is excited by a unit power, Monopole 4 is charged
  by Z_{load} and monopoles 1 and 2 act like parasitic elements.

All of this cases are programmable by pin diodes which allow to swich all
the time in the needed (θ_0, ϕ_0) direction until covered all 360 deg azimuthal
plan for reconfigurability. Cases as stated below by Figs. 7 and 8 are in order to
reconfigure the directivity, for 360 deg azimuthal plan coverage.

2.2 Simulation and Results

The antenna array as stated is an array of 4 monopoles 0.1λ spaced one from
others, in form of lozenge and linear 2 by 2 associated. Monopoles are used for
IoV at 5.9 GHz frequency (5.875 GHz–5.905 GHz), with an infinite ground plan
confused to vehicule's roof. Simulations are done as stated with Ansys HFSS.

Results show that array antenna has good bandwidth of more than 30 MHz
and −20 dB at 5.9 GHz resonant frequency as shown by Fig. 2. Figures 3, 4, 5 and
6 relate a supergain of about 8.2 dB reconfigurable as we can see it in a desired
direction. Situations 2 and 4 are respectively reconfigurable cases of situations
1 and 3. Thus, an integral coverage of all 360 deg of azimuthal plan is so far
obtained as stated by Figs. 7 and 8 with $s1$ meaning situation 1, $s2$ situation 2,
$s3$ situation 3 and $s4$ corresponding to situation 4.

References

1. Harrington, R.F.: On the gain and beamwidth of directional antennas. IRE Trans.
   IEEE Antennas Propag. **6**, 219–225 (1958)
2. Uzkov, A.I.: An approach to the problem of optimum directive antennae design.
   Comptes Rendus (Doklady) de l'Academie des Sciences de l'URSS **53**, 35–38 (1946)
3. Altshuler, E.E., O'Donnell, T.H., Yaghjian, A.D.: A superdirective array using very
   small genetic antennas. Digest, URSI General Assembly, Maestricht (2002)
4. O'Donnell, T.H., Yaghjian, A.D.: Electrically small superdirective arrays using parasitic elements. In: Proceedings of the International Symposium Antennas Propagation, Albuquerque NM, pp. 3111–3114 (2006)
5. Altshuler, E.E., O'Donnell, T.H., Yaghjian, A.D., Best, S.R.: A monopole superdirective array. IEEE Trans. Antennas Propag. **53**, 2653–2661 (2005)
6. Altshuler, E.E., ODonnell, T.H., Yaghjian, A.D.: Electrically smallsupergain end-
   fire arrays. Radio Sci. **43**, 1–13 (2008)

7. Best, S.R.: An efficient impedance matched 2-element superdirective array. In: Digest National Radio Science Meeting, p. 462, July 2005

8. Best, S.R.: The performance properties of electrically small resonant multiple-arm folded wire antennas. IEEE Antennas Propag. Mag. **47**, 13–27 (2005)

9. Abdullah, H., Ala, S., Sylvain, C., Pigeon, M., Mahdjoubi, K.: A design methodology for electrically small superdirective antenna arrays. In: IEEE Antennas and Propagation Conference (LAPC), 2014 Loughborough (2014)

10. Abdullah, H., Ala, S., Sylvain, C.: A design methodology for impedance-matched Electrically Small parasitic superdirective arrays. In: 2015 IEEE International Symposium Antennas and Propagation & USNC/URSI National Radio Science Meeting, pp. 1852–1853 (2015)

11. Abdullah, H.: Contribution to the study of directive or wide-band miniature antennas with non-Foster circuits (2016)

12. Yaru, N.: A note on super-gain antenna arrays. Proc. IRE **39**, 1081–1085 (1951)

13. Lim, S., Ling, H.: Design of a closely spaced, folded Yagi antenna. IEEE Antennas Wireless Propagat. Letts. **5**, 302–305 (2006)

14. Haviland, R.P.: Supergain antennas: possibilities and problems. IEEE Antennas Propagat. Mag. **37**, 13–26 (1995)

Online Courseware Development in Public Universities in Uganda: The Precepts of Active, Passive and Exclusive Participation

Benedict Oyo[1]([⊠]), Gilbert Maiga[2], and Paul Birevu Muyinda[3]

[1] Department of Computer Science, Gulu University, Gulu, Uganda
b.oyo@gu.ac.ug
[2] Department of Information Technology, Makerere University,
Kampala, Uganda
gmaiga@cis.mak.ac.ug
[3] Department of Open and Distance Learning, Makerere University,
Kampala, Uganda
mpbirevu@cees.mak.ac.ug

Abstract. Irrespective of the maturity or infancy of e-learning adoption in a university, the academic staff always have varying levels of commitment to online courseware development and delivery. Some will be actively engaged, some will be passively involved while others will remain ignorant about online courses' issues. This paper investigates trends in online courseware development in Uganda and classifies emerging participation levels into three, namely active, passive and exclusive engagement. The latter clustering followed a survey of 120 academic staff from six public universities in Uganda, with general findings indicating low participation of instructors in courseware development. For instance, whereas 60% of the respondents had been trained in the use of authoring tools, only about a half of them had continued to use these tools for courseware development. Essentially, the survey revealed that the variation in courseware development engagement is caused by both the individual and institutional strengths (active case) and weaknesses (passive and exclusive scenarios). As such, institutional support strategies for improvement in courseware development for each of these three categories are explored and discussed. Future researchers are encouraged to test the developed institutional support strategies in their e-learning or blended learning practice.

Keywords: E-learning · Blended learning · Courseware development · University education

1 Introduction

Electronic courseware development and delivery has become a prominent educational reform practice in university education. This has taken different forms including: the use of presentations (PowerPoint, video lessons and animated lessons); the use of learning management systems (e.g. Moodle, Edmodo, itslearning, Blackboard, WebCT, etc.); and more recently, the use of massive open online courses platforms

© ICST Institute for Computer Sciences, Social Informatics and Telecommunications Engineering 2019
Published by Springer Nature Switzerland AG 2019. All Rights Reserved
G. Mendy et al. (Eds.): AFRICOMM 2018, LNICST 275, pp. 12–23, 2019.
https://doi.org/10.1007/978-3-030-16042-5_2

(e.g. Coursera, edX, Udacity, etc.). While these developments are driven by the increasing use ICTs in education, academics still face challenges in acquiring and mastering information technology skills for the purposes of teaching. In this paper, we investigate these challenges and provide strategies for improvement that caters for the varying individual and institutional readiness levels in online courseware development.

Courseware development and delivery through a learning management system (LMS) is viewed as the basic requirement for teaching and learning in the 21st century universities [2, 16, 18]. As university education transitions to online and blended teaching modes, there is much discussion and pessimism of the capacity of universities in the developing countries to cope [4, 19]. Achieving this transition is particularly difficult because the traditional face-to-face contact mode cannot easily be adapted to online contexts without sufficient investment in ICT resources and competency of the instructors. This paper further examines the individual and institutional support strategies aligned with the real-life scenarios of active, passive and exclusive participation in online courseware development.

As a means of meeting the increasing demand for higher education and enroll more students, public universities in Uganda are encouraged to change the method of delivery of content from the traditional face-to-face (F2F) to online course delivery [6, 7]. Online course delivery as part of e-learning involves the use of computer networks to support teaching and learning remotely. Aside from the high demand for university education that can be met through e-learning, this mode of pedagogy is considered beneficial to higher education for a number of reasons including:

- Empowering institutions to flexibly support student learning without restriction of time, space and enrolment numbers [2].
- Supporting individual learner differences, allowing students to study at their pace and priorities [11, 12, 15].
- Compensating for scarcities of resources (e.g., human, lecture space, etc.) in traditional settings [8, 19].
- Building horizontal relationships amongst learners through discussion forums and vertical relationship with lecturers through online facilitation [20].
- Creating rapid and inexpensive distribution channels of educational courseware and knowledge within and outside national boundaries [1, 9].
- Improving the quality of teaching and learning as it complements the face-to-face teaching approaches [2, 15].

In contrast, online courseware development is affected by several factors that should holistically be managed for its successful utilization. These factors include: varied instructor readiness, institutional support challenges, technology accessibility issues, course content quality benchmarks, varied levels of demand for online courses by students and the society, and pedagogical changes in online delivery. Related research within East African countries have found some of these factors to be more profound. For instance, [10, 15], in their studies on the status and challenges of e-learning in Kenya, reveal that ICT infrastructure and technical competency are most significant challenges to e-learning adoption in Kenya. The same challenges with addition of staff and student attitude are reported in the Ugandan case study involving leading universities in e-learning adoption [5, 13]. The Tanzanian case is not any different as research finding indicate similar challenges of human resource capacity, infrastructural capacity and technology use capacity [3, 4, 19].

Whereas universities continue to engage in courseware development in order to create their own online learning resources for their students, the level of participation by staff varies significantly as already highlighted. This variation including lack of participation in courseware development forms the central thesis of this paper and hence clustered as active, passive and excluded courseware developers' continuum. In the subsequent sections of this paper, we further explore the latter typology.

1.1 The Problem

Online courseware development is a laborious, knowledge intensive, technology driven and costly process. It is capable of high returns on investment when tied to a business model and can also become a waste of money, intellectual energy and valuable time when un-strategically managed. In the context of the public universities in Uganda, there are a number of positive trends such as the existence of functional LMSs, improving technical competency and percentages of staff trained in courseware development. Despite these positive trends, the existing volume and quality of courseware developed is still low [5, 6]. Moreover, most of the courses with online presence are in the engineering and related fields where information technology competency is highest [13]. A number of the universities with functional LMSs do not have any courses in the Arts and Humanities fields. Furthermore, evidence of staff trained in online courseware development but have never hosted any course in an LMS are the norm rather than the exception. These realities point to the need to cluster courseware developers according to their levels of activeness and design appropriate strategies for support as addressed in this paper.

1.2 Objective

This research sought to investigate the state of online courseware development in public universities in Uganda in order to identify gaps and develop strategies for improvement. In pursuing this aim, a two sequence research strategy was followed. Firstly, inclusivity and/or exclusivity in online courseware development was investi-gated at university level. This was connected to the second sequence where inclusivity was further probed at individual/instructor level to reveal activeness or passiveness in online courseware development. The strategy implied here is reflected in Fig. 1 in the next section.

2 Courseware Development Participation Indicators

The level of participation in courseware development in this research was investigated in the context of institutional initiatives and individual effort. The institutional initia-tives include: hosting the preferred LMS; creating and facilitating a technical support unit for the LMS and other courseware development issues; training of staff on the use of LMS and course authoring tools; providing on-campus internet access through local area network (LAN) and/or wireless (Wi-Fi) points; supporting off-campus internet access through prepaid internet modems; development and implementation of online/blended learning policy; and provision of computers (desktop or laptop) for staff.

Similarly, individual/instructor initiatives in online courseware development include: gaining skills on the use of LMS and course authoring tools; delivering at least one course on the institutional/university LMS; sharing content developed through an online space; seeking support from the university's technical team; and collaborating with peers on online courses development. Figure 1 therefore shows how institutional and individual initiatives are responsible for active or passive engagement in courseware development.

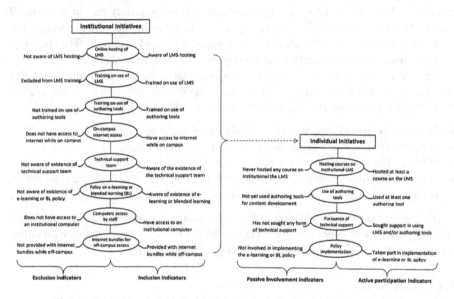

Fig. 1. Institutional and individual indicators of courseware development

The indicators of courseware development in Fig. 1, further guided the design of the data collection instrument as presented in the next section.

3 Methodology

3.1 Location of the Study

The study was carried out as part of the project title "Training for sustainable spatially enabled e-services in Uganda," under the objective "to increase on the number of e-learning researchers and managers in Public universities in Uganda." As such, the study sample was derived from academic staff of public universities in Uganda that have been in existence for over five years. Six public universities suited this criterion including, Makerere University, Gulu University, Kyambogo University, Makerere University Business School (MUBS), Busitema University and Mbarara University of Science and Technology (MUST).

3.2   Study Population, Validity and Reliability

A cross-sectional survey was used in this study. The survey focused on three related areas, namely, online courseware development, online course facilitation and online course management. An estimated number of academic staff in the aforementioned public universities was 4221. Using [7]'s sample determination table, a sample size of 351 respondents was targeted. However, 120 valid questionnaire responses were returned representing a response rate of 34%. The reason for this low response rate was due to the delay in validating the questionnaire and subsequently end of semester II examinations for 2016/2017 academic year coincided with the actual survey. The returned questionnaires were checked for completeness and accuracy. The data was analyzed using SPSS to generate the descriptive and inferential statistics.

Prior to the actual survey, validity of the questionnaire was established by engaging one expert in e-learning from each of the participating university. These experts examined the questionnaire against four criteria as outlined by [14]:

- Whether the questionnaire measured what it intended to measure;
- Whether the questionnaire represented the desired content;
- Whether the questionnaire was appropriate for the target population; and
- Whether the questionnaire was comprehensive enough to collect all the information needed to address the purpose and goals of the study.

Following successful validation of the questionnaire, a pilot test was carried out and reliability coefficient (alpha) of 0.89 obtained for the section of questionnaire on online courseware development issues in Ugandan public universities.

3.3   Study Sample

The sample comprised of 120 academic staff distributed as 40% (48) from Gulu University, 18% (22) from Kyambogo University, 11% (13) from MUBS, 11% (13) from Busitema University, 10% (12) from MUST and 10% (12) from Makerere University. The variation of responses was due to the timing of data collection whereby the participating universities were at various stages of administering end of semester II examinations for 2016/2017 academic year. The departments from which the respondents were drawn are shown in Fig. 2.

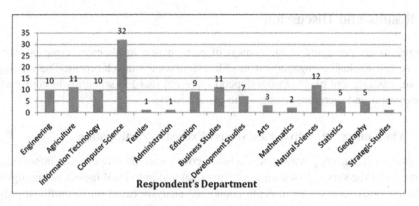

Fig. 2. Distribution of respondents by department

Other respondents' details on age group, gender, tenure are given in Table 1.

Table 1. Background characteristics of the respondents

Item	Category	Frequency	Percent
Respondents' age group	Up to 30	30	25.0
	31 to 35	23	19.2
	36 to 40	31	25.8
	41 to 45	15	12.5
	46 to 50	11	9.2
	Above 50	10	8.3
Gender of the respondents	Female	35	29.2
	Male	85	70.8
Academic rank of the respondents	Teaching assistant	21	17.5
	Assistant lecturer	25	20.8
	Lecturer	53	44.2
	Senior lecturer	19	15.8
	Associate professor	1	0.8
	Professor	1	0.8

Since this paper is particularly informed by the section on online courseware development in the survey, the level of participation in online courseware development was determined by the indicators in Fig. 1 based on institutional and individual factors.

4   Results and Discussion

The results are presented in the context of participation levels categorized as active, passive and exclusive engagement in online courseware development. The typology (active, passive, and excluded developers) represent real-life scenarios in courseware development and therefore worthy of in-depth analysis.

4.1   The Context of Active, Passive and Exclusive Participation

The context of active, passive and excluded courseware developers was informed by the results of the survey based on the institutional and individual factors as highlighted in the previous section. An in-depth contextual analysis based on institutional provisions for online courseware development is given in Table 2. From the institutional perspective, the active and passive participation is not important but rather inclusion and exclusion in institutional initiatives for improving online courseware development, as depicted in Table 2.

Table 2. Institutional initiatives for inclusive and exclusive participation in online courseware development

Institutional initiative	Inclusive context	Exclusive context
Online hosting of LMS	52% (62) respondents agreed that an institutional LMS was installed and hosted online. The actual LMS varied from Moodle, Edmodo, itslearning, WebCT to the one for Mbarara University (MUST-LMS)	48% (58) were not sure of LMS installation and hosting
Training on use of LMS	38% (46) had basic training in the respective LMS. Another 8 staff (7%) trained themselves on the use of LMS	57% (68) never participated in any LMS training
Training on use of authoring tools	60% (72) had training on use of authoring tools. This percentage includes those trained through institutional arrangements and others who learnt on their own. The authoring tools identified include: MS PowerPoint, eXe, Adobe Presenter, EasyProf, FlashPoint and Elucidat	40% (48) were ignorant about authoring tools and had never received training on their use
Provision of on-campus internet access	77% (92) could access internet on campus. There were general complaints of slow connectivity during peak hours (mid-morning to afternoon – 10:00 am to 4:00 pm)	23% (28) did not have access to internet while on campus

(*continued*)

Table 2. (*continued*)

Institutional initiative	Inclusive context	Exclusive context
Provision of off-campus internet access through prepaid internet bundles	100% not applicable response was recorded. Some of the respondents indicated that this is an unrealistic dream. Others provided resentful comments such as "only possible when university top management becomes: *.com, digital not analogue, and honest with ICT budgeting*"	
Existence of technical support team	46% (55) agreed that a technical support team exists. Some of the respondents further emphasized that the support team is centralised and easily accessible by staff of different units	54% (65) were either not sure of their existence or affirmed their non-existence
Existence of policy on e-learning or blended learning	20% (24) confirmed existence of guiding policy for e-learning or blended learning	80% (96) were not aware of the existence of such policy
Provision of computers for staff	18% (21) have access to a university's desktop or laptop computer. However, 74% (89) own laptops which they use for personal and university work	82% (99) do not have access to a university computer

Further analysis of the inclusive context was needed to discover the level of participation in online courseware development in terms active or passive engagement. To achieve this, the survey sought to investigate the level of individual participation by examining four constructs: actual use of the institutional LMS; actual use of course authoring tools; pursuance of technical support in using LMS and/or authoring tools; and engagement in e-learning/blended learning policy implementation. The results of this investigation are presented in Table 3 based on the corresponding sample sizes from the inclusive context in Table 2. For this reason, the respective sample sizes are indicated in Table 3.

Arising from the results in Table 3, we can safely suggest that measurement of the level of instructors' personal effort in courseware development can be determine by three constructs: actual use of the institutional LMS to host courses; actual use of course authoring tools to develop content; and pursuance of technical support in using LMS and/or authoring tools. The fourth construct on the level of engagement in e-learning/blended learning policy implementation, does not have definite boundaries and therefore not significant in establishing instructors' personal effort in courseware development.

Having discussed results of inclusivity and exclusivity in courseware development at institutional/university level as well as through instructors' efforts, the next section examines how instructors should be supported by their universities to become proactive courseware developers.

Table 3. Individual initiatives for active and passive participation in courseware development

Individual initiative	Active participation indicators	Passive participation indicators
Use of institutional LMS (n = 62)	53% (33) had hosted a course on the existing LMS. The 33 includes 25 out of 46 who were trained in existing LMS and 8 who learnt LMS by themselves. Further analysis on the extent of use of personal internet data for an online course activity while off-campus revealed that 14 out of 33 (42%) were involved	47% (29) were trained but never used the existing LMS on their own
Use of course authoring tools for content development (n = 72)	54% (39) used at least one course authoring tool for content development	46% (33) had not used these tools despite having undertaken basic training
Pursuance of technical support (n = 55)	42% (23) had sought support in using LMS and/or authoring tools	58% (32) had not sought any form of technical support in relation to courseware development
Engagement in e-learning/blended learning policy implementation (n = 24)	All the 24 (100%) indicated that they were not engaged in e-learning/blended learning policy implementation. Some supported this position with claims that the policies were either externally sourced through consultancy or merely drafted under donor funded projects for accountability but without involvement of the potential instructors	

4.2   Institutional Strategies for Improvement of Online Courseware Development

The low/no adoption of e-learning is directly linked to the level of scarcity of online courseware managed by the respective university. While the results of this study indicate that majority of the academic staff are either not engaged in online courseware development (excluded) or are at least passively involved, the ultimate goal is ensuring active participation in courseware development. This section therefore, presents a generic strategy for sustaining active online courseware development through institutional initiatives that uniquely support each category of developers (active, passive or excluded). Figure 3 represents this strategy as informed by the research results, e.g., the ratio of instructors engaged in courseware development decreases from the excluded category towards the active category. It (Fig. 3) depicts the relative distribution of staff by their prominence in online courseware development. Institutional initiatives are indicated in circles and aligned with corresponding context of courseware developers.

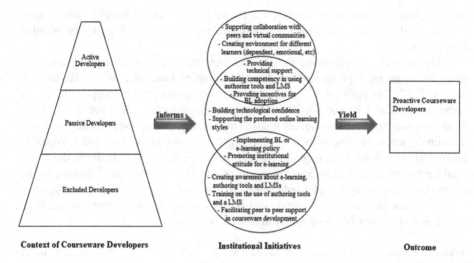

Fig. 3. Institutional strategies for attainment of proactive online courseware developers

Cross-cutting initiatives such as access to computers and provision of internet have been ignored in Fig. 3. The intersections of circles in Fig. 3 depict initiatives that are relevant to the interfacing categories. For instance the interface between active and passive developers reflects a real-life scenario where the referred active developer at the lower end of this continuum needs equal support as the developers with passive characteristics.

5 Conclusion

Online courseware development and delivery stems from instructors mastering content design techniques and delivery strategies that promote student-to-student interaction with minimal instructor intervention. Its success in turn depends on the university's commitment to technical and financial support for instructors. In the context of Uganda and emerging from this study, online courseware development has remained generally low despite evidence of mastery of content design techniques. Indeed 60% of the respondents in this study had been trained in the use of authoring tools and yet only about half of those trained had continued to use these tools to develop their content. This and related findings as presented in this paper confirmed the claim that irrespective of the maturity or infancy of e-learning adoption in a university, the academic staff will have varying levels of commitment to electronic courseware development and delivery. This research further contends that effective improvement strategies in courseware development by instructors are those that are unique to participation levels of the instructors, i.e., the active, passive and excluded instructors' clusters of courseware developers should be supported differently. This unique intervention strategy as articulated in Fig. 2, depicts the role of universities in supporting their instructors to become proactive courseware developers. Future researchers are therefore encouraged to test the developed institutional support strategies in their e-learning or blended learning practice.

This study also confirms the previous findings that the engineering and other sciences fields are more prominent in e-learning adoption than the Arts and Humanities fields [13, 17]. For instance, while 72 instructors had under gone training on the use of authoring tools and 39 had actually used the authoring tools, only 5 out of 39 (13%) were from the Arts and Humanities fields. This notable finding suggests that passivity in online courseware development is more significant among the Arts and Humanities instructors than those from engineering and other sciences fields. As such, there is a need for further investigation into the causes of variation in e-learning adoption by the different professionals in higher education. At the same time, qualitative studies that document best practices by the prominent online courseware developers especially in Africa would inform future adoption in related contexts.

Acknowledgment. The authors wish to acknowledge full funding for this research under Makerere University and Sweden Bi-lateral Programme (Mak-Sida) Grant No. 321.

References

1. Chang, C., Shen, H., Liu, E.Z.: University faculty's perspectives on the roles of e-instructors and their online instruction practice. Int. Rev. Res. Distrib. Learn. **15**(3), 72–92 (2014)
2. Garrison, D.R.: E-Learning in the 21st Century: A Framework for Research and Practice. Taylor & Francis, London (2011)
3. Kafyulilo, A., Fisser, P., Pieters, J.M., Voogt, J.: ICT use in science and mathematics teacher education in Tanzania: developing technological pedagogical content knowledge. Australas. J. Educ. Technol. **31**(4), 381–394 (2015)
4. Kafyulilo, A., Fisser, P., Voogt, J.: Factors affecting teachers' continuation of technology use in teaching. Educ. Inf. Technol. **21**(6), 1535–1554 (2016)
5. Kasse, J.P., Balunywa, W.: An assessment of e-learning utilization by a section of Ugandan universities: challenges, success factors and way forward. In: 5th Annual Conference on ICT for Africa 2013, Harare, Zimbabwe (2013)
6. Kahiigi, E.K.: A collaborative e-learning approach: exploring a peer assignment review process at the university level in Uganda (Doctoral thesis). Stockholm University (2013)
7. Krejcie, R.V., Morgan, D.W.: Determining sample size for research activities. Educ. Psychol. Measur. **30**, 607–610 (1970)
8. Makokha, G.L., Mutisya, D.N.: Status of e-learning in public universities in Kenya. Int. Rev. Res. Open Distrib. Learn **17**(3), 341–359 (2016)
9. Maqableh, M.M., Mohammed, A.B., Masa'deh, R.: Modeling teachers influence on learners self-directed use of electronic commerce technologies outside the classroom. Sci. Res. Essays **11**(3), 29–41 (2016)
10. Mutisya, D.N., Makokha, G.L.: Challenges affecting adoption of e-learning in public universities in Kenya. E-Learn. Digit. Media **13**(3–4), 140–157 (2016)
11. Oyo, B., Kalema, B.M.: MOOCs for Africa by Africa. Int. Rev. Res. Open Distance Learn. **15**(6), 1–13 (2014)

12. Oyo, B., Kalema, B.M.: A preliminary speech learning tool for improvement of African English Accents. In: International Conference on Education Technologies and Computers. IEEE Explore Digital Library, Lods, Poland (2014)
13. Oyo, B., Kalema, B.M., Byabazaire, J.: The MOOC for in-service teachers: the Uganda case and lessons for Africa. Span. J. Pedagog. (Rev. Esp. Pedagog.) **75**(266), 121–141 (2017)
14. Radhakrishna, R.B.: Tips for developing and testing questionnaires/instruments. J. Ext. **45** (1), 1–4 (2007)
15. Tarhini, A., Hone, K., Liu, X.: Factors affecting students' acceptance of e-learning environments in developing countries: a structural equation modeling approach. Int. J. Inf. Educ. Technol. **3**(1), 54–59 (2013)
16. Tarus, J., Gichoya, D., Muumbo, A.: Challenges of implementing e-learning in Kenya: a case of Kenyan public universities. Int. Rev. Res. Open Distrib. Learn. **16**(1), 120–141 (2015)
17. Zhu, C., Mugenyi, K.J.: A SWOT analysis of the integration of e-learning at a university in Uganda and a university in Tanzania. Technol. Pedagog. Educ. **24**(5), 1–19 (2015)
18. Medvedeva, T.A.: University education: the challenges of 21st century. Soc. Behav. Sci. **166**, 422–426 (2015)
19. Mwapachu, J.V.: Challenges facing African and Tanzanian universities. Development **53**(4), 486–490 (2010)
20. Gillett-Swan, J.: The challenges of online learning: supporting and engaging the isolated learner. J. Learn. Des. **10**(1), 20–30 (2017)

A 2-hop LoRa Approach Based on Smart and Transparent Relay-Device

Mamour Diop[1,2], Congduc Pham[1], and Ousmane Thiaré[2(⊠)]

[1] University of Pau, Pau, France
{mamour.diop,congduc.pham}@univ-pau.fr
[2] Gaston Berger University, Saint-Louis, Senegal
{mamour.diop,ousmane.thiare}@ugb.edu.sn

Abstract. LoRa is designed for long-range communication where devices are directly connected to the gateway, which removes typically the need of constructing and maintaining a complex multi-hop network. Nonetheless, even with the advantage of penetration of walls, the range may not sometimes be sufficient. This article describes a 2-hop LoRa approach to reduce both packet losses and transmission cost. To that aim, we introduce a smart, transparent and battery-operated relay-device that can be added after a deployment campaign to seamlessly provide an extra hop between the remote devices and the gateway. Field tests were conducted to assess relays' ability to automatically synchronize to the network without advertising their presence.

Keywords: LoRa · Low-power IoT · Low-cost IoT · Multihop · Rural area

1 Introduction

Recently, Low-Power Wide Area Networks (LPWAN) play a key role in the IoT maturation process. This is a broad term for a variety of technologies enabling power efficient wireless communication over very long distances. For instance, technologies based on ultra-narrow band modulation (UNB) – e.g. SigFox[TM] – or Chirp Spread Spectrum modulation (CSS) – e.g. LoRa[TM] [1] – have become de facto standards in the IoT ecosystem. Most of LPWAN technologies can achieve more than 20 km in line of sight (LOS) condition and they definitely provide a better connectivity answer for IoT by avoiding complex and costly relay nodes to be deployed and maintained.

In the context of the H2020 WAZIUP project, we developed a low-cost IoT generic platform using LoRa technologies to enable the deployment of smarter rural applications in developing countries [2–4]. From this generic platform, significant real-world deployments have already been realized in Senegal (Cattle Rustling), Ghana (Fish Farming, AGRI-Weather) and Pakistan (AGRI-Soil with multi-level soil moisture for crop irrigation). The feedback we have with these

G. Mendy et al. (Eds.): AFRICOMM 2018, LNICST 275, pp. 24–34, 2019.
https://doi.org/10.1007/978-3-030-16042-5_3

rural deployment experiences is that even with the longer range offered by LoRa, we encountered in many of these deployment campaigns connectivity issues with the gateway: there is no or very weak connectivity. In fact a clear LOS communication is hardly the case. Reasons are numerous, for instance there are constraints on gateway and gateway's antenna placement – e.g. in the farm office with power supply and wired Internet access – and some devices can become very isolated from the vast majority of deployed devices even when device's antenna can be placed higher than the device itself. Regarding the transmission power, there are also limitations in many countries. But it is not always desirable to use higher transmission power levels as it would result in severe energy consumption and reduced battery lifetime.

In this paper, we investigate a 2-hop LoRa approach to extend the coverage area and solve these connectivity issues of real-world IoT deployment in rural environments. Very importantly, the main objective is to design a smart, transparent and battery-operated intermediate node – *relay-device* – that can be added after a deployment campaign to seamlessly provide an extra hop between the remote devices and the gateway. That can significantly improve reliability of data transmission in non-line of sight (NLOS) scenarios. The remainder of the paper is organized as follows. Section 2 provides an analysis to the LoRa technology multi-hop schemes proposed in the literature. Section 3 describes the proposed approach based on low-power relay nodes. Performance evaluation and measurement results are discussed in Sect. 4. We conclude in Sect. 5.

2   Related Work

In a multi-hop network, every node can communicate with the other nodes. They provide routing for each other so that two nodes physically far away from each other can communicate using nodes between them. Multi-hop alternatives for the uplink in LPWANs technologies – particularly in LoRaWAN – have not yet been profoundly explored in networks operating at sub-1 GHz. In exploring the limits of LoRaWAN, the authors in [5] addressed the use of TDMA and multi-hop solutions in order to reduce both the number of collisions and the needed transmission power. From there, an extension of LoRaWAN protocol enabling relay-based communication to extend coverage area without the need of gateways and increase the performances of end-devices, is designed in [6]. LoRaBlink [7] is a protocol on top of LoRa's physical layer designed to support reliable and energy efficient multi-hop communications. Time synchronization is used to define slotted channel access. While downlink messages are distributed through flooding, nodes use a directed flooding approach for uplink communications.

In [8], the author analyzed the impact of introducing a forwarder node between an end device and a gateway to improve the range and quality of LoraWAN communications. As the forwarder aims to reduce the power consumption on end-nodes, the work mainly focused on an energy analysis. However, the device receive window must be increase to manage downlink packets. In [9], authors investigated the combination of LoRa and concurrent transmission

(CT) – a recently proposed multi-hop protocol that can significantly improve the network efficiency – to realize a reliable CT-based LoRa multi-hop network. On the one hand, the long transmission range of LoRa ensures the indoor coverage, reduces the number of redundant relay nodes, and keeps the transmission power small. On the other hand, the CT protocol helps to realize a simple but efficient one-to-any fast packet broadcast by introducing the synchronized packet collisions. [10] proposed a multi-hop uplink solution compatible with LoRaWAN specification, which can act as an extension to already deployed gateways. End nodes transmit data messages to intermediate nodes, which relay them to gateways by choosing routes based on a simplified version of DSDV routing.

These works propose centralized approaches controlled by the gateway, the network server or the initiator, which sets up both the relays and the devices through MAC commands. In addition, the synchronization mechanism requires message exchanges. In most of these works, end-devices act as relay depending on the needs. [10] introduces routing nodes (RNs) for relaying uplink packets from leaf nodes. However, RN are assumed not energy constrained. The purpose of this work is not to use the multi-hop concept to propose a new LPWAN protocol or an extension of LoRaWAN, to solve the aforementioned problems. In rural applications context for developing countries, gateways cannot act as relays as in [11] where more gateways are deployed to ensure multi-hop communication. This would lead to additional deployment cost since a gateway (a) is considered to be appropriately placed close to an unlimited power source, (b) requires an IP connection to operate and (c), is the most expensive component, even in our low-cost context. End-devices also don't act as relays because they run very specific sensing template code and must be placed according to sensing needs.

3   Smart 2-hop Relaying Mode

3.1   Principle

Our 2-hop LoRa relay approach consists, in a post deployment addition, of an extra hop between some end-devices and the gateway in NLOS scenarios as illustrated in crop fields for the Nestlé WaterSense project (the left part of Fig. 1). We propose to have *relay-devices* which are special low-power nodes different from the end-devices. However, similar to the end-devices, relay-devices are built from the generic hardware IoT platform but their unique feature is to extend the network coverage by performing data receive and forward operations. It does not take part in any data sensing, data processing nor aggregation tasks. One of the major considerations of a relay-device should be its appropriate location to cover areas where connectivity is either lost or unstable after the network deployment. We designed the relay-device with the following requirements:

– *Low power*: relay-devices are battery-powered and therefore energy constrained. Their hardware should be very similar to those used by low-cost end-devices (i.e. Arduino Pro Mini). Being battery-operated they must not listen continuously, which basically would make them gateways and this is not what we wanted.

- *Smart*: relay-devices must be designed to remain in low-power mode most of the time. Obviously, they have to wake-up at appropriate moments to catch uplink transmissions from specific devices in order to perform the relay operation. This is the major consideration of this work since missing uplink packets would make the network less reliable than it was. Therefore, a relay-device must be able to switch from sleep to active mode by smartly analyzing the uplink pattern from end-devices.
- *Transparent*: relay-device nodes must be transparent to the rest of the network: (*a*) no change in hardware or software for end-devices or gateway to support the new 2-hop approach; (*b*) no additional signaling traffic between relay-devices and end-devices or gateway. Therefore, end-devices should not be aware of the 2-hop relay mode, nor to perform any discovery and binding process to a nearby relay-device. A relay-device also does not need to exchange parameters with the gateway for advertising its presence. And, on the gateway side, no scheduling mechanism for end-devices and relay-devices is required. The presence of a relay-device should not be detected although it is possible to indicate its presence with a specific flag in the packet header if it is desirable for the gateway (or network server) to have this information. Our approach is not centralized, neither at gateway nor network server as in related works. Furthermore, withdrawal or failure of a relay-device leaves the network as functional as before its integration in the network.

Figure 1 (right part) depicts our proposed architecture for providing a transparent 2-hop LoRa connectivity. The red link means no direct connectivity while the orange link means unstable connectivity. The green links means high quality, stable connectivity. The main advantage of our smart relaying mode is related to the relay-devices' ability to adapt in complete autonomy and transparency to their deployment environment. This is realized with an autonomous and asymmetric synchronization approach. It does not require any time synchronization between the nodes, e.g. end-devices behavior remain unchanged as indicated previously. It is asymmetric in the sense that the synchronization work is done by the relay-device: only the relay-device has to learn wakeup periods of the end-devices.

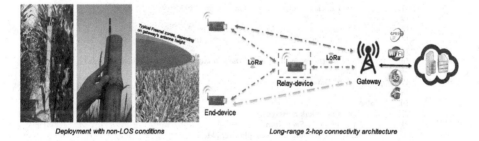

Deployment with non-LOS conditions   Long-range 2-hop connectivity architecture

Fig. 1. Long-range 2-hop connectivity architecture (Color figure online)

3.2 Implementation

In a typical telemetry LoRa network, end-devices periodically measure environmental parameters and transmit data packets mostly at regular intervals, being most of the time in deep sleep mode where they are unable to send nor receive packets. We assume here that end-devices wake-up at least once every 60 min – from their local time as there is no synchronicity between end-devices. When inserted in an existing LoRa network, relay-devices are responsible for forwarding data packets from end-devices with no prior knowledge of how end-devices will wake up. Once deployed, a relay-device discovers end-devices in its vicinity and will build a wake-up table. When powered-on a relay-device first runs an observation phase and then a data forwarding phase.

Observation Phase. This phase consists in observing network traffic for a specified duration. At start-up a relay-device usually does not know when it will receive an uplink packet, so it needs to be in receive mode during all the observation duration. This observation duration must be long enough to catch the various uplink packets from end-devices. Assuming that end-devices wake-up at least once every 60 min, an observation duration longer than 60 min is sufficient. The Arduino Pro Mini running at 3.3 V consumes about 15 mA in continuous receive mode, so 60 min of observation has little impact on the battery lifetime as this process is only performed on startup.

Algorithm 1. Observation stage

Input:
> *obs_duration*: appropriate time interval for observing the network traffic in order to synchronize with it.
> *Bound_Devices*: an array of bounded devices to the relay device, sorted in receiving packet order.

```
 1: while obs_duration ≥ current_time do
 2:    pkt ← Receive_Pkt()
 3:    if pkt ≠ Null then
 4:       if pkt.Src ≠ Gateway_id then
 5:          //it's an uplink data
 6:          if not is_bound(pkt.Src) then
 7:             //it's the first reception for this device
 8:             Record_Device(Bound_Devices, pkt.Src, timestamp)
 9:          else
10:             /*send back downlink message to pkt.Src device, if present. Then delete
                it */
11:             Send_Back_Downlink_Msg(Bound_Devices, pkt.Src)
12:
13:             /*update pkt.Src device in Bound_Devices */
14:             Update_Device(Bound_Devices, pkt.Src, timestamp)
15:          end if
16:          /*forward the received packet to the gateway by keeping the original packet
             header */
17:          Forward_Data(pkt)
18:
19:       else
20:          //it's a downlink message
21:          if is_bound(pkt.Src) then
22:             Store_Msg(Bound_Devices, pkt.Src, pkt.Msg)
23:          else
24:             Record_Device_Msg(Bound_Devices, pkt.Src, timestamp, pkt.Msg)
25:          end if
26:       end if
27:    end if
28: end while
```

In the observation phase a relay-device receiving an uplink packet from an end-device (a) sends to the device any cached downlink packet; (b) records relevant information of the uplink packet such as the source address, the timestamp, etc.; (c) forwards the packet to the gateway by keeping the original packet header. Note that packet forwarding from a relay-device to the gateway during this phase can also allow for transmission quality comparison if the original packet also reach the gateway. Note that the relay-device can also receive downlink packets from the gateway to specific devices. In this case, the relay-device stores this downlink packet and will forward it at the next uplink transmission from the corresponding end-device. The reason to do so, instead of directly forwarding the downlink packet to the device is because the device receive window probably does not take into account the additional delay introduced by the relay-device. This process, detailed in Algorithm 1, is repeated throughout the observation duration. When the observation phase is over the relay-device switches to the data forwarding phase.

Data Forwarding Phase. With the collected information during the observation phase, the relay-device is now able to determine wakeup time of the end-devices in its vicinity. It can determine its own activity schedule in each round to wakeup at appropriate moment to forward uplink packets and remain in low-power mode the rest of the time. Algorithm 2 shows how the sleep period is computed. In the data forwarding phase the relay-device determines the wakeup time T (using *sleep_period*) to wake up to catch the next uplink packet from device i. The relay-device will actually wake up at $T - T_{guard}$ in order to compensate for clock drift. T_{guard} must be kept small to reduce energy consumption. Once awake, the relay-device enters in receive mode waiting for the next uplink packet until time $T + T_{guard}$. When receiving the uplink packet it simply forwards the packet to the gateway. If it receives a downlink message in the receive window, it stores the message until the next upstream transmission from the corresponding end-device as explained previously for the observation phase. Note that upon reception of the uplink packet from device i the relay-device updates the wakeup time of device i accordingly to take into account any clock drift.

Algorithm 2. Computing sleep period

Input:
    Bound_Devices: an array of bound devices to relay device, sorted in receiving packet order.

Output:
    sleep_period

1:   min_time ← Bound_Devices[0].timestamp + Bound_Devices[0].reception_interval
2:   **for** i = 1 to *Bound_Devices.size()* **do**
3:     tmp_time ← Bound_Devices[i].timestamp + Bound_Devices[i].reception_interval
4:     min_time ← min(min_time, tmp_time)
5:   **end for**
6:   sleep_period ← min_time − current_time
7:   **return** sleep_period

---

4   Performance Evaluation

We performed field tests to assess the performance of the proposed 2-hop approach for increasing network reliability. The university campus with many veg-
etation and sparse buildings has been our rural environment of deployment.
We deployed at first a network consisting of 3 soil humidity end-devices (ED_1,
ED_2, ED_3) and one gateway (GW), as shown in the part (a) of Fig. 2. GW
was placed in the car park of the Faculty of Science and Technology, two meters
above the ground. End-devices have different transmission intervals: ED_1 sends
a data packet every 3 min, ED_2 every 5 min, ED_3 every 7 min. LoRa parameters
of the experiments were chosen as follows: spreading factor of 12, bandwidth
of 125 kHz and coding rate of 4/5, which is the usual setting that provides the
longest range. The transmission power for all tests has been set to 14dBm and all
measurements were done in NLOS conditions. Two relevant metrics have been
identified: packet error rate and power consumption.

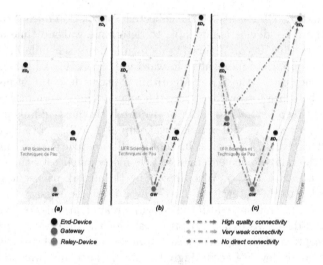

Fig. 2. Deployment scenarios

4.1   Network Reliability

In our first set of experiments, we adopted the standard LoRa one-hop communication scheme. In order to determine the network reliability, we simply measured the number of correctly received packets by the gateway GW. Results, as
shown in Fig. 3 (left part), indicate connectivity state of end-devices compared
to GW: high quality for ED_1, very weak for ED_2, no direct for ED_3. Part (b)
of Fig. 2 illustrates this network connectivity state. In order to assess our 2-hop
approach, we introduced a relay-device (RD) in the network so as to obtain
stable connectivity between the isolated nodes (ED_2, and ED_3) and RD, but
also between RD and the gateway. The part (c) of Fig. 2 shows this deployment

scenario. We first tested the network reliability by adopting our 2-hop approach with the relay-device in continuously listening mode waiting for uplink packets. As expected, results validated that adding an extra hop between isolated end-devices and gateway can significantly increase the link reliability in high packet error rate conditions. Indeed, all packets sent by end-devices have been correctly received on the gateway side. That means packets from ED_2 and ED_3 were catched by RD and forwarded to the gateway. Finally, we conducted tests to assess the relay-device's ability to automatically synchronize with the rest of the network by fully embracing our smart and transparent 2-hop approach.

As the relay-device should wakeup in advance (by T_{guard}) to safely catch the next uplink packet, the value for T_{guard} is critical: a too small value may make the relay-device miss the uplink packet while a too large value would consume more energy. By varying T_{guard} from 0 s to 5 s we measured the ratio of correctly received packets at the gateway, i.e. uplink packets catched and forwarded by RD to GW. The observation phase is set to 15 min and at least two packets per end-devices are expected to be catched. We ran each test during 1 h: the first 15mn for the observation phase and the remaining time for the data forwarding phase. Results are shown in Fig. 3 (right part).

Of course, during the observation phase all packets sent by the end-devices are correctly received and forwarded to the gateway. As shown in Fig. 3 (right part), there is a total desynchronization of the relay-device with the rest of the network when $T_{guard} \leq 2$ s. This is mainly due to the fact that the wakeup of the relay-device takes some time. When $T_{guard} \in [3, 4]$, synchronization is partial: at least 50% of packets can be correctly received but not more than 70%. This is due to a small clock drift. When $T_{guard} = 5$ s, it is possible to obtain 100% of correctly received packets.

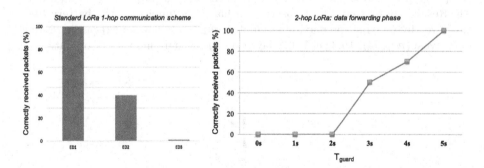

Fig. 3. Correctly received packets

4.2 Discussion on Radio Duty-Cycle

In Europe, electromagnetic transmissions in the unlicensed EU 863-870 MHz Industrial-Scientific-Medical (ISM) band used by Semtech's LoRa technology falls into the Short Range Devices (SRD) category. The ETSI EN300-220-1 document [12] specifies for Europe various requirements for SRD devices, especially those on radio activity. Basically, a transmitter is constrained to 1% duty-cycle (i.e. 36 s/h) in the general case. This duty cycle limit applies to the total transmission time, even if the transmitter can change to another channel. Obviously, a relay-device that has to forward uplink packets from n end-devices will have to transmit at least n packets/hour. Assuming that each transmission takes about 1.5 s (approximatively the time-on-air of a 20-byte payload packet – header included) then a relay-device can relay 24 packets/hour which is quite sufficient in most of the cases.

4.3   Discussion on Energy Consumption

The Arduino Pro Mini (in its 3.3 V and 8 MHz) with the LoRa module draws about 40 mA when active (taking a measure) and transmitting. The whole process takes about 2 s. In deep sleep mode, the board draws 5uA. Therefore an end-device that sends 1 measure every hour consumes in the average $(2 * 40\,mA + 3598 * 0.005\,mA)/3600 = 0.0272\,mA$. We have real devices running on AA batteries that have been functioning for more than 2 years at time of writing.

Observation Stage Consumption. In the observation phase, a relay-device must remain in continuous receive mode for a specified duration D_{obs}. The Arduino Pro Mini running at 3.3 V consumes about 15 mA in receive mode. Then, it has to forward the packet which has an energy consumption similar to the transmission from an end-device, i.e. 40 mA during 2 s. At the relay-device level, managing 3 isolated end-devices by relaying for example 3 packets for a duration $D_{obs} = 60\,min$, consumes in average $((3 * 2\,s) * 40\,mA + (3600\,s - 3 * 2\,s) * 15\,mA)/3600\,s = 15.04\,mA$. The left part of Fig. 4 shows the average consumption of a relay-device that relays n packets for a duration of 1 h, 2 h and 3 h. Results shows that 1 h of observation has little impact on the battery lifetime even by relaying the maximum number of packets per hour regarding radio duty-cycle ($n = 24$): 15.33 mA, 6.8 days over more than one year of operation.

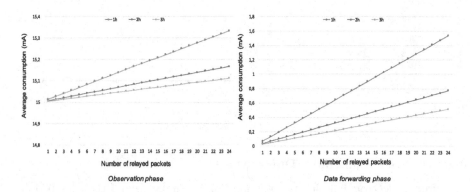

Fig. 4. Average consumption

Data Forwarding Stage Consumption. Regarding the relay-device, it has to wakeup and forward uplink packets. For each wakeup, there will be a continuous receive during $2 * T_{guard} = 10s$ at the maximum, then it has to forward the packet during 2 s. Therefore, for each uplink packet, the relay-device consumes in the average $(10 s * 15\,mA + 2 s * 40\,mA)/12 s = 19.16\,mA$. If we assume that a relay-device is used to relay a very small number of isolated end-devices, e.g. 3 end-devices, then the number of wakeup can be limited. For instance, with 3 end-devices, the relay-device has to wakeup 3 times per hour resulting in an average consumption of $(3 * 12 s * 19.16\,mA + (3600 s - 3 * 12 s) * 0.005\,mA)/3600 s = 0.196\,mA$ which still allows for more than a year of operation. As illustrated in the right part of Fig. 4, results are even better when the relay-device has to wakeup 3 times every 2 h (more than 2 years of operation) or every 3 h (more than 4 years of operation). While maintaining at least one year of operation, a relay-device can relay 4 packets if it has to wakeup every hour, 8 packets every 2 h and 13 packets every 3 h.

5   Conclusion

We described in this article a 2-hop LoRa approach to increase reliability in real-world deployment scenarios. We proposed a smart, transparent and low-power relay-device that can be added seamlessly into an existing LoRa network, between some end-devices and the gateway. Both end-devices and gateway are unchanged and can work with or without the relay-device. The experimental tests demonstrate the effectiveness of our approach, especially validating the relay-device's ability to synchronize in an automatic and asymmetric way with the rest of the network. Using low-cost hardware for the relay-device, the experimental tests also show that a safety wakeup of 5 s prior to the expected time of receiving an uplink packet is sufficient to significantly increase the network reliability.

Acknowledgments. This work was supported by WAZIUP project which was funded by EU Horizon 2020 research and innovation program under grant agreement No 687607.

References

1. Semtech: LoRa modulation basics. Rev.2 (2015)
2. Pham, C., Rahim, A., Cousin, P.: Low-cost, long-range open IoT for smarter rural African Villages. In: Proceedings of ISC2, Italy (2016)
3. Pham, C., Dupont, C.: IoT, an affordable technology to empower African addressing needs in Africa. In: Proceedings of the IST-Africa, Namibia (2017)
4. Pham, C., Rahim, A., Cousin, P.: WAZIUP: a low-cost infrastructure for deploying IoT in developing countries. In: Proceedings of AFRICOMM, Ouagadougou (2016)
5. Adelantado, F., Vilajosana, X., Tuset, P., Martinez, B., Melia-Segui, J.: Understanding the limits of LoRaWAN. IEEE Commun. Mag. **55**, 34–40 (2017)

6. Sanfratello, A.: Enabling relay-based communication in LoRa networks for the Internet of Things. Master thesis. University of Pisa, Italy (2016)
7. Bor, M., Vidler, J.-E., Roedig, U.: LoRa for the internet of things. In: Proceedings of EWSN 2016, Graz, Austria, 361–366 (2016)
8. De Velde, B.-V.: Multi-hop lorawan: including a forwarding node (2017)
9. Liao, C.-H., Zhu, G., Kuwabara, D., Suzuki, M.: Multi-Hop LoRa networks enabled by concurrent transmission. IEEE Access **5**, 21430–21446 (2017)
10. Dias, J.: LoRaWAN multi-hop uplink extension. Comput. Sci. **130**, 424–431 (2018)
11. Lundell, D.: Ad-hoc network possibilities inside LoRaWAN. Thesis. Lund U (2017)
12. ETSI: Electromagnetic compatibility and Radio spectrum Matters (ERM); Short Range Devices (SRD); Radio equipment to be used in the 25 MHz to 1 000 MHz frequency range with power levels ranging up to 500 mW; Part 1: Technical characteristics and test methods (2012)

Towards a Public Participatory GIS-Based Framework for Municipal Solid Waste Management

Irene Arinaitwe$^{(\boxtimes)}$, Gilbert Maiga, and Agnes Nakakawa

School of Computing and Informatics Technology, Makerere University,
Kampala, Uganda
irenedats@gmail.com, gilmaiga@gmail.com,
agnesnakakawa@gmail.com

Abstract. Municipal solid waste management (MSWM) is a global contro-versial environmental challenge globally. Participatory approaches in planning and decision making have been advanced as part of the strategies in order to attain sustainable waste management systems. However, achieving meaningful public participation for such systems is still a challenge. The need therefore remains to explore different ways in which public participation in MSWM can be enhanced. The use of Public Participatory GIS (PPGIS) has a potential to increase public participation in MSWM. However, its use still face hurdles from the social, institutional and political aspects that limit "public participation". This paper reports on a study that explores the social, political and institutional challenges affecting public participation in MSWM problem in Uganda. An exploratory study was conducted in Uganda's central region with key stake-holders in MSWM. The results were analyzed using thematic analysis based on the Enhanced Adaptive Structuration Theory (EAST-2) framework. The results show that knowledge and awareness, participant attitudes, institutional practices, political will and legislation are important for successful MSWM participatory planning process.

Keywords: Public participation · Geographic information systems ·
Participatory planning · Municipal solid waste management · Framework

1 Introduction

Participatory approaches in environmental planning are popular due to their support for sustainable development. The shift from top-down to bottom–up approaches that are participatory is motivated by the need to take care of location-specific concerns of stakeholders in policy making in a bid to solve environmental, economic and social problems [1]. Participatory approaches are relevant because environmental problems cannot be solved by only authorities, but by engaging stakeholders in the causes and solutions so as to secure democratic legitimacy of decision-making as a critical factor for good environmental governance [2].

© ICST Institute for Computer Sciences, Social Informatics and Telecommunications Engineering 2019
Published by Springer Nature Switzerland AG 2019. All Rights Reserved
G. Mendy et al. (Eds.): AFRICOMM 2018, LNICST 275, pp. 35–44, 2019.
https://doi.org/10.1007/978-3-030-16042-5_4

Using ICTs to support public participation refers to e-participation [3]. ICTs motivate and widen the participation spectrum of citizens, broaden their involvement in the policy process, generate real time qualitative and accessible information [4], pro-actively change spheres of public involvement [3], and motivated the discovery of Geographic Information System (GIS) to enhance environment management [5]. However, GIS has been criticized as an 'elite' technology that lacks suitable tools to solicit public views for effective planning and decision making, hence the introduction of Public Participatory GIS – PPGIS [5, 6]. PPGIS is a set of methods for integrating public knowledge of places to inform land use planning and decision making [6]. PPGIS is one of the e-participation tools that specifically support public participation in planning [7] and environmental decision-making processes [8, 9]. PPGIS facilitate understanding of environmental problems and allow players to highlight their points of view on maps [10].

Municipal Solid Waste Management (MSWM) is one of the environment chal-lenges whose planning process can be enhanced by use of participatory tools such as PPGIS [11]. PPGIS can enhance MSWM by supporting several executive, operational, environmental, social and managerial decisions such as the siting of waste processing and disposal units, selection of waste-treatment technologies, and allocation of waste flow to processing facilities and landfills [12]. Higgs [13] emphasizes that participative IT-based methods that combine GIS and multi-criteria evaluation techniques when involving the public in the decision-making process, support consensus building and reduce conflicts involved in siting waste facilities.

Although there has been commendable progress in developing methods to involve non-experts in planning and decision-making using PPGIS tools, the field still faces several challenges [14]. However, these challenges are not technological, but are social, economic and political; and call for the need to enhance PPGIS capabilities with conceptual theories on political, social and economic issues [15]. To address this need, Enhanced Adaptive Structuration theory version 2 (EAST-2) is adopted as the theo-retical framework to investigate political, social and economic hindrances of public participation. This investigation was contextualized by using MSWM as a case study. Section 2 presents related work on public participation and PPGIS in MSWM. Section 3 presents the design of an exploratory survey on public participation in MSWM, Sect. 4 presents results, Sect. 5 concludes the paper.

2 Related Work

2.1 Municipal Solid Waste Management (MSWM)

MSWM is the control of generation, storage, collection, transport or transfer, pro-cessing and disposal of solid waste materials by developing sustainable waste man-agement strategies [16]. However, its implementation and adoption varies across countries due to factors such as: population density, transportation infrastructure, social economics and environmental regulations [17].

2.2 Public Participation in Municipal Solid Waste Management

Public participation in MSWM is crucial because everyone generates waste and they are affected indirectly or directly by poor waste management. However, citizens are normally regarded passive recipients of government services which inhibit their ability to explore the different roles in government service delivery [18]. Amidst complex MSWM challenges faced by municipalities in developing countries, citizen participation is a necessary component of the remedy. Public involvement in waste strategy and planning helps to transform traditional consultation techniques to incorporate deliberative and participatory activities that involve lay communities in decision making [19]. According to Garnett and Cooper [20] changing existing waste management practices and behaviors that are inherent in communities requires broader public participation in decision making. Public participation in waste management in crucial because: (1) landfill space is now scarce and yet the communities also are less likely to accept landfills to be sited near their habitation for environmental and health reasons, (2) systematic sorting of waste at the different stages right from the source to the disposal sites is inadequate, (3) manner in which waste is disposed of especially in the developing world may only suit participation of the public in order to reverse the effects of poor solid waste disposal, (4) public participation helps to build trust and avoid controversy over decisions, (5) public support is needed to implement policies [21–23].

Although public participation is important for the success of any waste management system, it is faced with many challenges. Several studies [22, 24, 25] report challenges faced for public participation in waste management. Other studies [22, 23] classify these challenges. Besides the classifications used by these scholars, in this study we adopt a classification based on EAST-2 constructs as presented in Table 1.

Table 1. Challenges for public participation in MSWM

Classification based on EAST-2 convening constructs	Challenges reported in literature under each classification
Social-Institutional Influence includes issues associated with laws and regulations, institutional arrangements and resource distribution	• Inadequate funding that limits resources for public participation in waste management [25] • Lack of structures and clear policies [20] • Public institutions are not willing to involve the public in planning for waste management [22] • Poor waste management infrastructure [26, 27]
Public Participant Influence includes issues associated with public knowledge, trust, and interest in waste management initiatives	• Poor attitude towards public participation in MSWM [23, 28] • Limited Public knowledge and awareness about different waste practices [28–30]
PPGIS/technology influence involves ability to use technology, access to data, and the functionalities offered by ICT systems	• Limited use of ICTs in waste management [31] • Inadequate ICT waste infrastructure [29] • Low technology access [29]

2.3 PPGIS Support for Public Participation in MSWM

Modern Participatory processes are quite often associated with interactive platforms such as discussion forums, collaborative software, web-GIS/internet-GIS and PPGIS to promote two-way interaction among the citizens and local authorities [10]. However, PPGIS is the commonly used platform in environmental planning [10]. Planning for MSWM can benefit from the implementation and uptake of PPGIS because MSWM issues have locational attribute [32]. Thus, public participation should be focused on the locational aspects of waste management aided by PPGIS [32, 33]. Idris and Mohd [21] also noted that PPGIS enables citizen to record and follow up their feelings and spatial knowledge regarding main problems of the city such as MSWM. In addition, PPGIS can tackle several factors simultaneously which need to be considered while planning waste management [34].

The potential of PPGIS to support public participation in planning and decision making is widely recognized in literature [35–37]. However, the actual use of PPGIS still faces many obstacles that go beyond the technology aspects [15, 38]. Babelon et al. [15] noted that a theoretical understanding of the social-technical aspects associated with the implementation and use of PPGIS is crucial. These aspects include:

- Tool design and affordances are concerned with the design, application and use values of PPGIS applications. Affordances are influenced by the functionalities of the tool.
- Organizational capacity concerns financial resources and skilled staff to facilitate uses participatory planning.
- Organizational capacity which is determined by parameters such as incentives, resource allocation, knowledge and experience sharing, early PPGIS application in the planning stages and PPGIS adaptability in all planning stages.
- Governance issues such as municipal governance structures and context are crucial for the design and implementation of PPGIS applications.

According to Brown and Kyatta [14] technical, social and political issues affect the implementation and uptake of PPGIS and these include: (1) Understanding and increasing participation rates, (2) Evaluating the effectiveness of PPGIS (the focus has been largely put on evaluating the technology not the process outcomes), and (3) Improving "PP" in PPGIS.

Sieber [6] developed a framework for analyzing PPGIS implementations. It considers coproduction of PPGIS as an integration of several aspects such as:

- Place and people dimension considers cultural influences, stakeholder relations and influences important for PPGIS implementation and subsequent acceptance.
- Technology and data dimension considers accessibility of data, representation of data, the cost of hardware and software and the extent of GIS technology for operationalization of PPGIS.
- Process outcome and evaluation considers discursive goals such as empowerment, social capacity and inclusion, equity and redistribution and expanded participation.

2.4 Applications of EAST 2

Public participation can be framed using complex decision situation. Enhanced Adaptive Structuration Theory EAST [39] and EAST-2 [40] are the frameworks that have been used to analyse and understand technology use in large group decision making situations. EAST-2 includes eight constructs that characterize complex decision. These constructs are categorised as convening, process and outcome. All EAST-2 constructs helps us to understand that information technology use in public participation is influenced by rather broad-based set of issues. Chang and Li [41] critiqued EAST 2 for not being robust to explain real-time synchronous geo-collaborations and suggested that participant profiles, task information, access to information and communication among participants are important for real time geo-collaborations. Porwol et al. [42] suggested that public participation process and real time geo-collaborations can benefit from dynamic capabilities orchestrated by the World Wide Web (WWW) such as ubiquitous participation and remote monitoring. Wang [43] applied EAST 2 to analyse Volunteered Geographical reporting systems and concluded that Participant's trust, beliefs (public participants influence aspects) and the role of convenor (social-institutional aspects) are not crucial. Modifications advanced [41–43] have been considered to adapt EAST-2 framework shown in Fig. 1.

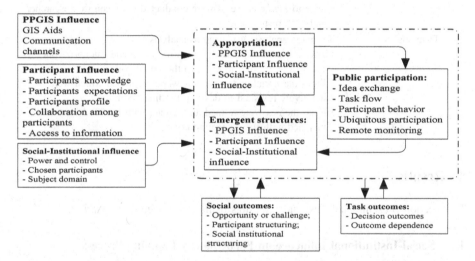

Fig. 1. Conceptual Framework PPGIS implementation in MSWM (Extension of EAST-2 by Jankowski and Nyerges [38])

3 Set up of the Exploratory Survey

The study sought to establish the factors influencing public participation in a participatory planning process for MSWM in Uganda. Qualitative exploratory study was done through conductive interviews with key stakeholders involved in planning for MSWM. The Interviews were conducted between January and March 2018. Table 2 shows key factors that were considered when designing the exploratory survey.

Table 2. Design of the exploratory interviews on challenges of public participation in MSWM

#	Parameter	Instantiations of the parameter in the study
1	Target population	• Solid waste officers, environmental officers, physical planners, field/landfill officers, managers and directors of waste collection contracted officers and landfill operators • The respondents were from Mukono, Entebbe and Kampala capital city Authority
2	Sample size	• Permission to conduct an exploratory study on public participation in MSWM was sought • The principle of saturation point in qualitative studies was based on to select 25 participants
3	Sampling method	Purposive sampling was used. Selection criteria for subjects that participated in the interviews were: • The availability or willingness of a respondent to allocate time to respond to Interview questions through a face-to-face dialog with the researcher • Having knowledge on waste management and also being involved in planning for MSWM
4	Data collection instrument	• A semi-structured interview guide to keep the researcher consistent with the flow of the questions • Face to face interviews were conducted (between the researcher and each respondent)
5	Data analysis	Thematic analysis was used to analysis [44] • Transcriptions were used to identify, name and categorize phrases and words in order to develop the initial codes • From the initial codes, themes were developed which were iteratively revisited to develop the final themes • Final themes were refined and named with EAST-2 view and matched with the convening constructs

4   Results

This section presents analyzes study findings using components of EAST 2.

4.1   Social-Institutional Influence on Participatory Planning Process

Results relating to social-institutional influence include: availability of resources, institutional practices and norms, legislation and mandate and political will.

Institutional practices and norms have an impact on public participation. Current municipal practices and norms in regard to planning for MSWM do not cater for involvement of stakeholders. *"It is a common practice with institutions not to involve stakeholders; however, there is a change where majority stakeholders are being brought on board"* (solid waste officer 1).

Availability of resources has an effect on Public participation in MSWM. Time, funds and human resources are needed to conduct successful participatory planning process. *"It is time consuming and costly to involve the stakeholders"* (solid waste officer 3). Availability of resources has an effect on a participatory planning and the subsequent outcomes because it has an impact on the number of stakeholders that can be involved in the process *"Budget constraints limit us on the number of stakeholders to involve in council meetings"* (solid officer 3).

Legislation and guidelines – A set of well established guidelines and procedures are needed prior to establishing a participatory planning process. Guidelines and legislations held to demonstrate the relevancy of stakeholders at each stage in planning and the premises of participation. At least 13 respondents reported lack of guidelines as one of the reasons for not involving stakeholders in planning for MSWM.

Political will – Municipal authorities are reluctant to involve stakeholders in the planning processes. *"Public participation hinders development so most institutions are not ready to involve the public and other stakeholders"* (solid waste officer 1).

4.2 Participant Influence on Participatory Planning Process

Results show that participant's knowledge and awareness of the existing MSWM practices has an influence on the participatory planning process. Participants give views based on the knowledge and experience they have. However, solid waste 2 and 4 noted that. *"Some stakeholders are at times not ware of existing MSWM practices and initiatives and some lack knowledge of MSWM principles"* In addition, public attitude towards municipal solid waste management initiatives and projects has an effect on participatory planning process. The public resist municipal solid waste initiatives. Thus, sensitization campaigns and negotiations have to be first carried out in order to prepare the public for change. *"Most people think that handling municipal waste is not their responsibility so they are not concerned"* (Field officer 1).

4.3 PPGIS and the Participatory Planning

Respondents reported limited application of ICTs especially GIS in MSWM practices; although ICTs are necessary component of any sound municipal solid waste system. *"ICTs such as GIS are rarely used. The entire process is still manual"* (solid waste officer 1). Also, views were collected on the awareness of the roles of GIS in waste management. All the 23 respondents agreed that they were aware of the roles GIS plays in municipal solid waste management processes especially in the selection of suitable sites for waste disposal, route scheduling and optimization, waste disposal site monitoring and management.

5 Discussions and Conclusions

The study investigated the social, institutional and technology aspects that affect participatory planning processes. The key aspects are legislation, institutional practices and norms, political will, knowledge and awareness challenges and attitude. Results show that the current institutional practices and norms do not favor participatory planning process. The current practice is that institutions make decisions without involving stakeholders especially the general public. These results are in line with findings of Minn et al. [27] who noted that decisions regarding planning and implementation of waste management strategies are made by municipalities without taking into consideration the concerns of the general public. In addition, results show that there is lack of knowledge on the general principles and practices in MSWM needed for public participation. Mukama et al. [25] also found that practices, concerns, and attitudes of residents in slum areas indicate lack of sufficient knowledge about good waste practices and their responsibilities in MSWM.

From the findings, participant's attitude towards a participatory planning process affects the process itself and the subsequent outcomes. The public feel it is the mandate of municipal authorities to handle all the municipal solid waste aspects and hence they are not interested in participating in any of the initiatives. Minn et al. [25] findings show people have indifferent attitude towards keeping public places clean and they too lack interest in participating in the drive for sustainable MSWM. Thus, change in attitude and behavior is critical for the success of public participation initiatives for MSWM.

We conclude that PPGIS implementations for successful public participation in MSWM require: sensitization of public on waste management practices, setting up ICT infrastructure and advocate for adoption of ICTs in MSWM, equip staff with skills to conduct participatory processes, allocate funds to conduct citizen participation projects and establish procedures for recruiting participants. At this preliminary stage, the study did not consider views of citizens so as to enrich views of institutions responsible for MSWM. Hence a limitation, that is to be explored in future work.

References

1. Sabatier, P.A., Leach, W.D., Lubell, M., Pelkey, N.W.: Theoretical frameworks explaining partnership success. In: Swimming Upstream Collaborative Approaches to Watershed Management, pp. 173–200 (2005). R, F.: Article title. Journal 2(5), 99–110 (2016)
2. Bulkeley, H., Mol, A.P.: Participation and environmental governance: consensus, ambivalence and debate. Environ. Values 12(2), 143–154 (2003)
3. Tambouris, E., Liotas, N., Kaliviotis, D., Tarabanis, K.: A framework for scoping eParticipation. In: 8th Annual International Conference on Digital Government Research, Bridging Disciplines & Domains, pp. 288–289 (2006)
4. Islam, M.S.: Towards a sustainable e-Participation implementation model. Eur. J. e-Pract. 5(10), 1–12 (2008)
5. Butt, M.A., Li, S.: Developing a web-based, collaborative PPGIS prototype to support public participation. Appl. Geomat. 4(3), 197–215 (2012)

6. Sieber, R.: Public participation geographic information systems a literature review and framework. Ann. Assoc. Am. Geogr. **96**(3), 491–507 (2006)
7. Nooshery, N.R., Taleai, M., Kazemi, R., Ebadi, K.: Developing a web-based PPGIS, as an environmental reporting service. In: International Archives of the Photogrammetry, Remote Sensing & Spatial Information Sciences, p. 42 (2017)
8. Brown, G.: An empirical evaluation of the spatial accuracy of public participation GIS (PPGIS) data. Appl. Geogr. **34**, 289–294 (2012)
9. Floreddu, P., Cabiddu, F., Pettinao, D.: Public participation in environmental decision-making: the case of PPGIS. In: Information Technology and Innovation Trends in Organizations, pp. 37–44 (2011)
10. Jankowski, P.: Towards participatory geographic information systems for community-based environmental decision making. J. Environ. Manage. **90**(6), 1966–1971 (2009)
11. Al-Shehhi, A., Aung, Z., Woon, W.L.: Argument visualization and narrative approaches for collaborative spatial decision making and knowledge construction: a case study for an offshore wind farm project. In: Woon, W.L., Aung, Z., Madnick, S. (eds.) DARE 2015. LNCS (LNAI), vol. 9518, pp. 135–154. Springer, Cham (2015). https://doi.org/10.1007/978-3-319-27430-0_10
12. Ghiani, G., Laganà, D., Manni, E., Musmanno, R., Vigo, D.: Operations research in solid waste management: a survey of strategic and tactical issues. Comput. Oper. Res. **44**, 22–32 (2014)
13. Higgs, G.: Integrating multi-criteria techniques with geographical information systems in waste facility location to enhance public participation. Waste Manage. Res. **24**(2), 105–117 (2006)
14. Brown, G., Kyttä, M.: Key issues and research priorities for public participation GIS (PPGIS): a synthesis based on empirical research. Appl. Geogr. **46**, 122–136 (2014)
15. Babelon, I., Ståhle, A., Balfors, B.: Toward Cyborg PPGIS: exploring socio-technical requirements for the use of web-based PPGIS in two municipal planning cases, Stockholm region, Sweden. J. Environ. Plan. Manage. **60**(8), 1366–1390 (2017)
16. Environmental Protection Agency: Waste Classification (2014). http://www.epa.ie/waste/municipal/wasteclass. Accessed 02 Aug 2017
17. Sakai, S.: Municipal solid waste management in Japan. Waste Manag. **16**, 5–6 (1996)
18. Tadesse, S.: The economic value of regulated disclosure: evidence from the banking sector. J. Account. Public Policy **25**(1), 32–70 (2006)
19. Cotton, M.: Shale gas—community relations: NIMBY or not? Integrating social factors into shale gas community engagements. Nat. Gas Electr. **29**(9), 8–12 (2013)
20. Garnett, K., Cooper, T., Longhurst, P., Jude, S., Tyrrel, S.: A conceptual framework for negotiating public involvement in municipal waste management decision-making in the UK. Waste Manag. **66**, 210–221 (2017)
21. Idris, A., Mohd, N.: Overview of waste disposal and landfills/dumps in Asian countries. J. Mater. Cycles Waste Manage. **6**(2), 104–110 (2004)
22. Mukisa, P.K.: Public participation in solid waste management: challenges and prospects: a case of Kira Town council, Uganda. Master's thesis, Universitetet i Agder, University of Agder (2007)
23. Mukama, T., et al.: Practices, concerns, and willingness to participate in solid waste management in two urban slums in central Uganda. J. Environ. Public Health **2016**, 7 pages (2016)
24. Gorsevski, P.V., Torregrosa, A.M.: Android-based multi-criteria evaluation approach for enhancing public participation for a wind farm site selection. In: Sarjakoski, T., Santos, M.Y., Sarjakoski, L.T. (eds.) Geospatial Data in a Changing World. LNGC, pp. 87–103. Springer, Cham (2016). https://doi.org/10.1007/978-3-319-33783-8_6

25. Amasuomo, E., Tuoyo, O.J.A., Hasnain, S.A.: Analysis of public participation in sustainable waste management practice in Abuja. Nigeria Environ. Manag. Sustain. Dev. **4**(1), 180 (2015)
26. Kinobe, J.R., Gebresenbet, G., Niwagaba, C.B., Vinnerås, B.: Reverse logistics system and recycling potential at a landfill: a case study from Kampala City. Waste Manag. **42**, 82–92 (2015)
27. Okot-Okumu, J., Nyenje, R.: Municipal solid waste management under decentralization in Uganda. Habitat Int. **35**(4), 537–543 (2011)
28. Shukor, F.S.A., Mohammed, A.H., Sani, S.I.A., Awang, M.: A review on the success factors for community participation in solid waste management. In: Proceeding of International Conference on Management, Penang, Malaysia (2015)
29. Kaza, Y., Mrkgraf, C.: Five ways to increase citizen participation
30. Hannan, M.A., Al Mamun, M.A., Hussain, A., Basri, H., Begum, R.A.: A review on technologies and their usage in solid waste monitoring and management systems: issues and challenges. Waste Manage. **43**, 509–523 (2015)
31. Minn, Z., Laohasiriwong, W.: Promoting people's participation in solid waste management in Myanmar. Res. J. Environ. Sci. **4**(3), 209–222 (2010)
32. Ganapati, S.: Uses of public participation geographic information systems applications in e-government. Public Adm. Rev. **71**(3), 425–434 (2011)
33. Labib, S.M.: Volunteer GIS (VGIS) based waste management: a conceptual design and use of web 2.0 for smart waste management in Dhaka City. In: Research in Computational Intelligence and Communication Networks (ICRCICN), Third International Conference 2017, pp. 137–141. IEEE (2017)
34. Ahmed, A.: Field Testing Volunteer Geographic Information Collection–The Viability of Community Mapping (2011)
35. Mansourian, A., Taleai, M., Fasihi, A.: A web-based spatial decision support system to enhance public participation in urban planning processes. J. Spat. Sci. **56**(2), 269–282 (2011)
36. Kahila-Tani, M., Broberg, A., Kyttä, M., Tyger, T.: Let the citizens map—public participation GIS as a planning support system in the Helsinki master plan process. Plan. Pract. Res. **31**(2), 195–214 (2016)
37. Simao, A., Densham, P.J., Haklay, M.M.: Web-based GIS for collaborative planning and public participation: an application to the strategic planning of wind farm sites. J. Environ. Manage. **90**(6), 2027–2040 (2009)
38. Bugs, G., Granell, C., Fonts, O., Huerta, J., Painho, M.: An assessment of Public Participation GIS and Web 2.0 technologies in urban planning practice in Canela, Brazil. Cities **27**(3), 172–181(2010)
39. Nyerges, T.L., Jankowski, P.: Enhanced adaptive structuration theory: a theory of GIS-supported collaborative decision making. Geogr. Syst. **4**, 225–260 (1997)
40. Jankowski, P., Nyerges, T.: Toward a framework for research on geographic information-supported participatory decision-making. URISA J. **15**(1), 9–17 (2003)
41. Chang, Z., Li, S.: Geo-social model: a conceptual framework for real-time geo-collaboration. Trans. GIS **17**(2), 182–205 (2013)
42. Porwol, L., Ojo, A., Breslin, J.G.: An ontology for next generation e-Participation initiatives. Gov. Inf. Q. **33**(3), 583–594 (2016)
43. Wang, M.: Volunteer geographic information reporting system: a cross-case comparison, Doctoral dissertation (2015)
44. Braun, V., Clarke, V.: Using thematic analysis in psychology. Qual. Res. Psychol. **3**, 77–101 (2006)

LTE-Advanced Random Access Channel Congestion Detection Method for IoT

Goni Mahamadou Bouba[1], Jerôme Mbainaibeye[2],
James Kouawa Tamgno[3(✉)], and Claude Lishou[1]

[1] LTI Laboratory, ESP/UCAD, Dakar, Senegal
bouba.mahamadou@ucad.edu.sn
[2] Université de DOBA, Doba, Tchad
mbai_jerome@yahoo.com
[3] LTI & RSI Research Group, ESMT, Dakar, Senegal
james.tamgno@esmt.sn

Abstract. The Long Term Evolution - LTE - is one of the very last evolutions in mobile communication systems that offer a much wider bandwidth than its predecessors. That is why it is very much in demand for a massive deployment of the Internet of Things (IoT) also called Machine to Machine communication or Machine Type Communication (MTC). With the IoT, the network is subject to recurrent congestion when densely charged which is due to increased uplink solicitation. MTC devices must complete the RACH process to access the network. Collisions occur during this process that leads to the congestion which, in turn, has a negative impact on the quality of service. The Third Generation Partnership Project (3GPP) provided some solutions to alleviate the problem. In this paper we propose a congestion detection method since 3GPP only proposed contention resolution methods. We first determine the interval of use of preambles during which the success rate is the highest. By doing so, we determine the maximal preamble utilization threshold (Rlimit) beyond which quality of service is no more guaranteed. The novelty with this method is that once Rlimit threshold is reached, a contention resolution scheme could be activated and will remain so until the threshold drops below Rlimit. Our method can give better results if applied to contention resolution methods. Moreover it is simple, less complex and easy to implement in the LTE. Moreover, it does not require large investments.

Keywords: Machine Type Communication (MTC) ·
Long Term Evolution (LTE) · Radio Access Network (RAN) overload ·
Random Access Channel (RACH) · Congestion

1 Introduction

The Internet of Things (IoT) is a recent communication paradigm that envisions a near future, in which everyday objects will be equipped with microcontrollers, transceivers for digital communication, and appropriate protocol stacks that will make them able to communicate with each other, with users or with a remote server, becoming part of the Internet [1]. These objects are able to collect, store, transmit and process data from the

G. Mendy et al. (Eds.): AFRICOMM 2018, LNICST 275, pp. 45–55, 2019.
https://doi.org/10.1007/978-3-030-16042-5_5

physical world. It is a paradigm that finds its application in many different areas, such as home automation, industry, medical aid, mobile health care, help for the elderly, intelligent energy management and smart grids, automobiles, agriculture, traffic management, and many others [2]. Several standardization bodies, among which IEEE and 3GPP, are working to set standards for it [3]. Its deployment on the LTE network is exponentially increasing, which is not without causing enormous challenges when we know that the LTE is designed for basic Human-to-Human (H2H) communications type (large downlink bandwidth and narrow uplink bandwidth). The IoT is meanwhile very greedy in the uplink band as the MTC devices transmit much more packets than they receive. We are talking about 26 [4] to near 50 [5] billion of connected objects by 2020. MTC devices have to compete for resources to get access to network. This is done through RACH process where congestion often happens.

2 Background

2.1 Random Access Procedure

In the LTE system, access to the network is through a RACH process in which UEs use preambles broadcasted at regular time slots by the base station (a total of 64 preambles). The preambles are generated from the sequences of the Zadoff-Chu algorithm include a cyclic prefix CP, a sequence and a guard time as in Fig. 1.

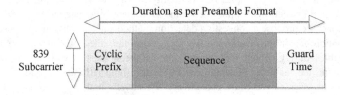

Fig. 1. RA preamble structure [6]

Two types of access exist in LTE:

- **Contention-free access:** Among the 64 preambles, 10 are dedicated to specific uses of high priorities in contention-free access. During contention-free access, the connection is initiated by the base station which, at the same time, provides the UE with the necessary resources. This is applied to priority communications such as emergency alert messages and specific uses.
- **Contention-based access:** In the case of contention-based access, UEs compete for the remaining 54 preambles in the RACH process. The random access request consists of this preamble, which is a digital signature transmitted by the UEs in a time slot. The RACH process is consist of four steps [7]:

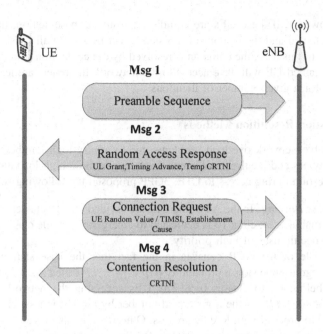

Fig. 2. RACH process

Figure 2 describes the four steps of the Random Access Channel process:

Step 1 (Preamble Send): In this step, each UE sends the access request by sending one of the 54 orthogonal predefined preambles, as well as a temporary identity RA-RNTI (Random Access - Radio Network Temporary Identifier) which is actually based on the time interval in which the preamble is issued.

Step 2 (Random Access Response): In this step, the base station transmits the access response that contains the detected preamble index, the timing for step 3, the time offset (so the UE can modify its schedule to compensate for round-trip delay), and the uplink resources necessary for UE to perform step 3.

Step 3 (Connection Request): After obtaining the resources in Step 2, the UE sends a connection request to the base station. This message contains the identity of the cell (C-RNTI) in which the UE is located and the reason of the request.

Step 4 (Contention Resolution): The base station responds with a contention resolution message. Each device that has received this message compares the identity in the message with the identity passed in the previous step. In case of correspondence between these identities access is granted. In case of non-correspondence, the UE back-off and go back to step 1.

When two or more UEs use same preamble collisions can be detected by the base station, based on the difference in preamble transmission delays. Then it will not send a response for this preamble. The UEs concerned will then be required to resume the operation. However, if these UEs are equidistant from the base station, the collision will not be detected and the response from step 2 will be sent to all UEs having used this preamble. In this case, the collision is resolved by the contention resolution in step 4. Only the retained UE will have access to the network, the others are led to resume the operation for a given number of iterations.

2.2 Congestion Resolution Methods

In order to solve network overload problems due to a very high number of requests from MTC devices and recurrent collisions that occur in these high-load environments causing congestion during access to LTE, 3GPP proposed the following solutions [8]:

(1) Access Class Barring: In the ACB, the UEs are divided into 16 classes. Classes 0–9 are called normal classes; class 10 is dedicated to emergencies while classes 11–15 are dedicated to specific uses of high priority.

The principle of the ACB consists in the fact that the base station (eNodeB) broadcasts at regular time slots a probability **p** *(p ∈ [0 − 1])* called ACB factor towards all the UEs belonging to classes 0–9. The UEs accessing the network generate a number q *(q ∈ [0 − 1]))*. If the q generated number by the UE is less than *p (q < p),* UE is allowed to proceed with RACH process. Otherwise, it has to wait a $T_{barring}$ time (barring time) before resuming the process. By this way it is possible for the base station to control the collisions and network overloads by assigning an optimal value to *p*. $T_{barring}$ can be calculated as follows [8]:

$$T_{barring} = (0.7 + 0.6 * rand) * ac\_BarringTime$$

Where rand is a random number generated by the MTC device after passing a first failed ACB check and before a second attempt. The values of *ac_BarringTime* can range from 4 s to 512 s.

Several improved versions of the ACB have been performed to increase its performance. The separate approach of ACB for M2M and H2H [9, 10]. Improvements of Extended Access Barring (EAB) have also been proposed in [11, 12]. For UEs under cover of several base stations, a cooperative approach has been proposed [13] to allow an optimal choice of E-NodeB for the EU. [14, 15] provide priority random access joined to the dynamic ACB mechanism to improve the performance of the random access channel. The improvement of the ACB in most cases leads to an increase in the access time on which, once a certain threshold is reached can be a real problem. In order to overcome this problem, the authors of [16] have developed a scalable ACB system based on the game is proposed.

(2) Separate RACH Resources for MTC: This scheme separates resources for H2H and M2M. When resources are not shared, the network is subject to recurring congestion. The separation of RACH resources between H2H and M2M reduces the impact of each other. A study of the separation of resources is done in [17]. It proposes 2 methods: First method, called "Method 1", consists of completely dividing all available preambles into two disjoint subsets. The other method, called "Method 2",

also consists of dividing the set into two subsets, but one of them is shared by the H2H and MTC clients, meaning one is reserved for the customers H2H and the other shared between H2H and MTC.

However, the division of RACH resources into 2 groups does not seem efficient. This is a method that can very quickly become ineffective if the M2M traffic becomes excessively high and the H2H traffic remains low and vice versa.

(3) Dynamic Allocation of RACH Resources: In this scheme, resources are allocated to M2M and H2H devices. The network can predict in advance whether the network will be overloaded by excessive access attempts caused by the large number of MTC devices. The network then dynamically allocates additional resources for the RACH procedure. As proposed in [18], M2M devices are categorized by types. In this approach, when the base station accepts the access request of an M2M device, in addition to granting access, it also allocates certain resources to devices of the same type, in which M2M devices of the same type can be content with access resources. Compared to the regular static RACH allocation, the dynamic resource allocation provided a big improvement [19] in the probability of successful access as well as time access. It is a solution that can be effective to some extent. However, it is limited by the unavailability of additional resources.

(4) Backoff Specific Scheme: In this scheme, a lower backoff time is assigned to conventional UEs than to MTC devices. This reduces the collision and congestion in the access network. Unfortunately, this pattern causes considerable delays, which negatively impacts high priority applications that are very sensitive to delays. The authors of [20] suggested a pure back-off scheme as well as a mixed back-off and ACB scheme based on cell load information. This system can provide performance improvements when the network is experiencing a low level of congestion in the RACH. It cannot, however, solve very high congestion levels [21].

(5) Slotted Access: This is an approach that defines access slots for MTC devices, so that the MTC device can perform RACH process only at the beginning of its dedicated time slot. This means that an MTC device cannot access the network when it wants, but only in its predefined time slot. This solution also reduces access level congestion. In [22], the authors have shown that randomly assigning slots to H2H and M2M devices may reduce the performance of this approach, while pre-assigning resources can increase efficiency up to three times.

(6) Pull based Access (Paging): In this scheme RACH process is not initiate by the M2M devices but rather by the base station. M2M devices are in idle mode. M2M servers trigger the random access process via the network (Paging) to collect data from M2M devices. This is a useful mechanism when it comes to, for example, reading smart meter data [23] in the smart gird network. Although it can simply mitigate overload problems at RACH, it can create an overload in the paging channel. Over-loading of the paging channel is discussed in [24, 25]. The authors of [26] developed an analytical model for evaluating the performance of group paging in LTE.

3 System Model

During the RACH access process in a low-load network environment, the success rate of requests is very high with low delay. But as soon as a strong load is felt this rate decreases very quickly to reach a critical threshold and the delay with to reach inconceivable levels. Since the 3GPP has not proposed a method of detection or prevention of overload, we propose an overload detection method so that the network can anticipate an overload situation to enable it to set up a suitable overload resolution solution on optimal time. Our method is first to determine the resource utilization interval (preambles) in which the success rate is highest $R_1 \leq R_{used} \leq R_{limit}$ (see Sect. 4). Assuming the network not loaded at the beginning, eNodeB monitors the number of preambles used. If the preamble utilization threshold reaches R_{limit}, we assume that the threshold is reached; meaning that the collision rate is going very high in contrary of success rate which drop down drastically. On that point of view, we envisage activation of contention resolution method, which will remain so until the number of used preambles (R_{used}) drops below the R_{limit} threshold (Fig. 3).

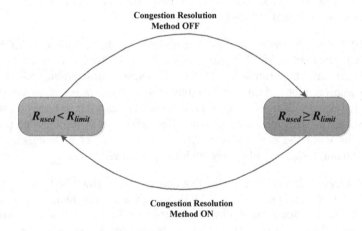

Fig. 3. Proposed congestion detection scheme

We assume a stable power for the MTC and the base station, we also assume that the base station is not able to successfully decode any type of transmission where a preamble is selected by more than one MTC in the same interval access time and therefore does not send any response to the corresponding MTCs. Note that random access can only take place in a frequency block specified by the base station. That is, the Physical Random Access Channel (PRACH) which is the physical layer responsible for mapping the RACH. In our work the RACH configuration index is 6. This means that the RACH occurs every 5 ms in a frequency band of 180 kHz for duration of 1 ms to 3 ms. We denote by R the number of available preambles and N the number of MTCs transmitting the preambles in a time interval T_A called activation time

$0 \leq t \leq T_A$, with a probability p(t) during which p(t) follows a beta distribution with parameters $\alpha = 3$, $\beta = 4$ as in [9].

$$p(t) = \frac{t^{(\alpha-1)}(T_A - t)^{\beta-1}}{T_A^{\alpha+\beta-1} Beta(\alpha, \beta)} \tag{1}$$

Where **Beta (α, β)** is a beta function.

It is considered that there is I_A access in the activation time interval and that the access time is smaller than the interval between two access channels. I_A is divided into several activation times where the first activation time starts at $t_{(i-1)}$ and ends at t_i.
The number of supposed new arrivals is given by [8]:

$$\lambda_i = N \int_{t_{i-1}}^{t_i} p(t)dt \tag{2}$$

where $i = 1, 2, 3, \ldots, I_A$.

Equiprobable preambles (1/R) are considered. The probability that one of the N MTCs chooses one and only one preamble successfully is given by the binomial law:

$$P_{success} = \binom{N}{1}\left(\frac{1}{R}\right)^1\left(1 - \frac{1}{R}\right)^{N-1}$$
$$P_{success} = \frac{N}{R}\left(1 - \frac{1}{R}\right)^{N-1} \tag{3}$$

The probability that one of the N MTCs does not transmit any preamble (Idle) is given by the binomial law:

$$P_{Idle} = \binom{N}{0}\left(\frac{1}{R}\right)^0\left(1 - \frac{1}{R}\right)^{N-0}$$
$$P_{Idle} = \left(1 - \frac{1}{R}\right)^N \tag{4}$$

Success (successfully transmitted queries) can be achieved by multiplying the probability of success (Eq. 1) by the amount of available resources:

$$Success = R * P_{success}$$
$$Success = R * \frac{N}{R}\left(1 - \frac{1}{R}\right)^{N-1}$$
$$Success = N\left(1 - \frac{1}{R}\right)^{N-1} \tag{5}$$

Probability of collision will then be:

$$
\begin{aligned}
P_{Collision} &= 1 - P_{success} - P_{Idle} \\
&= 1 - \frac{N}{R}\left(1 - \frac{1}{R}\right)^{N-1} - \left(1 - \frac{1}{R}\right)^{N} \\
&= 1 - \frac{N}{R}\left(1 - \frac{1}{R}\right)^{N-1} - \left(\frac{R-1}{R}\right)\left(1 - \frac{1}{R}\right)^{N-1} \\
&= 1 - \left(1 - \frac{1}{R}\right)^{N-1}\left(\frac{N}{R} + \frac{R-1}{R}\right)^{N-1} \\
&= 1 - \left(\frac{N+R-1}{R}\right)\left(1 - \frac{1}{R}\right)^{N-1}
\end{aligned}
\tag{6}
$$

From previous equations, it is clear that the quantity of resources used is the product of the total number of resources by the probability of use $(1 - P_{Idle})$:

$$
\begin{aligned}
R_{used} &= R * (1 - P_{Idle}) \\
R_{used} &= R\left(1 - \left(1 - \frac{1}{R}\right)^{N}\right)
\end{aligned}
\tag{7}
$$

4   Discussion and Performance Analysis

In this section we determine the resource (preambles) utilization interval in term of the success rate of RA transmissions. Simulations (Fig. 4) from Eqs. (5) and (7) show that this interval is located between $R_{used} = 18.93$ and $R_{used} = 46,5$ gives a higher success rate when considering this rate above 15 and when taking N = 300 (MTC devices) and R = 54 as in [8]. From that interval it is clear that beyond $R_{used} = 18.93$ (the threshold called Rlimit in our work) the success rate falls down badly and considered non-viable for the network. So we consider that threshold the point from which congestion resolution method can be applied. By doing so, performances of system can be improved when comparing to the case when congestion resolution method is applied without taking in account the Rlimit threshold. In this section we determine the resource (preambles) utilization interval in term of the success rate of random access transmissions. Simulations (Fig. 4) from Eqs. (5) and (7) show that this interval is located between $R_{used} = 18.93$ (Y = 18.9) and $R_{used} = 46,5$ (Y = 46.5) gives a higher success rate when considering this rate above 15 and when taking N = 300 (MTC devices) and R = 54 as in [8]. From that interval, and considering $R_{used} = 18.93$ as R_1, it is clear that beyond $R_{used} = 46,5$ (the threshold called R_{limit} in our work) the success rate falls down badly and considered non-viable for the network. So we consider that threshold the point from which congestion resolution method can be applied. By doing so, performances of system can be improved when comparing to the case when congestion resolution method is applied without taking in account the R_{limit} threshold.

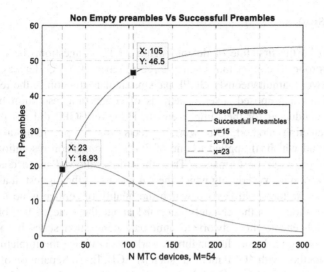

Fig. 4. Rused vs Success

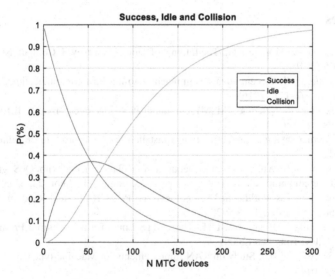

Fig. 5. Success-Collisions-Idle

Figure 5 shows that success probability (Eq. (3)) reaches its highest value at N = 50 and decreases when the number of MTC devices is going high. At that point, congestion is detected. So if no congestion resolution is applied, the collision probability (Eq. (6)) goes increasingly high from reaching its highest value when N increasing towards 300. At the same time Idle probability (Eq. (4)) decreases from higher value to 0 when N is going high.

5 Conclusion

Considered to be the first line of defense against LTE congestion, the LTE RACH procedure is prone to congestion when a large number of MTC devices attempt to access the network simultaneously. 3GPP pays particular attention to the resolution of congestion. Thus it proposed several methods of congestion resolution from which research was conducted for their improvement. However 3GPP did not provide any congestion detection method. Our work corrects this by providing a congestion detection method which, if applied to one of 3GPP's congestion resolution methods, will greatly improve its performance. The simulations allowed us to determine the preamble utilization interval during which the RA success is the highest. It also allowed us to determine the threshold beyond which the quality of service is no longer guaranteed. The method gets the eNodeB informed about the state of use of preamble resources, which enable the network to anticipate congestion states by activating a congestion resolution scheme. In our future work, we envisage the implementation of our detection method with 3GPP methods such as ACB, EAB, Separation of Resources or Backoff Scheme to improve its performance.

References

1. Atzori, L., Iera, A., Morabito, G.: The Internet of Things: a survey. J. Comput. Netw. **54**(15), 2787–2805 (2010)
2. Xia, N., Yang, C.-S.: Recent advances in machine-to-machine communications. J. Comput. Commun. **4**, 107–111 (2016)
3. IEEE: Machine to Machine (M2M) communications technical report. IEEE 802.16p-10/0005, November 2010
4. Gartner: Gartner says the internet of things installed base will grow to 26 billion units by 2020 (2013)
5. Han, X., Lim, T.J., Xu, J.: Heterogeneous access class barring with QoS guarantee in machine-type communications. Trans. Emerg. Telecommun. Technol. **28**, e2959 (2015)
6. http://www.rfwireless-world.com/Terminology/LTE-PRACH-Physical-Random-Access-Channel.html. Accessed 12 Apr 2017
7. Sesia, S., Toufik, I., Baker, M.: LTE–The UMTS Long Term Evolution: From Theory to Practice. Wiley, Hoboken (2009)
8. GPP TR 37.868 V11.0.0: Study on RAN Improvements for Machine-type Communications, September 2011
9. GPP:R2-100182: Access control of MTC devices. 3GPP TSG RAN WG2 Meeting 68bis, Valencia, Spain (2010)
10. GPP:R2-103143: Discussion on separating RACH resources for MTC. Alcatel-lucent Shanghai Bell, Alcatel-lucent (2010)
11. Larmo, A., Susitaival, R.: RAN overload control for machine type communications in LTE. In: 2012 IEEE GLOBECOM Workshops (GC Workshops), pp. 1626–163 (2012)
12. Cheng, R., Chen, J., Chen, D., Wei, C.: Modeling and analysis of an extended access barring scheme for machine-type communications in LTE-A networks. IEEE Trans. Wirel. Commun. **14**(6), 2956–2968 (2015)
13. Lien, S.-Y., Liau, T.-H., Kao, C.-Y., Chen, K.-C.: Cooperative access class barring for machine-to-machine communications. IEEE Trans. Wirel. Commun. **11**(1), 27–32 (2012)

14. Jiang, T., Tan, X., Luan, X., Zhang, X., Wu, J.: Evolutionary game based access class barring for machine-to-machine communications. In: 2014 16th International Conference on Advanced Communication Technology (ICACT), pp. 832–835, February 2014
15. Cheng, J.-P., Lee, C., Lin, T.-M.: Prioritized random access with dynamic access barring for RAN overload in 3GPP LTE-a networks. In: 2011 IEEE GLOBECOM Workshops (GC Workshops), pp. 368–372 (2011)
16. Lin, G.-Y., Chang, S.-R., Wei, H.-Y.: Estimation and adaptation for bursty LTE random access. IEEE Trans. Veh. Technol. 65, 2560–2577 (2015)
17. Lee, K.-D., Kim, S., Yi, B.: Throughput comparison of random access methods for M2M service over LTE networks. In: 2011 GLOBECOM Workshops (GC Workshops), December, pp. 373–377
18. GPP:R2-113328: Dynamic separate RACH resources for MTC. 3GPP TSG RAN WG2 74. Institute for Information Industry (III), Coiler Corporation (2011)
19. Pang, Y.-C., Chao, S.-L., Lin, G.-Y., Wei, H.-Y.: Network access for m2m/h2h hybrid systems: a game theoretic approach. Commun. Lett. 18(5), 845–848 (2014)
20. Jian, X., Jia, Y., Zeng, X., Yang, J.: A novel class-dependent back-off scheme for machine type communication in LTE systems. In: 2013 22nd Wireless and Optical Communication Conference (WOCC), pp. 135–140 (2013)
21. Lien, S.-Y., Chen, K.-C., Lin, Y.: Toward ubiquitous massive accesses in 3GPP machine-to-machine communications. IEEE Commun. Mag. 49(4), 66–74 (2011)
22. GPP:R2-112247: Merits of the slotted access methods for MTC. Alcatel-lucent Shanghai Bell, Alcatel-lucent (2011)
23. G. R. 104873: Comparing push and pull based approaches for MTC. 3rd Generation Partnership Project (2010)
24. GPP:R2-104007: Pull vs push approach for MTC. 3GPP TSG RAN WG2 70bis, Stockholm, Sweden (2010)
25. GPP:R2-102781: Paging and downlink transmission for MTC. 3GPP TSG RAN WG2 Meeting 70, Montreal, Canada (2010)
26. Wei, C.-H., Cheng, R.-G., Tsao, S.-L.: Performance analysis of group paging for machine-type communications in LTE networks. IEEE Trans. Veh. Technol. 62(7), 3371–3382 (2013)

Contribution to Improving the Presence Base of VoIP Servers for Sending and Receiving Messages

Latyr Ndiaye[(✉)], Kéba Gueye, Samuel Ouya, and Gervais Mendy

LIRT Laboratory, Higher Polytechnic School, University of Dakar,
Dakar, Senegal
{latyrndiaye,keba.gueye}@esp.sn,
samuel.ouya@gmail.com, gervais.mendy@ucad.edu.sn

Abstract. The purpose of this article has been emphasized on the SIP Signaling Protocol in order to contribute to the improvement on sending and receiving message about the services provided by the VoIP servers. The current configuration of VoIP servers has allowed us to see that if a user connected by wifi to the VoIP server has disconnected involuntarily from the network without disconnecting his SIP client from the server, the server can not remove him from his base presence, where it stores all connected users, and cost the message that is sent to him is not stored and no longer he does not receive it.

To overcome this, we couple the Freeswitch intelligence used as a VoIP server coupled to a presence detection server and a MySQL database. This platform makes it possible to retrieve all messages with a non-connected recipient and store them in a database, then wait for their reconnection to send them the messages that concern them.

Keywords: Freeswitch · VoIP · SIP · MySQL · Wifi · Message

1 Introduction

Session Initiation Protocol (SIP) is an increasingly used protocol in the world of voice over IP. It is a signaling protocol used to open sessions in an IP environment, modify and close them. A session can simply be a telephone call (in reception and transmission) or a connection between several multimedia supports at the same time. The role of SIP is to open, modify, and release sessions. SIP, although widely used, must become even more mature. However, SIP-compatible VoIP products are becoming more numerous and more diverse. The choice of SIP in an IP environment comes from the fact that this protocol is extensible and easily integrates into different architectures. This protocol now has an important place in telecommunications. Specialists quickly became aware of its limitations and its need to interact with other protocols to be fully functional. The technological revolution noted in recent years in the telecommunications and networks sector allows researchers in the field to direct research in protocols such as the SIP protocol [1–3].

© ICST Institute for Computer Sciences, Social Informatics and Telecommunications Engineering 2019
Published by Springer Nature Switzerland AG 2019. All Rights Reserved
G. Mendy et al. (Eds.): AFRICOMM 2018, LNICST 275, pp. 56–66, 2019.
https://doi.org/10.1007/978-3-030-16042-5_6

This is why our research on the SIP protocol will allow us to detect flaws in it. These flaws noted compared to the connection by WIFI are a big problem for users and it is important to correct them. In this article, we will explain how this flaw was found and how we came up with a solution.

2 Motivation

A SIP study will allow us to understand the different methods, queries, and messages used. This will allow us to detect some flaws that this protocol is facing. This is why our article deals with the study of the SIP protocol and particularly with the MES-SAGES events (sending and receiving messages). So we conducted experiments that allowed us to note some problems that the SIP protocol has. Different scenarios have been experimented and the results obtained have allowed us to see the problems that the SIP protocol faces. In the current SIP configuration, sending and receiving a message requires the direct connection of both clients to the SIP telephony server [5, 6].

2.1 IP-PBX

An IP-PBX is a professional telephone system designed to transmit voice or video over a data network and interact with the normal public switched telephone network (PSTN). The traditional PBX is based on the hardware circuit switch while the IP PBX is an IP telephony system that uses software switching [7, 8].

The system converges the voice and data backbone, simplifies network and service management, provides flexible/scalable solutions, and most importantly, many customizable service packages. There are many proprietary IP-PBX systems such as 3CX, Freeswitch, Kamailio (former OpenSER), IP-PBX Matrix, IP-PBX Magiclink, VoIP software, and so on [9]. However, it is still desirable to have an open source solution that will offer the freedom of customization if needed as well as keep the cost low.

2.2 SIP Signaling

Session Initiation Protocol (SIP) is a signaling protocol defined by the Internet Engineering Task Force (IETF) for establishing, releasing, and modifying multimedia sessions [4, 10]. SIP is used in VoIP PBXs and also in IMS as a signaling protocol for session control and service control. It therefore replaces both ISDN User Part (ISUP) and Intelligent Network Application Part (INAP) protocols in the world of telephony by providing multimedia capability [11]. SIP is the unifying protocol of VoIP architectures. Its use involves associated protocols, especially SDP, for session description, and RTP/RTCP, for real-time transport (and control) of multimedia data streams.

At the PABX level, SIP is used by network devices such as IMS (CSCF in particular) to control the call (establishment, modification, end) during any multimedia session. A session is established when two or more participants exchange data. SIP can handle multi-recipient, group or automatic calls. In any type of network, there are always four types of signaling:

Registration signalling: by it, a terminal registers in the network. It contains the procedures for downloading the profile and managing the location. It is performed by the SIP registration procedure (SIP REGISTER) (Fig. 1).

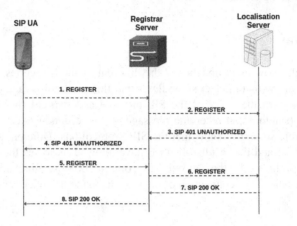

Fig. 1. REGISTER SIP registration procedure

Call signaling: it establishes an end-to-end association between the endpoints wishing to communicate. This type of signaling is characterized by reference exchange. This is done in IMS and PBXs through the SIP INVITE procedure (Fig. 2).

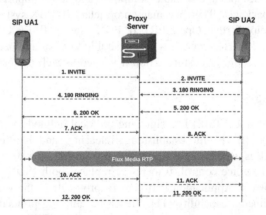

Fig. 2. INVITE session setup procedure

Connection signaling: this is the assignment of a support service to a call. Gradually we will reserve resources in the network according to the QoS required for the service. In SIP, this signaling is done through SDP headers that describe the traffic and resources required. At the transport level, the RSVP (Resource Reservation Protocol) and DiffServ (Differentiated Services) mechanisms are used to ensure the quality of service in the IP network.

Intelligence signaling: it allows substitution treatment compared to normal call processing. In a similar way to intelligent networks of RI (INAP) or CAMEL type, services are executed by the equivalent of service platforms that are application servers (AS) [11].

3   Studies of SIP Protocol Vulnerabilities

In the current SIP configuration, sending and receiving a message requires the direct connection of both clients to the SIP server. The architecture in the following implements this configuration of a SIP server (Fig. 3).

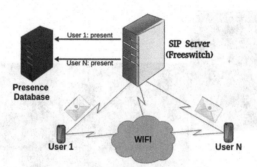

Fig. 3. Initial architecture of a SIP server

In this architecture, User 1 and User N are all connected to the SIP telephony server. It has a presence database where it will store all users connected. Once a user connects, the server detects its connection and records it at the presence database so it has information about its presence, that is, REGISTER events. When the connected User 1 sends a message to the User N, the server consults its presence database to obtain the information on the User N. If it sees that it is present at the presence base, it retransmits it. the message that is intended for him. Otherwise, if the User N is absent at the presence database, the message intended for him is lost. The following figures show illustrations of faults noted on users' attendance servers in VoIP PBXs.

3.1   Sending Message Between User: Both Connected (User 1000 and User 1001)

To do the tests, we used the CSipSimple SIP client (Fig. 4).

Fig. 4. Registration of user 1000 and 1001

The user 1000 sends a message to the connected user 1001 (Fig. 5).

Fig. 5. Sending message from user 1000 to user 1001 and Receipt of the message by the user 1001

For this initial configuration of the SIP server, if all users are connected to the SIP server, the sent messages always arrive at their destination as we can see for the message sent by the user 1000 to the user 1001. This example is the case where both users are connected, we will now see the case where one of the users is not connected.

3.2 Sending Message Between User: One Connected (1000) and the Other Disconnected (1001)

The user 1000 sends a message to the user 1001 not connected (Figs. 6 and 7).

Fig. 6. Send message from the user 1000 to the user 1001 not connected

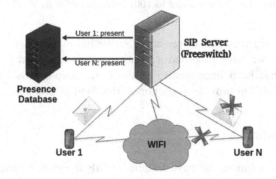

Fig. 7. Informations from the server

After sending this message, we will consult our server and this thanks to its console, we observe the error messages.

Figure 8 shows the messages at the log level of our server and that the message sent to the user 1001 has not arrived at the destination. We note that this message sent without connection of the User N has not arrived at its destination.

Fig. 8. Architecture on the noted connection problem

It is found that another problem arises, if the user disables its WIFI indicator, the server does not have disconnection information to be able to properly disconnect the user from the presence database. From the cost, he continues to see it as this one was still connected to the server. The figure below implements the enumerated phenomenon.

The User N decides to disable his WIFI light and as we see the server continues to register as present at its base of presence. The message sent by User 1 to User N did not arrive at destination. This is simply because the server still has User N registration information in its presence database, so it tries to send the message when it is not actually connected. From the cost this message will not be received by the User N.

The following figures present the different steps that led to this study. In this figure, both users are connected to the telephony server. They are present at the level of the presence base (Fig. 9).

	call id	sip user	sip host	presence hosts	contact	st
1	QWN-Q4PPA755	1000	192.168.1.7	192.168.1.7,19:	"" <sip:1000@1	Re
2	c7gHjeB2EQsXO	1001	192.168.1.7	192.168.1.7,19:	"" <sip:1001@1	Re

Fig. 9. The presence base of the telephony server

The experiment implemented is that if the user 1001 decides to disable only are WIFI LED. If we update our presence base, we continue to have its presence at the level of it. The user 1000 will send him a message. We notice at the level of the logs of our SIP server that the sent message does not reach its destination. The following figure shows the message sent by the user 1000 to the user 1001 (Fig. 10).

```
2018-06-13 09:42:32.355696 [INFO] switch_cpp.cpp:1365 *******    Evenement Message    *********
2018-06-13 09:42:32.355696 [INFO] switch_cpp.cpp:1365 ipv4 : 192.168.1.7
2018-06-13 09:42:32.355696 [INFO] switch_cpp.cpp:1365 sender : 1000
2018-06-13 09:42:32.355696 [INFO] switch_cpp.cpp:1365 recipient : 1001
2018-06-13 09:42:32.355696 [INFO] switch_cpp.cpp:1365 message : Hello you're there?
```

Fig. 10. Message sent to 1001 which disables its WIFI

We notice that the message arrives at the server but the user will never receive it. To overcome this, we have proposed a solution that is described in detail with the architecture that has been implemented in the next section. This leads us to do a thorough study of SIP to provide a solution to this kind of problem.

4 Implementation

To implement this solution, we have installed a SIP freeswitch server that we have exploited by sending requests and thanks to its ESL module (Event Socket Library), we manage to listen on MESSAGES type events. This listening of events allows us to detect the various faults noted in the previous section.

To solve the flaws, we developed a script in python and adapted to SIP servers as freeswitch and asterisk, we also set up a MySQL database that will be used to store messages whose owners are not registered at the SIP server. In this script, we listen to the MESSAGES events of freeswitch so that the flaws we noted relate to message reception problems in case of bad connection. This script listen infinitely loop on these events, it allows us to recover any event that arrives on our telephony server in order to exploit it, either we send it to the recipient or it is to store in a MySQL database.

This database also allows us to have the traces of the different messages exchanged. As soon as the recipient who was absent reconnects, our script receives the event reconnection message, it checks in the database if the user in question has no messages store in absence. If this is the case then the script retrieves the message (s) from the database and reformats it to send it to its recipient. If this is not the case, the script notifies in the SIP server console that the user does not have a missed message. The proposed architecture is given in the following figure (Fig. 11).

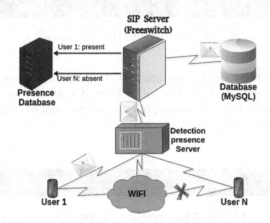

Fig. 11. Architecture of the proposed solution

5   Results and Discussions

Following the problem identified earlier, we will propose a solution that will allow us to overcome this. The architecture below shows how the solutions have been implemented and a description of this solution will be provided. In this architecture, there is the presence of another server that is called here "presence detection server". This server works as follows:

It sends a ping every five seconds to users connected to the SIP server.

- If the User N, who was previously connected to the server, decides to disable his WIFI LED, automatically the presence detection server by sending him a Ping gets as UNREGISTERED answer.
- He then contacts the SIP server to notify him of the disconnection of the User in question.

The SIP server consults its presence base, which always sees the User as logged in, and informs him of the disconnection of the latter by asking him to update the new information. User information is therefore updated, and is therefore absent from the presence database. If a message is sent to this User N, then the presence detection server retrieves the message, retransmits it to the SIP server and it will simply store the message in the MySQL database while waiting for the User to reconnect. N. The following figure shows that both user 1000 and 1001 are well connected to the SIP server and a ping is sent to them at every moment to see their presence detected (Fig. 12).

Fig. 12. User 1000 and 1001 connection

We note for our two users the messages succeeded Ping sent. Now if the user 1000 disables its WIFI simply, our Ping allows us to know if it is well connected or not. The following figure shows the return messages after the ping sent to the user 1000 which disables his WIFI (Fig. 13).

Fig. 13. Return message after ping to 1000

The user 1000 is removed from the server's presence database. This allows us to be able to know if a user is connected or not in order to be able to take measurements in relation to the messages he receives. If the user 1001 sends a message to the user 1000, the message is retrieved and stored in the database. MySQL data. The following figure shows the message sent to the user 1000 (Fig. 14).

Fig. 14. Message sent to the user 1000 after our modification.

We note that the message is well saved in the database to wait for the good connection of the user 1000. The following Fig. 16 shows the reconnection of the user 1000, the message that was stored is sent to him (Fig. 15).

Fig. 15. Message sent after reconnecting the user 1000

One faith the user in question reconnects, he receives the message (s) which were stored in the database and which had for recipient him.

Fig. 16. Message sent after reconnecting the user 1000

6 Conclusion

The global study of the SIP protocol concerning the sending and the receiving of the SIP messages made it possible to note the problems of reception of the message sent in case the recipient is not connected. We found that this message is lost and never reaches its destination in this case. This resulted in the solution we propose in this article. A solution we tested with the SIP server freeswitch but it remains adapted to other SIP servers as an asterisk. So today we can say that this solution can greatly contribute to the improvement of SIP message sending and reception conditions and therefore to a perfect reliability of SIP MESSAGES events, which is for us an advantage in a context where we tend towards IP at all with the arrival of the fourth generation (4G) and the prospects of a fifth generation (5G).

References

1. Abbasi, T., Prasad, S., Seddigh, N., Lambadaris, I.: A comparative study of the SIP and IAX VoIP protocols. In: Canadian Conference on Electrical and Computer Engineering, Saskatoon, Sask, pp. 179–183 (2005). https://doi.org/10.1109/ccece.2005.1556904
2. Saliha, M., Amina, Z., Chafia, Y.: A new authentication and key agreement protocol for SIP in IMS. In: 2015 IEEE/ACS 12th International Conference of Computer Systems and Applications (AICCSA), Marrakech, pp. 1–7 (2015). https://doi.org/10.1109/aiccsa.2015.7507136
3. Yang, L., Lei, K.: Combining ICE and SIP protocol for NAT traversal in new classification standard. In: 2016 5th International Conference on Computer Science and Network Technology (ICCSNT), Changchun, pp. 576–580 (2016). https://doi.org/10.1109/iccsnt.2016.8070224
4. Rosenberg, J., et al.: SIP: Session Initiation Protocol, IETF RFC3261, June 2002
5. Yu, L.: Improving query for P2P SIP VoIP. In: 2012 IEEE 11th International Conference on Trust, Security and Privacy in Computing and Communications, Liverpool, pp. 1735–1740 (2012). https://doi.org/10.1109/trustcom.2012.183
6. Hosseinpour, M., Seno, S.A.H., Moghaddam, M.H.Y., Roshkhari, H.K.: Modeling SIP normal traffic to detect and prevent SIP-VoIP flooding attacks using fuzzy logic. In: 2016 6th International Conference on Computer and Knowledge Engineering (ICCKE), Mashhad, pp. 274–279 (2016). https://doi.org/10.1109/iccke.2016.7802152
7. Hersent, O., Gurle, D., Petit, J.P.: IP Telephony Packet-Based Multimedia Communication Systems. Wiley, Hoboken (2005)
8. Johnston, A.B.: SIP: Understanding the Session Initiation Protocol. Artech House, Boston (2007)
9. List_of_SIP_software#Proprietary_license (n.d.). Wikipedia. http://wikipedia.org/wiki/List_of_SIP_software#Proprietary_license
10. Ansari, A.M., Nehal, M.F., Qadeer, M.A.: SIP-based interactive voice response system using FreeSwitch EPBX. In: 2013 Tenth International Conference on Wireless and Optical Communications Networks (WOCN), Bhopal, pp. 1–5 (2013). https://doi.org/10.1109/wocn.2013.6616224
11. Imène ELLOUMI: Management of mobility between access networks and Quality of Service in an NGN/IMS approach. Thèse doctorat: University of Carthage (Tunisie) (2012)

Towards a Spatial-Temporal Model of Prevalence of Nodding Syndrome and Epilepsy

Kizito Ongaya[1]($\boxtimes$), Paul Ssemalullu[1], Benedict Oyo[2], Gilbert Maiga[1], and Augustus Aturinde[3]

[1] College of Computing and Information Sciences,
Makerere University, Kampala, Uganda
k.ongaya@gu.ac.ug1
[2] Department of Computer Science, Gulu University, Gulu, Uganda
[3] Department of Physical Geography and Ecosystem Science,
Lund University, Lund, Sweden

Abstract. Nodding syndrome is an emerging disease which have unknown transmission patterns and no properly established mechanisms for diagnosis leading to numerous hypothetical postulations. It has affected thousands of children in Uganda with debilitating effect and serious economic consequences. Spatial-temporal analysis may provide a quick mechanism to establish comparative understanding of the various hypotheses ascribed to nodding syndrome and any other emerging diseases with similar clinical manifestation. There is considerable suspicion that "nodding syndrome is a form of epilepsy", a hypothesis that has hardly been investigated in literature. The *aim* of the study described in this paper is to establish spatial-temporal relationships between ailments diagnosed as nodding syndrome and ailments diagnosed as epilepsy. An *exploratory cross section* survey in three districts of Northern Uganda was done. Spatial data of health centers were recorded and ArcGIS was used for display. The *findings* show significant spatial-temporal correlation of diagnosis reporting of nodding syndrome to epilepsy. The regression statistics overall, epilepsy significantly ($p < 0.05$) ex-plains about 58% of Nodding syndrome variability. The F-statistic shows a very highly significant value ($p = 8.20481E-13$; $p < 0.05$), meaning that the output of the regression is not by chance.

Keywords: Nodding syndrome · Emerging diseases · Surveillance · Spatial-temporal · Geographic information system

1 Introduction

Space-time mapping and analysis of disease data has historically involved the search for patterns in aggregated data to identify how regions of high and low risk change through time [16]. Mapping of space and time analysis of aggregated data has great value, but represents only a subset of space time epidemiologic applications. Technological advances for tracking and mapping individuals (e.g., global positioning systems) have introduced mobile populations as an important element in space time

© ICST Institute for Computer Sciences, Social Informatics and Telecommunications Engineering 2019
Published by Springer Nature Switzerland AG 2019. All Rights Reserved
G. Mendy et al. (Eds.): AFRICOMM 2018, LNICST 275, pp. 67–77, 2019.
https://doi.org/10.1007/978-3-030-16042-5_7

epidemiological modelling [19]. The importance mapping, place, and time came in light more than 200-years ago when Dr. John Snow modelled a map of cholera deaths in relation to London's water pumps. This was one of the first, and perhaps the most celebrated, disease maps model. His history of disease mapping is filled with examples of maps that helped provide etiological clues to diseases from cholera to lung cancer. With the help of his famous map model, Snow was not only able to track the source of what he called "the most terrible outbreak of cholera which ever occurred in this kingdom," but he was able to convince authorities to act against the disease (Snow 1855). Analyzing and mapping spatial and temporal dynamics of infectious diseases features mathematical and spatial modeling approaches that integrate applications from various fields such as geo-computation and simulation, spatial analytics, mathematics, statistics, epidemiology, and health policy [5] provides great insights to understanding disease outbreaks.

In recent years, transmission of diseases has exhibited new spatial and temporal patterns [20]. Emerging diseases like nodding syndrome with unknown transmission patterns and mechanisms for diagnosis are being discovered more often. There is therefore need to harness geographical information system (GIS) capabilities to establish insights into patterns of spatial transmission.

Nodding Syndrome is a childhood neurological disorder which affects communities in Northern Uganda [13]. It is a poorly understood neurologic disorder of unknown aetiology that affects children and adolescents in Africa [21]. It is an emerging illness that has eluded surveillance models in Africa for over six decades since its discovery in the 1960's [7, 14]. There is hardly any surveillance model for investigating spatial diffusion and supporting geographical knowledge on how to intervene on the outbreak of nodding syndrome. Many authors agree that its spatial diffusion patterns, and transmission models are not properly understood [18], the characteristics, risk factors as well as aetiological factors are also not well established [4, 15, 18] complicating surveillance efforts. Up to the year 2012, when the Ministry of Health Uganda recognized the ailment as a public health concern, it had affected estimated thousands of children in Northern Uganda [4, 10]. The surveillance form used in health centers and hospitals for Integrated Disease Surveillance and Response lacked provision for nodding syndrome for all the years before 2012. The ailment became endemic in the population and the disease reached a threshold after over a decade to warrant public health concern.

There is considerable suspicion that nodding syndrome is a form of epilepsy [6, 11, 18]. Much as these findings are of biological significance, there is limited literature on spatial models comparing spatial prevalence of nodding syndrome and associated epilepsy. The Ministry of Health of Uganda and partner organizations identified the gaps in knowledge of nodding syndrome that "the actual geographic coverage and distribution is not known, and that there is need for surveillance in other areas outside the current foci and the overlap of areas of distribution of nodding syndrome, etiological, potential risk factors and other information of interest [15]. Also, the burden of nodding syndrome in the currently reported three foci and surrounding areas are also not known. The increasing prevalence of nodding syndrome in northern Uganda has generated a wide range of speculations with respect to aetiology and natural history and best possible medical treatment for this mysterious seizure disorder. Despite in-depth investigations by the United States Centers for Disease Control and Prevention and the Ministry of Health in Uganda, agree that no clear causal factors have emerged [15].

The spatial epidemiological prevalence of nodding syndrome particularly in Northern Uganda is inaccurately presented by different organizations [1]. For instance, the independent charity organization; Kitgum District NGO Forum, which first announced the outbreak of nodding syndrome, estimates that as many as 5,000 children are infected by the disease in Kitgum district alone, while government officials report; there are only 3,200 infected children, Other scholars put the total number of cases of nodding syndrome in the 3 districts of study at 1,876 [9]. These news reports and some clinical scholarly research examined above, clearly lack systematic spatial and temporal analysis of nodding syndrome. Furthermore, many scholars believe that "nodding syndrome is a form of epilepsy" [8, 11, 14], and [12]. However, these reports and researches hardly critically examined the distribution of the two diseases over time in-order to contrast them and make spatial correlation to deduce conclusion and inter-vention plans.

The compelling issues of this paper therefore are: (i) The need to determine whether nodding syndrome is being reported by the different health facilities in Northern Uganda, (ii) The need to establish spatial prevalence of nodding syndrome and epilepsy reporting and model the overlapping (scaffolding) relationship; and (iii) Propose a method for surveillance mechanism for nodding syndrome.

2   Methodology

This paper is a cross section studies comparing spatial-temporal diagnoses of diseases identified as nodding syndrome and those that have been identified as epilepsy in three districts of Gulu, Omoro, and Kitgum in Northern Uganda. Purposive sampling of health centers was used to identify facilities that are relevant for the study. Twelve (12) health centers were identified for the study based on Ministry of Health IDSR (Integrated Disease Surveillance and Reporting tool). Two questionnaires were used for data collection with the first one designed for health workers interfacing with nodding syndrome patients. It was to elicit basic information on the gravity of nodding syn-drome in the communities and also provide some statistical overview of patients attended to from a particular health center. The second was designed for health centers and hospitals data managers. It was particularly tailored to examine the depth of information available from a particular health center identified as receiving nodding syndrome victims. Environmental System Research Institute (ESRI) ArcView Software was used for analysis and display of the data on a map. ANOVA and Spreadsheet were used for trend and regression analysis. Analysis was done consecutively for five years to establish the spatio-temporal aspects.

3 The Study Findings

We can observe that health centers, began reporting on nodding syndrome incidences especially in West of Aswa river basin in 2012. In Kitgum, Pajimo and Tumangu also began reporting around the same period. The Local NGO Hope for Humans was established in Odek because the cases were very many in the area and spear headed advocacy program about the outbreaks and scientific research.

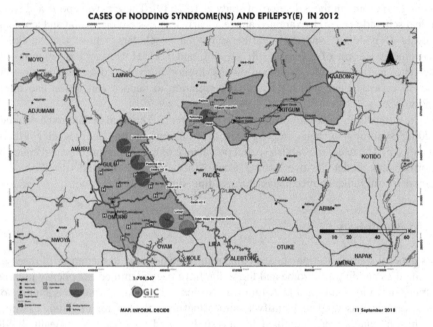

Fig. 1. A map of health centers reporting nodding syndrome and epilepsy in 2012

The number of health centers reporting the ailments increased in the following years mostly along the span of Aswa River. The patients that were in Omoro were referred to Hope for Human Centre which was thought to have better facilities and specialized in treatment of nodding syndrome patients. While others that were in Kitgum district were referred to Kitgum Hospital. Most health facilities however, continued recording epileptic also patients across the region. By the year 2016 (Fig. 2), the spatial-temporal reporting was widely spread across the three districts.

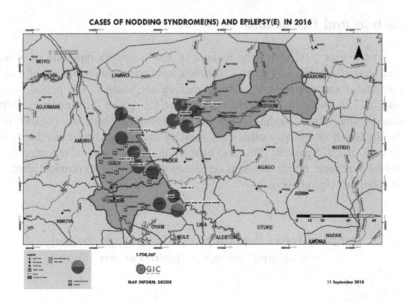

Fig. 2. A Map of health centres reporting nodding syndrome and epilepsy in 2016.

In 2017 (Fig. 3), it appears that diagnosis of nodding syndrome was very low across the region, however, the associated epilepsy were distributed across. On the other hand, the Referral Hospital in Kitgum and Hope for Human Centre had high number of diagnosis of epilepsy.

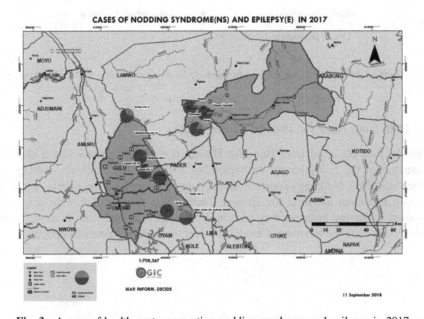

Fig. 3. A map of health centres reporting nodding syndrome and epilepsy in 2017

4 Analysis and Discussions

A shown from Figs. 1, 2 and 3 the number of health centers reporting of nodding syndrome were rising. We can observe that the spatial-temporal prevalence of nodding syndrome and associated epilepsy were mimicking one another. The period between 2015 and 2017 is special in that there was massive Campaign for support to nodding syndrome victims. Since nodding syndrome manifests with epilepsy, the turn up of patients diagnosed as epilepsy other than nodding syndrome were exceedingly high with the peak of 7,725 patients. This also explains the anomaly in the reporting figures for nodding syndrome by the different organization partnering to provide health services in Northern Uganda (Fig. 4).

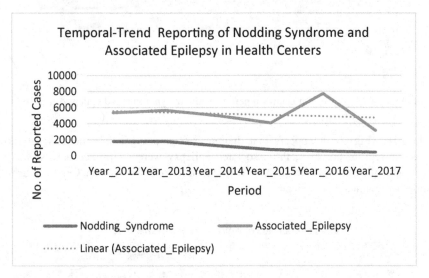

Fig. 4. Temporal Graph with line of best-fit showing Nodding syndrome & associated epilepsy reporting.

4.1 Data from Hope for Human Center (Odek)

Diagnoses data collected from Hope for Human (Fig. 5) Center provides a classical comparison of the two ailments. In September 2013 saw the diagnosis overlap one another (scaffold). Nodding syndrome dropped down epilepsy as the patients continue receiving treatment at Hope for Human Center. The patients that were originally diagnosed as having both nodding plus epilepsy improved and nod no more. Some recovered and left the treatment Center, however, some have remained epileptic.

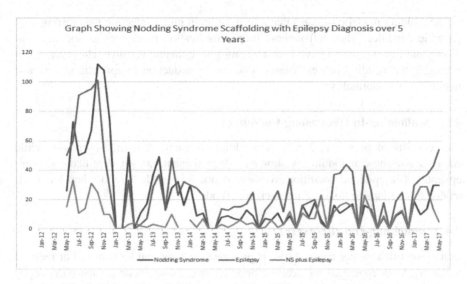

Fig. 5. Temporal scaffolding pattern of nodding syndrome and epilepsy

4.2 Scaffolding Model of Nodding Syndrome and Associated Epilepsy

Distinguishing nodding syndrome and epilepsy reporting shows some succinct details in that, there is scaffolding/ overlap between the two ailments. Much as epileptic conditions are clear, nodding is equally clear and it seems they influence each other. Figure 6 is an attempt to show distinctions and relationships between the two conditions.

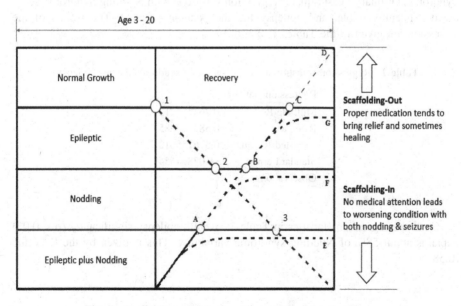

Fig. 6. Scaffolding model of nodding syndrome and epilepsy

Scaffolding model postulates that a form of brain injury/infection manifesting with epileptic condition when left without proper medication progresses to nodding syndrome and can worsen to have both nodding plus epileptic seizures. However, when managed, the nodding process ceases followed by reduction in epileptic seizure and may recover to normality.

4.3   Scaffolding-In (Worsening Condition)

This consists of nodes (1, 2 &3) as condition worsens. A normally growing child comes in contact with nodding syndrome etiological agent (not yet identified), becomes epileptic. The epileptic condition overlaps to nodding (node 1) and when left unattended to overlaps to nodding plus seizures (node 3).

4.4   Scaffolding-Out (Recovery)

In the event that proper medical care is provided, seizures can be removed or reduced (node A). With continued medication, nodding also ceases (node B) and all epileptic conditions may be reduced (node C), and at times full recovery may result (node D). Some patients have only reduced nodding and epileptic conditions (node E) while others recover from nodding conditions (node G), but epileptic conditions remains unsolved problem (node G). Majority of the patients from Hope for Humans Center have fully recovered and have either returned home and were able to go back to school.

4.5   Regression Analysis

To evaluate the strength and nature of the association between epilepsy and Nodding Syndrome, Ordinary Least Squares regression was done with Nodding Syndrome being the dependent variable, and epilepsy the independent variable. The results of the regression are given in the Tables 1, 2 and 3.

Table 1. Regression statistics summary (nodding syndrome against epilepsy)

Regression statistics	
Multiple R	0.763688212
R Square	0.583219685
Adjusted R Square	0.576155612
Standard error	16.07864554
Observations	61

From the regression statistics in Table 1, overall, epilepsy significantly ($p < 0.05$) explains about 58% of Nodding syndrome variability. This is given by the R^2 value (0.58).

Table 2. Analysis of variance (nodding syndrome against epilepsy)

	df	SS	MS	F	Significance F
Regression	1	21344.00476	21344.00476	82.56138826	8.20481E-13
Residual	59	15252.8477	258.5228424		
Total	60	36596.85246			

From the ANOVA results in Table 2, the F-statistic shows a very highly significant value (p = 8.20481E−13; p < 0.05), meaning that the output of the regression is not by chance. This means that epilepsy significantly influences the distribution of Nodding Syndrome, and this influence is not by chance.

Table 3. Linear-regression results (nodding syndrome against epilepsy)

	Coefficients	Standard error	t Stat	P-value	Lower 95%	Upper 95%	Lower 95.0%	Upper 95.0%
Intercept	−0.5720	3.0641	−0.1867	0.8525	−6.7032	5.5592	−6.7032	5.5592
Epilepsy (x)	0.7741	0.0852	9.0863	8.20481E-13	0.6036	0.9446	0.6036	0.9446

Results from Table 3 show that the contribution of epilepsy to Nodding Syndrome is highly significant (p < 0.05). The overall equation for this Epilepsy-NS association is given by Eq. (1). However, the intercept obtained is not reliable as it is statistically insignificant (p = 0.8525 > 0.05). From Eq. (1), it can be observed that overall, for every one unit increase in epilepsy, there is a 77% increase in Nodding Syndrome. This seemingly explains the relationship observed in (Fig. 6) where an increase in one disease resulted in an increase in the other.

$$y = -0.572 + 0.7741(x) \tag{1}$$

5 Conclusion

From this preliminary investigation, we have established that reporting on nodding syndrome by the different health facilities started in the year 2012 following recognition as a public health threat. Beyond 2012, no record exists in the reporting tools provided by Ministry of Health Uganda especially in the Integrated Disease Surveillance and Response (IDSR) form. In fact, there was no provision in the IDSR form beyond 2012.

As we can observe, the trend of prevalence of nodding syndrome and epilepsy over the period of four years were very much the similar. However, there was exceptional peak trend in associated epilepsy between 2015–2016 due to mass political assertion to intervene on the outbreak. Also, because nodding syndrome usually first manifests as epileptic conditions, the diagnosis and reporting in health facilities were not upright nodding syndrome, but rather epilepsy in the reporting tools provided by the Ministry of Health Uganda.

The study shows that there is scaffolding relationship in prevalence diagnosis of nodding syndrome and epilepsy especially with critical evaluation of data from Hope for Human Nodding Syndrome Center. The spatial-temporal analysis of diagnosis and reporting by the different health facilities, the study confirms that spatial-temporal distribution nodding syndrome is associated with spatial-temporal distribution of epileptic condition. This is also in line with other scientific establishment such as [6, 11, 18] and [8] through clinical studies which established that nodding syndrome is a form of epilepsy.

Therefore, we can affirm that due to relationships that exist as seen in scaffolding pattern, surveillance of nodding syndrome must go hand in hand with surveillance of epilepsy. The existing Integrated Disease Surveillance mechanisms can be improved to consider nodding syndrome, epilepsy as well as conditions that manifest both. And when there appears to be an outbreak of epilepsy, it may be a sign that infection that may result to nodding syndrome is in a community.

At the same time, we can also affirm that in the event of occurrence of emerging disease, when there is no established clinical diagnosis, geographical information systems (GIS) approaches can be effective alternative investigation mechanisms to establish relationships between hypothetically similar outbreaks.

References

1. Bemmel, K.V.: The rise and fall of nodding syndrome in public discourse: An analysis of newspaper coverage in Uganda. Critique Anthropol. **36**(2), 168–196 (2016). https://doi.org/10.1177/0308275X15614635. Sage publication. http://coa.sagepub.com. Accessed 13 May 2016
2. Bemmel, K.V., Derluyn, I., Stroeken, K.: Nodding syndrome or disease? On the conceptualization of an illness-in-the-making. Ethn Health **19**, 100–118 (2014)
3. Center for Disease Control – CDC: Nodding syndrome. Emerging Infectious Diseases, vol. 19, No. 9, September 2013. doi: http://dx.doi.org/10.3201/eid1909.130401, www.cdc.gov/eid. Accessed 18 Aug 2017
4. Center for Disease Control (CDC): Technical guidelines for integrated disease surveillance and response in the African Region. In: 2nd ed. Center for Global Health Division of Public Health Systems and Atlanta, Georgia, USA (2010)
5. Chen, D., Moulin, B., Wu, J.: Analyzing and modeling spatial and temporal dynamics of infectious diseases. In: Chen, D., Moulin, B., Wu, J. (eds.), 496 p. Wiley (2014). ISBN: 978-1-118-62993-2
6. Colebunders, R.: Prevalence and distribution of river epilepsy in the Orientale Province in the Democratic Republic of the Congo (DRC). In: 2nd International Conference on Nodding Syndrome, July 26–31, 2015. Gulu University (2015)
7. Colebunders, R., Hendy, A., Mokili, J.L., et al.: Nodding syndrome and epilepsy in onchocerciasis endemic regions: comparing preliminary observations from South Sudan and the Democratic Republic of the Congo with data from Uganda. BMC Res. Notes **9**, 182 (2016). https://doi.org/10.1186/s13104-016-1993-7. http://www.sciencedirect.com

8. Gazda, S.: Hope for humans, caring for children with nodding syndrome (2016). http://
    hopeforhumans.org/our-history/. Accessed 21 Sep 2017
9. Global Health Governance, vol. VI, Issue 1 (Fall 2012). http://www.ghgj.org
10. Idro, R., et al.: Nodding syndrome; a new (infectious?) disease entity of the CNS in Eastern
    Africa. J. Neurol. Sci. **333**, e1–e64 (2013). https://doi.org/10.1016/j.jns.2013.07.184
11. Idro, R.: Proposed guidelines for the management of nodding syndrome. In: 2nd International
    Conference on Nodding Syndrome, July 26–31, 2015. Gulu University (2015)
12. Kitara, D.L.: History and the distribution of nodding syndrome in Uganda. In: 2nd
    International Conference on Nodding Syndrome, July 26–31, 2015. Gulu University (2015)
13. Kitara, D.L.: Nodding Syndrome (NS) and Onchocerca Volvulus (OV) in Northern Uganda.
    Pan Afr. Med. J. **28**, 1 (2017). https://doi.org/10.11604/pamj.2017.28.1.13554. http://www.
    panafrican-med-journal.com/content/article/28/1/full/
14. Korevaar, D.A., Visser, B.J.: Reviewing the evidence on nodding syndrome, a mysterious
    tropical disorder. Int. J. Infect. Dis. **17**, e149–e152 (2013). http://www.elsevier.com /
    locate/ijid
15. Ministry of Health-MoH: About Uganda Ministry of Health (2016). http://health.go.ug/
    about-us/about-ministry-health
16. Meliker, J.R., Sloan, C.D.: Spatio-temporal epidemiology: Principles and opportunities. Sci.
    Dir. **2**(1), 1–9 (2010). Elsevier. https://doi.org/10.1016/j.sste.2010.10.001 Accessed 30 Jan
    2018
17. Snow, J.: On the Mode of Communication of Cholera. John Churchill, London (1855)
18. Spencer, P.S. Palmer, V.S., Jilek-Aall, L.: Nodding syndrome: origins and natural history of
    a longstanding epileptic disorder in Sub-Saharan Africa (2015)
19. Stevens, K.B., Pfeiffer, D.U.: Spatial modelling of disease using data - and knowledge-
    driven approaches. Pubmed. **2**(3), 125–133 (2011). https://doi.org/10.1016/j.sste.2011.07.
    007. Epub 2011 Jul 19. Accessed 30 Jan 2018
20. Samphutthanon, R., Tripathi, N.T., Ninsawat, S., Duboz, R.: Spatio-temporal distribution and
    hotspots of Hand, Foot and Mouth Disease (HFMD) in Northern Thailand. Int. J. Environ.
    Res. Public Health **11**, 312–336 (2014). https://doi.org/10.3390/ijerph110100312. ISSN
    1660-4601. http://www.mdpi.com/journal/ijerph. Accessed 31 Jan 2018
21. World Health Organization (WHO): Proposed guidelines for the management of nodding
    syndrome. African Health Sciences, **13**(2), June 2013. http://www.who.int/neglected_
    diseases/diseases/Proposed_guidelines_management_nodding_syndrome.pdf

Proposal of a SIP-Based Method to Supervise Free Roaming Calls

Said Hassani, Samuel Ouya, Ahmath Bamba Mbacke[✉],
Gervais Mendy, and Kéba Gueye

LIRT Laboratory, Higher Polytechnic School, University of Dakar,
Dakar, Senegal
saidhassani75@yahoo.fr, samuel.ouya@gmail.com,
{ahmathbamba.mbacke,keba.gueye}@esp.sn,
gervais.mendy@ucad.edu.sn

Abstract. This paper proposes an optimised method to supervise free roaming calls. Since November 28th, 2016, West African countries and members of the Economic Community of West African States (ECOWAS) have decided to ban roaming charges among mobile phone users in these countries. Its implementation however poses a problem of performance costs of their visibility for certain actors such as regulatory authorities (R.A.). To improve this matter we proposed to set up a SIP proxy (Session Initiation Protocol) at the regulatory authorities in order to recover only the signaling of received calls in roaming. The SIP proxy is implemented by Kamailio. Compared to the literature, this article brings a new method of supervision by controlling and following the evolution of calls received in roaming. The results obtained have produced positive effects as only concerned calls will be supervised through the proxy. The proposed solution will facilitate regulators to perform their duties as taxing operators and resolving conflicts between them. It will allow end-users to have visibility into their calls.

Keywords: Free roaming · Signalization protocol · SIP · Supervision system · Kamailio

1 Introduction

Since March 31, 2017, africans traveling to some member countries of the Economic Community of West African States (ECOWAS) can call without worrying about their phone bill. Initiated on November 28th in Abidjan and put into practice on March 31st 2017, free roaming now concerns several countries in West Africa such as: Senegal, Guinea, Mali, Togo, Burkina Faso, Benin,... etc. A call from another ECOWAS member country during a trip to a "Free Roaming" country is no longer surcharged, so callers will no longer have to pay extra fees once they leave their country; despite some restrictions [13]:

- Once abroad, the subscriber will be able to receive free calls for a period of 300 min and within one month,
- Outgoing calls will be billed by the local operator as if he has billed his subscriber,

© ICST Institute for Computer Sciences, Social Informatics and Telecommunications Engineering 2019
Published by Springer Nature Switzerland AG 2019. All Rights Reserved
G. Mendy et al. (Eds.): AFRICOMM 2018, LNICST 275, pp. 78–87, 2019.
https://doi.org/10.1007/978-3-030-16042-5_8

- A call made to a country that is not a party to free roaming will be surcharged,
- Free roaming does not apply to internet data.

However the implementation of this "Free Roaming" poses a problem of performance to obtain their visibility through filtering. Visibility issues include subscribers who do not have a way to track their calls duration for the next 300 min, which can engender unexpected bills. They (visibility issues) also include the regulatory authorities, such as Senegal's regulatory authority, whose signaling tools for "Free Roaming" calls are jumbled up with that of international calls. This affects their processes performances (reporting delays and precision) in taxing operators and generates conflicts with them [11, 12].

Existing studies show generally that the implementation of Free Roaming causes many problems and stresses the importance of finding solutions. In Europe, Patrick Maillé et al. have raised two issues arising from the application of free roaming:a problem of relationship between users and service providers and economic in the operators [1, 2]. On the same continent, Jonathan Spruytte et al. have raised a lot of problems after the establishment of Roaming Like At Home (RLAH) and proposed to implement the Roaming Like At Local (RLAL) [3]. As a limit to the RLAL, they emphasized the lack of transparency for consumers. These studies did not indicate a technical solution. Other studies propose solutions but within known limits. Biswas et al. have raised the problem of free roaming by proposing cloud-based system to reduce the communication costs between users when one of the two users is in roaming [4]. By making use of technology, a robust system has been developed that automatically identifies a roaming mobile number and blocks any unknown number but notifies at either end [4, 5]. After the adoption of SIP protocol (Session initiation protocol) in WIMAX networks Cheng et al. pointed out an expensive transfer time when a subscriber is roaming and changing a network to another. When the subscriber changes a network, he sends a RE-INVITE request to register for the new network. They proposed as solution the establishment of a SIP hierarchical domain (HSIP). This means that multiple networks must be managed by a single HSIP server to form an administration domain [6]. Beaubrun et al. have detected an increase in roaming signaling traffic in Next Generation (NG) wireless networks. They proposed to set up a special gateway called the Wireless Interworking Gateway (WING) to facilitate interoperability between the heterogeneous subsystems of NG wireless systems [7].

These solutions do not control and do not track the evolution of calls in terms of their duration. However architectures they propose are to be taken into account for their robustness. Interviews show that some regulators such as Senegal have a system to oversee incoming and outgoing international communications. The defect of this system is that the signaling of free roaming calls is mixed with that of the others.

This paper proposes a method to separate the signaling, to control and monitor the evolution of the meter for 300 min combining robust architecture with filtering of signalization for specific roaming calls.

In this article, Sect. 2 presents the method and architecture proposals, Sect. 3 trains results, Sect. 4 discusses the results and Sect. 5 gives a conclusion to this actual work.

2   Technical Proposition and Design

2.1   Objectives and Steps

As emphasized in the introduction, this paper aims to propose a method to supervise free roaming calls. This means a method to separate the signaling of free roaming calls from that of others; and control/monitor the evolution of their meter for 300 min. Principles of this solution are based on the implementation of a SIP proxy at each regulatory authority that will only recover and process the signaling of calls from "Free Roaming". A program will be implemented on that proxy to process calls counter through these SIP proxies. We then propose to interconnect regulatory authorities systems.

In short the regulatory authorities will build a intra-network that will be used to route calls from "Free Foaming" to the destination.

To do so, the SIP proxy need the following functions:

- retrieve call signaling to a roaming subscriber,
- process the signaling and route the call to the authority of the country where the roaming subscriber is located,
- The proxy of the authority of the country where the subscriber is located will route the call to the visited operator.

Architecture of Proposed Solution. To design the architecture, we used the works of Cheng et al. and that of Beaubrun et al. [6, 7]. We proposed and compared the following two architectures.

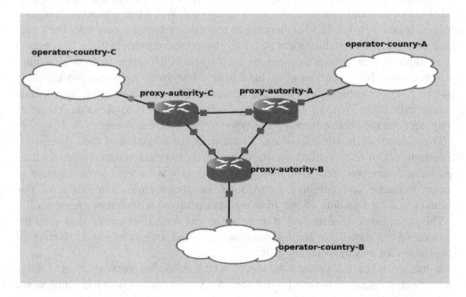

Fig. 1. Basic architecture : Regulation authorities direct proxy interconnexion

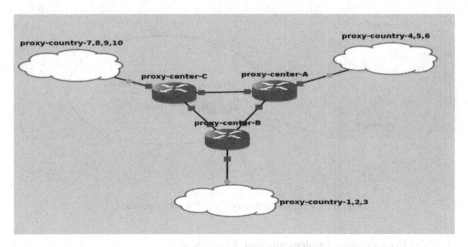

Fig. 2. Advanced architecture : Shared proxy centers interconnexion

Example of Call Processing

If for example, a call is made to a subscriber Jean of a country C op-C operator roaming in a visited network of an op-A operator in country A, the scenario below will be observed:

- The operator op-C will direct the call to the authority authority-country-C,
- Country-authority-C will perform the processing and route the call to authority authority-country-A:
    - Through a direct interconnexion with authority-country-A 's proxy (Fig. 1)
    - Through a shared proxy center network covering multiple countries (Fig. 2)
- The authority authority-country-A will route the call to the operator op-A,
- The operator op-A to make the call to the subscriber Jean,
- John will then have the choice of answering or not answering.

Entities Needed to Operate the SIP Proxy

The SIP proxy will be combined with a database system on which it will store information from the signatory countries of the "Free Roaming" (that will serve as its routing information) and the information of the recipient (for the control of the 300 min). Its tables will store the recipient information's and his calls duration sum in minutes (its values will be incremented at the end of each call) (Fig. 3).

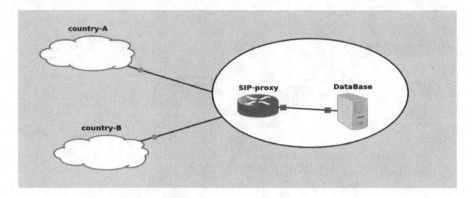

Fig. 3. Elements necessary for SIP proxy operation

2.2   SIP Protocol and Implementation Algorithm

SIP Protocol

As pointed out above, the solution is based on the SIP protocol. SIP (Session initiation Protocol) is an application layer control protocol that can establish, modify and terminate multimedia sessions [8]. SIP works in client-server mode. Like the HTTP protocol, the client sends commands and the server responds with response codes. Unlike HTTP, a SIP entity is in most cases both client and server. Between the client and the server (between the two communicators), there may be servers called proxy servers such as [8, 9]:

- Proxy server: it receives requests from clients that it processes itself or that it sends to other servers,
- the redirection server: this is a server that accepts SIP requests, translates the destination SIP address into one or more network addresses and returns them to the clients,
- The user agent "UA, User Agent": it is an application on a user equipment that sends and receives SIP requests,
- Registrar: This server registers users. It also updates the location database,
- B2BUA (Back To Back User Agent): it is like a proxy with the difference that the B2BUA establishes communication and monitors.

Consider a call between Alice and Bob. It is assumed that Alice wants to communicate with Bob (Fig. 4).

1. Alice sends a SIP INVITE message to her operators proxy (orange).
2. Alice Proxy sends the request to Bob's proxy server (tigo.sn),
3. Bob's proxy server sends the request to Bob,
4. being available Bob responds with a 200 OK response and this response goes through the same entities,
5. Alice sends an ACK confirmation message and start to communicate.

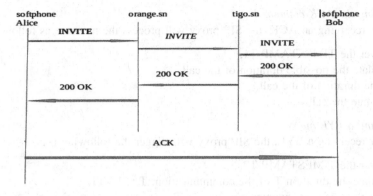

Fig. 4. Session setup between two users who do not have the same provider

Algorithm for Setting up the SIP Proxy

The SIP proxy will process a call in three phases: when receiving SIP INVITE, ACK and BYE commands. Let the table APPEL (id, uri-dest, counter) the table used to store the recipient's information, the INVITE, ACK and BYE messages will be processed as follows: (a) processing an INVITE, (b) then an ACK and (c) finally a BYE.

Processing an INVITE

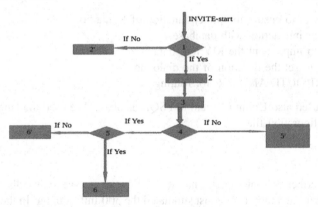

1: check if the country of destination is part of the signatory countries of "Free Roaming"

2 ': reject the call

2: continue treatment

3: retrieve the recipient's UR

4: check if the user is in the database (table CALL)

5 ': create an entry in the CALL table and route the call

5: check if the meter is less than 300 min

6 ': redirect the call

6: get the counter and route the call.

Processing the ACK command

After receiving an ACK, the SIP proxy will process the message as follows:

- recover the TIMESTAMP T1,
- calculate the possible duration of the call,
- set the duration of the call,
- Continue the call.

Processing a BYE query

After receiving a BYE, the SIP proxy will trigger the following processes:

- recover the TIMESTAMP T2,
- calculate the duration T of the communication: $T = T2\text{-}T1$,
- Update the counter: counter = counter + T.

3 Implementation and Results

3.1 Implementation

We propose the Kamailio SIP proxy as an implementation. Kamailio is a telephony server based on the SIP signaling protocol [10]. To work, Kamailio uses several modules and those we will use are:

- RTPPROXY: to ensure the proxy function of Kamailio,
- SQLOP: for interaction with databases,
- MYSQL: to implement the MYSQL database,
- DIALOG: to set the duration of the dialogue,
- CARRIERROUTE AND RR: for routing.

We have used also Ubuntu.14 and MYSQL database. We used the language of the Kamailio configuration file.

3.2 Results

When a subscriber is roaming, he has the ability to receive free calls for the first 300 min and within a month. We just simulated the 300 min counter. In the simulation, we used two SIP servers and the proxy in their middle (Fig. 5).

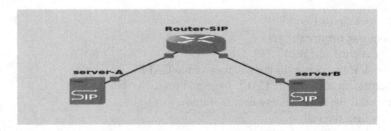

Fig. 5. Architecture simulation

In the architecture above, the servers simulate the operators and R-SIP simulates the SIP proxy. We will begin by viewing the description of the CALL table on which the recipient's call information is stored (Fig. 6).

```
mysql> desc 'CALL';
+---------+-------------+------+-----+---------+----------------+
| Field   | Type        | Null | Key | Default | Extra          |
+---------+-------------+------+-----+---------+----------------+
| id      | smallint(6) | NO   | PRI | NULL    | auto_increment |
| login   | varchar(60) | NO   |     | NULL    |                |
| counter | varchar(60) | NO   |     | NULL    |                |
+---------+-------------+------+-----+---------+----------------+
3 rows in set (0.00 sec)
```

Fig. 6. Structure of the CALL table

At the counter time is expressed in seconds.
We will now view the evolution of the counter after two successive calls.

```
mysql> select * from 'CALL';
+----+------------------------+---------+
| id | login                  | counter |
+----+------------------------+---------+
| 46 | sip:1002@192.168.43.65 | 35      |
+----+------------------------+---------+
1 row in set (0.00 sec)
mysql> select * from 'CALL';
+----+------------------------+---------+
| id | login                  | counter |
+----+------------------------+---------+
| 46 | sip:1002@192.168.43.65 | 98      |
+----+------------------------+---------+
1 row in set (0.00 sec)
```

Fig. 7. Evolution of the counter

We see that the first call lasted 35 s and this duration was recorded in the CALL table. After the second call, the counter was incremented to 98 s, which meant the call lasted 63 s.

To simulate the call control, we will now view the behavior of the KAMAILIO router when receiving a call to a recipient who has consumed its 300 min. We simulated the 300 min at 5.

```
09:41:42.669 GRAVE: [569] impl.protocol.sip.OperationSetBasicTelephonySipImpl.pr
ocessResponse().589 Received error: 403 your corespondent has consumed his 5mn
```

Fig. 8. Rejection of an INVITE

We sent a message to the caller informing him that the called party had consumed his 300 min of receiving the call. It was just to show that we can reject or redirect the call.

To conclude, this section has presented the proposed solution and its implementation. The next part will discuss the obtained results.

4 Discussion

Our main objectives are: to separate the signaling of the calls, to control and to follow the evolution of the calls (evolution of the counter) in the case of roaming situations. The implementation of a SIP proxy at the regulatory authorities seems to be a functioning control and supervision solution.

Its deployment through the proposed architectures (Figs. 1 and 2) allows to physically separate the signaling of the calls as shown in the results (Fig. 7). It also facilitates calls control (Fig. 8) in a separate infrastructure, distributing performances costs in regulator authorities' infrastructures. By this mean a subnetwork linking countries members of the free roaming zones is also created with costs reduction in case of central proxy sharing (Fig. 2).

Compared to the literature [6, 7], the similarities are on the proposed architecture (Figs. 1 and 2). We therefor beneficiate of the robustness induced by the flow calls separation. We also added monitoring and tracking calls support for the regulators; and notification functionalities for callers as our main contributions (visibility).

This proposal allows regulatory authorities to perform their duties such as taxation and management of conflicts between operators (Fig. 7) by automated data processing (mainly semi-automated in case of non filtering solution). It also allows roaming end-users to follow the evolution of the meter (Fig. 8) in real-time.

However a study must be made to evaluate routing and By Passing problems.

5 Conclusion

The purpose of this article was to propose a method to supervise free roaming calls in west of Africa. We can conclude from the results obtained that setting up a SIP proxy, on either the basic (Fig. 1) or advanced (Fig. 2) architecture is a good method to fulfill those goals within that specific context.

The results obtained show that the proposed algorithm allows to separate call flows processing in a specific server, reducing the impact on the regulator authorities infrastructure with a possible cost reducing through sharable SIP proxy centers. Compared to previous works, the proposed solution improves the calls visibility and allows regulatory authorities to perform their obligations as taxation operator and conflict manager between operators by providing efficient tools. It also allows consumers to have visibility on their calls in a roaming context.

However a study must be made to avoid routing and By Passing security risks.

The proposed architecture seems also to provide a deployable service in a single (sub)regional network context.

References

1. Maillé, P., Tuffin, B.: Enforcing free roaming among UE countries: an economic analysis. In: 13th International Conference on Network and Service Management (CNSM), November 2017, Tokyo, Japan (2017)
2. Maillé, P., Tuffin, B.: How does imposing free roaming in EU impact users and ISPs' relations?. In: 8th International Conference Network of the Future, November 2017, London, United Kingdom (2017)
3. Spruytte, J., Van der Wee, M., de Regt, M., Verbrugge, S., Colle, D.: International roaming in the EU: current overview, challenges, opportunities and solutions. Telecommun. Policy **41**, 717–730 (2017)
4. Biswas, S., Mukherjee, A., Roy Chowdhury, M., Bhattacharya, A.B.: Cloud computing technology as an auto filtration system for cost reduction while roaming. In: Satapathy, S.C., Bhateja, V., Udgata, SK., Pattnaik, P.K. (eds.) Proceedings of the 5th International Conference on Frontiers in Intelligent Computing: Theory and Applications. AISC, vol. 516, pp. 437–445. Springer, Singapore (2017). https://doi.org/10.1007/978-981-10-3156-4_45
5. Shrivastava, P., Sahoo, L., Pandey, M.: Recognition of telecom customer's behavior as data product in CRM big data environment. In: Somani, A.K., Srivastava, S., Mundra, A., Rawat, S. (eds.) Proceedings of First International Conference on Smart System, Innovations and Computing. SIST, vol. 79, pp. 165–173. Springer, Singapore (2018). https://doi.org/10.1007/978-981-10-5828-8_16
6. Chenga, F.H., Chang, F.-M., Kao, S.J.: Efficient hierarchical SIP mobility management for WiMAX networks. Comput. Math. Appl. **64**, 1522–1531 (2012)
7. Beaubrun, R., Pierre, S., Conan, J.: An approach for managing global mobility and roaming in the next-generation wireless systems. Comput. Commun. **28**, 571–581 (2005)
8. RFC 3261. https://www.rfc-editor.org/info/rfc3261
9. SIP. http://www.efort.com
10. KAMAILIO. https://www.kamailio.org/w/
11. Code des télécommunications. https://www.sec.gouv.sn/code-des-télécommunications
12. Décret n° 2014-770 du 14 juin 2014 précisant certaines obligations des opérateurs quant aux droit droità l' information des consommateurs. https://www.artpsenegal.net/sites/default/files/textes_refs/decret_sur_le_droit_a_linformation_des_consommateurs.pdf
13. Lancement du «free roaming». https://senepeople.com/2017/03/30/free-roaming-effectif-demain-31-mars-2017/

Contribution to the Setting up of a Remote Practical Work Platform for STEM: The Case of Agriculture

Bessan Melckior Degboe[✉], Ulrich Hermann Sèmèvo Boko,
Kéba Gueye, and Samuel Ouya

LIRT Laboratory, High Polytechnic School,
University Cheikh Anta Diop of Dakar, Dakar, Senegal
bessanmelckior.degboe@ucad.edu.sn,
bulrich91@gmail.com, mamekeb@gmail.com,
samuel.ouya@gmail.com

Abstract. Several approaches have been proposed to make practical work available in e-learning trainings. The visits of field represent an indispensable complement to the theoretical course given to students in the natural sciences and life sciences. Biodiversity areas may be politically unstable and potentially dangerous for non-residents. The purpose of this paper is to contribute to the improvement of distance education in agricultural sectors by providing a collaborative platform for virtual field visits and even sharing resources.

To do this, we combine the intelligence of the Web of Things (WoT) with the power of WebRTC. Our contribution applies first to distance education in agriculture. However, our experimental results may be relevant for other STEM disciplines.

This platform, based on the WebRTC Kurento multimedia server and the Web of Things (WoT), allows the teacher and a group of students to go to the field to carry out practical work. The results of this outing are broadcast in real time for other students who are not on site.

Keywords: WoT · STEM · WebRTC · Kurento

1 Introduction

Previous research has demonstrated the positive impact of practical work on students' knowledge [1, 2]. This is why in recent years research on line labs has become very popular. In fact, online labs are distributed and flexible computing environments that allow a learner to conduct experiments alone or in collaboration with other participants in a distance learning context.

Several approaches have been proposed to make practical work available in e-learning courses [3, 4]. Each approach solves a specific problem [5]. There are certain disciplines such as biology and agriculture where it is difficult to do e-learning. In the case of e-agriculture training, field visits are an indispensable complement to the theoretical course given to students. However, the areas where biodiversity is sought may be politically unstable and potentially harmful to non-residents.

G. Mendy et al. (Eds.): AFRICOMM 2018, LNICST 275, pp. 88–97, 2019.
https://doi.org/10.1007/978-3-030-16042-5_9

Thus, the purpose of this paper is to contribute to the improvement of distance learning in agricultural sectors by providing a collaborative platform for virtual field visits and even sharing of resources. To do this, we combine the intelligence of the Web of Things (WoT) with the power of the WebRTC Kurento multimedia server. The proposed solution allows teachers/tutors and students to do remote labs.

The rest of the article is structured as follows: Sect. 2 gives an overview of previous work using WoT in the field of agriculture. Section 3 describes the technologies used to implement the proposed platform. Section 4 presents the architecture of the model. Section 5 outlines the methodology for implementing the KMS-IoT-Agriculture platform. Finally, Sect. 6 provides the conclusion and future work.

2 Related Works

In the literature, studies have shown that precision electronic agriculture can be used to improve watering, soil fertilization and crop yield. The authors of [6–8] propose solutions based on arduino and sensors (pH sensor, water level sensor, servo …) to save the use of water and fertilizers on small cultivable areas. Those of [9] have set up a LoRa and bluetooth-based transmission system to retrieve sensor information (temperature, humidity, CO2, brightness) in a field. This information is stored in a database and can be viewed using a smartphone. In article [10, 11], the authors propose a website to regulate the sale of agricultural products. The authors of the article [12] propose an online learning module to train farmers on the right choice of seeds, pest control, side effects of pesticide use, etc. Despite the relevance of this work, few solutions are focused on distance education of students in agricultural sectors.

3 Technology

The first part presents the technology used to establish communication between the different users of the system. Then, the Web of Things allows to control and interact with different intelligent objects of architecture.

3.1 Web of Things

The Web of Things (WoT) is a specialization of the Internet of Things (IoT). On the one hand, it provides an abstraction of the connectivity of smart objects. On the other hand, WoT adds a standard web standards-based application layer to simplify the creation of IoT applications. In IoT, the communication protocols are multiple (MQTT, CoAP, ARMQP …), which creates groups of users.

The main interests of using WoT instead of IoT are the simplicity of development using APIs, standardization and simple coupling. The idea is that all intelligent objects can communicate using a Web language through an API. This API can be present in the intelligent object itself or in an intermediary that can act on behalf of the intelligent object [13]. This has become possible with the improvement of embedded systems. Nowadays, we can run small servers such as lighttpd [14] and Nginx [15] inside constrained devices.

3.2   Kurento Media Server

Traditional WebRTC applications are standardized so that browsers can communicate directly without the mediation of third-party infrastructures. This is sufficient to provide basic multimedia services, but features such as group communications, stream recording, streaming, or transcoding are difficult to implement. For this reason, the most interesting applications require the use of a multimedia server.

There are many other services we can offer with media servers: augmented reality, computer vision and alpha blending. These services can add value to applications in many scenarios such as e-agriculture, e-learning, security, entertainment, games or advertising. Kurento Media Server (KMS) is an evolution of traditional media servers that provides a modular architecture where other features can be added as modules.

Kurento is an open source WebRTC multimedia server that allows you to create media processing applications based on the pipeline concept. Media pipelines are created by interconnect modules called Media Elements. Each Media Element provides a specific feature. KMS contains Media Elements capable of recording and mixing streams, computer vision, etc.

From the point of view of the application developer, Media Elements are like Lego pieces: just take the necessary elements for an application and connect them according to the desired topology. This type of modularity is new in the field of RTC multimedia servers.

Kurento Media Server offers the capabilities of creating media pipelines through a simple JSON-RPC-based network protocol. However, to further simplify developer work, a client API that implements this protocol and directly leverages Media Elements and pipelines is provided. Currently, the Java and JavaScript client API is ready for developers [16].

Taking into account the integrated modules, the Kurento Toolbox is detailed in Fig. 1.

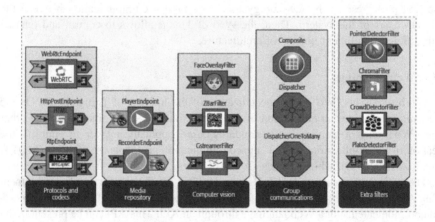

Fig. 1. Kurento media elements toolbox

4   Presentation of the Proposed Architecture

To exploit the advanced features of the WebRTC, the proposed architecture integrates Kurento Media Server (KMS). During a WebRTC multimedia session, the solution provides access to the information collected by the sensors and sends it to the other end of the communication in real time. The Fig. 2 describes the architecture of the proposed system.

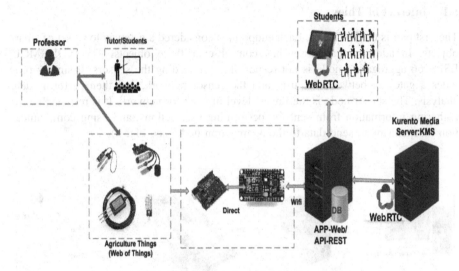

Fig. 2. Proposed system architecture

Distance education in the field of agriculture, biology, etc. is faced with many technical and logistical difficulties. Field visits are an indispensable complement to the theoretical course given to students. Biodiversity areas may be unstable and potentially dangerous for non-residents. The proposed solution allows students of the National School of Agriculture (ENSA) Thies to conduct an educational excursion to study the biodiversity of southern Senegal. To do this, a group resident in the region is selected for taking measurements (soil moisture, chemical composition, ambient temperature, etc.) under the supervision of a tutor. The collected data is directly transmitted to the application and then shared in real time with the other students via the platform. With the help of a connected computer, tablet or smartphone, any student can view the measurements and follow in real time the comments/explanations of the tutor. Each student can also interact by asking questions.

5   Implementation

A platform using Node.js and KMS is implemented in this paper. On the one hand, it allows to establish a multimedia communication between several users by simply using their browser. On the other hand, it allows users to access data from predefined connected objects. The proposed architecture consists of three distinct entities: Internet of Things, API and Web Application.

5.1   Internet of Things

The first part is the WoT part. Each endpoint is considered a gateway to its set of smart objects. In addition, each user has control over these objects. The NODEMCU ESP8266 aggregation node is not responsible for reading the sensors. It simply provides a gateway between the user and the sensor network, and then performs data analysis. The sensor node is the lowest level of a sensor network. It is responsible for gathering information from sensors, performing user actions, and using communication mechanisms to send data to the aggregation node (see Fig. 3).

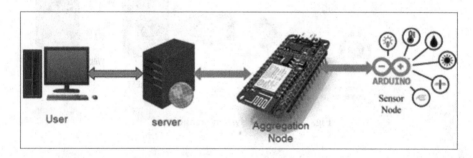

Fig. 3. Architecture WoT

The ESP8266 gateway can then communicate with the sensors using one of the well-known communication protocols (Lora, Zigbee, Bluetooth, WIFI …). In the current platform, a DHT11 humidity and temperature sensor, sensors for the chemical composition of the soil and an HD camera to visualize the medium can be used. These are connected to the NODE MCU Gateway (ESP8266) which sends data using 4G or WIFI. Using the current architecture, the implementation of a remote pedagogical outing is possible, where a tutor communicates with students using Kurento Media Server. Figure 4 shows the wiring of the Node MCU Gateway with the DHT11 temperature and humidity sensor.

Fig. 4. Wiring the ESP8266 with the DHT11

5.2 API

We have developed a REST API capable of retrieving information collected by sensors and storing it in a MongoDB database. MongoDB belongs to the NoSQL family Document-store, developed in C++. It is based on the concept of a key-value pair. The document is read or written using the key. MongoDB supports dynamic queries on documents. Since this is a document-oriented database, the data is stored as JSON, BSON style [17].

According to recent work [18–20], NoSQL database systems are non-relational databases designed to provide great accessibility, reliability and scalability to huge data. NoSQL databases can store unstructured data such as e-mails and multimedia documents. MongoDB has many security risks that can be overcome by a good, secure cryptographic system [21].

5.3 Web Application

To set up the web application, we use the NodeJs and Kurento Media Server technologies. This platform allows teachers/tutors and students to register and authenticate themselves to access Kurento Media Server features. Once connected, students can view the sensor data and media streams of the tutor in charge of the educational output. Figures 5 and 6 show the authentication principle on the KMS-IoT platform.

The web application can also collect information from the database and display it. Connected users can then view sensor data. Figures 7 and 8 show that actors can access the temperature and humidity sensor information. The same mechanism is applicable to any other sensor.

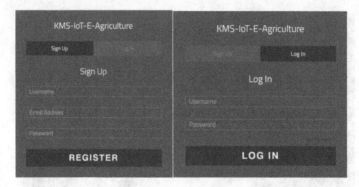

Fig. 5. Authentication and login on the KMS-IoT-E-Agriculture

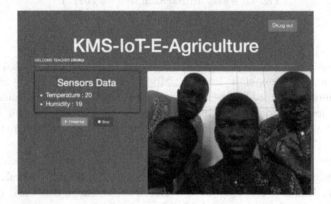

Fig. 6. Communication between teacher and students: teacher side

Fig. 7. Communication between teacher and students: student side

Figures 8 and 9 show the authentication and communication steps between the students and the teacher on the KMS-IoT-E-Agriculture platform.

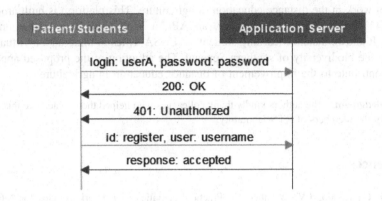

Fig. 8. Authentication flow

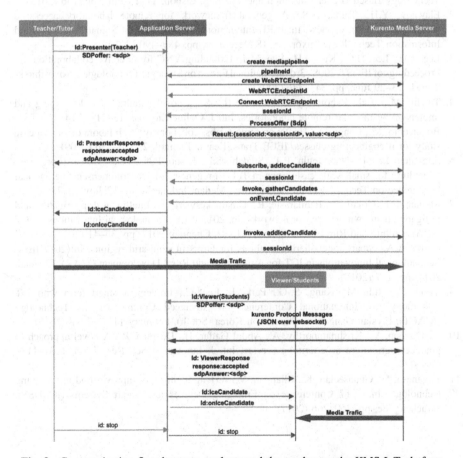

Fig. 9. Communication flow between students and the teacher on the KMS-IoT platform.

6 Conclusion

In this article, we propose the platform KMS-IoT-Agriculture which allows to do practical work in the distance education of agriculture. This platform is built around a WebRTC Kurento multimedia server, an API, a Web application and connected objects. It allows distance learning students at ENSA Thiès to undertake a virtual tour to study the biodiversity of southern Senegal. The adoption of the proposed approach could contribute to the improvement of distance education in agriculture.

Acknowledgment. The authors kindly thank colleagues who helped them to achieve this paper, especially the members of RTN laboratory.

References

1. Coti, C., Loddo, J.V., Viennet, E.: Practical activities in network courses for MOOCs, SPOCs and eLearning with Marionnet. In: International Conference on Information Technology Based Higher Education and Training, Lisbon, 11–13 June, pp. 1–6 (2015)
2. Elawady, Y.H., Talba, A.S.: A general framework for remote laboratory access: a standarization point of view. In: IEEE International Symposium on Signal Processing and Information Technology, Luxor, 15–18 December, pp. 485–490 (2010)
3. Lee, T.H., Lee, H.C., Kim, J.H., Lee, M.J.: Extending VNC for effective collaboration. In: Proceedings of IFOST-2008 - 3rd International Forum on Strategic Technologies, Novosibirsk-Tomsk, 23–29 June, pp. 343–346 (2008)
4. Tawfik, M., et al.: Laboratory as a service (LaaS): a novel paradigm for developing and implementing modular remote laboratories. Int. J. Online Eng. **10**, 13–21 (2014)
5. Bochicchio, M., Longo, A.: Hands-on remote labs: collaborative web laboratories as a case study for it engineering classes. IEEE Trans. Learn. Technol. **2**, 320–330 (2009)
6. Simanjuntak, P.P., Napitupulu, P.T., Silalahi, S.P., Kisno, P.N., Valešová, L.: E-precision agriculture for small scale cash crops in Tobasa regency. In: 1st Nommensen International Conference on Technology and Engineering, Medan, Indonesia, 11–12 July 2017
7. Mohanraj, I., Gokul, V., Ezhilarasie, R., Umamakeswari, A.: Intelligent drip irrigation and fertigation using wireless sensor networks. In: 2017 IEEE Technological Innovations in ICT for Agriculture and Rural Development (TIAR), Chennai, 2017, pp. 36–41 (2017)
8. Garba, A.A.: Smart water-sharing methods for farms in semi-arid regions. In: 2017 IEEE Technological Innovations in ICT for Agriculture and Rural Development (TIAR), Chennai, 2017, pp. 1–7 (2017)
9. Yoon, C., Huh, M., Kang, S.-G., Park, J., Lee, C.: Implement smart farm with IoT technology. In: International Conference on Advanced Communications Technology (ICACT), Elysian Gangchon, Chuncheon Korea (South), February 11–14 2018 (2018)
10. Vijayarajan, V., Krishnamoorthy, A., Abdul Gaffar, H., Deepika, R.: A novel approach to practices agriculture as e-farming service. Int. J. Innovation Sci. Res. **7**(01), 1131–1134 (2018)
11. Jaiganesh, S., Gunaseelan, K., Ellappan, V.: IOT agriculture to improve food and farming technology. In: 2017 Conference on Emerging Devices and Smart Systems (ICEDSS), Tiruchengode, pp. 260–266 (2017)

12. Sreeja, M., Sreeram, M.: Teacher less classroom: a new perspective for making social empowerment a reality. In: 2017 IEEE Technological Innovations in ICT for Agriculture and Rural Development (TIAR), Chennai, 2017, pp. 186–193 (2017)
13. Garcia, B., Lopez-Fernandez, L., Gallego, M., Gortazar, F.: Kurento: the Swiss army knife of WebRTC media servers. IEEE Commun. Stan. Mag. 1(2), 44–51 (2017)
14. Guinard, D., Trifa, V.: Building the Web of Things. Manning Publications Co. (2016)
15. lighttpd, \lighttpd (1993). http://www.lighttpd.net/
16. nginx, \nginx. nginx.org
17. Truică, C.O., Boicea, A., Trifan, I.: CRUD operations in MongoDB. In: International Conference on Advanced Computer Science and Electronics Information, pp. 347–348 (2013)
18. Chopade, M.R.M., Dhavase, N.S.: Mongodb, couchbase: performance comparison for image dataset. In: 2017 2nd International Conference for Convergence in Technology (I2CT), Mumbai, 2017, pp. 255–258 (2017)
19. Jose, B., Abraham, S.: Exploring the merits of NoSQL: a study based on mongodb. In: 2017 International Conference on Networks & Advances in Computational Technologies (NetACT), Thiruvanthapuram, 2017, pp. 266–271 (2017)
20. Patil, M.M., Hanni, A., Tejeshwar, C.H., Patil, P.: A qualitative analysis of the performance of MongoDB vs MySQL database based on insertion and retrieval operations using a web/android application to explore load balancing—Sharding in MongoDB and its advantages. In: 2017 International Conference on I-SMAC (IoT in Social, Mobile, Analytics and Cloud) (I-SMAC), Palladam, 2017, pp. 325–330 (2017)
21. Kumar, J., Garg, V.: Security analysis of unstructured data in NOSQL MongoDB database. In: 2017 International Conference on Computing and Communication Technologies for Smart Nation (IC3TSN), Gurgaon, India, 2017, pp. 300–305 (2017)

Snapshot Setting for Temporal Networks Analysis

Ahmed Ould Mohamed Moctar[1]([✉]), Idrissa Sarr[1], and Joel Vaumi Tanzouak[2]

[1] Department of Mathematics and Computer Science, Cheikh Anta Diop University,
Dakar - Fann, BP 5005, Dakar, Senegal
{ahmed.ouldmoctar,idrissa.sarr}@ucad.edu.sn
[2] Department of Mathematics and Computer Science, University of Ngaoundere,
BP 454, Ngaoundere, Cameroun
joel.tanzouak@univ-ndere.cm

Abstract. Temporal networks can be used to model systems that evolve over longer time scales such as networks of disease spread, for instance, HIV/AIDS disease that is propagated within the population over a relatively long period. Analyzing temporal networks can be done by considering the network either as a series of snapshots (aggregation over a time window) or as a dynamic object whose structure changes over time. The first approach is used in this paper and requires specifying a size of time window that delimits snapshot size. To our best knowledge, there is not yet studies on setting the size of the window in a methodical basis. In real, existing works rely on a static or a regular value of time window size to capture snapshots over time.

This work is conducted to identify dynamically snapshots over time in a directed and weighted network. That is, we aim to find out the right time to start and to end capturing a new snapshot. To this end, we define a quality function to evaluate the network state at anytime. Then, we rely on time series to predict the quality scores of the network over time. A significant changes of the network state is interpreted as the start and/or end of a snapshot. Our solution is implemented with R and we use a real dataset based on geographical proximity of individuals to demonstrate the effectiveness of our approach.

Keywords: Time window size · Temporal networks · Quality function

1 Introduction

Most of the networks such as the one of Facebook, LinkedIn and YouTube deal with hundreds of millions of users that interact hugely day in day out. The creation or the birth of these networks is a dynamic process in which the network evolves over time. Analyzing such a dynamic process unveils the intrinsic temporal aspects of the network. To analyze a temporal network, one may see the network as a static view in which all the links in the final network are present

© ICST Institute for Computer Sciences, Social Informatics and Telecommunications Engineering 2019
Published by Springer Nature Switzerland AG 2019. All Rights Reserved
G. Mendy et al. (Eds.): AFRICOMM 2018, LNICST 275, pp. 98–107, 2019.
https://doi.org/10.1007/978-3-030-16042-5_10

throughout the study. This is a very simplifying assumption for a network which is built instantly and does not evolve frequently over time. However, if the network evolves over longer time scales, it is worthwhile to take into account the fact that ties may be temporary, and the network structure can change at many points of time and have an impact on the final network status. For example, an individual with zero or very few contacts at a single time t may see his contacts growing significantly at time $t + 1$. Therefore, temporal analysis is challenging at many points such as how to track and/or represent changes over time, how to manage the time in order to report the right times within which the network undergoes through the main phases of its creation. To analyze the network evolution, one may consider either a series of network snapshots and assess whether changes occur between snapshots or track continuously the changes that occur over time. The first choice that we use in this work requires to define a time interval, called "time window", allowing to determine the time from which network updates are studied. Even though many studies point out the impact of the time window size on the quality of snapshots, they don't address particularly such an issue. Rather, existing works used to rely on a fixed time interval to capture snapshots.

The goal of this paper is to propose a strategy of setting time window for capturing a snapshot. In opposite to existing solutions, our approach does not define a fixed time window but a dynamic one based on the amount of reported changes. The reason of doing so is to make an earlier detection of the main phases of the network creation process. That is, our solution eases an on-time follow-up that alerts once significant changes occur rather than postponing them till a given time is reached. Such an approach sounds well for monitoring applications like dealers group monitoring, which requires rapid and instant reaction based on the organization size and/or status. This is also the case for epidemic surveillance systems. The main contributions of this work can be summarized as follows:

- a time-based quality function that evaluates the network quality at any given time t. The quality function takes into account the cohesion aspect as well as the communication intensity of nodes during a period of time.
- a prediction strategy that estimates scores of the network quality at time $t+1$ based on network composition at t. Two time series are used. The first one predicts the next quality score of the temporal network while the second one is used to correct the prediction by minimizing the error of prediction;
- a snapshot setting based on the prediction of the quality score values over time. Our solution work by supposing that two snapshots have to be different so as their quality scores. Therefore, we compute the variation of the scores at t and $t + 1$ and if it is beyond a given threshold, thus, $t + 1$ is the start of a new snapshot.
- an implementation of our solution using R to assess and validate our algorithms over a real data set. The quality of the predictions as well the snapshot bounding show the feasibility and performances of our approach.

The remainder of this paper is as follows. Firstly, we review the related works in Sect. 2. Secondly, we propose our quality function in Sect. 3. Thirdly, we explain in Sect. 4 our methodology for decomposing the network evolution. To validate our solution, we present our experiments in Sect. 5 before concluding in Sect. 6.

2   Related Work

Even though several studies explain the effect of time window size on snapshot setting [3,4,6]. To our best knowledge, there is not yet work focusing on estimating the time window size based on a methodological reasoning. In existing works, the time window size is fixed in a static manner without providing any argumentation. Let us give the following examples of periods: one day [2], one month [6] or multiple timescales [3].

Indeed, time window management can be done by using:

1. A static method, which decomposes the network evolution into several snapshots having all the same size.
2. A dynamic method that subdivides the network evolution into several snapshots whose size of each one may be different from that of other.

The static method has the advantage of being simple and easy to implement. However, if the network does not change during a given period, the snapshots obtained over this period will contain exactly the same structure. Thus, we are wasting time and resources searching for new changes while network has not changed. In addition, if network structure evolves irregularly, choosing a static time window size can be problematic: a small size may lead to snapshots that don't capture important connections, while a big size would hide the precise moments of significant changes of network structure.

To avoid the problem of time window size balancing as well as favor relevant captures that incorporate enough changes, we propose a strategy able to capture dynamically snapshots throughout the network evolution. To this end, we define a quality function allowing to quantify the network changes at a given time. Our method captures a new snapshot if the quality difference of network between two moments exceeds a given threshold. We use a time series to predict the moments from which the quality score reaches the defined threshold.

3   Quality Function

In this section, we propose a quality function allowing to evaluate a snapshot relevance in term of cohesion aspect as well as the communication intensity between nodes. We consider that a snapshot is a static network including all nodes/links that have appeared at least once during a time interval. If an interaction appears several times during the time internal, we represent it by a single link whose weight is equal to sum of links weights that correspond to different appearances.

The quality function we present here is a reformulation of the one we proposed in [1]. The difference between these two functions is that the first one evaluates the quality of a local community in a static network while the reformulated function evaluates the quality of a temporal network at a given instant t.

Let $\mathcal{N}$ a temporal network and $\mathcal{N}_t$ the network snapshot at instant t. To get an idea of the communication intensity between nodes within $\mathcal{N}_t$, we calculate the inverse of all links weights sum $\frac{1}{\sum_{w_{\mathcal{N}_t}}}$. The intuition behind is that more communication is intense within snapshot $\mathcal{N}_t$ (high values of links weights), more $\frac{1}{\sum_{w_{\mathcal{N}_t}}}$ tends to 0.

Regarding the internal cohesion of $\mathcal{N}_t$, we consider that more the topological structure of a snapshot at time t is similar to a clique, more the snapshot is considered cohesive. Therefore, the proportion $\frac{|V_{\mathcal{N}_t}|}{|E_{\mathcal{N}_t}|}$ allows to evaluate at what level the snapshot $\mathcal{N}_t$ is cohesive. $|V_{\mathcal{N}_t}|$ is the number of nodes in $\mathcal{N}_t$ and $|E_{\mathcal{N}_t}|$ the number of links.

Our quality function is defined as follows:

$$\psi(\mathcal{N}_t) = \frac{1}{\sum_{w_{\mathcal{N}_t}}} \times \frac{|V_{\mathcal{N}_t}|}{|E_{\mathcal{N}_t}|} \tag{1}$$

4   Methodology

We consider a network represented by a weighted digraph where a link weight states for the intensity (number of exchanges for instance) of two nodes and the orientation indicates which node has initiated the interaction. While assuming that the network is a temporal one, the overall structure shaping is assimilated as an evolution process within which a series of moments of significants changes are reported. A specific moment bringing numbers of changes can be seen as the delimitation of two snapshots. We name such a moment a *"switch moment"* since it indicates a precise time where changes make a great impact on the overall structure. Actually, the purpose of this work is to characterize, and moreover, to predict *"switch moment"*. In this respect, we define a time-based function that measures the quality of the network at anytime. Hence, if the network quality score varies beyond a given threshold between t and $t+1$, thus, we consider that we reach a *"switch moment"* at $t+1$. In other words, the score of the quality remain almost the same for a network without and/or with a few significant changes during a period of time. We notice the quality function is a continuous one so that it affords the possibility to detect a *"switch moment"* once it happens. Furthermore, to be able predicting whether a new *"switch moment"* will occur, we need to foresee the quality scores evolution over time. To this end, we rely on exponential smoothing that helps us estimating upcoming score values based on the previous and detecting any variation beyond the fixed threshold. Finally, since the quality scores predictions give us *"switch moment"*, we can monitor where one has to start or ending capturing a snapshot. In the following sections we portray the definition and prediction method of our quality function.

The optimal size of time window should enable us to decompose the network evolution into several snapshots, each one includes a considerable number of changes. To this end, we propose a strategy that works in two steps:

1. measure network changes during a time period using the quality function;
2. model the changes rate across a threshold η. If the network quality difference between two instants exceeds the threshold value, that means that the network has been considerably modified.

Formally, we consider that the network has undergone a considerable change if the difference between its quality at instant t and that at instant $t+1$ becomes higher than threshold η:

$$|\psi(\mathcal{N}_t) - \psi(\mathcal{N}_{t+1})| \geqslant \eta \qquad (2)$$

Note that more higher the threshold value, more the changes number increases between each two successive snapshots.

4.1 Quality Scores Prediction

The principle of our method is to predict the quality score at instant $t+1$ from instant t. In other words, we try to predict the next quality score before the network reaches the next instant. To predict the next quality score, we use a time series built from quality scores over time. The prediction model we used is the simple exponential smoothing. Formally, our time series is defined as:

$$\hat{P}(t) = \alpha Q(t) + (1 - \alpha)\hat{P}(t-1) \qquad (3)$$

Such as:

- $\hat{P}(t)$ means the predicted quality score at instant $t+1$;
- $\alpha \in]0,1[$ represents the smoothing coefficient;
- $Q(t)$ indicates the observed quality score at instant t;
- $\hat{P}(t-1)$ is the predicted quality score at instant t.

If α is closest to 0 (respectively if α is closest to 1), it means that to predict the next quality score, the most oldest (respectively most recent) predicted values will be taking into account.

By using the expression 3, the algorithm will learn based on the history of predicted quality scores over time. In order to improve these predictions, we used a second series that allows to correct the prediction of $\hat{P}$ based on the history of prediction errors.

4.2 Correction of Our Predictions

To correct the prediction, our algorithm first calculates the prediction error, defined by the difference between observed quality score and predicted quality score. Then, it predicts the next prediction error using a time series based on the history of prediction errors.

4.2.1   Prediction Error

The prediction presented in the previous section sometime could be inaccurate because of important fluctuation of quality scores. To improve the future predictions, we try to correct our prediction using a second time series that learns from past prediction errors. To this end, we define the prediction error given by the expression below:

$$E(t) = Q(t) - \hat{P}(t-1) \tag{4}$$

We defined also a second time series to estimate the predicted error in the future according to the error recorded in the past:

$$\hat{L}(t) = \beta E(t) + (1 - \beta)\hat{L}(t-1) \tag{5}$$

Such as:

- $\hat{L}(t)$ means the predicted error at instant $t+1$;
- $\beta \in \,]0,1[$ represents the predicted error coefficient;
- $E(t)$ is the prediction error at instant t;
- $\hat{L}(t-1)$ is the predicted error at instant t.

If β is closest to 0 (respectively if β is closest to 1), it means that to estimate the next predicted error, the most oldest (respectively most recent) predicted values will be taking into account.

4.2.2   Correction of Predicted Quality Scores

After predicting the error, we are then able to make some correction of the prediction according to the context which is materialized by the value of the error. Our algorithm considers that the corrected prediction is equal to the sum of predicted score and predicted error:

$$\hat{C}(t) = \hat{P}(t-1) + \hat{L}(t-1) \tag{6}$$

Finally, it should be noted that results of our time series $\hat{L}(t)$ et $\hat{C}(t)$ improve by learning from past predicted values. Thus, the wider the history, the better the predicted futures will be.

5   Experimentation

The purpose of this section is to evaluate the effectiveness of our solution. To this end, we implemented our solution with R platform. The dataset we used includes more than 2 million mobile phone interactions between 80 students who lived in undergraduate dormitory [5]. These interactions were collected between September 05, 2007 and July 16, 2009. In the following, we present two experiments. The objective of the first one is to show that our predictions provide very close scores, often identical to observed quality scores. The second experiment aims to present some detected snapshots during the network evolution. These two experiences are presented in Sects. 5.1 and 5.2.

5.1   Quality Scores Prediction

The use of the time series P and L requires two parameters, namely, the prediction coefficient α and the coefficient of predicted error β. In our experiments, we chose the coefficient $\alpha = 0.5$ for the next prediction to be influenced, equitably, by oldest past values and the near past values. Regarding the β coefficient, we chose it so that momentary fluctuations do not have a significant impact on the predicted error of the next prediction. Thus, $\beta = 0.1$. The goal of the first experiment we conducted is to assess the accuracy of short-term prediction. To this end, we predicted network quality scores between September 05, 2007 and April 17, 2008, a period of approximately 7 months and two weeks. During this period, there were 2000 interactions.

Figure 1 presents the observed quality scores (black colored curve), the predicted quality score (red colored curve) and the corrected predictions (green colored curve). The x-axis indicates the times at which the network has undergone a change. The y-axis represents the corresponding quality scores. On Fig. 1, we noticed that the prediction is acceptable when there are fluctuations. However, the prediction becomes good if the quality scores curve is somehow linear. On the curves, we remark that prediction are sometime more accurate than correction. It can be explained by the fact that, since the correction of prediction is base on error prediction, it means that if the prediction of the error is bad, then the corrected prediction will be inaccurate. When the quality function values have important fluctuation in a short time, the error predicted becomes bad, so this inaccuracy is propagated to correction.

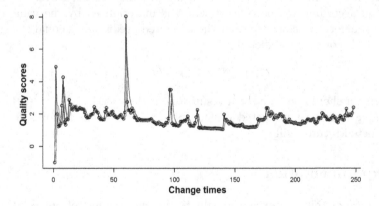

Fig. 1. Predicted and observed quality scores between September 05, 2007 and April 17, 2008 (Color figure online).

To evaluate the effectiveness of our long-term prediction, we conducted a second experiment. This time, we observed all the interactions that took place between September 05, 2007 and October 03, 2008, a period of one year and four weeks. This period includes 10000 interactions. The number of times the

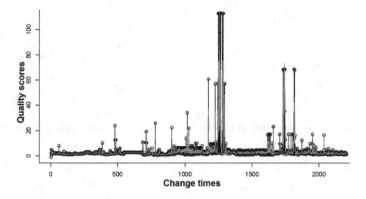

Fig. 2. Predicted and observed quality scores between September 05, 2007 and October 03, 2008.

network has undergone a change is equal to 2205. Figure 2 presents the curves of this experiment.

Note that in long-term, correction of prediction becomes almost identical with observed quality scores. This proves the effectiveness of our prediction algorithm.

5.2   Examples of Detected Snapshots

The objective of this experiment is to show the difference between our solution and the static method that decomposes the network evolution using a regular time interval. To this end, we consider that the time interval is 30 min. Thus, we make a new snapshot every 30 min.

Figure 3a, b, c and d show the network state, respectively, after 30 min, one hour, one hour and a half and two hours. The value displayed on each link represents its weight during the time window. For readability reasons, we did not display the link weights in Figs. 3c and d. We find out that the network did not change during the first two snapshots and a slight change occurred during last two snapshots. This experiment illustrates the irrelevance of the static method since it can capture identical snapshots over time, which involves a waste of time and resources. To overcome this weakness, we present in the following a few snapshots captured by our solution. To this end, we consider that rate of quality changes needed to capture a new snapshot is $\eta = 0.8$. Remember that our method that allows to decompose the network evolution according to the degree of changes that takes place.

Figures 3e, f, g and h show four snapshots captured at different times. The value displayed on each link represents its weight during the time window. For readability reasons, we did not display the link weights in Figs. 3g and h. From these figures, we clearly see that the time window size is dynamic. It varies according to changes degree of network. The considerable difference between the size of these windows is due to the network changes degree over time.

(a) Captured snapshot after 30 minutes.   (b) Captured snapshot after 60 minutes.

   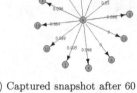

(c) Captured snapshot after 90 minutes.   (d) Captured snapshot after 120 minutes.

(e) First time window representing the ini-
tial state of temporal network. This time (f) Second time window captured on
window is captured on September 05, 2007 September 05, 2007 at 14:12:33. The inter-
at 14:02:11.   val of this window is 10 minutes.

(h) Fourth time window captured on Jan-
(g) Third time window captured on Jan- uary 26, 2008 at 06:37:50. The size of this
uary 23, 2008 at 14:27:42. The size of this time window is 3 days.
window is 4 months.

Fig. 3. Examples of captured snapshots by the static method VS those one captured
by our solution.

6   Conclusion

In this paper, we proposed a solution that answers two fundamental questions,
namely:

1. how to measure the temporal network quality during a given period?
2. how to determine at what moment we need to capture a new snapshot?

To answer the first question, we proposed a quality function allowing to evaluate the internal cohesion and the communication intensity between nodes in a temporal network. Regarding the second question, we proposed a new strategy based on time series to predict the next moment corresponding to a new snapshot.

In perspectives, we are interested in making an experiment in order to determine the optimal threshold of a given dataset. In addition, we intend to study the time window size in relation to the local changes of some ego-communities. Finally, we will also experiment our solution on several datasets to determine the impact of the network kind on the time window size.

References

1. Ould Mohamed Moctar, A., Sarr, I.: Ego-centered community detection in directed and weighted networks. In: Proceedings of the 2017 IEEE/ACM International Conference on Advances in Social Networks Analysis and Mining 2017, pp. 1201–1208, New York, NY, USA, 2017. ACM (2017)
2. Génois, M., Vestergaard, C.L., Fournet, J., Panisson, A., Bonmarin, I., Barrat, A.: Data on face-to-face contacts in an office building suggest a low-cost vaccination strategy based on community linkers. Network Sci. 3(3), 326–347 (2015)
3. Holme, P.: Modern temporal network theory: a colloquium. Eur. Phys. J. B 88(9), 234 (2015)
4. Krings, G., Karsai, M., Bernhardsson, S., Blondel, V.D., Saramäki, J.: Effects of time window size and placement on the structure of an aggregated communication network. EPJ Data Sci. 1(4), 1–16 (2012)
5. Madan, A., Cebrian, M., Moturu, S., Farrahi, K., et al.: Sensing the "health state" of a community. IEEE Pervasive Comput. 11(4), 36–45 (2012)
6. Psorakis, I., Roberts, S.J., Rezek, I., Sheldon, B.C.: Inferring social network structure in ecological systems from spatio-temporal data streams. J. R. Soc. Interface 9, 3055–3066 (2012)

Access Control Model Based on Dynamic Delegations and Privacy in a Health System of Connected Objects

Jeanne Roux Ngo Bilong[✉], Kéba Gueye, Gervais Mendy,
and Samuel Ouya

LIRT Laboratory, Higher Polytechnic School,
University of Dakar, Dakar, Senegal
{jeanneroux.ngobilong, gervais.mendy}@ucad.edu.sn,
keba.gueye@esp.sn, samuel.ouya@gmail.com

Abstract. The Internet of Things (IoT) promotes the development of new platforms, services and applications that connect the physical world to the virtual world. Defining access control policies for these platforms remains a challenge for researchers, as security gaps are still observed in several domains, including health. There are much scientific work on systems for remote patient monitoring and most of them have technological limits in access control of patients' personal and confidential information. Moreover, these systems do not allow collaborative work because the doctor, in case of unavailability or in case of need of collegial decision, cannot delegate his role to another doctor having the same skills and the same attributes as him. In this paper, we propose a model based on dynamic role delegation, emphasizing on collaborative work and the protection of patients' privacy. This model is a redefinition of the ORBAC model taking into account the notion of user attributes. We use first order logic and non-monotonic logic T-JCLASSIC$\delta\varepsilon$ to perform an axiomatic interpretation of the model. We implement the model with WebRTC, Node.js and Kurento Media Server technologies to facilitate real-time communication between users, and raspberry pi for collecting biometric information received from sensors.

Keywords: Access control · Delegation · IoT · E-health

1 Introduction

Access controls are still relevant for the management of intelligent structures involving several domains, in this case that of telemedicine [1–3]. In addition, the environments integrate more and more different miniaturized devices as well as mobile communication technology. This allows you to deploy services anywhere, anytime and for anyone. This evolution imposes new security requirements and challenges in these dynamic, context-aware, intelligent environments [1]. Access control models such as Mandatory Access Control (MAC), Discretionary Access Control (DAC) and Role Based Access Control (RBAC) proposed so far do not take into account the dynamic side of access controls [4], neither the management of obligations or recommendations, nor the rules specific to the organization. These are static access control models.

© ICST Institute for Computer Sciences, Social Informatics and Telecommunications Engineering 2019
Published by Springer Nature Switzerland AG 2019. All Rights Reserved
G. Mendy et al. (Eds.): AFRICOMM 2018, LNICST 275, pp. 108–119, 2019.
https://doi.org/10.1007/978-3-030-16042-5_11

In order to improve access control policies, researchers have been working on dynamic access control models such as OrBAC, GeoRBAC (Geographic Role Based Access Control), Context Role Based Access Control (CRBAC), Multi-OrBAC, Poly OrBAC [1]. These models each represent an extension of RBAC, but are not entirely satisfactory because they do not make it possible to manage the delegation of roles, especially in a context of telemedicine that requires the availability of staff dealing in real time. In our work, we have implemented the DORBAC model which is an extension of the OrBAC model, taking into account the role delegation issue and the administration issue for the assignment of license and role. The rest of our work is organized as follows: Sect. 2 presents the state of the art of access control models. Section 3 deals with the description of the proposed model. In Sect. 4, we implement the model. Section 5 concludes our paper with an opening for future work.

2   State of the Art of Access Control Models

2.1   Discretionary Access Control (DAC)

Discretionary Access Control policies are based on the concepts of subjects, objects and access rights. Access rights to each piece of information are manipulated by the information owner. This access control model is flexible because a subject with access rights can grant access rights to any other user. The granting or revocation of privileges is regularized by a decentralized administrative policy [5].

Limits: difficulty of administration and limitation of the access to the objects according to the identity of the user.

2.2   Mandatory Access Control (MAC)

The MAC model has a security policy which is set and managed by an authority, and cannot be modified by users. This excludes problems related to information leaks (using Trojans) observed in the DAC model. This is mainly due to not allowing users to interfere with the access control policy [5]. Unlike discretionary access control policies, subjects of a mandatory access control policy do not own the information which they have access to. Moreover, the operation allowing the delegation of rights is controlled by the rules of the policy. Subjects no longer have control over the information they handle. The subject has access to information only if authorized by the system [1].

Limits: Vulnerable to hidden channels, does not taking into account the administration component in role management, does not take into account delegation issues and level of trust

2.3   Role-Base Access Control (RBAC)

The role-based access control model, or RBAC, is seen as an alternative approach to mandatory access control (MAC) and discretionary access control (DAC). Its security policy does not apply directly to users [2, 8, 11]. The RBAC model is centered on the role [9, 10, 12]. The latter represents in an abstract way a function or a profession within an organization, which associates the authority and responsibility entrusted to a person who plays this role (for example, Professor, Director, Engineer, Technician …). Each role is assigned permissions (or privileges), which are a set of rights corresponding to the tasks that can be performed by that role. A role can have multiple permissions, and a permission can be associated with multiple roles. Just as a subject can have several roles, a role can be performed by several subjects [5].

Limits:

- No role delegation [7].
- Preserving Privacy not taken into account.
- Doesn't express prohibitions, recommendations or obligations.

2.4   Organization Based Access Control (OrBAC)

In any organization, the administrator is responsible for managing each user's access to a resource, applying security rules. But managing access rights becomes complex as the number of users, resources and activities increases. In this context, the OrBAC model solves this problem by creating abstract entities (Role, View, activity) separated into concrete entities (Subject, Object, Action). The objective of this separation is to apply the security rules to abstract entities, and to each such entity, a concrete entity is associated. OrBAC defines four types of safety rules: Permission, obligation, prohibition and recommendation [6, 10].

Limitations: No delegation nor preserving privacy.

Figure 1 below shows the OrBAC model.

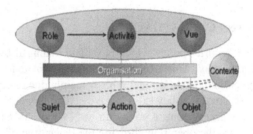

Fig. 1. Structure of OrBAC model

2.5   Synthesis of the Literature Review

We made a study of the most famous access control models. Each of them presents benefits and limits. The static access control models, the most advanced of which is RBAC, have a large limit due to its none-dynamicity. Several models, such as TrustBAC, TRBAC, have been proposed with the aim of partially improving it, but none of them to our knowledge integrates the parameters concerning the delegation and preserving privacy. We introduced too Dynamic access control models, the most advanced of which is OrBAC. Unfortunately, the latter, despite its dynamic side and its ability to manage permissions, prohibitions, obligations, recommendations, doesn't take into account some important parameters already existing in the RBAC model extensions and also like RBAC, delegation and data privacy. The limitations observed in this synthesis justify our choice to propose a dynamic model that will take into account delegation and data privacy.

3 Proposed Model (DORBAC)

3.1 Description of Non-monotonic Logic T-JClassic$\delta\varepsilon$

The non-monotonic logic T-JClassic$\delta\varepsilon$ was developed to permit a better management of the time aspect in a variety of domains such as reasoning about actions and plans, enhancing natural languages comprehension and also allowing the improvement of access control. T-JClassic$\delta\varepsilon$ allows representing temporal concepts while having default knowledge. It's Differing from the existing temporal description logics where temporal components are added to classical description logics. T-JClassic$\delta\varepsilon$ consists of: a set of atomic concepts P and atomic roles R, the two constants $\top$ (Top) and $\perp$ (Bottom) that represent respectively the universal and the bottom concept, a set of individuals called 'classic individuals', the concepts C and D, the unary connectives δ(Default) and ε(Exception), the binary conjunction π , the quantifier that enables universal quantification on role values, and the temporal qualifier @ to represent the interval 'X' at which a concept C applies, u is a real number, n is an integer, "Ii" are 'classic individuals' [3].

3.2 Description of Proposed Model

The Delegation and Organization Based Access Control Model (DORBAC) is an extension of the OrBAC model. The central element of this model is delegation, while taking into account confidentiality. We describe our model in an environment of e-health in which several nurses and doctors are involve. Whereas the nurse is a key player in the manipulation of patient data, here the role of the latter is limited to the material level. He will then be responsible for connecting the sensors to the patients and thus the collected information will be stored directly in a database. The doctors, licensing by the delegation, will then be able to delegate the roles. We define the doctor as follows:

$$\text{Doctor} \equiv \text{Staff\_Member} \sqcap \text{Attribute\_Member} \sqcap \text{Licence\_assigment} \sqcap \text{Role\_Assigment} \sqcap \delta\text{Permission} \tag{1}$$

The definition of the user Doctor gives to him the right of access to the services of the environment of the connected objects. Each doctor receives a license that will allow him to delegate his role to another doctor with the same attributes and/or additional attributes.

Role assignment can be considered as the first step of authorization. The assignment of license is considered as the second step. This gives the right to a user, to delegate his role to his colleague, who has the same attributes as him. The definition of a role and a permission translates into the following axioms:

- Role: given U_P the universe of all permissions, role R is the finite permission set. In other words,

$$R = \Sigma P_i / \, Pi \in U_P \tag{2}$$

- Permission: given U_{OIoT} the universe of all the objects of the Internet of Things, U_s the universe of services offered by the connected objects and U_{OPS} the universe of all operations allowed to a subject, a permission P is represented by the triplet (O_i, S_i, OPS_i) where $O_i \in U_{OIoT}$, $S_i \in U_s$ and $OPS_i \in U_{OPS}$.

$$P = \Sigma O_i + \Sigma S_i + \Sigma OPS_i \tag{3}$$

$$\delta Permission = ObjectConntedP.permission \sqcap ServiceP.permission \sqcap \\ OperationP.permission \tag{4}$$

3.2.1 Assignment of Role and License

- Role assignment for the doctor:

$$\delta Role\_Assigment \sqsubseteq OrgR.Assignee \sqcap AssigneeR.assigment \sqcap RoleR.assigment \sqcap \\ \delta PrivilegesR.Service \sqcap \delta PrivilegesR.ObjectConnected \tag{5}$$

- Licensing of the doctor

$$\delta Licence\_Assigment \sqsubseteq OrgL \sqcap AssigneeL.assigment \sqcap LicenceL.assigment \sqcap \\ \delta PrivilegesL.Action \sqcap CibleL.Objet \sqcap ContextL \tag{6}$$

3.2.2 Role Delegation

In our work, we consider the total delegation of role in which physicians with the same attributes can delegate themselves roles. Attributes represent the set of characteristics to determine a subject, a service or an object. A doctor may also delegate his role to another doctor with more attributes than him. Role delegation is represented by the following axiom:

$$Empower \sqsubseteq UserRD.Role\_Delegation \sqcap AttributeRD.Role\_Delegation \sqcap \\ AssignmentRD.Role \sqcap ServiceRD.Service \sqcap Object\_ConnectedRD.Object \sqcap \quad (7) \\ AssigneeRD.Grantor \sqcap Working\_HourRD.hour$$

The revocation of delegation can be represented as follows:

$$\delta\text{Permission} \sqsubseteq \text{UseL.License\_Delegation} \sqcap \text{AssigneeL\_Assignee} \sqcap$$
$$\text{AttributeRD.Role\_Delegation} \sqcap \text{DurationEndL.Licence\_Delegation} \sqcap \quad (8)$$
$$\text{PermisionD.GD\_Revoke}$$

3.2.3 Privacy

Privacy is another important issue [18] to considering domains such as crisis management. In the context of the management of data collected via connected objects (sensors), the protection of privacy in access control takes into account two dimensions, namely, the privacy of the connected object and the privacy of the subject (patient).

Preserving the privacy of the connected object is close to trust issue. Thus, a record stored in a database via the sensors is protected by a user if the user requests access to the information for a purpose other than that associated with him. The protection of the privacy of the object states that the access of a subject will affect the attributes assigned to him. The privacy of the patient is preserved in that the information is received at the sensor and stored directly in the database without the intervention of a data entry agent.

Purpose assignment function:

$$\text{Purp\_assign}(\text{subject.ATTR}, O_{IOT}.\text{ATTR}, \text{Ops.ATTR}, \text{service.ATTR}) = \text{purp\_attr}$$
$$(\text{subject.ATTR}) \subseteq \text{purp\_attr} \ (\text{service.ATTR}) \subseteq \text{purp\_attr} \ (O_{IOT}.\text{ATTR}) \subseteq \text{purp\_attr} \quad (9)$$
$$(\text{service.ATTR}) \in \{0, 1\}$$

Purp_attr is a function that returns the attribute of the set of goals of a subject, a connected object, a service, or an operation.

3.3 Comparison Between DORBAC and State-of-the-Art Models

Table 1 shows that compared to the models presented in the state of the art, our model is more comprehensive and reliable in terms of flexibility and privacy. Moreover, it is easy to implement.

Table 1. Comparison between DPORBAC and other models

Criteria of comparison	DAC	MAC	RBAC	ORBAC	DORBAC
Contrôle d'accès	✓	✓	✓	✓	✓
Contextual rules	x	x	x	✓	✓
Centralized administration	x	✓	x	x	✓
Privacy	x	x	x	x	✓
Dynamic	x	x	x	✓	✓
Delegation/revocation	x	x	x	x	✓
Permission, recommendation, prohibition, obligation	x	x	x	✓	✓
Collaboration	x	x	x	x	✓

Concerning the flexibility of our model, consultations and decisions are not the responsibility of only a single physician. Collaborative work between physicians is taken into account and role delegation is done dynamically. Confidentiality is also taken into account. We can deduce that our model has additional advantages compared to the models presented above in the state of the art.

4 Implementation of Our Model

4.1 Description of the Proposed Architecture

The architecture above allows to set up a platform using Node.js, Kamailio-IMS and KMS. This platform makes it possible, on the one hand, to establish a multimedia communication between two users simply by using their browser or their SIP account and, on the other hand, it allows the users to access the data of the predefined connected objects. The proposed architecture consists of three distinct entities: Web of Things (WoT), Application Programming Interface (API) and Web Application (Fig. 2).

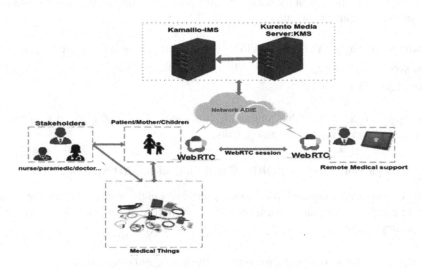

Fig. 2. Architecture of the proposed solution

4.2 Entities of the Proposed Architecture

WoT: represents the first part. Each endpoint is considered a gateway to its set of smart objects. In addition, each user has control over these objects. The NODEMCU ESP8266 aggregation node (Raspberry) is not responsible for reading the sensors. It simply provides a gateway between the user and the sensor network, and then performs data analysis. The sensor node is the lowest level of a sensor network. It is responsible for gathering information from sensors, performing user actions, and using communication mechanisms to send data to the aggregation node.

The ESP8266 gateway can then communicate with the sensors using one of the well-known communication protocols (Lora, Zigbee, Bluetooth, WIFI …). In the platform we put in place, a DHT11 humidity and temperature sensor is used. The latter is connected to the NODE MCU gateway (ESP8266) which sends the sensor data using WIFI.

In the case of e-health scenarios, we just need portable medical sensors. They can communicate via any protocol, since the WoT summarizes the complexity of the connectivity of objects.

Using the current architecture, an implementation of the remote clinical examination is possible. The doctor can then communicate with a patient using Kurento Media Server. The specialist or generalist doctor has access to a set of sensors. It can process the information collected by these sensors in real time, using the K-2I-E-health platform. Finally, these data can be analyzed and commented by the actors.

Figure 3 below shows the wiring of the Node MCU Gateway with the DHT11 temperature and humidity sensor.

Fig. 3. Wiring the ESP8266 with the DHT11

4.3   API

We have developed a REST API capable of retrieving information collected by a connected medical device and storing it in a MongoDB database. MongoDB belongs to the NoSQL family Document-store, developed in C++. It is based on the concept of a key-value pair. The document is read or written using the key. MongoDB supports dynamic queries on documents. Since this is a document-oriented database, the data is stored as JSON, BSON style [13].

According to recent work [14–16], NoSQL database systems are non-relational databases designed to provide great accessibility, reliability and scalability to huge data. NoSQL databases can store unstructured data such as e-mails and multimedia documents. MongoDB has many security risks that can be overcome by a good, secure cryptographic system [17].

4.4   Web Application

To set up the web application, we use the NodeJs and Kurento Media Server technologies. This platform allows doctors and patients to register and authenticate themselves to access Kurento Media Server features. Once connected, the specialist physician (pediatrician) can view the sensor data and the patient's media flow (Figs. 4, 5 and 6).

Fig. 4. Authentication on the K-2I-E-health   **Fig. 5.** Login on the K-2I-E-health

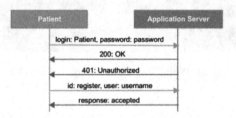

Fig. 6. Patient Authentication on the E-health Platform

The web application can also collect information from the database and display it. Connected users can then view sensor data. Figure 7 shows that actors can access the temperature and humidity sensor information. The same mechanism is applicable to any other sensor (Fig. 8).

Fig. 7. Communication between Doctor toto and patient Boko Ulrich

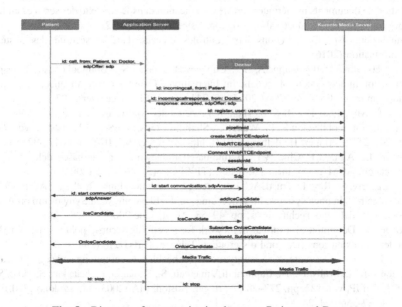

Fig. 8. Diagram of communication between Patient and Doctor

5   Conclusion

In this paper, we have proposed the DORBAC model, which is an extension of the
OrBAC model. Our model makes it possible to take in to account the delegation of
roles while ensuring the protection of the privacy of the patient. Thus, the proposed
model allows for delegation only between physicians. The application of our model
does not allow patient data capture by a health worker or assistant. The risk of seizure

error is thus eliminated and the confidentiality of the patient preserved. Once the patient is connected to the sensors, its data are analyzed by the sensor network using the ESP8266 gateway, collected by the sensor node before being stored in the database. The patient or doctor with the required permissions can view the stored data via the application interface. The doctor can follow the patient and make a decision based on information received from the sensors. A videoconferencing session is then possible between the patient and the doctor.

References

1. Zerkouk, M.: Modèles de contrôle d'accès dynamiques (Doctoral dissertation, University of sciences and Technology in Oran) (2015)
2. El Kalam, A.A., et al.: Or-BAC: un modèle de contrôle d'accès basé sur les organisations. Cahiers francophones de la recherche en sécurité de l'information **1**, 30–43 (2003)
3. Bettaz, O., Boustia, N., Mokhtari, A.: Dynamic delegation based on temporal context. Procedia Comput. Sci. **96**, 245–254 (2016)
4. Abakar, M.A.: Etude et mise en oeuvre d'une architecture pour l'authentification et la gestion de documents numériques certifiés: application dans le contexte des services en ligne pour le grand public (Doctoral dissertation, Saint Etienne) (2012)
5. Ennahbaoui, M.: Contributions aux contrôles d'accès dans la sécurité des systèmes d'information (2016)
6. Ghorbel-Talbi, M.B., Cuppens, F., Cuppens-Boulahia, N., Bouhoula, A.: Managing delegation in access control models. In: International Conference on Advanced Computing and Communications. ADCOM 2007, pp. 744–751. IEEE, December 2007
7. Ray, I., Mulamba, D., Ray, I., Han, K.J.: A model for trust-based access control and delegation in mobile clouds. In: Wang, L., Shafiq, B. (eds.) DBSec 2013. LNCS, vol. 7964, pp. 242–257. Springer, Heidelberg (2013). https://doi.org/10.1007/978-3-642-39256-6_16
8. Zhang, L., Ahn, G.J., Chu, B.T.: A rule-based framework for role-based delegation and revocation. ACM Trans. Inf. Syst. Secur. (TISSEC) **6**(3), 404–441 (2003)
9. Chakraborty, S., Ray, I.: TrustBAC: integrating trust relationships into the RBAC model for access control in open systems. In: Proceedings of the Eleventh ACM Symposium on Access Control Models and Technologies, pp. 49–58. ACM, June 2006
10. Miege, A.: Definition of a formal framework for specifying security policies. The Or-BAC model and extensions (Doctoral dissertation, Télécom ParisTech) (2005)
11. El Kalam, A.A., Deswarte, Y.: Security model for health care computing and communication systems. In: Gritzalis, D., De Capitani di Vimercati, S., Samarati, P., Katsikas, S. (eds.) SEC 2003. ITIFIP, vol. 122, pp. 277–288. Springer, Boston, MA (2003). https://doi.org/10.1007/978-0-387-35691-4_24
12. Barka, E., Sandhu, R.: A role-based delegation model and some extensions. In: Proceedings of the 23rd National Information Systems Security Conference, vol. 4, pp. 49–58, December 2000
13. Truică, C.O., Boicea, A., Trifan, I.: CRUD Operations in Mon-goDB. In: International Conference on Advanced Computer Science and Electronics Information, pp. 347–348 (2013)
14. Chopade, M.R.M., Dhavase, N.S.: Mongodb, couchbase: performance comparison for image dataset. In: 2017 2nd International Conference for Convergence in Technology (I2CT), Mumbai, pp. 255–258 (2017)

15. Jose, B., Abraham, S.: Exploring the merits of NoSQL: a study based on mongodb. In: 2017 International Conference on Networks & Advances in Computational Technologies (NetACT), Thiruvanthapuram, pp. 266–271 (2017)
16. Patil, M.M., Hanni, A., Tejeshwar, C.H., Patil, P.: A qualitative analysis of the perfor-mance of MongoDB vs MySQL database based on insertion and retriewal operations using a web/android application to explore load balancing—Sharding in MongoDB and its advantages. In: 2017 International Conference on I-SMAC (IoT in Social, Mobile, Analytics and Cloud) (I-SMAC), Palladam, 2017, pp. 325–330 (2017)
17. Kumar, J., Garg, V.: Security analysis of unstructured data in NOSQL MongoDB data-base. In: 2017 International Conference on Computing and Communication Technologies for Smart Nation (IC3TSN), Gurgaon, India, 2017, pp. 300–305 (2017)
18. Smari, W.W., Clemente, P., Lalande, J.F.: An extended attribute based access control model with trust and privacy: application to a collaborative crisis management system. Future Gener. Comput. Syst. **31**, 147–168 (2014)

Secure, Transparent and Uniform Mobile Money for Internet-Underserved Areas Using Sporadically-Synchronized Blockchain

Sankalp Ghatpande[1], Hadja Ouattara[2], Daouda Ahmat[3], Zakaria Sawadogo[2], and Tegawendé F. Bissyandé[1,2(✉)]

[1] SnT, University of Luxembourg, Luxembourg City, Luxembourg
sankalp.ghatpande@uni.lu
[2] Université Ouaga I Pr. Joseph Ki-Zerbo, Ouagadougou, Burkina Faso
hadja.ouattara@gmail.com, zakaria.sawado@gmail.com,
bissyande@fasolabs.org
[3] Université Virtuelle du Tchad, N'Djamena, Tchad
daoudique@gmail.com

Abstract. This position paper presents the design and outline of the implementation of a mobile money scheme that adapts to the realities of Internet-underserved Areas while exploiting the benefits of Internet protocols. In particular, we implement security and transparency in mobile money transactions using a lightweight permissioned Blockchain infrastructure. Nevertheless, due to network latency and potential connectivity issues, the design of the platform accepts semi-offline transactions: it leverages USSD, a 2nd Generation mobile protocol, only as a back-up channel to force writing of offline transactions to the permissioned ledger and ensure smooth synchronization of the blockchain.

Keywords: Mobile money · Blockchain · ICT4D · Internet-underserved areas

1 Introduction

Electronic payments have experienced a rapid development in the last decade with hundreds of customers worldwide [7]. Mobile banking services, in particular, are now widely adopted within developing countries where they enabled far remote population (e.g., in rural areas) to reach financial services which were not available due to the absence of infrastructure from the traditional banking institutions.

Electronic cash has been a hotbed for investigation in academia as well as industry since the early 90s with the seminal paper by Chaum [6]. Cryptographic techniques were heavily used to provide security for such electronic cash,

© ICST Institute for Computer Sciences, Social Informatics and Telecommunications Engineering 2019
Published by Springer Nature Switzerland AG 2019. All Rights Reserved
G. Mendy et al. (Eds.): AFRICOMM 2018, LNICST 275, pp. 120–130, 2019.
https://doi.org/10.1007/978-3-030-16042-5_12

including protecting against forgery and addressing the double-spending problem. However, in general, the solutions that were being introduced required a trusted third-party such as banks to generate, distribute and validate the digital cash. Bitcoin [12] is a pioneer electronic cash system that neither relies on banks (or any other form of central authority) for the issuance of the coins, neither for their distribution, nor for validating the transactions. There are now over thousands of merchants worldwide that accept bitcoins as currency [4] and has an increasingly large support from payment processors.

In recent years, Bitcoin has been thoroughly studied by researchers and industry practitioners for its use, going from a rigorous analysis in terms of security [9] to analysis of its economic impact [11]. Moreover, a number of alternative cryptocurrencies (altcoins) have been proposed that made considerable changes to the initial design and goals of the Bitcoin. For example, ZCash[1], CryptoNote[2] have been designed with the goal of providing more privacy. Litecoin[3] makes use of different mining mechanisms while others like Ethereum[4] extend the Bitcoin transaction capabilities to enable more flexible approach towards novel transactions scenarios such as Smart contracts.

The challenging aspects of digital currency security, including forgery and double-spending, are addressed in Bitcoin using asymmetric cryptography and a distributed time-stamping mechanisms that is based on Proof-of-Work. As a result a transaction cannot be considered to be confirmed as soon as they are received on the blockchain because it takes some time for the network to verify and integrate them in an atomic state that is hard to change. Consequently, the recipient of any blockchain-based transaction requires an online connection with its underlying blockchain network in order to confirm the validity of the transaction, which takes a certain amount of time[5]. **This makes offline payments with cryptocurrencies extremely challenging** despite offline payment being highly desirable in real world (e.g., in internet-underserved areas). Additionally, Bitcoin payments are increasingly used at many Point-of-Sale (PoS) terminals for immediate payments, where purchased assets are released within a few minutes after the payment and before the transaction confirmation have been generated by the network, although it was already shown that such deployments are vulnerable to double-spending attacks [10]. This has led for the introduction and wide-spread use of permissioned-ledgers, i.e., blockchains that make use of assets *other* than fully-decentralized Bitcoins and where nodes are vetted before they can participate in the blockchain, reducing the requirement for majority consensus before a transaction is validated.

---

[1] https://z.cash/.

[2] https://cryptonote.org/.

[3] https://litecoin.com.

[4] https://ethereum.org/.

[5] Currently the validation delay takes on average 10 min.

This Paper. In this paper, we present the design of a new protocol that will enable secure payments with electronic cash, based on blockchain, in semi-offline settings and in scenarios where payments/transactions needs to be immediately validated. In particular, our contribution is proposing a *solution for semi-offline payments* that is possible on permissioned ledger. To the best of our knowledge, this is the first solution that does not require both the payer and the payee to be online (either over internet or any another form of communication). The solution relies on an offline wallet (device) of the payee that uses cryptographic signatures to provide the assurance of a valid transaction between two parties even when they are not connected at transaction-time to the underlying blockchain.

2   Background

In this section, we provide a brief overview of the basics of blockchain, as well as the current state of the SIGMMA project for blockchain-based mobile money.

2.1   Blockchain Basics

The Bitcoin ecosystem consists of two types of users: Normal users and miners. A normal user utilizes the Bitcoin network for exchanging bitcoins with another user by means of transaction, either being the sender or recipient in such a transaction. These users are identified using their unique addresses which are associated with asymmetric key pairs. In practice, a single transaction may consists in transferring funds between several accounts at once, i.e. it can involve several senders and receivers. Nevertheless, for reasons of simplicity we will assume throughout the paper that a transaction has one sender and one recipient only.

The miners in the Bitcoin ecosystem are the actual backbone of the network. These miners work on validating the transactions and including them into the public history of all the successful transactions into a *blockchain*. These miners have no special account but rather normal user account where they receive rewards for their efforts in verifying transactions. In the case of permissioned ledgers, the role of miners is effectively taken by validators who work similarly as the miners but *without receiving any rewards for their efforts*. The validators have the authority to encode new transactions into a permissioned-blockchain.

The blockchain is simply a logical sequence of blocks that are chained to each other which is extended by appending new valid blocks at its end. Each block within the chain references the previous valid block, which defines the unique order of blocks within the chain. Appending a new block requires the miners to solve a cryptographic puzzle, which itself requires a significant computational effort depending on the consensus protocol which is used. Such a puzzle is then different for the different altcoins: for instance, the Bitcoin requires finding an input towards a hash function of a random nonce which results in a hash value less than a specific target value. This requires the miners to usually have a large computational capabilities where they have to compute a number of hashes until a solution is found. The target value for the puzzle is a security parameter which regulates the difficult of the puzzle, which is adjusted by the network based on the computational power within the network. For more comparative details, we refer the reader to our comparative enumeration of consensus protocols [13].

Once a block has been created and appended to the blockchain, all the transaction included within this block are considered to be confirmed by the network. Subsequent blocks will be appended to the current block making it harder to tamper with the past transaction as ti would require recomputing all the subsequent blocks within the chain. There are different ways to verify the transaction. The miners and validators can perform a full verification (i.e., check for all the blocks within the chain), mobile clients that are incapable of large computation performs a lightweight processing known as simple payment verification (SPV). As opposed to full verification, SPV users verify only the transaction and its confirmed issued by the network i.e. it checks for headers of the blocks for validation without checking all the transaction included within such block, which is considered to be sufficient to ensure that the blocks are part of the blockchain and were generated correctly.

2.2 Mobile Money and the SIGMMA Project

Digitization of payments, transfers, and remittances is key to transparent and inclusive economic growth in low income countries, as it will increase customer convenience, reduce transaction costs substantially, and minimize the need for unaffordable physical infrastructure (e.g., local bank branches). Various stakeholders across the financial and IT ecosystems are expected to be impacted by the penetration of Mobile money. For example: (1) a vast portion of the economy involving person-to-person (P2P) payments in networks of families and friends will benefit from the security and efficacy of remote transactions; (2) the enormous amount of businesses in the informal sector who are trading today but who do not have access to the formal payment infrastructure will be served; (3) governments will gain in reduced payment costs and increased transparency; (4) banks and financial institutions will finally be able to tap into the economic potential of unbanked populations; (5) finally, broad acceptance of digital-payment platforms should benefit stakeholders beyond the payment industry, as it will incite innovation and spur growth.

Over the last decade, the continent has been positioning itself as a leader in Mobile money–cashless electronic payment that use mobile telephones as the main payment mechanism, rather than using a smartphone only as a conduit to a user's bank or credit card account. The GSM Association (GSMA) Mobile Money programme, based on data collected from its network of 850 operators around the world, has recently stated that: *Mobile money has done more to extend the reach of financial services in the last decade than traditional "bricks and mortar" banking has in the last century.* [3]: While, by 2015, mobile money was available in 93 countries, more than half the mobile money companies are operating in Africa. The biggest success story in Africa is Kenya-based M-Pesa, a service launched by UK-based Vodafone for SafariCom in 2007. Within two years, about 38% of Kenya's adult population was using M-Pesa. By 2015,

M-Pesa had 13.9 million active users – with an estimated 40% of Kenya's GDP flowing through its network [1].

M-Pesa's growth however is based on special circumstances, as reported by The Economist Intelligence Unit: "M-Pesa was started by a mobile phone operator that already had a very high market share [of 70%]. Financial regulations around these types of services in Kenya were very loose at the time. The government was very supportive, as it was keen to use mobile financial services to make government payments throughout the country" [15]. In a piece for the BBC's Matter of Life & Tech, Burkman even argues that M-Pesa, "the poster child of mobile money in Africa", paints a false picture of the continent since the reality is that "mobile money has only really taken off in one country out of 55 on the continent" [2]. In other countries, the quest to replicate Kenyan M-Pesa success remains a difficult struggle. Even attempts to launch M-Pesa in neighbouring countries like Tanzania and South Africa have faced a range of obstacles [2]. Throughout the region (i.e., sub-Saharan Africa), several mobile money systems initiated by telecom operators and banks, and often based on SMS/USSD technologies as in M-Pesa, are beginning to pay off (although at a lesser scale than M-Pesa). We enumerate four limiting factors that currently prevent a full-blown adoption of mobile money in sub-Saharan Africa:

1. Mobile money payments are currently made using interfaces that target feature phones. Yet, smartphone penetration in Africa has rapidly evolved [8], and user-friendly apps can now help to improve adoption.
2. SMS/USSD messages are easily hacked by malware on smartphones which have become common among users. Besides, in case of fraud, it is impossible to track money flows beyond cash-out desks/agents [5].
3. Client and service provider accounts are tightly associated to network operators or banks. This situation challenges the possibility of transactions across operators while hindering innovation: service creation is not open to the large public [16].
4. There is little participation of low income country consumers to the global financial market; E.g., limitations on cross-border transactions challenges the access to online resources such as MOOC courses.

In 2017, the SnT Interdisciplinary centre at the University of Luxembourg has initiated, together with partners from Universities in Senegal, Burkina Faso, Cote d'Ivoire and Netherlands, a project for Secure, Interoperable Mobile Money in sub-Saharan Africa (SIGMMA) based on the blockchain technology. The SIGMMA platform is a digital vehicle to fiat currencies produced by the central bank. Thus, it is not a bitcoin-like platform where cryptocurrencies are mined (i.e., generated based on the computing power put forth to resolve complex algorithmic problems). Instead, our similarity with bitcoin is only related to the use of the underlying technology of blockchain to validate transactions and store them in a distributed ledger for transparency. Currencies get in and out of the system through cash-in/cash-out points where exchange operations are performed

Table 1. Bitcoin vs e-Money (©CGAP report [14])

	Bitcoin	e-Money
Accessibility	Largely limited to internet connection	Access to electronic devices such as mobile phones, and an agent network
Value	Determined by supply and demand, and trust in the system	Equal to amount of fiat currency exchanged into electronic form
Customer ID	Anonymous	Financial Action Task Force standards (especially KYC rules) apply for customer identification (though such standards permit simplified measures for lower risk financial products)
Production	Mathematically generated, "mined" by peer network	Digitally issued against receipt of equal value of fiat currency of central authority
Issuer	Community of developers, called "miners"	Legally established e-money issuer
Regulator	None	Regulated by central authority, typically central bank

by traditional financial service providers. We now describe differentiating points between different models in digital currencies, in order to better position the SIGMMA platform as cryptocurrency-based e-Money platform. The following table is an excerpt of the CGAP report on "Bitcoin vs Electronic money" [14] (Table 1).

SIGMMA is implementing an e-money platform on top of the blockchain technology: the cryptocurrencies transacted should then be considered as digital fiat currencies. Indeed, these are typical e-Money currencies (whose value is equal to the amount of exchanged fiat currency), but which are circulating in a blockchain network allowing to guarantee transparency, security and interoperability across systems.

Figure 1 illustrates screenshots from the current app of the SIGMMA prototype. The core technology for validating transactions is based on the Exonum[6] framework. Although promising, the current prototype did not support offline payments which are necessary for internet-underserved areas where connectivity is unstable. This paper presents our idea for moving SIGMMA for supporting semi-offline payments with a sporadically-synchronized blockchain.

---

[6] https://exonum.com/.

2.3   Challenges Towards Offline Payments

1. The first challenge towards offline mobile money payments that are based on blockchain relates to the use of *constrained devices*. As an order of comparison, for full bitcoin wallets it can take days to download and validate the whole blockchain even on modern desktop personal computers. Wallets on mobile devices may not even be able to perform Simple Payment Verification as they may not have enough resources to store the block headers. This itself makes it challenging to ensure that the device is capable of validating the transaction in some manner.

2. The second challenge relates to the need to guarantee the synchronization of the blockchain whenever the disconnected party goes online. Malicious parties may explore the possible to roll back some transactions while offline so as to repudiate any block that will be associated with the client.

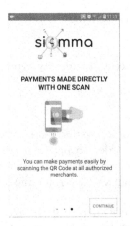   

(a) Support of payment with QR code   (b) Support for Person-to-person payments

Fig. 1. Screenshots from the SIGMMA app

3   Semi-offline Blockchain-Based Mobile Money

The SIGMMA platform already ensures interoperability by allowing legacy mobile money operators to plug in, enabling cross-operators transactions. Transparency and Security are assured by the underlying transparent ledger of the blockchain, while uniformity (i.e., the possibility to undertake any financial operations) is provided through an Application Programming Interface (API) on top of which new services can be built (e.g., person-to-person payments, Point-of-sale payment, online banking services, etc.). Unfortunately, currently the SIGMMA app does not fully account for instability in internet connection with the fragile infrastructure available in sub-Saharan Africa.

3.1   Model of the System

The system used can be represented in the traditional four-layer model which can be developed within the Exonum framework:

- *Network*: This layer tracks the adresses and connection routes to the different computing nodes that participate in maintaining the blockchain.
- *Protocol*: This layer defines the basic rules that define the behaviour of participants within the network. It formalizes the features such as immutability, byzantine fault tolerance and scalability of transactions.
- *Data*: This layer implements the blockchain storage. The blockchain itself will include the identities, transactions, account balances, contracts and its states that users of the network has stored.
- *Application*: This layer defines how services can be implemented by offering APIs.

Concretely, our system consists of a permissionned blockchain infrastructure which includes a blockchain **B** and validators **V**. These validators are similar in as miners in the traditional bitcoin-based blockchain. Validators, contrary to miners, are not rewarded since they are part of the system with the function to ensure integrity of the chain while finalizing the different transactions as state within the chain. We have multiple users (Alice and Bob here) where Alice wants to send an offline transaction τ to Bob. Both users have their handheld devices which are registered on the blockchain with a unique identity: typically, this is seamlessly done via the installation of the SIGMMA app. The unique identity is a public key used to identify the user on the network. Each of the device is also capable of performing a computational operation that can generate a unique secret key for each user and can apply signature on a piece of data.

Additionally, the handheld devices are connected to validators (which are operated by the service provider) either via normal 3G cellular network or using Wi-Fi capabilities. Furthermore, each of the device has a certificate that presents legitimacy of the validator to which the user is subscribed to.

3.2   Proposed Protocol Design

We present protocol design for each phase of our solution: committing-coins, offline transaction confirmation and pushing to the underlying blockchain.

Notations. We denote an operation as $A(in) \longrightarrow out$, where A is the name of operation, in is the input requires and out the output of the operation, which may be a boolean value. We have $sig(sk; d) \longrightarrow \sigma$ to denote signature on the data d using the signature key sk which can be verified using the operation $verify(pk, d, \sigma) \longrightarrow false, true$. Figure 2 shows the overall flow of offline and online validations.

In the committing-coins phase of the protocol, the payer Alice first indicates the amount b that she would like to load in her sub-wallet W_s. Next the wallet creates a transaction τ_1 that transfers b coins to this sub wallet and pushes this towards the underlying blockchain.

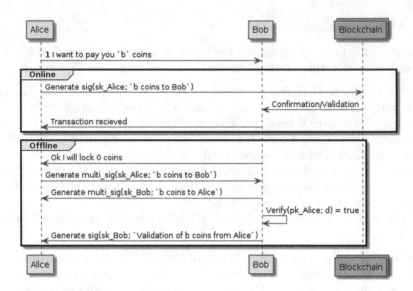

Fig. 2. Online vs offline protocols with the blockchain

As both Alice and Bob may not have any online connection during the payment, the offline transaction τ is sent using local interfaces that are commonly available in majority of the handheld devices (such as Bluetooth and NFC) for peer-to-peer connectivity recognized by the SIGMMA app available in both devices. Nevertheless, if both are online (in any form) then the transaction would be directly pushed towards the blockchain like normal blockchain transactions. However, both parties are bound to occasionally online, e.g., Alice goes online to receive a transaction to her account, and Bob to redeem the offline transaction that he received after payment. Finally, to prevent any roll-back of transactions made offline (which would lead to inconsistencies), once a transaction is made offline, a USSD message is committed by the SIGMMA app towards a telecom operator gateway. Since USSD message are always successful (in the sense that they get queued and cannot be canceled by the user, and will be sent out once cellular network connectivity appears), no offline transaction can be removed from the ledger. We further put a threshold on the number of transactions that a single user can make offlines before it must synchronize against the blockchain, so as to avoid latency in complex merging of blocks.

4   Concluding Remarks

There is a huge effort within the academia and industry towards democratizing the use of Blockchain on the one hand, and improving mobile money on the other hand.

Mobile money business has helped drive a large improvement towards achievement in providing the access towards financial services to those who are generally unreachable. Services through informal, yet technically sound systems, such as the micro-credit association or community driven savings club which are often refereed as powerful means to drive low-income people towards the traditional financial institutions. These alternative ways do not require the mandatory identification requirements and in many cases relay on mobile technologies that allow conducting transactions without the need of being physically present at the bank or other financial entity. Currently, mobile operator services are generally not interoperable with other operators, which means that transactions are limited *only* within the operator's system. Furthermore, the operators tend to charge transaction fees to establish monopoly within the economy of a particular region.

Blockchain projects have been known for its ability to store and transmit values across national and trans-national borders at large scale at relatively low cost but would require a logical approach and understanding of its underlying technology including access to stable Internet access and a relatively modern smartphone. In developing countries, people tend to live on daily wages that are approx 10$ per month where the requirement of 100$ smartphone along with Internet charges make it out of scope for majority of the population.

The SIGMMA project is working towards a sustainable solution to the security, interoperability, transparency and cross-border issues of Mobile money in sub-Saharan Africa. We plan to roll out a test prototype of the proposed solution for sporadically-synchronized blockchain which accounts for the realities of constraints of internet-underserved areas.

References

1. Telecoms in Kenya: A new East Africa campaign. https://goo.gl/H3cFyR
2. Making mobile money pay in Africa (2017). https://goo.gl/vl1WDi
3. GSM Association: State of the industry report on mobile money (2015). https://goo.gl/xdJj79
4. Barber, S., Boyen, X., Shi, E., Uzun, E.: Bitter to better — how to make bitcoin a better currency. In: Keromytis, A.D. (ed.) FC 2012. LNCS, vol. 7397, pp. 399–414. Springer, Heidelberg (2012). https://doi.org/10.1007/978-3-642-32946-3_29
5. Central Bank of Kenya: Launching of the financial geospatial mapping survey (2015). https://goo.gl/MF9rUU
6. Chaum, D.: Blind signatures for untraceable payments. In: Chaum, D., Rivest, R.L., Sherman, A.T. (eds.) Advances in Cryptology, pp. 199–203. Springer, Boston (1983). https://doi.org/10.1007/978-1-4757-0602-4_18
7. Dunn, E.: Advanced payments report (2017). http://edgardunn.com/wp-content/uploads/2017/06/EDC_AdvancedPaymentA4_2017.pdf
8. Ericsson: Ericsson report: Mobile internet use doubling year-on-year in sub-Sahara Africa. https://goo.gl/0iITaZ
9. Eyal, I., Sirer, E.G.: Majority is not enough: bitcoin mining is vulnerable. In: Christin, N., Safavi-Naini, R. (eds.) FC 2014. LNCS, vol. 8437, pp. 436–454. Springer, Heidelberg (2014). https://doi.org/10.1007/978-3-662-45472-5_28
10. Karame, G.O., Androulaki, E., Capkun, S.: Double-spending fast payments in bitcoin. In: Proceedings of the 2012 ACM Conference on Computer and Communications Security, pp. 906–917. ACM (2012)

11. Kroll, J.A., Davey, I.C., Felten, E.W.: The economics of bitcoin mining, or bitcoin in the presence of adversaries. In: Proceedings of WEIS, vol. 2013, p. 11 (2013)
12. Nakamoto, S.: Bitcoin: a peer-to-peer electronic cash system (2008)
13. Ouattara, H.F., Ahmat, D., Ouedraogo, F.T., Bissyande, T.F., Sie, O.: Blockchain consensus protocols - towards a review of practical constraints for implementation in developing countries. In: EAI International Conference on e-Infrastructures and e-Services for Developing Countries (AFRICOMM) (2017)
14. Parker, S.R.: Bitcoin vs electronic money, CGAP report (2014). https://goo.gl/po06th
15. The Economist Intelligence Unit: Mobile money in Africa: Promise and perils. https://goo.gl/DUI47i
16. World Bank Development Research Group, the Better Than Cash Alliance, and the Bill & Melinda Gates Foundation: The opportunities of digitizing payments (2014). https://goo.gl/wTlECK

Internet Development in Africa:
A Content Use, Hosting
and Distribution Perspective

Enrico Calandro[1]([✉]), Josiah Chavula[2], and Amreesh Phokeer[3]

[1] Research ICT Africa, Cape Town, South Africa
ecalandro@researchictafrica.net
[2] University of Cape Town, Cape Town, South Africa
jchavula@cs.uct.ac.za
[3] AFRINIC, Ebene, Mauritius
amreesh@afrinic.net

Abstract. Although a considerable investment in broadband infrastructure has improved broadband speeds across many African countries, the reliability and performance that users ultimately receive is determined also by the interconnection between networks and Internet Service Providers (ISPs) and by where the content, services and applications are hosted. Often, high latencies to remote destinations introduce significant performance bottlenecks, suggesting that, in addition to investments in higher throughput links, effort should be devoted to improving interconnection between ISPs and locating content closer to the users. By untangling the complexity of content access, use, hosting and distribution in Africa, this study offers three main contributions. First, it discusses challenges related to usage, hosting, distribution of local content and services in Africa, by developing a case on African local news websites. Second, it makes publicly available measurement data and indicators for local content use, hosting, and distribution across all African countries. And third, it provides points of policy recommendations on how to improve internet access and use, and infrastructure performance from a content perspective.

Keywords: Local content · Web hosting · Latency · Peering ·
Content infrastructure

1 Introduction

Between 2013 and 2017, Africa experienced the most rapid growth of international internet bandwidth in comparison to other regions, growing at a compound annual rate of 44% [1]. However, the majority of the African population continues to be offline due to high data costs [2–5] lack of local content [6], and poor network performance [7,8], despite a number of investments and projects

G. Mendy et al. (Eds.): AFRICOMM 2018, LNICST 275, pp. 131–141, 2019.
https://doi.org/10.1007/978-3-030-16042-5_13

to expand and upgrade undersea cables, and the new investments in terrestrial fibre network capacity. The average Round-Trip Times (RTT or latency) is still high, due to poor Internet peering infrastructure [9] and topological inefficiencies [10]. Not only is the peering fabric of the continent uneven, but also content infrastructure in Africa requires significant development. Studies suggest that content is a dominant component of network traffic, but local content is a major bottleneck to African connectivity [11].

While this significant investment in broadband infrastructure [12] and data centres [13,14] in Africa has improved throughput across the continent, most content in the continent, even local websites, are hosted and are delivered from overseas [15]. A number of factors have been postulated to be the reason for remote hosting of African websites. Foremost, hosting services and infrastructure have not been pervasive in Africa, rendering the provision and management of web content within the continent unattractive [16]. Although it is generally cheaper to host with remote/foreign companies than with local hosting companies, content hosted abroad must be routed back to the country of origin over international Internet transit links that, in spite of significant infrastructure investments in recent years, are still expensive. The resulting high costs to access content hosted abroad are generally borne by Internet Service Providers (ISPs), and ultimately by Internet users. The result is a negative externality, where the economic decisions of content providers to host abroad have a negative impact on ISPs' costs, which in turn increases the cost of Internet usage and limits Internet content demand [16].

1.1 Research Questions

This paper seeks to untangle the complexity of content use, hosting and distribution in Africa. More specifically, it poses the following key questions:

1. What type of content do African people consume?
2. Where is local African content hosted? Taking into account local news website, how much of the content is hosted locally vs globally?
3. How is content hosted in Africa?
4. What routes are used to access locally hosted content?
5. What is the latency for content hosted in various regions?

1.2 Contribution of the Study

In answering these key research questions, this paper makes three contributions: First, it offers a discussion on challenges related to usage, hosting, distribution and accessing of local content in Africa. Secondly, this study makes publicly available measurement data the web content infrastructure in Africa, and at the same time it illustrates what the factors affecting performance when accessing Africa's digital content are. The third contribution of this study is the provision of specific policy recommendation points on how to improve Internet adoption and infrastructure performance from a content perspective. To achieve this, the study undertakes an active Internet measurements campaign to characterize the latencies and to geolocate web servers and routes used for Africa's online content, focussing on local news websites in each country. This paper explores the hosting patterns and performance associated with a large sample of about 1,100 local news websites. To test assumptions on content use from a user's perspective, it draws on nationally representative ICT access and use surveys conducted by Research ICT Africa (RIA) in 2017 in seven African countries.

2   Research Methods and Data Sources

The study makes use of Internet measurements, household surveys data and pricing data as the three main data sources.

First, in order to measure what type of content people in Africa consume, the study draws on the Research ICT Africa (RIA) #AfterAccess survey[1], which delivers nationally representative results for households and individuals. The survey is based on enumerator areas (EA) of national census sample frames as primary sampling units. Through the survey, we could establish what type of content African people consume.

Second, Internet measurements were conducted to gather information regarding where Africa's web content is hosted, as well as to assess the associated performance and cost implications. The first task was therefore to identify websites that would be considered representative of Africa's local web content. In this study, Africa's web content is defined as content that is primarily generated and consumed within each African country. It was decided therefore to study local news and media websites, which by definition constitute a significant body of local content in Africa. A list of local news websites made for every African country was compiled from ABYZ News Links[2], an online directory of links to online news sources from around the world organized on a geographical basis.

Third, to answer to the question of whether local news websites are locally hosted within their countries or not, Traceroute data was analysed to determine the networks that host each of the measured websites, as well as the networks through which traffic flows between the websites and the measurement vantage points. Subsequently, the geographical location of each web-hosting server was determined. MaxMind[3] geolocation database was used to obtain the network information, which includes the networks' Autonomous System Numbers (ASNs) and network names. The geolocation database was also used to identify the countries related to each IP in the dataset, both the websites' web-servers and routers along the paths to the websites. The country-level geolocation was preferred as it has been shown to have relatively higher accuracy compared to city-level geolocation [17,18]. The Traceroute measurements were repeated over a five-day period, resulting in about 19,299 successfully measurements between

---

[1] https://researchictafrica.net/2017/08/04/beyond-access-surveys-questionnaires-methodologyand-timeframe/.

[2] Available at the following link: http://www.abyznewslinks.com/.

[3] https://www.maxmind.com/en/geoip2-country-database.

the probes and the websites. Each Traceroute measurement returns three final hop RTTs, meaning that in total, there were 57,897 end-to-end RTTs. A Traceroute measurement is considered successful if an IP route can be determined from the source to the web-hosting network, thereby also being able to reveal a delay estimate to the website. Each successful measurement contains the IP address of a website's hosting server, a series of IP hops from the vantage point up the server, as well as the delays (round-trip time, RTT) at each hop (router). Also, each Traceroute result is made up of multiple records, one record for each of the multiple hops on the path. Consequently, the final dataset was made up of 256,654 records, with each record comprising source and destination addresses, as well as the IP hop and RTT from the source to that hop.

3   Data Analysis

3.1   Internet Users' Perspective

Table 1 below shows that mobile phone penetration in African countries has not reached the 100% as reported by ITU for some African countries. The mobile phone technology continues nevertheless to scale rapidly with more than 50% of the African population owning a mobile phone. Migration to higher speed networks and smartphones continues apace, with mobile broadband connections set to reduce the historical digital divide. In four of the seven countries surveyed, more than 20% of respondents have used the Internet, in contrast to the 3 poorest of the countries surveyed, Mozambique, Rwanda, and Tanzania, which recorded 9,70%, 8,21%, and 13,53% respectively.

As the vast majority of people in all seven countries access the Internet through their mobile phone, the low Internet penetration in these countries can be attributed to low smartphone penetration which, except for Tanzania, is lower than 20% compared to South Africa (55,53%), Ghana (34,27%), Kenya (27,57%) and Nigeria (23,83%). Surprisingly, Tanzania's smartphone penetration is above 20% but Internet penetration remains lower. This could be attributed to supply-side issues such as data prices or the dearth of skills to enable Internet use.

In terms of barriers to internet use (Table 2 below), as expected, data cost has been reported as the main obstacle. For a number of respondents, internet is considered a time-consuming activity, as it seems that lack of time is another relevant barrier to internet use. In Tanzania (28.36%), South Africa (24.22%), and Mozambique (36.5%), instead, the users perceive that internet speed is not sufficient for a seamless internet access. Lack of content in local language, on the other hand, and in contrast to previous studies on local content in Africa, is not considered one of the main obstacles to internet use, except in Rwanda, where 8,49% of the respondents expressed some concern related to lack of content in local languages.

Table 1. Mobile phone, smartphone, and internet use across 7 African countries. (Source: #AfterAccess RIA surveys, 2017)

Country	Mobile phone (%)	Smartphone (%)	Internet use (%)
Ghana	73,87	34,27	26,00
Kenya	86,94	27,57	25,59
Mozambique	39,73	17,01	9,70
Nigeria	64,42	23,83	30,22
Rwanda	48,16	9,02	8,21
South Africa	83,84	55,53	49,72
Tanzania	58,52	22,12	13,53

Table 2. What does limit you to from using the internet? (Source: #AfterAccess RIA surveys, 2017)

	Ghana	Kenya	Mozambique	Nigeria	Rwanda	South Africa	Tanzania
No limitation	11,96	16,95		19,92	21,58		
Lack of time	21,78	20,16	11,59	15,65	18,13	10	25,62
Data cost	51,51	45,42	43,28	32,25	48,7	47,15	40,64
Lack of content in my language	**3,59**	**1,96**	**6,43**	**0,26**	**8,49**	**3,32**	**3,68**
Speed of internet	7,53	11,63	36,5	18,11	1,01	24,22	28,36
Privacy concern	0,47	0,51	2,44	2,98	2,08	3,18	0,89
Worried about getting virus/malware	0,6	0,74	8,85		9,97	3,77	0,85
Not allowed to use it (by family/spouse)	0,69	0,07	5,45	1,02	2,95	2,88	0,57
Find it difficult to use	1,87	0,95	5,36	1,65	5,99	2,23	4,14

3.2   Geolocation of African News Content Hosting

The hosting and geolocation analysis indicates that about 85% of the news websites are hosted outside the countries in which they belong, i.e. the website is owned and it is local to one country, but is hosted in another country. This is, hereafter, referred to as remote hosting. Analysis of remote hosted websites reveals that most of them are hosted in Europe and the US.

Figure 1 below shows a country-level distribution of locally hosted websites versus remotely hosted. Almost all the countries in the sample have less than 30% of their websites hosted locally, and about half of all the countries have less than 10% local hosting. South Africa (ZA) appears to have a high percentage of local hosting with 46%.

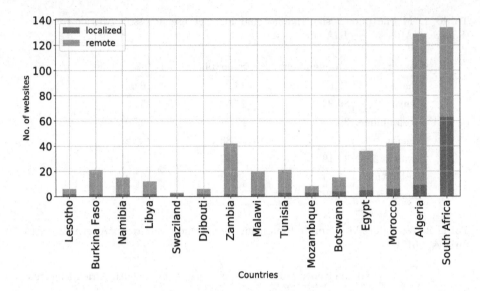

Fig. 1. Number of websites per country local vs remote

We observe that the US takes the lion's share in hosting African content, with about 58% of all the websites being hosted by American companies. Within Africa, South Africa leads in the content hosting business, hosting about 14% of all of Africa's remotely hosted news websites (i.e. minus those that belong to South Africa). The rest of the websites, about 20% are hosted in various countries in Europe (notably, 9% in France, 4% in Germany, and 3% in Great Britain). This signals low participation of the continent's companies in content hosting. Most of the websites that were observed to be hosted within Africa were based in South Africa, while the majority of the rest are hosted in either the US or Europe.

We also found that about 45% of all the IP hops (i.e. Internet path) for accessing African websites from African countries traversed outside African clients' home countries. Internet packets travel mostly through US networks, and about 23% pass through European networks. South Africa takes about 8% of all IP hops for traffic traversing to other African countries.

3.3   Network-Level Analysis of Africa's News Sites

Similar to the geolocation analysis, network-level analysis shows that most of the websites are hosted by foreign companies. Taking into consideration all the sampled African news websites, Cloudflare Inc. (US) takes the biggest share of the market, hosting about 22% of the websites. Following in the far distance is OVH SAS (France) with 8%, OPTINET (South Africa) at 6%, Google LLC and GoDaddy.com (both US) at 5% each, and Unified Layer (US) at 4%, and HETZNER (South Africa) at 3%.

With regards to the hosting market share, i.e. if only remotely hosted websites are considered, Cloudflare take an even bigger share of 26%, followed by OVH SAS (9%), Google LLC (6%), GoDaddy.com (5%) and Unified Layer (5%). What is interesting to note is that the leading providers for Africa's remote hosted news websites are largely based on Cloud infrastructure and make use of content distribution networks.

3.4 Delay Analysis (Round Trip Times) to Access Locally and Remotely Hosted Content

Analysis of round-trip times (RTTs) when accessing the websites from each of the countries shows significant RTT differences between locally hosted websites and those remotely hosted as shown in Fig. 3. The maps in Fig. 2 below highlights country-level RTT differences for local and remote hosting. The median RTTs for locally hosted websites is about 50 ms, whereas for remote hosted websites, the median RTTs range between 100 ms and 300 ms.

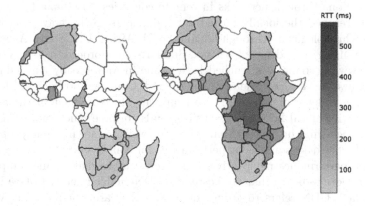

Fig. 2. National median RTT comparing locally (left) vs remotely (right) hosted content

The range of median RTTs shows significant differences between countries for websites hosted within each country. We found out that out of the 22 countries where local hosting performance was measured, 16 countries registered local median RTTs of less than 50 ms, while the other 6 countries (Angola, Malawi, Lesotho, Algeria, Cameroon, Morocco, and Ghana) had local median RTTs ranging between 50 ms and 200 ms. The analysis shows that in some countries, the median RTTs for locally hosted websites is higher than for websites that are remotely hosted. Examples include Ghana, where the median RTT for locally hosted websites was found to be 205 ms, whereas for remote websites, the median RTT was 127 ms; and Morocco, where the local median RTT was 152 ms against a remote median RTT of 68 ms. RTTs of over 100 ms for locally hosted websites

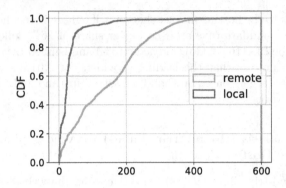

Fig. 3. RTT to access locally vs remotely hosted websites

could suggest circuitous path, where locally hosted websites are accessed through Internet paths that traverse other countries.

This further indicates a lack of peering, where interconnections between local network is done through networks in remote countries. In Ghana for example, one probe reached the locally hosted www.ghana.gov.gh by traversing remote networks, chronologically through Ghana, South Africa, UK, South Africa, and Ghana, resulting in a delay of 380 ms. Similarly in Morocco, a locally hosted website www.leseco.ma was reached by a probe in Morocco by traversing four networks, first in Morocco, then France, Ireland, Canada, and back to Morocco, experiencing a delay of 160 ms. These examples illustrate that in the absence of local peering, local hosting of websites tends to force much more circuitous routes for accessing the content than when the websites are in foreign countries, resulting higher delays and poor performance for consumers.

From a performance perspective, it is interesting to make some comparison between remote websites that are hosted by CDN-enabled networks (see Fig. 4). In a nutshell, CDN refers to groups of servers that are distributed in various geographic locations and work together to provide fast delivery of Internet content. The CDN takes content that is otherwise hosted on a single server, and replicates it to a set of distributed servers that are deemed to be closer to the intended consumers of such content. On the other hand, content that is not supported by CDN infrastructure generally remains within its original server location. This means that, while locally hosted content will be closer to the local consumers, CDN-based content can be brought closer to consumers even if the original servers are in distant locations. The expectation, therefore, is that level of delays for CDN-based websites should be similar to locally hosted websites. Of course, this assumes that the CDNs have nodes within or close to the respective countries. In this regard, the South African case is worth of a mention. Although the country has only about 46% of the news websites hosted locally, it can be seen the median RTTs for local and remote websites are almost the same; 22 ms and 25 ms respectively. As was mentioned earlier, the leading remote hosting providers for Africa (Cloudflare, OVH SAS, Google LLC, GoDaddy.com and Unified Layer) operate on Cloud infrastructure and distribute their content via CDN services. It is also worth noting that South Africa hosts a number of CDN nodes, including Cloudflare, which has two; one in Cape Town and another node in Johannesburg[4]. This means that although the original web hosting is in remote countries, the actual website content is generally served from within the country. CDNs are helpful primarily to bring content hosted overseas closer to its users, and the increasing in local traffic might become an incentive for local ISPs to peer locally.

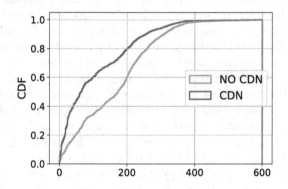

Fig. 4. RTT for websites using CDN vs NO CDN

4 Discussion

As opposed to previous studies on Internet adoption, this study does not find evidence of lack of content in local languages as one of the main obstacles to internet use, except in Rwanda. 85% of the African local news websites are hosted outside of their respective countries, mostly Europe and US, while the majority of the websites that were observed to be hosted within Africa were based in South Africa. Almost all the countries in the sample have less than 30% of their websites hosted locally, and about half of all the countries have less than 10% local hosting. 68% of all the Internet path for accessing African websites from African countries traversed outside Africa, mostly through US and European networks. A network-level analysis showed that most of the local African news websites are hosted by foreign companies.

The leading providers for Africa's remote hosted news websites are largely based on Cloud infrastructure and make use of content distribution networks to mirror the content locally. One direct consequence of remote hosting is that African network operators have to use significant levels of international bandwidth to fetch African content for their clients. The cost of this international bandwidth is in the end passed on to the Internet users in Africa.

Furthermore, geolocation of website hosting has significant implication on performance. The median RTTs for locally hosted websites is generally lower

---

[4] https://www.cdnplanet.com/geo/south-africa-cdn/.

than the RTTs for remote hosted websites. However, in some countries, the median RTTs for locally hosted websites is higher than for websites that are remotely hosted. High RTTs levels for locally hosted websites is an indicator of circuitous paths, which are due to lack of local ISP peering. Rather, in these cases interconnections between local networks is done through networks in remote countries. In the absence of local peering, local hosting of websites tends to resolve into circuitous routes for accessing the content than when the websites are in foreign countries, resulting in higher delays and therefore in poor performance for Internet users. By bringing remotely hosted content closer to the users, CDN-enabled networks reduce delays for CDN-based websites. Although level of delays for CDN-based websites are similar to locally hosted websites, CDNs do not improve the performance of locally hosted content in cases where there is lack of local peering. While access network infrastructure has improved in Africa, the content infrastructure has lagged behind. There is a considerable difference between access infrastructure and content infrastructure. While supply-side policy and regulatory interventions have positively affected access infrastructure (notably the roll out of mobile networks in the case of Africa), content infrastructure has not always been enabled by national policy and regulatory interventions resulting in most of the content in Africa being hosted and accessed from overseas. This configuration is not ideal, as it increases latency levels, and costs to access content. Not having a reliable hosting infrastructure affects also in-country delivery infrastructure. Without the necessary local peering, locally hosted content can exhibit equally higher access latencies.

5   Conclusion and Policy Implications

This study has provided empirical evidence on the current configuration of web content hosting, access, and distribution in Africa, and has demonstrated that the status of the African content infrastructure is alarming. All African countries heavily rely on foreign services, both to host, to access, and to distribute local content in Africa. Latency levels to remotely hosted local content are high as well as costs of accessing remotely hosted local content. Most of the public policy strategies on improving local content in Africa focused on demand-side interventions, such as the creation of content in local languages, and on developing skills on web content production and consumption. While these policies are important, bodies in charge of the governance of the internet are urged to identify ways of facilitating local markets for content hosting, access and distributions by focusing on: (1) incentivising investments on data centres and web farms in Africa, to stimulate economies of scale for the local web hosting market; (2) encouraging local news websites to move the content closer to the users in Africa, by incentivising the use of CDN-enabled networks and by reducing prices for local hosting, (3) Facilitating peering relationships between ISPs and investing in local exchange points to reduce latency; and (4) incentivising ISPs to peer in local exchange points.

References

1. Mauldin, A.: International Internet Capacity Growth Just Accelerated for the First Time Since 2015 (2018). https://blog.telegeography.com/international-internet-capacity-growth-just-accelerated-for-the-first-time-since-2015. Accessed 12 Nov 2018
2. Mothobi, O.: Botswana telecommunications limp a decade after policy changes (2017)
3. Mothobi, O.: South African data prices static for two years but consumers not flocking to cheapest product offering (2017)
4. Mothobi, O.: SADC not bridging digital divide, policy brief 6 (2017)
5. A4AI: 2017 Affordability Report: Regional Snapshots & Country-Specific Highlights. https://a4ai.org/2017-affordability-report-regional/. Accessed 15 Nov 2018
6. Amos, I.: Is the Lack of Local Content Hindering Internet Adoption in Afrika? (2016). https://www.iafrikan.com/2016/09/21/is-the-lack-of-local-content-hindering-internet-adoption-in-afrika-2/. Accessed 15 Nov 2018
7. Chetty, M., Sundaresan, S., Muckaden, S., Feamster, N., Calandro, E.: Measuring broadband performance in South Africa. In: Proceedings of the 4th Annual Symposium on Computing for Development, p. 1. ACM (2013)
8. Fanou, R., Francois, P., Aben, E.: On the diversity of interdomain routing in Africa. In: Mirkovic, J., Liu, Y. (eds.) PAM 2015. LNCS, vol. 8995, pp. 41–54. Springer, Cham (2015). https://doi.org/10.1007/978-3-319-15509-8_4
9. Chavula, J., Phokeer, A., Formoso, A., Feamster, N.: Insight into Africa's country-level latencies. In: AFRICON 2017, pp. 938–944. IEEE (2017)
10. Formoso, A., Chavula, J., Phokeer, A., Sathiaseelan, A., Tyson, G.: Deep diving into Africa's inter-country latencies. In: IEEE INFOCOM 2018 - IEEE Conference on Computer Communications, pp. 2231–2239, April 2018
11. OECD/ISOC/UNESCO: The relationship between local content, internet development and access prices (217) (2013)
12. Song, S.: The Internet is U-Shaped (2017)
13. Data Cent. Dyn. Africa Tracks the Growth of the African Colo and Cloud Markets (2018). https://www.datacenterdynamics.com/news/dcdafrica-tracks-the-growth-of-the-african-colo-and-cloud-markets/. Accessed 15 Nov 2018
14. Nelson, V.: MainOne to Build Three New Data Centres Across West Africa (2014). https://thestack.com/data-centre/2018/09/06/mainone-to-build-three-new-data-centres-across-west-africa/. Accessed 15 Nov 2018
15. Bram, U.: Why Your Internet Connection is Slow Wherever You are in Africa (2015). https://qz.com/africa/472028/why-your-internet-connection-is-slow-wherever-you-are-in-africa/. Accessed 15 Nov 2018
16. Kende, M., Rose, K.: Promoting local content hosting to develop the internet ecosystem. ISOC report (2015)
17. Poese, I., Uhlig, S., Kaafar, M.A., Donnet, B., Gueye. B.: IP geolocation databases: unreliable? ACM SIGCOMM Comput. Commun. Rev. 41(2), 53–56 (2011)
18. Shavitt, Y., Zilberman, N.: A geolocation databases study. IEEE J. Sel. Areas Commun. 29(10), 2044–2056 (2011)

The (Missing?) Role of Health Information Systems (HIS) in Patient Care Coordination and Continuity (PCCC): The Case of Uganda

Grace Kobusinge[1,2(✉)], Raymond Mugwanya[2], Kalevi Pessi[1],
and Dina Koutsikouri[1]

[1] AIT, University of Gothenburg, 412 96 Gothenburg, Sweden
gkobusinge@gmail.com, {grace.kobusinge,kalevi.pessi,
dina.koutsikouri}@ait.gu.se
[2] COCIS, Makerere University, 7062, Kampala, Uganda
ray.mugwanya@gmail.com

Abstract. In Uganda, patients receive care from different health facilities. However, most facilities struggle to exchange patient information across boundaries because their health information systems (HIS) operate in silos. Yet to meet the needs of a patient who receives care from different health facilities the participating facilities ought to collaborate, share and exchange patient information in order to enhance patient care coordination and continuity (PCCC) across the continuum of care. Using qualitative interviews we examine five HIS to investigate the problematic issues that could be raised during HIS active involvement in PCCC across the continuum of care. Results highly indicate that the existing HIS in the country do not enhance PCCC, and below are some of the challenges realized: interoperability objective not given priority during system design, HIS operating in silos, lack of a national standard for the patient record, health facilities exercising ownership of the data and other non-technical challenges. The main implication of these findings is that focusing on the interoperability objective as a design requirement during HIS implementation would potentially repress all other challenges and revive the active role of HIS involvement in PCCC.

Keywords: Health information systems ·
Patient care coordination and continuity

1 Introduction

Health information systems (HIS) are increasingly being implemented at most health facilities in order to promote quality healthcare delivery [1, 2]. However, even with increased HIS implementations, health facilities still struggle to share and exchange patient information amongst themselves. An assessment of the current HIS integration schemes, reveals that existing HIS are operating in silos, are fragmented and non-interoperable [3–6] since they do not support information sharing and exchange between each other [3] across the continuum of care. For example, in case of referrals patients repeat tests due to lack of past records to aid care continuity [7]. "Rarely, can

© ICST Institute for Computer Sciences, Social Informatics and Telecommunications Engineering 2019
Published by Springer Nature Switzerland AG 2019. All Rights Reserved
G. Mendy et al. (Eds.): AFRICOMM 2018, LNICST 275, pp. 142–151, 2019.
https://doi.org/10.1007/978-3-030-16042-5_14

health facilities access electronic medical information from other facilities even within the same geographic setting" [8]. Such lack of coordination among healthcare facilities delays decision making [9], and further impedes patient care coordination and continuity (PCCC) [1, 10].

Therefore, given that patients receive assistance from different health facilities across the continuum of care [11, 12], it is necessary for all participating facilities to be able to collaborate, share and exchange patient medical information [11, 13] in order to enable patient care coordination and continuity (PCCC). According to Haggerty and Lou [14, 15] patient care continuity can be described as the extent to which knowledge about the diagnosis and management of patient health problems is experienced as coherent, connected and conveyed forward in time. In addition care coordination has been defined as "the deliberate integration of patient care activities between two or more participants involved in a patient's care plan" [16]. Therefore, to achieve PCCC past patient medical information should be coherent, connected and conveyed forward through deliberate integration efforts between participating facilities [14–16].

Expediently, deliberate HIS integration efforts can pave way for PCCC and quality healthcare [17] as seen in well planned HIS that have restructured the way healthcare professionals process and manage patients' medical information [18, 19]. Moreover, several other studies have highlighted ICTs' potential in improving the healthcare system and scaling up healthcare initiatives [20]. However, several existing HIS operate in silos, and this has led to the need of research that focuses on: HIS developments that move away from vertical silos to horizontally integrated systems [21], and research that examines the challenges and opportunities for information systems integration in healthcare [1]. Consequently, an investigation in Uganda of 2018, answered by 41 respondents consisting of software developers, system users and ministry of health officials was carried out to establish problematic issues that can be raised concerning HIS involvement in PCCC. This inquiry concluded that almost all the existing HIS within the country could not enhance PCCC and further discussed potential challenges of HIS involvement in PCCC.

This rest of the paper is structured as follows: Sect. 2 presents a discussion of the concept of HIS involvement in PCCC and Sect. 3 highlights the research approach. This is followed by a presentation of the findings in Sect. 4 and a brief discussion of the missing role of HIS in PCCC in Sect. 5. Finally, a conclusion is given and a direction for future works.

2   HIS Role in PCCC

2.1   HIS Role in Healthcare

A Health Information Systems (HIS) is a set of procedures organized to process and disseminate timely information that improves the health care management decision making process [22, 23]. Indeed health information systems have been heavily implemented [1] for their renowned potential in scaling up healthcare initiatives [20]. According to Berg [24], HIS play a great role in bringing about synergy between primary and secondary care hospital roles. These HIS can be categorised under clinical or managerial HIS [22]. Clinical HIS can enhance patient care activities whereas health management information systems can enhance managerial secondary care activities [2, 25]. PCCC can be harnessed by implementation of clinical HIS like the electronic patient records' system that can process and avail a patient record [26]. Furthermore, [26] states that comprehensive electronic health records can enhance continuous high quality patient care. Subsequently, when HIS take on their role of information processing and dissemination of vital patient medical information across care providers they can certainly enhance PCCC. [2, 7] argue that HIS ought to be interconnected in order to gather and disseminate relevant health information across providers for continued and integrated quality patient healthcare. To have these HIS interconnected, we need 'interoperability' – which is the ability for them to exchange and use that information [27]. This interoperability can at times be facilitated by pre-arranged protocols or a team that works very closely [28]. In such a plan, the patient receives one coherent and logical medical record to inform the ongoing treatment. To this cause, several authors have called for the implementation of integrated and interoperable HIS [2, 22] capable of enhancing PCCC within the continuum of care.

2.2   PCCC Role in Healthcare

One of the major processes within primary healthcare, is the 'primary-care-process'. This process according to [29, 30] consists of: access, integration, continuity and comprehensiveness of care. It is within this primary care process that patient care coordination and continuity (PCCC) is pursed in order to aid informed decision making within the continuum of care. PCCC is a term coined to mean care coordination and care continuity. Care continuity according to Lou [15] is when past medical history is conveyed forward in time between the participating facilities. According to Haggerty and Schang [14, 31], care continuity is enhanced by 'care coordination' at both information and managerial levels. The information level ensures that information is recorded and used across the continuum of care while the managerial-coordination ensures longitudinal follow-ups across care providers. This implies that to achieve quality healthcare, patient care should be both coordinated and continued within the continuum of care.

When patient care is coordinated and continued across providers, the patient receives up-to-date medical treatment that is logically informed by their past medical histories [14]. Currently patients need timely updates on their personal health more than ever before [1]. A patient "medical record is a dynamic informational entity that enables continuous monitoring of the health condition of a patient which aggregates all the information from the clinical history and treatments" [2] and this comprehensive patient record supports continuous high quality patient care within the continuum of care [26, 32]. On the contrary, lack of PCCC can delay ongoing treatment as the health professionals seek out for past patient medical information to guide the process [3, 7, 32], or leads to uninformed treatment whereby the later has critical effects of the patients' health as expressed [33] that coordinated care between and across health facilities is often a matter of life and death.

3   Research Approach

3.1   Study Setting

The study was carried out in Uganda and is part of an ongoing study that is investigating the interoperability of health information systems used in the country. Health services in the country are offered by both government and private owned health facilities, from the national referral to regional referral through district hospitals to health center levels [34]. In Uganda, patients can visit any health facility for treatment. Apparently, each health facility operates independently and implements its own HIS which has resulted into a pool of HIS within the country [5]. Therefore, this study focused on HIS that are actively used at health facilities. Consequently, the investigation was done by visiting the system proprietors and developers at their head offices, systems users at the health facilities and ministry of health key informants at the Ministry of Health headquarters.

3.2   Case Description

To identify health information systems for the case study, an exploration of the implemented health information systems within the country was carried out during the period of July to December 2017. It was discovered that many systems in Uganda do not go beyond the piloting stage, due to lack of sustainability funds after the funded

Table 1. Description of the health information systems under study.

HIS	Description
DHIS2	The District Health Information System-DHIS2, this is a health management system "which provides a coherent platform for data entry and processing, and presentation of data to planners" [36]. It is highly recommended by the MoH for reporting about health indicators to the MoH
HeleCare2x	HeleCare2x was customized for Uganda, from Care2x which is an Integrated Hospital Information System including Surgery, Nursing, Outpatient, Wards, Labs, Pharmacy, Security, Admission, Schedulers, Repair and Communication among others [37]. Current client base are health facilities under the Uganda catholic medical bureau private non for profit (http://care2x.org/)
NGANISHA	Nganisha health information system: a comprehensive health facility management information system developed locally in Uganda to provide real time and complete data of a health facility. Current pilots are in government health facilities
UgandaEMR	UgandaEMR is an OpenMRS based electronic medical record system customized for Uganda. It is a system recommended by the ministry of health as the nation's patient records' system. http://emrportal.mets.or.ug/
Clinic Master	This is an integrated health information management and medical billing software that automates patients' transactions at the clinic on a visit basis and daily procedures. Current client base in Uganda are private health facilities. https://clinicmaster.net/about-us/

project ends [35]. Subsequently looking at system sustainability, system coverage and usage across health facilities and insights from the ministry of health, five outstanding health information systems were chosen for this study. The five systems chosen included: District Health Information System -DHIS2, Clinic master, Nganisha health information system, HeleCare2x and UgandaEMR. The following Table 1 gives the description of the HIS for the case study.

3.3 Method

The study followed a qualitative case study approach [38] with an interpretation of the study findings done by the researcher [39]. Through a case study approach, new discoveries were verified with existing knowledge in the area of HIS involvement in PCCC [40]. Data for the study was collected through semi-structured interviews and focused group discussions. Interviews were used for soliciting information regarding the functionality of the health information systems and their role in enhancing PCCC. The study participants included health officials from the ministry of health (MoH), system developers and users from each of the five studied HIS. A total of 5 MoH key informants, 22 system developers and 14 system users were interviewed. Interviews, which on average took 30–60 min, were carried out with the use of an interview guide and an audio recorder, and interviewer took field notes whenever it was necessary. For purposes of validation, at the end of each interview both parties would do a recap of what had transpired during the session in order to have the same understanding.

Furthermore the interviews were transcribed and analysed through the general inductive analysis approach according to Thomas [41]. Guided by this approach we read the transcript over and over and captured brief summaries of categories from the text relating to our study objectives. Throughout the analysis exercise responses concerning each HIS were compared first, followed by comparisons across the studied HIS.

4   Findings: Challenges of HIS Involvement in PCCC

From the interviews we found out challenges associated to HIS involvement in PCCC as presented in the subsections that follow.

4.1   Interoperability Objective Not a Design Priority

For all the systems studied, it was discovered that the interoperability objective was never considered as a design requirement. Most of these systems were designed to manage and store patient records at the facility level. However, some systems were designed to promote patient information flow within the facility not across facilities. Therefore, for such systems sharing a patient record across facilities becomes a challenge, as illustrated in the following verbatim quote by our respondents.

> "So it was mainly to harbor patient information and use as an information system to manage patient records that was the main aim it did not have anything to do with data exchange before".

4.2 HIS Operate in Silos

Most health facilities in the Uganda implement independent health information systems that are usually not interoperable. Sometimes different sections of the same health facility implement independent systems. This is in many cases attributed to donor pressure. Respondents stated that most systems in the country serve a section of the care process according to donor needs and most of them are silos as indicated in the verbatim quotes below.

"There were systems that were running but they were specific to programs, there were not general". "Systems are silos, which is not talking to each other".

"Another problem why people have different systems is because of the funders".

This is further exacerbated by the lack of country uniform HIS implementation guidelines that would certainly lead to standardized systems that are capable of being interoperable as illustrated in the following verbatim quote.

"We lack regulations that determine the design of electronic systems at least by Uganda national bureau of standards."

4.3 Lack of a National Standard for the Patient Record

All the existing health information systems in the country are developed without uniform standards and so the patient information is recorded in various formats that are non-interoperable. Consequently, each system holds some kind of patient record different from the others and so there is no standard patient record for exchange. One respondent stated that:

"If we are to share what should we share and what should we not share"

The situation is worsened by the lack of a national patient identification that would help in identifying the patient as the same across the continuum of care.

4.4 Data Ownership by Health Facilities

Each health facility records its own data in its own format, and therefore has sole ownership over the data. Respondents perceived this as the common practice especially in private health facilities that have no will to share patient data as illustrated in the following verbatim quote.

"Currently the client base is private everyone wants to keep their information for themselves, they wouldn't want the sharing....private hospitals want their data".

With such mentality, it becomes hard to harness HIS to improve PCCC across the continuum of care.

4.5 Non-technical Challenges

There are a number of challenges encountered in the use of HIS for PCCC. For example, challenges to do with cost of purchasing and maintaining computing equipment is usually high for health facilities. In developing countries, infrastructure is still a big challenge, with intermittent and inadequate internet and electricity supplies. Others include lack of skilled technology savvy personnel as indicated in the respondent's verbatim quotes.

"They cut off power even before we completed the pilot"

"We left because there was no equipment and support"

Another respondent noted the presence of the policies that do not support patient data exchange across facilities.

"But the challenge comes, in with policy, policy of Uganda especially health does not allow clouding patient information. That means it does not allow remote access of patient information but rather have patient information strictly at health centers."

Yet another challenge is resistance to change from the old way of doing things to new ways of using technology.

5   Discussion: The Missing Role of HIS in PCCC

By their nature, information systems should facilitate information processing from data creation to information dissemination to all relevant stakeholders for purposes of decision making [1, 22, 23]. Indeed, they have been heavily employed in processing health data in order to promote quality healthcare. One example is the electronic medical records system which according to Heavin [1] provides a unified single view of patient data, and they have currently restructured the way patients' medical data is handled at a given health facility.

However, amidst rapid HIS implementations, there are challenges encountered that have led to the missing role of HIS in PCCC, as discussed below. Findings reveal interoperability issues as being the greatest challenge of HIS involvement in PCCC [32, 42]. Though several state policies address interoperability issues, in practice system implementers do not consider interoperability aspects during HIS implementation. In Uganda policies that support system interoperability are under development though the current ones do not support exchange of patient data across facilities [35, 43]. The lack of active interoperability policies, standards and implementation guidelines, leaves health facilities no choice but to implement independent HIS, that end up operating in silos and not capable of exchanging data [3–5, 35, 43]. Consequently, all systems are developed following different implementation standards [42] and therefore have no uniform patient record to exchange across the continuum of care for PCCC. Therefore, the missed interoperability objective during HIS design potentially leads to the missing role of HIS in PCCC, as patient records will be dispersed and not exchangeable across the various health facilities [10].

Additionally, since health facilities implement their own independent HIS, they tend to own their data and are not willing to share it across facilities. Hence these particular HIS will not actively participate in PCCC. These challenges combined with other non-technical challenges like: lack of technology-savvy labour, high costs of computing equipment, poor infrastructure [34, 44, 45], and inadequate policy guidelines [35, 43] all together justify the missing role of HIS in improving PCCC.

6 Conclusion and Future Works

This study set out to discover the missing role of health information systems (HIS) in PCCC. This was carried out by discovering the problematic issues of HIS involvement in PCCC. Certainly, through an empirical case study approach, the study validated both new and previously known challenges through a discussion of the missing role of HIS in PCCC. Important to note is that internal interoperability in some health facilities existed but interoperability across facilities emerged as the greatest challenge, hence the missing role of HIS in PCCC within the continuum of care.

Amidst an array of challenges, HIS have ended up missing their unique and fundamental role of enhancing PCCC. Therefore, there is a need for future research to revive this great role of HIS involvement in PCCC, by investigating how these challenges can be overcome and most importantly, on how interoperability across facilities can be achieved and prioritized.

References

1. Heavin, C.: Health information systems–opportunities and challenges in a global health ecosystem. J. Midwest Assoc. Inf. Syst. 2017(2), 1 (2017)
2. Jardim, S.V.: The electronic health record and its contribution to healthcare information systems interoperability. Procedia Technol. 9, 940–948 (2013)
3. Adebesin, F., et al.: A review of interoperability standards in e-Health and imperatives for their adoption in Africa. S. Afr. Comput. J. 50(1), 55–72 (2013)
4. Bygstad, B., Hanseth, O., Le, D.T.: From IT silos to integrated solutions. A study in e-health complexity. In: ECIS (2015)
5. Kiberu, V.M., Mars, M., Scott, R.E.: Barriers and opportunities to implementation of sustainable e-Health programmes in Uganda: a literature review. Afr. J. Prim. Health Care Fam. Med. 9(1), 1–10 (2017)
6. Kuziemsky, C.E., Weber-Jahnke, J.H.: An eBusiness-based framework for eHealth interoperability. J. Emerg. Technol. Web Intell. 1(2), 129–136 (2009)
7. Jeong, J.-S., Han, O., You, Y.-Y.: A design characteristics of smart healthcare system as the IoT application. Indian J. Sci. Technol. 9(37) (2016). 102457 – 219695-1-PB
8. Halamka, J., et al.: Exchanging health information: local distribution, national coordination. Health Aff. 24(5), 1170–1179 (2005)
9. Van Lerberghe, W.: The World Health Report 2008: Primary Health Care: Now More Than Ever. World Health Organization (2008)
10. Rexhepi, H., Åhlfeldt, R.-M., Persson, A.: Challenges and opportunities with information system support for healthcare processes–a healthcare practitioner perspective. In: 8th IADIS International Conference on Information Systems, Madeira, Portugal, 14–16 March 2015
11. Bourgeois, F.C., Olson, K.L., Mandl, K.D.: Patients treated at multiple acute health care facilities: quantifying information fragmentation. Arch. Intern. Med. 170(22), 1989–1995 (2010)

12. Coleman, E.A.: Falling through the cracks: challenges and opportunities for improving transitional care for persons with continuous complex care needs. J. Am. Geriatr. Soc. **51**(4), 549–555 (2003)

13. Coleman, E.A., et al.: The care transitions intervention: results of a randomized controlled trial. Arch. Intern. Med. **166**(17), 1822–1828 (2006)

14. Haggerty, J.L., et al.: Continuity of care: a multidisciplinary review. BMJ Br. Med. J. **327** (7425), 1219 (2003)

15. Lou, W.W.: A new measure for continuity of care: the Alpha index. Health Serv. Outcomes Res. Method. **1**(3–4), 277–289 (2000)

16. Agency for healthcare research and quality. National Healthcare Quality Report (2010). U.S. Department of Health and Human Services, pp. 2635–2645 (2010)

17. Brandt, P., et al.: A proportional interoperability framework as an appropriate growth strategy for eHealth in sub-Saharan Africa. In: Jordanova, M., Lievens, F. (eds.) Global Telemedicine and eHealth Updates: Knowledge Resources, vol. 8 (2015)

18. Demirci, U., Wang, S., Inci, F.: Editorial for advanced health care technologies. Adv. Health Care Technol. **1**, 1–2 (2015)

19. Demiris, G., et al.: Patient-centered applications: use of information technology to promote disease management and wellness. A white paper by the AMIA knowledge in motion working group. J. Am. Med. Inform. Assoc. **15**(1), 8–13 (2008)

20. Blaya, J.A., Fraser, H.S., Holt, B.: E-health technologies show promise in developing countries. Health Aff. **29**(2), 244–251 (2010)

21. Adenuga, O.A., Kekwaletswe, R.M., Coleman, A.: eHealth integration and interoperability issues: towards a solution through enterprise architecture. Health Inf. Sci. Syst. **3**(1), 1–8 (2015)

22. Aghazadeh, S., Aliyev, A., Ebrahimnezhad, M.: Comprehensive review of information systems, medical institutions. Int. J. Comput. Theory Eng. **4**(6), 862 (2012)

23. World Health Organization: Developing Health Management Information Systems: A Practical Guide for Developing Countries (2004)

24. Berg, M.: Implementing information systems in health care organizations: myths and challenges. Int. J. Med. Inf. **64**(2), 143–156 (2001)

25. Krickeberg, K.: Principles of health information systems in developing countries. Health Inf. Manag. J. **36**(3), 8–20 (2007)

26. Knaup, P., et al.: Section 2: Patient records: electronic patient records: moving from islands and bridges towards electronic health records for continuity of care. Yearb. Med. Inf. **16**(01), 34–46 (2007)

27. IEEE (Institute of Electrical and Electronics Engineers): Standard computer dictionary a compilation of IEEE standard computer glossaries (1990)

28. Blount, A.: Integrated primary care: organizing the evidence. Fam. Syst. Health **21**, 121–134 (2003)

29. Kringos, D.S., et al.: The breadth of primary care: a systematic literature review of its core dimensions. BMC Health Serv. Res. **10**(1), 65 (2010)

30. Starfield, B.: Primary Care: Balancing Health Needs, Services, and Technology. Oxford University Press, New York (1998)

31. Schang, L., Waibel, S., Thomson, S.: Measuring care coordination: health system and patient perspectives: report prepared for the Main Association of Austrian Social Security Institutions, LSE Health, London (2013)

32. Kohli, R., Tan, S.S.-L.: Electronic health records: how can IS researchers contribute to transforming healthcare? MIS Q. **40**(3), 553–573 (2016)

33. Christodoulakis, C., Asgarian, A., Easterbrook, S.: Barriers to adoption of information technology in healthcare (2016)

34. Mukasa, N.: Uganda Healthcare system profile: background, organization, polices and challenges. J. Sustain. Reg. Health Syst. **1**, 2–10 (2012)
35. Omaswa, C.: Uganda National eHealth Strategic Plan 2012/2013–2014/2015 (2012). http://www.ubts.go.ug/assets/publications/Uganda%20National%20eHealth%20Strategic%20Plan_April%202013.pdf, Accessed 20 June 2018
36. Braa, J., et al.: Developing health information systems in developing countries: the flexible standards strategy. MIS Q. **31**, 381–402 (2007)
37. Kanagwa, B., Ntacyo, J., Orach, S.: Towards paperless hospitals: lessons learned from 15 health facilities in Uganda. New Advances in Information Systems and Technologies. AISC, vol. 445, pp. 23–32. Springer, Cham (2016). https://doi.org/10.1007/978-3-319-31307-8_3
38. Hennink, M., Hutter, I., Bailey, A.: Qualitative Research Methods. Sage, Los Angeles (2010)
39. Klein, H.K., Myers, M.D.: A set of principles for conducting and evaluating interpretive field studies in information systems. MIS Q. **23**, 67–93 (1999)
40. Rowlands, B.: Employing interpretive research to build theory of information systems practice. Australas. J. Inf. Syst. **10**(2), 3–22 (2003)
41. Thomas, D.R.: A general inductive approach for analyzing qualitative evaluation data. Am. J. Eval. **27**(2), 237–246 (2006)
42. Alkhaldi, B., et al.: Barriers to implementing eHealth: a multi-dimensional perspective. Stud. Health Technol. Inf. [e-Health-For Continuity of Care] **205**, 875–879 (2014)
43. Ministry of Health Uganda: Health Sector Development Plan 2015/16–2019/20, September 2015. http://www.health.go.ug/sites/default/files/Health%20Sector%20Development%20Plan%202015-16_2019-20.pdf
44. Ngafeeson, M.N.: Healthcare information systems opportunities and challenges. In: Khosrow-Pour, M. (ed.) Encyclopedia of Information Science and Technology, 3rd edn., pp. 3387–3395. IGI Global, Hershey (2015)
45. Nyella, E.: Challenges in health information systems integration: Zanzibar experience. In: 2009 International Conference on Information and Communication Technologies and Development (ICTD). IEEE (2009)

Performance Barriers to Cloud Services in Africa's Public Sector: A Latency Perspective

Josiah Chavula[1]([✉]), Amreesh Phokeer[2], and Enrico Calandro[3]

[1] University of Cape Town, Cape Town, South Africa
jchavula@cs.uct.ac.za
[2] AFRINIC, Ebene, Mauritius
amreesh@afrinic.net
[3] Research ICT Africa, Cape Town, South Africa
ecalandro@researchictafrica.net

Abstract. Cloud computing allows individuals and organizations to lease storage and computation resources remotely and as needed. For such remote access to work efficiently, there is need for reliable and low-delay delivery of Internet traffic. By carrying out month-long Internet measurement campaign, this paper investigates location and latencies of cloud-based web hosting in the public sector of five African countries. Results of the study show that a large percentage of public sector websites are hosted in cloud-based infrastructure physically located in America and Europe. Analysis of latencies shows significant differences between local and remote hosted websites, and that delays are significantly lower for countries that host CDN nodes. The results also indicate high delays for local websites that are accessed circuitously.

Keywords: Latency · Internet measurements · Cloud services

1 Introduction

Cloud computing broadly refers to applications delivered as services over the Internet as well as the hardware and systems software that provide such services [1]. Cloud computing makes possible the provision of large-scale services using remote and shared servers to store and process data. By facilitating ubiquitous and on-demand remote access to externally managed computing resources, the cloud computing helps to eliminate the need for individuals and organisations to own and maintain their own computing infrastructure. This enables organisations that have minimal capital, to deploy their services more rapidly and successfully [2]. By the same token, cloud computing provides an opportunity for developing countries that have limited financial resources, to utilize remote IT infrastructure, such as data centres and applications, to rapidly scale public

© ICST Institute for Computer Sciences, Social Informatics and Telecommunications Engineering 2019
Published by Springer Nature Switzerland AG 2019. All Rights Reserved
G. Mendy et al. (Eds.): AFRICOMM 2018, LNICST 275, pp. 152–163, 2019.
https://doi.org/10.1007/978-3-030-16042-5_15

service provision through electronic means [11]. Despite the perceived opportunities for the public sector, the rate of cloud computing adoption in the public sector has significantly lagged behind that of the private sector. A survey in 2012 [12] found that only 12% of the government departments had spent more than 10% of the total IT resources on cloud services.

Prior studies have suggested that limited availability, accessibility and affordability of the underlying Internet technology is a key hindrance to the adoption of cloud computing developing countries [8,13]. Apart from the limited access to the Internet infrastructure, concerns related to security and privacy of cloud based information processing have been cited as a critical factors slowing adoption of the cloud. For the South African, survey results by Brenda Scholtz *et al.* [13] suggested that 'system performance' and 'privacy of data' were the biggest technical concerns that could hamper implementation of cloud computing in the public organisations. Similarly, Gillwald *et al.* [8] identified limited and costly broadband as major barriers to adoption of cloud computing services in South Africa, Tunisia, Nigeria, Ghana, and Kenya.

The aim of this study was to quantify Internet latency as a barrier to the adoption of cloud computing services by the public sector. This will highlight the quality of service for accessing content hosted in various networks and geographical locations, including cloud-based infrastructure. The rationale is that the success of cloud-based services for the public sector will depend on the ability to achieve high performance connectivity to the cloud. This study therefore provides insight into the readiness of the public sector in the selected countries to interact with cloud-based services. After characterising the network performance - the study will also explore the causality behind any observed sub-optimal performance (e.g. high delays), and the possible cloud-computing readiness steps that need to be undertaken. In particular, the study seeks to characterise the level of when accessing public sector's online public resources. Performance data was collected via Internet measurement campaigns targeting public sector websites sampled from five countries: Nigeria, Ghana, Kenya, Zambia and South Africa.

The three key questions addressed in this paper are as follows:

1. In which networks and countries are the public sector websites currently being hosted. This question is meant to provide some insight on the current hosting practices in the public sector, particularly regarding the extent to which websites are hosted locally within a country, or remotely. This will also shed light on the locality of networks that are dominating the public sector hosting market in Africa.
2. What are the characteristics of country specific Internet latencies to web servers of the public sector? This question is meant to provide country specific delay characteristics and comparison for public sector websites hosted in various networks and countries.
3. What is the extent of circuitous routing when accessing locally hosted websites, and what impact does this circuitous routing have on the Internet delays?

2 Related Work

Past studies have highlighted general performance challenges in Africa's Internet, including high latencies and generally poor quality of experience. A recent study by Formoso *et al.* (2018) showed that many parts of Africa still experience excessively high Internet delays, often exceeding 300 ms. A study by Fanou *et al.* [7] also showed that Internet performance on the continent is largely characterised by slow download speeds and high delays. Other studies have highlighted traffic engineering problems in Africa's Internet topology, showing a lack of direct interconnection amongst Africa's ISPs, resulting in suboptimal performance for intra-country and cross-border communication, a well as high cost of Internet access [3–5,9]. Apart from the lack of direct network-level and country-level interconnections, other studies have looked at inefficient DNS configurations, as well as lack of local content caching servers across the African continent [6,10,16].

3 Measurement Methodology

This section describes the process for conducting measurements to gauge readiness of the public sector to utilize cloud-based resources. The first step involves identifying the appropriate set of performance metrics that can reveal the readiness of the public sector to utilize cloud-based services. This is followed by the process of selecting the appropriate tools and platform for conducting the measurements. After selecting the measurement platform, it is necessary to select the locations from which to observe performance (i.e. measurement vantage points), as well as appropriate measurement targets.

3.1 Performance Metrics

The public's high concern for "system performance" as reported in the study of Brenda Scholtz *et al.* [13] highlights the perceptions that Internet infrastructure in many African countries is not developed and robust enough to provide reliable and high performance access to computing resources and information stored in cloud. One aspect of this relates to high end-to-end delays (latencies) that impact responsiveness and quality of experience (QoE) for online interactions. Latency is an important metric for cloud computing as it gives insight into responsiveness of interactions between cloud servers and Internet clients.

3.2 Measurement Platform and Vantage Points

A number of Internet measurement platforms have deployed thousands of probes in access and backbone networks, as well as behind residential gateways, globally. Researchers are able to make use of these platforms to conduct Internet measurement campaigns, using the specialized network devices (probes) as vantage points from which to launch tests towards specified targets. Recent measurement platforms use dedicated hardware-based probes, and these probes are used to run continuous measurements with minimal end-user participation. When selecting a distributed Internet measurement platform for a large scale campaign, it is important to consider the number and distribution of vantage points in networks that are to be measured [14]. Shavitt *et al.* (2011) showed that extensive topology sampling from a broad and distributed vantage points is required for obtaining an unbiased and accurate topology characteristics. A more widely deployed hardware-based measurement platform is the *Ripe Atlas*[1], which consists of thousands of probes that perform active measurements. As of December 2017, RIPE Atlas had around 230 active probes in 36 African countries. On this basis, this study made use of Ripe Atlas for topology characterization, measuring latency to public sector websites for five African countries. During each measurement episode, 10 Ripe Atlas probes were randomly selected as vantage points for each of the countries.

3.3   Selecting Measurement Targets

The next step in the study was to identify and select prominent websites from the public sector in each of the target countries. This was obtained through the AlexaTop[2], a website that ranks websites based on a combined measure of page views and unique site users. For each country, a filter was applied for 'Government' websites to list the prominent public sector websites, such as those for government departments and parastatal organisations. For example, 'category/Top/Regional/Africa/Kenya/Government' would list the most popular government related websites in Kenya. In some cases, expert local knowledge was sought to determine prominent public sector in each of the five countries. In total, 86 websites were identified as measurement targets across; 10 in Kenya, 9 in South Africa, 10 in Zambia, and 48 in Nigeria.

3.4   Launching Measurements

Traceroute measurements were then launched from each of the selected Atlas probes, towards each the country's selected public sector websites. The actual measurement was performed towards the IP address of web server for each website. To obtain IP addresses, a DNS lookup was performed for each website domain. In order to mitigate the effects of location based load balancing, where requests for a domain are directed to different web servers based on location of Internet clients, the DNS lookups/resolution were performed from the vantage points (i.e. from each Atlas probe).

For each measurement episode, four Traceroutes were launched successively from each Atlas probe to all of the country's selected websites, and this was repeated 4 random times a day for one month in December 2017. While not all Traceroute measurements could reach the final destination, a Traceroute measurement was considered successful it is was able to reach the hosting network,

---

[1] https://atlas.ripe.net/.

[2] https://www.alexa.com/topsites.

i.e. if the last hop in the Traceroute was inside the hosting company's network. In the end, a total of 13790 Traceroute measurements were successfully completed; 2570 in Ghana, 3073 in Kenya, 2790 in Nigerian, 3341 in South Africa, and 2016 Zambia.

4   Results

This section describes results of a measurement study on public sector websites carried out in the five selected countries. The results describe the remote locations and networks where the websites are hosted, the nature of routes for accessing the public sector websites in the respective countries, as well as the performance (delay) observed for each situation. The initial step in the data analysis involved attaching network and geolocation information to each target IP address (obtained from the websites' DNS lookups performed from the vantage point), as well as every router hop in the traceroute data. The RIPE Routing Information Service (RIS) and the MaxMind GeoLite2-City database[3] are used to obtain the Autonomous System Number (ASN) and the geographical location (country) of each IP address. While it is well known that geolocation databases do contain inaccuracies, the analysis in this study is restricted to country-level geolocation which has relatively much higher accuracy.

4.1   Geolocation of Web Hosting for the Public Sector

One of the key goals of this study was to examine the ASN and geographical distribution of web hosting servers used by the public sector in Africa and to evaluate the performance implication of such a distribution. This should also reveal the strengths and weaknesses of the web hosting environment in the selected African countries. The first step in the analysis was therefore to compute the geographical and network distribution of public sector websites per country.

The first observation from the analysis was that, on overage, 66% of the sampled public sector websites were hosted outside their respective countries, i.e. remote hosting. It was also noted that the level of remote hosting varies widely among the countries, ranging between 4 and 82%. Figure 1 shows the percentages of remote and locally hosted public sector websites in each of the five countries. Of the five, South Africa had the lowest percentage of remote hosting at 4%, whereas Nigeria and Ghana had the highest remote hosting of 61 and 82%, respectively.

From Fig. 2, it can be seen that most of the remote website hosting is situated in USA, UK, Germany, Canada and Ireland. Figure 2a shows that Nigeria, for example, had 75% of the websites hosted in US based companies, mostly through New Dream Network (14.8%), RackSpace (9%), GoDaddy (8%), and Unified Layer (7%). For Ghana, the remotely hosted websites are mostly in the US (26.5%), Germany (25%) and Canada (10%). Kenya and Zambia have a higher

---

[3] https://www.maxmind.com/en/geoip2-city.

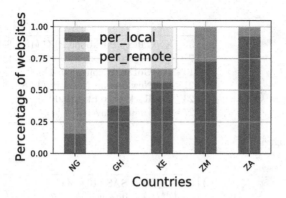

Fig. 1. Percentage of local and remote hosting of public sector websites per country.

percentage of public sector websites locally hosted. Interestingly for the both, local hosting of public sector websites appears to be supported by their respective National Research and Education Networks (NRENs); in Kenya, 37.9% of the websites were hosted in KENET (Fig. 2c), whereas in Zambia, 25.3% of the websites were inside ZAMREN (Fig. 2d).

South Africa had only one of the sampled websites hosted outside the country, in Ireland (Fig. 2e). The remote website was hosted in the Amazon cloud infrastructure, using their data centre in Ireland. The result for South Africa was as expected, particularly considering its significantly more developed web-hosting infrastructure compared to other African countries. It also needs to be noted that the much robust Internet infrastructure in South Africa has also attracted many more foreign and cloud-based hosting companies, the result of which is that, while these companies appear to have presence in the country, some of the content hosted by such networks is physically located in remote data centres. For example, while Amazon Web Services (AWS) has become popular in the South African market, the company does not operate a data centre within the country, meaning content hosted within the AWS infrastructure is remotely hosted.

4.2 Latency to Public Sector Websites

It is important to highlight that choice of hosting provider, and where it is located, can have significant consequences on the level of delay experienced by Internet clients. The websites hosted in more remote places generally experience higher delays. While many of the dominant hosting providers make use of cloud-based infrastructure, and therefore claim to have global presence, the absence of data centres and CDN (Content Delivery Networks) nodes in most of African countries means that hosting in such networks results in high overall delays. The table below shows the range of delays for websites hosted in different networks. Many of the local hosting networks can be seen to have delays that are less than 100 ms, whereas the higher delays are mostly for websites hosted by the large international operators. The high delays are particularly prevalent in situations

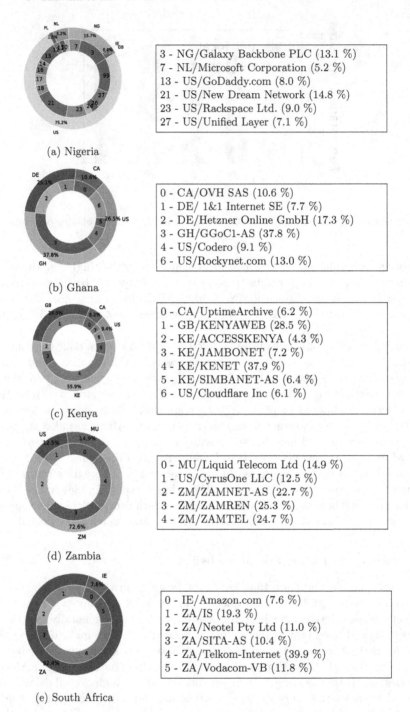

Fig. 2. Pie-charts showing hosting countries and networks most used by each vantage country

where the remote hosting is not supported by CDN infrastructure that would otherwise push the content closer to where the intended audience is, i.e. closer to the countries owning the websites.

Figure 3 shows that hosting companies with average delays of over 200 ms are mostly based in the US, including *Microsoft Corporation, LunarPages, RackSpace, GoDaddy,* and *New Dream Network.* On the other hand, *CloudFlare,* which is also US-based, runs a number of data centers in Africa, including in South Africa and Kenya, and this is reflected in the lower median delay of 110 ms when their content is accessed by Internet clients in Africa.

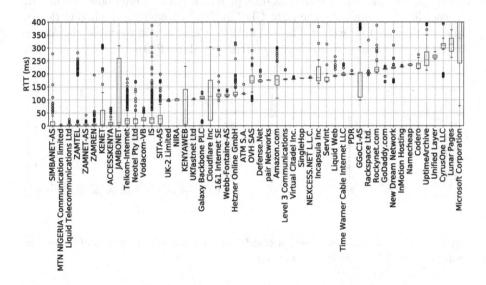

Fig. 3. Distribution of round-trip-times for websites hosted in different networks.

Figure 4a below presents a summary of RTTs to the sampled public sector websites as measured from each of the five countries. As is observed in Fig. 4a, Ghana and Nigeria, the two countries with the highest remote hosting percentages in the sample, also had the highest median RTTs of 199 ms and 177 ms respectively. In contrast, Kenya, which had an almost 50-50 split between local and remote hosting, had a lower mean RTT of 50 ms. The best lowest mean RTT of 3 ms was observed in Zambia, which also had much lower remote hosting of 25%.

4.3 Impact of Hosting Locations

It is worth analysing the extent to which different host hosting countries result in different levels of delay for the selected African countries. Figure 4b shows the delays to websites hosted in different countries, and illustrates how websites hosted remotely, such as in USA, Canada and Netherlands experience significantly higher delays. As would be expected, the lowest delays were within each of the vantage countries. The only exception was Ghana, whose special case circuitous routing discussed later. In general, the further away a website's hosting country is, the higher the delays. It can be observed that the highest delays are for websites hosted in Canada and the USA (median RTT of 230 ms and 220 ms respectively), the two countries are geographically the furthest of the hosting countries from any of the five vantage countries in this study. The cumulative distribution in the left plot of Fig. 5 shows that about 50% of the delay samples in Ghana and Nigeria were above 200 ms. In comparison, only 20% in Kenya, 19% in Zambia, and less than 1% of samples in South Africa were above 200 ms. About 10% of the samples in all countries, except South Africa were above 300 ms. In terms of hosting countries, the right CDF in Fig. 5 shows that the higher delays are more prevalent for websites hosted in USA, Canada, and Netherlands. About 50% of the delay samples to these countries are above 250 ms.

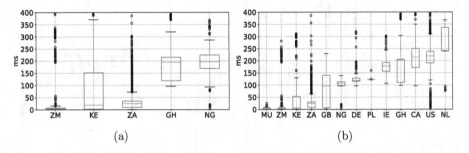

(a)   (b)

Fig. 4. Figure a showing distribution of delays to per vantage country; and b showing distribution of delays per hosting country

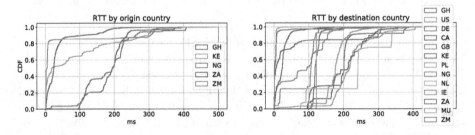

Fig. 5. Cumulative distribution of latency values for each vantage country (left), as well as for each hosting country (right)

Different countries experience different delays to websites hosted in the remote locations. Figure 6 presents delays from the vantage countries to websites hosting countries. The differences can be attributed to the differences in geographical distances, as well as varying logical topologies. Among the countries hosting in the USA, it can be seen that Zambia experiences the highest median delay of 314 ms. This should be expected given Zambia's geographical distance from the USA, compared to Ghana, Nigerian and Kenya, which experience median delays to the USA of 221 ms, 200 ms, and 174 ms respectively. In the case of South Africa, the only remote hosted website was in the Republic of Ireland, where *AWS* has a data centre. In terms of performance, the median delay between South Africa and the Republic of Ireland is observed to be 180 ms.

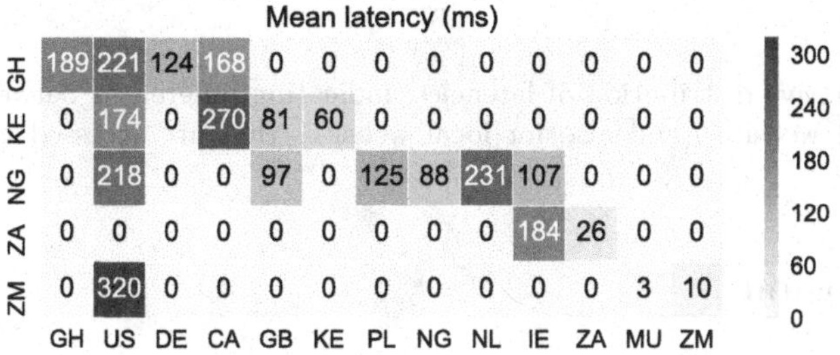

Mean latency (ms)

	GH	US	DE	CA	GB	KE	PL	NG	NL	IE	ZA	MU	ZM	
GH	189	221	124	168	0	0	0	0	0	0	0	0	0	300
KE	0	174	0	270	81	60	0	0	0	0	0	0	0	240
NG	0	218	0	0	97	0	125	88	231	107	0	0	0	180
ZA	0	0	0	0	0	0	0	0	0	184	26	0	0	120
ZM	0	320	0	0	0	0	0	0	0	0	0	3	10	60
														0

Fig. 6. Matrix of mean latencies from the vantage countries (x-axis) to website hosting countries (y-axis)

4.4   Impact of Circuitous Routing

It is generally the case that local hosting provides lower delay compared to remote hosting, and the dataset from Zambia and Kenya exhibit this expectation, with local delays of 2 ms and 9 ms respectively. Ghana and Nigeria, on the other hand, go against this trend. In the case of Ghana, there was a median delay for locally hosted websites of 201 ms, while the country's websites hosted in Great Britain had a lower median delay 118 ms. Similarly, while the local median delay for Nigeria was observed to be 107 ms, a slightly lower median delay of 97 ms was observed for websites hosted in Great Britain.

To evaluate this phenomenon, another aspect of this study was to look at the extent and impact of circuitous routing when accessing public sector websites. In this context, circuitous routing is when a website that is locally hosted is accessed by local Internet clients through paths that traverse other countries. Overall, 23% of the websites were accessed circuitously, but this is more prevalent some countries than others. For example, the Ghana dataset had the highest percentage of circuitous routes at about 33%, while Kenya was at 16% and Nigeria at 11%. Figure 7 shows a distribution of RTTs for the three categories of routes. The general distribution does show that locally hosted websites that are accessed through circuitous routes, i.e. routes that leave and come back to the vantage country, experience higher delays than websites that are remotely hosted.

Circuitous access of locally hosted websites, and the result high latencies are symptomatic of lack local peering of networks within a country. With locally hosted websites appearing to perform worse than remotely hosted websites, the lack of peering has the potential to not only discourage local hosting, but also inhibit success local content initiatives.

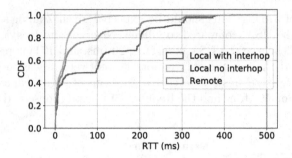

Fig. 7. Cumulative distribution of latencies, indicating differences between local and remote hosted websites, and also for local websites that are accessed via circuitous routes.

5   Conclusion

This study has shown that in some African countries, access to public sector websites is largely characterised by high Internet delays. In addition, a large proportion of public sector websites are currently being hosted remotely, i.e. in other countries. It was also observed that of the five countries surveyed, Nigeria and Ghana had the highest percentage of remote hosting and experienced the highest latencies. A large portion of the remote websites were hosted in USA, Canada, Germany, UK, and South Africa. While the hosting networks generally have global operations, they do not necessarily have physical infrastructure in most of the African countries. This means that while offering the convenience of cloud-based hosting, lack of physical infrastructure in Africa entails that Africa's web content gets to be stored in remote locations. Remote storage of web content has a negative implication on the sovereignty of African countries in that they loose control of their data. In addition, the burden of fetching content from remote locations falls on local network operators, the cost of which get passed on the users. This ultimately has negative implications on the local economies, and also in terms of poor quality of experience due to high latencies as reported in this study.

To reduce these latencies, and to help improve performance of cloud-services in Africa, there is need for leading cloud infrastructure providers to deploy infrastructure in Africa. The advantage of local deployments is demonstrated in the results from Kenya, which although had a relatively high percentage of remote hosting (42%), appeared to have a much lower median web delay of 50 ms. In comparison, Nigeria and Ghana had mean latencies of almost 200 ms. However, for African countries to fully take advantage of cloud infrastructure that is domiciled on the continent, there is need for better peering and interconnectivity at national and continental level.

References

1. Armbrust, M., et al.: A view of cloud computing. Commun. ACM **53**(4), 50–58 (2010)
2. Berman, S.J., Kesterson-Townes, L., Marshall, A., Srivathsa, R.: How cloud computing enables process and business model innovation. Strat. Leadersh. **40**(4), 27–35 (2012)
3. Chavula, J., Feamster, N., Bagula, A., Suleman, H.: Quantifying the effects of circuitous routes on the latency of intra-Africa internet traffic: a study of research and education networks. In: Nungu, A., Pehrson, B., Sansa-Otim, J. (eds.) AFRICOMM 2014. LNICST, vol. 147, pp. 64–73. Springer, Cham (2015). https://doi.org/10.1007/978-3-319-16886-9_7
4. Chavula, J., Phokeer, A., Formoso, A., Feamster, N.: Insight into Africa's country-level latencies. In: AFRICON, 2017 IEEE, pp. 938–944. IEEE (2017)
5. Fanou, R., Francois, P., Aben, E.: On the diversity of interdomain routing in Africa. In: Mirkovic, J., Liu, Y. (eds.) PAM 2015. LNCS, vol. 8995, pp. 41–54. Springer, Cham (2015). https://doi.org/10.1007/978-3-319-15509-8_4
6. Fanou, R., Tyson, G., Francois, P., Sathiaseelan, A.: Pushing the frontier: exploring the African web ecosystem. In: Proceedings of the 25th International Conference on World Wide Web, pp. 435–445. International World Wide Web Conferences Steering Committee (2016)
7. Formoso, A., Chavula, J., Phokeer, A., Sathiaseelan, A., Tyson, G.: Dissecting the African internet: an intra-continental study
8. Gillwald, A., Moyo, M.: The cloud over Africa. Research ICT Africa (2014)
9. Gupta, A., Calder, M., Feamster, N., Chetty, M., Calandro, E., Katz-Bassett, E.: Peering at the internet's Frontier: a first look at ISP interconnectivity in Africa. In: Faloutsos, M., Kuzmanovic, A. (eds.) PAM 2014. LNCS, vol. 8362, pp. 204–213. Springer, Cham (2014). https://doi.org/10.1007/978-3-319-04918-2_20
10. Kende, M., Quast, B.: Promoting content in Africa. ISOC report (2016)
11. Kshetri, N.: Cloud computing in developing economies. Computer **43**(10), 47–55 (2010)
12. Sahu, B.L., Tiwari, R.: A comprehensive study on cloud computing. Int. J. Adv. Res. Comput. Sci. Softw. Eng. **2**(9), 33–37 (2012)
13. Scholtz, B., Govender, J., Gomez, J.M.: Technical and environmental factors affecting cloud computing adoption in the South African public sector. In: CONF-IRM, p. 16 (2016)
14. Shavitt, Y., Weinsberg, U.: Quantifying the importance of vantage point distribution in internet topology mapping (extended version). IEEE J. Sel. Areas Commun. **29**(9), 1837–1847 (2011)
15. Weins, K.: Cloud computing trends: 2016 state of the cloud survey. Right Scale (2016)
16. Zaki, Y., Chen, J., Pötsch, T., Ahmad, T., Subramanian, L.: Dissecting web latency in ghana. In: Proceedings of the 2014 Conference on Internet Measurement Conference, pp. 241–248. ACM (2014)

Impact of ZRP Zone Radius Value
on Wireless Network Performance

Tiguiane Yélémou[1(✉)], Boureima Zerbo[2], Mesmin Toundé Dandjinou[1],
and Oumarou Sié[2]

[1] University Nazi BONI, Bobo-Dioulasso, Burkina Faso
`tyelemou@univ-bobo.bf, dandjimes@yahoo.fr`
[2] University Ouaga 1 Professeur Joseph Ki-Zerbo, Ouagadougou, Burkina Faso
`bzerbo@gmail.com, oumarou.sie@gmail.com`

Abstract. In this paper, we highlight the impact of the routing load on the performance of ad hoc wireless networks. Specifically, we analyze Zone Routing Protocol (ZRP) routing load and the impact of zone radius value on this protocol performance. First, we show that performance parameters curves such as routing overhead, Packet Delivery Ratio and End-to-End Delay don't evaluate monotonously according to zone radius value. In our test context, we note optimal values for routing overhead and Packet Delivery Ratio (PDR) when $R = 3$. For delay, minimal values are observed when $R = 1$ and $R = 4$. Second, we study this hybrid protocol routing overhead according to network density and compare it to pure on-demand and table-driven routing approaches. Contrary to that is largely presented, in realistic wave propagation model context, taking into account obstacles and their effects such as multi-path one, proactive routing approach performs better than reactive one. In fact, in lossy link context, route request and route error packets broadcasted are significant. In dense network, ZRP, due to its multitude control packets, performs the worst for routing overhead and packet delivery ratio (PDR) parameters.

Keywords: Wireless networks · Routing algorithm ·
Zone Routing Protocol · Zone radius · Realistic simulation conditions

1 Introduction

Wireless networks are characterized by their mode of communication and limited bandwidth. To transmit data to a destination, source node proceeds by diffusion. This blind broadcast added to multi-paths effect, due to obstacles in the propagation medium, generates a high level of interference. Specifically, signaling mechanisms used to avoid collisions [1] and to update neighbors set, negatively impact on throughput and transmission delay. In this context, routing protocols play an important role. They determine in particular the network overhead, then the proportion of bandwidth consumed by control messages. Most of routing

© ICST Institute for Computer Sciences, Social Informatics and Telecommunications Engineering 2019
Published by Springer Nature Switzerland AG 2019. All Rights Reserved
G. Mendy et al. (Eds.): AFRICOMM 2018, LNICST 275, pp. 164–173, 2019.
https://doi.org/10.1007/978-3-030-16042-5_16

protocols used in wireless communications are from the adaptation of those already used in wired networks. These include proactive protocols like Open Shortest Path First protocol (OSPF) and reactive protocols like Routing Information Protocol (RIP).

Proactive protocols, also call table-driven protocols, maintain an updated routing table they exploit when needed communication. For that, the various nodes in the network must periodically exchange topology control messages. To transmit data, a route is immediately available but maintenance of the routing table leads to an important routing overhead.

Considering reactive routing protocols, also call on-demand routing protocols, to transmit data, the source node must, first, initiate a route discovery process and wait a route is found before starting data transmission. This waiting time helps increase communication delay. In an erroneous environment, network topology is unstable, established routes break very fast. Broadcast Route ERROR (RERROR) messages for restoring paths also becomes frequent.

Hybrid routing protocols have been developed to overcome the shortcomings of these two families of protocols. They use the proactive routing approach for establishing and maintaining routes with the nearest neighbors witch are defined by a zone radius parameter. Thus the distribution of topology control message is limited to the area defined by the zone radius value. For communications with remote locations, the on-demand routing approach is used. Route REQuest (RREQ) messages are broadcast for route discovery. Periodic broadcasting of control messages is limited by the zone radius value, but then we are left with a multitude of control messages.

Zone Routing Protocol (ZRP) is one of the most used hybrid protocol. In the literature, very few studies have focused on optimal zone radius determination in realistic transmission conditions. In this article, we conduct a detailed study of the significance and components of this protocol routing load and we present the impact of the neighborhood zone radius value on routing overhead.

The main contributions of this paper are:

- a detailed analyze of ZRP routing load components,
- a comprehensive assessment of the impacts of zone radius value on the protocol performance parameters (routing overhead, Packet Delivery Ratio and delay),
- the optimal value determination of zone radius.

The remainder of this paper is organized as follows: in Sect. 2, we present related work. In Sect. 3, we analyze ZRP protocol routing load. We present our simulation conditions and analyze simulation results in Sect. 4, then we conclude in Sect. 5.

2 Related Work

Routing protocols used in Mobile Ad hoc NETwork (MANET) [2] are mostly derived from an adaptation of those already used in wired networks. Thus Optimized Link State Routing (OLSR) protocol [3] is based on OSPF and Ad hoc

On-demand Distance Vector (AODV) protocol [4] is inspired from RIP. Because of the transmission mode (blind diffusion) in wireless networks, optimization solutions should take into account interference and congestions. OLSR, for example, introduces the Multi-Point Relay (MPR) mechanism [5]. The goal of this mechanism is to limit routing overhead, by selecting a subset of nodes which are the only ones allowed to broadcast topology control (TC) messages. Despite this mechanism, the routing load is always important for this protocol. It is a critical component for achieving good performance in wireless communications. Negative impact of congestion on the performance of wireless networks has been noted in several studies [6–9].

Hybrid protocols have been proposed to overcome full control messages dissemination of proactive routing protocols.

ZRP is a well-known hybrid routing protocol [10]. It is characterized by its zone radius R which determines the scope of topology control messages broadcasting. For communications to close neighbors (to less than R range), table-driven routing approach is used. For communications with more remote nodes, on-demand routing approach is used. Thus, ZRP implementation has tree components: IntrAzone Routing Protocol (IARP), Interzone Routing Protocol (IERP) and Bordercast Resolution Protocol (BRP). IARP is a limited-scope proactive routing protocol [11]. Since each node monitors changes in its surrounding R-hop neighborhood (routing zone), global route discovery processes to local destinations can be avoided.

IERP is the reactive routing component of ZRP [12]. It adapts existing reactive routing protocol implementations to take advantage of the known topology of each node (surrounding R-hop neighborhood). The availability of routing zone routes allows IERP to pass over route queries for local destinations. A BRP allows a node to send a route request packet to each of its peripheral nodes by unicast or multicast system [13]. By employing query control mechanisms, route requests can be directed away from areas of the network that already have been covered [10,14].

Duc et al. present congestion as a dominant cause of packet loss in Mobile Ad hoc NETworks (MANET). They propose a Congestion adaptive Routing Protocol (CRP) [15]. A key in CRP design is the bypass concept. A bypass is a sub-path connecting a node and the next non-congested node. If a node is aware of a potential congestion ahead, it finds a bypass that will be used in case the congestion actually occurs or is about to. Part of the incoming traffic will be sent on the bypass, making the traffic coming to the potentially congested node less.

In [16], it is proposed a Dynamic Probabilistic Route Discovery (DPR) scheme based on neighbor coverage. In this approach, each node determines the forwarding probability according to the number of its neighbors and the set of neighbors which are covered by the previous broadcast. This scheme only considers the coverage ratio by the previous node, and it does not consider the neighbors receiving the duplicate RREQ packet. Rajeeve et al. [17] propose a rebroadcast technique for reducing routing overhead in wireless network. In their approach, they enhance route request packet with two parameters: rebroadcast delay and rebroadcast probability to define the neighbor coverage knowledge in the network. RREQ message also plays the role of Hello message to detect neighbors.

Authors in [18–20] analysed zone radius impact in ZRP performance. They concluded that the zone radius should be configured to as low as 2 hops in case of low traffic and mobility scenarios, but as the traffic increases so must the zone radius. But, as performance parameter, they are mainly limited to estimating the network load. For us, parameters such as transmission end-to-end delay and packet delivery ratio (PDR) are more decisive. Their simulation environment also has not been sufficiently presented.

Authors in [21] conduct a study on the impact zone radius on the performance of ZRP. The results explanations do not stick to the obtained curves. These results contradict some widely recognized facts. For example, the delay and jitter are recognized the best for table-driven protocols because paths are immediately available for data transmissions and are more stable. They have not been detailed. In [22] it is reminded that the accuracy of the optimal zone radius computation would still be limited by the quality of the network model used.

3 Analyze

For communication with close neighborhood, ZRP uses the table-driven approach thanks to IARP. For remote destinations, it use the on-demand approach thanks to IERP. The radius area determines the close neighborhood (limited to neighbors at most R hops). This zone radius value R is an important parameter for this protocol. The larger it is, more the protocol behaves as pure table-driven protocol like OLSR protocol. The less it is, its route search process is simular to pure on-demand routing protocol like AODV protocol. It determines the scope of control messages dissemination and then routing load. It is expected for ZRP, a better control of the routing load compared to OLSR one (control packet dissemination is limited) and a better transmission delay compared to AODV. However, due to its multitude control messages, the routing overhead can be important. It includes topology control messages broadcasted periodically for the local networking, route search queries: route request, route reply an route error packets. On the other hand if the topology is too unstable, it creates consistency for the membership or not of a node to the neighboring and hence the existence of a pre-established route.

Which value to assign to this zone radius for better performance ? Very few studies have addressed the question.

To demonstrate such effects in a simulation requires the use of a realistic physical layer and a realistic propagation model. Therefore, in our tests, we enhanced Network Simulator (NS2) with CRT simulator [23]. CRT software implementes a realistic model of wave propagation taking into account environment characteristics.

In the next section, we analyse and evaluate ZRP routing overhead components and the impact of zone radius on the protocol performances in realistic simulation conditions.

4   Performance Evaluation

4.1   Experimental Setup

The global parameters for the simulations are given in Table 1.

Table 1. Simulation parameters.

Parameter	Value
Network simulator	ns-2
Simulation time	66 s
ZRP zone radius	2–6
Simulation area	1000 m * 1000 m
Transmission power	100 mw
Data type	CBR
Data packet size	512 bytes
MAC/physical layer	802.11a
Mac rate	24 Mbps

We have also used a realistic model of the Munich town (urban outdoor environment, see Fig. 1.), obstacles (building, etc) are printed red. Points represent nodes.

In this paper, we focused only on fixed nodes scenario. This fixed-nodes scenario facilitates the study and analyse of node route choice during routing process. Ten simultaneous unicast data transmissions occurred during 66 s. Beyond, time has no significant impact on the evolution of trends.

We analyze ZRP Routing Overhead (RO) and its impact on transmission End-to-End Delay and Packet Delivery Ratio (PDR). Then, we study the impact of ZRP zone radius value (R) on network performance. PDR is the ratio of the number of successfully delivered data packets over the number of sent data packets. End-to-End Delay concerns only successfully delivered packets. This includes delays caused by buffering during route discovery latency, queuing at the interface queue, retransmission delays at MAC layer, and propagation and transfer times. Routing Overhead (RO) is the number of routing protocol control packets. It permits to evaluate the effective use of the wireless medium by data traffic.

Fig. 1. Simulation environment with number of nodes = 60. Obstacles are printed red. (Color figure online)

4.2   Simulation Results

For these tests, number of nodes is fixed to 60. The average node density is 3.1. The ten simultaneous communications are selected so that source-destination distance vary from 2 to 6 hops. We observe ZRP performance when zone radius value varies from 1 to 6.

We see in Fig. 2 that, contrary to that is presented in the among of related work, routing overhead curve evolution according to zone radius is not monotonous. RO decreases with R until R = 3, then it is growing beyond. The optimal value of R is 3. Simulation trace files analysis shows that most of the routing load concerned Route REQuest (RREQ) and Route ERROR (RERROR) messages (on-demand routing approach of ZRP). We bear in mind that the routing load has essentially two components: control messages related to the reactive routing approach (RREQ, RERROR and route reply packets of IERP) and control messages related to the table-driven routing approach (IARP). When the radius R increases, naturally, the number of topology control (TC) messages increases. The solicitation of the proactive approach (IARP) and the scope of TC messages diffusion increase. For very high values of R (6 for example), the routing load due to these TC messages is very important. It nears the purely proactive approach as OLSR. This is not enough to justify the current values of number of control messages (see Fig. 2). The analysis of trace files shows that the number of route request and route error messages also increases. The dissemination of these messages is due to the non-existent paths between source-destination, therefore not included in the routing tables. For requests of transmission from a source to an unreachable destination, the purely proactive routing like OLSR reports the failure of communication while the reactive approach tried unsuccessfully a path establishment. This is the case for ZRP. With on-demand routing approach, route breaking causes a RERROR messages broadcasting to notify and apply for routing tables purification while the proactive approach initiates a local repapration the broken route.

In addition, when links are very unstable (in lossy link context), the bordercasting mechanism [13, 24] is ineffective. It produces a lot control packets to keep up to date neighborhood nodes defined by R. Remind that this process support ZRP IERP process [24]. Thank to query control mechanisms of ZRP BRP, route requests can be directed away from areas of the network that already have been covered [14].

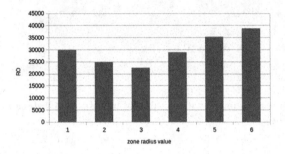

Fig. 2. Routing overhead evolution according to zone radius value

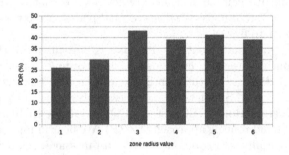

Fig. 3. PDR evolution according to zone radius value

The RO curve is consistent with the PDR one (see Fig. 3). The two curves are inversely proportional. A significant data packet loss due to lack of route, means that ZRP has used IERP process, so to multitudes RREQ and ERROR messages broadcast.

The same curve trend is observed for PDR (Fig. 3) and delay (Fig. 4). The optimal value is observed for PDR at R = 3. For delay, the best value is observed when R = 1. At the moment ZRP behaves as OLSR, established links are more reliable.

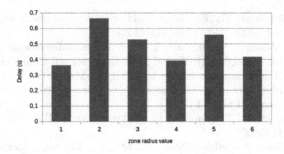

Fig. 4. Average delay evolution according to zone radius value

With these results, we can say that we must challenge the notion of optimal value of the ZRP. It must be determined for each desired performance parameter.

5 Conclusion

Congestion is one of the main cause of ad hoc wireless network cons-performance. This congestion is mainly due to the blind broadcast of routing control messages. By considering a realistic wave propagation environment, we conducted a comprehensive study on ZRP routing load and impact of zone radius value on the performance of this hybrid routing protocol. Thus, we highlight that when we take into account the lossy nature of wireless links, the on-demand routing approach generates more routing overhead than proactive approach.

We show that, in realistic conditions, the curve of routing overhead is not monotonically increasing with the neighborhood area defined by the zone radius value R. The optimal value is observed when $R = 3$. For packet delivery ratio parameter, the optimal value is 3. For delay there are 1 (equivalent at this time to OLSR) and 4. When the obstacles in the propagation medium are taken into account, the radius zone has not mean the same as the physical distance as seen in the free-space model.

These poor results of ZRP are also due to an inconsistency in the routing. Indeed, IARP can be acted to manage the routing while the concerned destination is no longer in the vicinity of the source node.

As prospects, we plan to study the impact of mobility on the optimal value of ZRP.

References

1. Karn, P.: MACA a new channel access method for packet radio. In: Computer Networking Conference, vol. 9, pp. 134–140 (1990)
2. Chlamtac, I., Conti, M., Liu, J.J.N.: Mobile ad hoc networking: imperatives and challenges. Ad Hoc Netw. **1**(1), 13–64 (2003)
3. Clausen, T., Jacquet, P.: Optimized link state routing protocol (OLSR), IETF RFC 3626, October 2003

4. Perkins, C., Belding-Royer, E., Das, S.: Ad hoc on-demand distance vector (AODV) routing protocol, iETF RFC 3561, July 2003
5. Yélémou, T., Meseure, P., Poussard, A.-M.: A new BER-based approach to improve OLSR protocol. In: Eighth IEEE and IFIP International Conference on Wireless and Optical Communications Networks (WOCN), May 2011
6. Parissidis, G.: Interference-aware routing in wireless multihop networks, Ph.D. dissertation, University Paris VI (2008)
7. Gupta, P., Kumar, P.: The capacity of wireless networks. IEEE Trans. Inf. Theory **46**(2), 388–404 (2000)
8. Jain, K., Padhye, J., Padmanabhan, V., Qiu, L.: The impact of interference on multi-hop wireless network performance. In: Proceedings of the 10th Annual International Conference on Mobile Computing and Networking (MOBICOM), vol. 11, pp. 471–487, September 2003
9. Hekmat, R., Van Mieghem, P.: Interference in wireless multi-hop ad-hoc networks and its effect on network capacity. J. Wirel. Netw. **10**(4), 389–399 (2004). (Proceedings of Conference on Ad hoc networking)
10. Beijar, N.: Zone Routing Protocol (ZRP). Helsinki University of Technology, Finland, Networking Laboratory (2002). http://citeseer.ist.psu.edu/538611.html
11. Haas, Z.J., Pearlman, M.R., Samar, P.: The intrazone routing protocol (IARP) for ad hoc networks, Networking Laboratory, Helsinki University of Technology, Finland, IETF Internet-Draft, draft-ietfmanet-zone-iarp-02.txt, July 2002
12. Haas, Z.J., Pearlman, M.R., Samar, P.: The interzone routing protocol (IERP) for ad hoc networks, Networking Laboratory, Helsinki University of Technology, Finland, IETF Internet-Draft, draft-ietfmanet- zone-ierp-02.txt, July 2002
13. Haas, Z.J., Pearlman, M.R., Samar, P.: The bordercast resolution protocol (BRP) for ad hoc networks, Networking Laboratory, Helsinki University of Technology, Finland, IETF Internet-Draft, draft-ietfmanet-zone-brp-02.txt, August 2002
14. Haas, Z., Pearlman, M.: The performance of query control schemes for the zone routing protocol. IEEE/ACM Trans. Netw. **9**(4), 427–438 (2001)
15. Tran, D., Raghavendra, H.: Congestion adaptive routing in mobile ad hoc networks. IEEE Trans. Parallel Distrib. Syst. **17**(11), 1294–1305 (2006)
16. Abdulai, J.-D., Ould-Khaoua, M., Mackenzie, L., Mohammed, A.: Neighbour coverage: a dynamic probabilistic route discovery for mobile ad hoc networks. In: International Symposium on Performance Evaluation of Computer and Telecommunication Systems, SPECTS 2008, June 2008, pp. 165–172 (2008)
17. Dharmaraj, R., Mohan, S.: A rebroadcast technique for reducing routing overhead in mobile ad hoc network. Int. J. Inf. Comput. Technol., 797–804 (2014). http://www.irphouse.com
18. Giannoulis, S., Antonopoulos, C., Topalis, E., Koubias, S.: ZRP versus DSR and TORA: a comprehensive survey on ZRP performance. In: 10th IEEE Conference on Emerging Technologies and Factory Automation, ETFA 2005, vol. 1, pp. 8 (2005)
19. Loutfi, A., ElKoutbi, M.: Evaluation and enhancement of ZRP performances. In: 2011 International Conference on Multimedia Computing and Systems (ICMCS), pp. 1–6 (2011)
20. Patel, B., Srivastava, S.: Performance analysis of zone routing protocols in mobile ad hoc networks. In: 2010 National Conference on Communications (NCC), pp. 1–5 (2010)
21. Lakhtaria, K.I., Patel, P.: Analyzing zone routing protocol in MANET applying authentic parameter, pp. 114–118 (2008)
22. Pearlman, M., Haas, Z.: Determining the optimal configuration for the zone routing protocol. IEEE J. Sel. Areas Commun. **17**(8), 1395–1414 (1999)

23. Delahaye, R., Pousset, Y., Poussard, A.-M., Chatellier, C., Vauzelle, R.: A realistic physic layer modeling of 802.11g ad hoc networks in outdoor environments with a computation time optimization. In: Proceedings of the Eleventh World Multi-Conference on Systemics, Cybernetics and Informatics (WMSCI), Orlando, Florida, USA (2007)
24. Yélémou, T., Meseure, P., Poussard, A.-M.: Improving ZRP performance by taking into account quality of links. In: IEEE Wireless Communications and Networking Conference (WCNC), April 2012

Classification and Prediction of Arrhythmias from Electrocardiograms Patterns Based on Empirical Mode Decomposition and Neural Network

Abdoul-Dalibou Abdou[1]($\boxtimes$), Ndeye Fatou Ngom[2], and Oumar Niang[2]

[1] LTISI-EPT, Univerté de Thies, Thies, Senegal
abdould.abdou@univ-thies.sn
[2] Laboratoire Traitement de l'Inforrmation et Systémes Intelligents (LTISI),
Ecole Polytechnique de Thies (EPT), Thies, Senegal
{fngom,oniang}@ept.sn

Abstract. Diagnosis of heart disease rests essentially on the analysis of the statistical, morphological, temporal, or frequency properties of ECG. Data analytical techniques are often needed for the identification, the extraction of relevant information, the discovery of meaningful patterns and new threads of knowledge from biomedical data. However for cardiovascular diseases, despite the rapid increase in the collection of methods proposed, research communities still have difficulties in delivering applications for clinical practice. In this paper we propose hybrid model to advance the understanding of arrhythmias from electrocardiograms patterns. Adaptive analysis based on empirical Mode Decomposition (EMD) is first carried out to perform signal denoising and the detection of main events presented in the electrocardiograms (Ecg). Then, binary classification is performed using Neural Network model. However in this work, the Ecg R-peak detection method, the classification algorithm are improved and the chart flow include a predictive step. Indeed, the classification outputs are used to perform prediction of cardiac rhythm pattern. The proposed model is illustrated using the MIT-BIH database, compared to other methods and discussed. The obtained results are very promising.

Keywords: ECG classification · Neural networks · Predictive models · Empirical mode decomposition · Arrhythmia

1 Introduction

An electrocardiogram (ECG) is a representation of the electrical impulses due to ionic activity in the heart muscles of the human heart (Fig. 5). And the analysis (statistical, morphological, temporal or frequency aspects of P, Q, R, S, T waves) of the ECGs shape is a key step during the investigation of symptoms related to heart anomalies [1]. An anomaly is an abnormality or irregularity

G. Mendy et al. (Eds.): AFRICOMM 2018, LNICST 275, pp. 174–184, 2019.
https://doi.org/10.1007/978-3-030-16042-5_17

that occurs when the behavior of the system is unusual and significantly different from normal previous behavior [3,21]. As heart disease is one of the leading cause of death around the world, the understanding of hearth anomalies is a main subject of research in the field of cardiac care and information processing [2]. For this purpose, many approaches have been proposed for anomaly detection, classification and prediction. Classical methods for anomalies detection use external probe [12,13] or internal components that periodically send heartbeats or store logs of relevant events when certain conditions occur [3]. The classification can be done through adaptive methods such as Harr descriptor, empirical mode decomposition and Neural Network models [1,2]. Unlike the detection and classification methods, the predictive approach gives indicators for possible abnormalities before the symptoms occur from historical data and an intelligent system [4,11]. The main approaches for prediction of anomalies are based on the statistics, information theory, data mining and machine learning (HMM, Bayesian networks, ARMA model, SVM) [3–5,17,21]. Several studies have shown the effectiveness of the statistical approach to machine learning and data mining [21]. Statistical techniques assume that data have predefined distributions and use the distribution gap to find an anomaly [4]. In this paper, we improved the model proposed in [1] for anomalies detection and ECG classification with empirical mode decomposition and neural network. The main contributions are the ECGs morphological properties taken as input during the classification and the predictive model based on heart rate frequency analysis. The proposed cardiac abnormalities prediction uses linear regression from the neural network outputs classifier. The results are illustrated using MIT-BIH database and discussed.

The body of the paper is organized as follows. First, Sect. 2 presents the architecture of our methodology, the basics of the empirical mode decomposition and the neural network classifier. Secondly, Sect. 3 describes the parameters extraction. Thirdly, Sect. 4 presents the classification method. Next, Sect. 5 describes the predictive model. Then, Sect. 6 shows and discuss the results obtained with our methodology. Finally, Sect. 7 draws conclusions and perspectives of work.

2   Model Presentation

The chart flow of the proposed classification and prediction approach for cardiac abnormalities is presented in the Fig. 1.

The inputs of our system (Fig. 1) are ECGs. For the MIT-BIH database, the each ECG includes three components: time samples, MLII signals and V5 signals. For the classification, we first extract the V5 signal, then denoise the signal through filtering and compute input parameters (Negative form, maximum amplitude, minimum amplitude, maximum width and minimum width) for the neural network classifier. The outputs of the classifier are then used during the prediction step. For this purpose, we first compute the ten previous heart rate, then we estimate the next heart rate to predict the existence or not of cardiac abnormality.

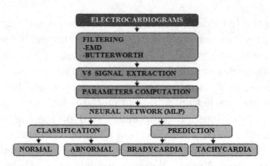

Fig. 1. Chart flow of the proposed classification and predictive approach.

2.1 Empirical Mode Decomposition

EMD decomposes iteratively a complex signal s(n) into components elementary AM-FM Types, called Intrinsic Mode Functions (IMFs) [10,16,18,20].

$$s\left(n\right) = r_k\left(n\right) + \sum_{k=1}^{K} imf_k\left(n\right) \tag{1}$$

Where imf_k is the kth mode or IMF of the signal and r_k is the trend residual. Figure 2 illustrates the empirical decomposition of ECG 100 [1].

h

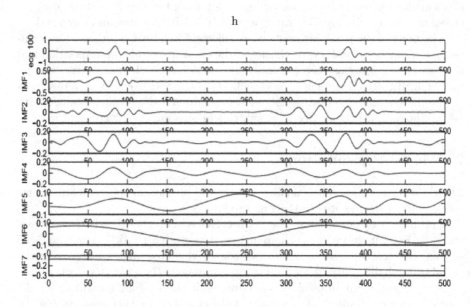

Fig. 2. Empirical mode decomposition of ECG 100 [1]

The sifting procedure generates a finite number of IMFs. The underlying principle of the EMD is to identify locally in the signal the fastest oscillations defined as the waveform interpolating the local maxima and minima. To do this, these last points are interpolated with a cubic spline to produce the upper and lower envelopes. The average envelope is subtracted from the initial signal and the same interpolation scheme is reiterated.

2.2 Neural Network

A neural network is a mathematical function, see Fig. 3 [1].

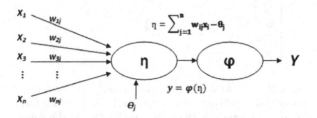

Fig. 3. Representation of an artificial neuron [1]. Inputs are multiplied by their weight. The products are added to give the weighted sum. The threshold of the node is subtracted from the weighted sum to determine the output of the node.

To set up a neural network, there must be defined input data, the activation function and the thresholds of the nodes. Each data (node) is associated with a weight. A neural network works as follows:

1. Computation of the weighted sum of the inputs and their weights;
2. Computation of the difference between the threshold and the weighted sum;
3. Computation of the image of the difference with the activation function.

In this paper, we propose a neural network composed of six nodes, corresponding to morphological properties of the complex QRS (negative form, maximum amplitude, minimum amplitude, maximum width, minimum width) and arrhythmia class. Figure 4 illustrated the network component.

3 ECG Patterns Detection

Intrinsic parameters are used for ECG patterns detection that can leads the classification that will be further performed. Indeed, statistical properties (mean, variance, standard deviation, energy and power) are often used as input parameters for classification [1]. However these parameters are global descriptors of data. Unlike statistical properties, morphological attributes allow local analysis. Thus, in this work, we used a set of morphological properties (negative form, maximum amplitude, minimum amplitude, maximum width, minimum width) of the complex QRS (Fig. 5) and the step activation function for classifying the ECG.

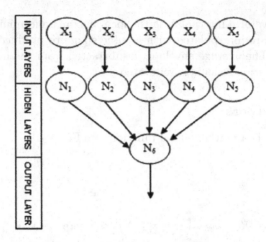

Fig. 4. Architecture of the neural network. The variables $X_1 \ldots X_5$ represent the morphological properties of the QRS complex, respectively the negative form, the maximum amplitude, the minimum amplitude, the maximum width and the minimum width. The variables $N_1 \ldots N_5$ represent the intermediate nodes. The Node N_6 determines the class of the signal.

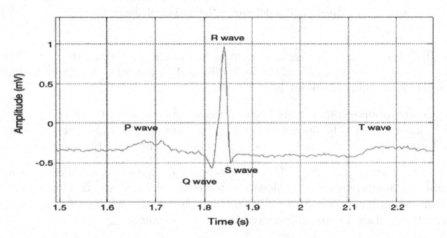

Fig. 5. Illustration of the morphological properties with ECG: P, Q, R, S and T waves represent a heartbeat [19].

3.1 Filtering

The signal are denoised using method based on empirical mode decomposition (EMD) and Butterworth filtering [1]. We subtract the first IMF (IMF_1) to eliminate the high frequency [10,18,20] and apply the Butterworth filter to smooth the signal [22]. The main operations are:

1. Inputs: ECGs
2. EMD based filtering

- Empirical mode decomposition (EMD);
- Remove the IMF_1;
- Subtract the IMF_1 from ECG.
3. Butterworth Filtering:
    - Compute the filter order;
    - Compute the filter coefficients;
    - Apply the filter.
4. Outputs: Denoised ECG.

3.2   Parameters Vector

The Algorithm 1 describe the detailed step processing of the morphological properties computation.

Algorithm 1. Parameters

1: function vecteur(s)
2: $e \leftarrow extrema(s)$
3: $l \leftarrow largeur(e)$
4: $a \leftarrow rdetecter(e)$
5: $n \leftarrow rnegative(e)$
6: $ln \leftarrow min(l)$
7: $lm \leftarrow max(l)$
8: $an \leftarrow min(a)$
9: $am \leftarrow max(a)$
10: $v \leftarrow [n, ln, lm, an, am]$
11: return v

- Algorithme 1 takes as input an ECGs and computes the maximums, the minimums of the widths and amplitudes of the QRS complexes. It detects a negative R-wave if it occurs and returns a parameters vector for the neural network.
- The extrema() function is used to compute the ECG local extrema (maximum and minimum).
- The function width() takes as input the ECG extrema, detects the waves (Q and S) and returns the QRS complex width.
- The rdetect() function takes as input the ECG extrema, computes the absolute maximum, uses a threshold of 75% of the absolute maximum to detect the R waves and returns the ECG R waves.
- The rnegative function() takes as input the ECG extrema, computes the absolute extrema (maximum, minimum, the ratio of the minimum and the maximum) and returns the index of a negative R wave if the ratio is greater than 0.75.

The parameters given by the output of Algorithm 1 are used as input for the cardiac abnormalities prediction (Algorithm 2).

Algorithm 2. Heart Rate

1: function frequence(e)
2: $s \leftarrow e(2, :)$
3: $sp \leftarrow abs(s)$
4: $l \leftarrow length(s)$
5: $r \leftarrow []$
6: $m \leftarrow max(sp)$
7: **for** $i \leftarrow 1$ to l **do**
8:     $q \leftarrow sp(i)/m$
9:     **if** $q \geq 0.50$ **then**
10:         $r \leftarrow [r, s(i)]$
11:     **end if**
12: **end for**
13: $fc \leftarrow length(r)$
14: return fc

The function frequence() (Algorithm 2) takes the extremum of an ECG, counts the number of R waves and returns the heart rate and the number of beats per minute.

4   Classification

The classification involves two functions: the network function and the classifier function. The implemented neural network uses H(x), the step activation function with a threshold (s) for each parameter: $H(x) = 0$ *si* $x < s$ *and* $H(x) = 1$ *si* $x \geq s$. The parameters are negative form, minimum width, maximum width, minimum amplitude and maximum amplitude which are respectively associated to the following thresholds 0, 0.06, 0.10, 0.5 and 2.5 [9]. The network function is composed of six neurons. It takes as input a parameters vector and returns zero (0) for normal or one (1) for abnormal. The classifier iterates the network function and detects an anomaly when there is [9]:

1. a negative R wave;
2. a minimum width is less than 0.06;
3. a maximum width is greater than 0.10;
4. a minimum amplitude is less than 0.5;
5. a maximum amplitude is greater than 2.5.

This proposed process improves the classification method proposed in [1] by 6.25%. The improvement is due to the use of the morphological parameters on the one hand and the step function on the other hand. The morphological parameters allow to perform local analysis with defined thresholds.

5   Abnormalities Prediction

The detection and prediction of anomalies are very important in monitoring the patients and ensure a good patient care. Several techniques exist for the detection and prediction of cardiac abnormalities. In this section, prediction based on linear regression [8] is presented. A linear regression model can be described by Eq. (2):

$$y = a + bx$$
$$a = \bar{y} - b\bar{x}$$
$$b = \frac{\sum(x-\bar{x})(y-\bar{y})}{(x-\bar{x})^2} \tag{2}$$

where, y is the estimated frequency and x the prediction horizon. The frequency prediction is done through the following steps:

1. Computation of the 10 previous heart rates;
2. Estimation of the next heart rate;
3. Classification of the estimated cardiac frequency with a network of neurons;
4. Prediction of a cardiac abnormality (Tachycardia or Bradycardia).

The prediction base is constructed by extracting the samples from last 10 min and computing the corresponding heart rates. The cardiac frequency is estimated using the Algorithm 3.

Algorithm 3. Prediction Method

1: function predire(dfc,t)
2: $y \leftarrow dfc$
3: $x \leftarrow 1 : 10$
4: $mx \leftarrow mean(x)$
5: $my \leftarrow mean(y)$
6: $n \leftarrow 0$
7: $d \leftarrow 0$
8: **for** $i \leftarrow 1$ *to* 10 **do**
9:     $n \leftarrow n + (i - mx) * (y(i) - my)$
10:     $d \leftarrow d + (i - mx) * (i - mx)$
11: **end for**
12: $b \leftarrow n/d$
13: $a \leftarrow my - b * mx$
14: $fcp \leftarrow a + b * t$
15: return fcp

The function (Algorithm 3) takes ten previous frequencies and t (horizon prediction). It estimates the heart rate at t (prediction horizon). When the estimated heart rate is less than 50 beats per minute, Bradycardia is predicted [7]. And when the estimated heart rate is higher at 100 beats per minute, tachycardia is predicted [7].

6   Results and Discussion

6.1   Data Description

For the learning, testing, evaluation and validation of our classifier, we use the ECG of the MIT-BIH Arrhythmia database [1,15]. It is a waveform and class completed references databases of physionet.org. It is composed of 48 signals recorded on a half-hour. The MIT-BIH Arrhythmia database ECG can be downloaded from physionet.org. It is a set of 48 data files, 48 annotations files and 48 head files. The files have 64800 items including 21600 samples (time), 21600 MLII signals and 21600 V5 signals.

We considered 70% of ecg for learning and 30% for testing and evaluation. The learning base is composed of 33 ecg including 19 ecg normal and 14 ecg abnormal. The test base is composed of 15 ecg including 6 abnormal ecg and 9 ecg normal. Our goal, during testing, is to be able to detect all abnormal ECGs.

6.2   Classification and Prediction

We first use dual filtering based on the EMD and the Butterworth filter during the preprocessing step. Then, we compute the classification parameters (Table 1) and estimate the heart rate (Table 3) for the prediction. We have computed the parameters for the Forty-eight (48) ECG signals from the MIT-BIH database. Table 1 shows, as exemple, the parameters of the five ECG signals (100, 102, 104, 106 and 108).

Table 1. Characteristic vectors for the classification

ECG	FORME NEGAT	LARG MIN	LARG MAX	AMPLIT MIN	AMPLIT MAX
100	−0.5860	0.0660	0.1270	−0.5860	0.7350
102	−3.3040	0.1310	0.5550	−3.3040	−3.0240
104	−0.9310	0.0500	0.4330	−0.9310	0.8870
106	−0.4280	0.0560	0.0950	−0.4280	0.5220
108	−2.3600	0.1610	0.3000	−2.3600	−1.8170

Table 2. The performance indices

Classifier	TP	FP	TN	FN	Ac	Se	Sp	Pp
SPNNC [1]	5	1	2	7	47%	42%	22%	83%
This work	6	0	4	5	67%	55%	44%	100%

For evaluating the performance of the classifier, we have computed the standard familiar metrics [6,14] like Accuracy (Ac), Sensitivity (Se), Specificity (Sp),

Positive Predictivity (Pp) using True Positive (TP), True Negative (TN), False Negative (FN) and False Positive (FP). Compared (Table 2) to our previous work [1], we see an improvement in all performance indices, particularly anomaly detection, represented by the positive predictivity (Pp).

Table 3. Frequencies estimated for the prediction

ECG	FC 1	FC 2	FC 3	FC 4	FC 5	FC 6	FC 7	FC 8	FC 9	FC 10	FC ESTIMÉE
100	17	46	4	35	7	51	363	110	56	113	163.26
101	185	107	186	283	110	140	67	13	95	83	44.06
118	36	51	40	82	36	59	74	47	83	52	69.40

We have computed and estimated the frequencies for the forty-eight (48) ECG signals from the MIT-BIH database. We compute ten heart rates for the forty-eight ECG and we estimated their heart rates. In Table 3, we gave the example of the three cases of estimation of the cardiac frequency. The estimated frequencies will be given as parameters of the neural network to predict a cardiac anomaly.

Table 3 contains the ten heart rates and the estimated frequency of three ECG signals (100, 101 and 118). For ECG 100, the estimated heart rate is 163.26. This frequency predicts tachycardia. The frequency 44.06 predicts a bradycardia for the ECG 101. And ECG 118 is predicted normal by the frequency 69.40.

7   Conclusion

In this work, we proposed an approach based on empirical mode decomposition (EMD), the neural network and linear regression for classification and prediction of cardiac abnormalities. The main contributions are the ECGs morphological properties taken as input during the classification and the predictive model based on heart rate frequency analysis. The output of our approach gives promising results for the classification and prediction of cardiac abnormalities such as tachycardia and bradycardia. In future works, the predictive model will be combined with a stochastic model to better understand the behavior of ECG signals.

References

1. Abdou, A.D., Ngom, N.F., Sidibé, S., Niang, O., Thioune, A., Ndiaye, C.H.T.C.: Neural networks for biomedical signals classification based on empirical mode decomposition and principal component analysis. In: Kebe, C.M.F., Gueye, A., Ndiaye, A. (eds.) InterSol/CNRIA -2017. LNICST, vol. 204, pp. 267–278. Springer, Cham (2018). https://doi.org/10.1007/978-3-319-72965-7_25

2. Atibi, M., Bennis A., Boussaa M., Atouf, I.: ECG image classification in real time based on the haar-like features and artificial neural networks. In: The International Conference on Advanced Wireless, Information, and Communication Technologies (AWICT 2015), vol. 73, pp. 32–39 (2015)
3. Bovenzi, A.: The on-line detection of anomalies in mission-criticial software system, April 2013
4. Zhang, Y., Hong, D., Zhao, D.: The entropy and PCA based anomaly prediction in data streams. In: 20th International Conference on Knowledge Based and Intelligent Information and Engineering Systems, vol. 96, pp. 139–146 (2016)
5. Gupta, S., Phung, D., Nguyen, T., Venkatesh, S.: Learning latent activities from social signals with hierarchical Dirichlet processes
6. Ramanujam, E., Padmavathi, S.: Naïve bayes classifier for ECG abnormalities using multivariate maximal time series motif. Procedia Comput. Sci. **47**, 222–228 (2015)
7. Dubois, R.: Application des nouvelles méthodes d'apprentissage à la détection précoce d'anomalies cardiaques en électrocardiographie (2004)
8. Gaudoin, O.: Principes et methodes statistiques, p. 145
9. Desnos, M., Gay, J., Benoit, P.: l'électrocardiograme: 460 tracés commentés et figures, pp. 30–32 (1990)
10. Jin, F., Sugavaneswaran, L., Krishnan, S., Chauhan, V.S.: Quantification of fragmented qrs complex using intrinsic time-scale decomposition. Biomed. Signal Process. Control **31**, 513–523 (2017)
11. Moya, J.M., Ayala, J.L., Pagan, J., Risco-Martín, J.L.: Modeling methodology for the accurate and prompt prediction of symptomatic events in chronic diseases. J. Biomed. Inform. **62**, 136–147 (2016)
12. Rish, I., Brodie, M., Ma, S.: Optimizing probe selection for fault localization, in operations et management. In: 12th International Workshop on Distributed System, pp. 88–98 (2001)
13. Rish, I., et al.: Adaptive diagnosis in distributed systems. IEEE Trans. Neural Networks **16**(5), 1088–1109 (2005)
14. Markazi, A.H.D., Anaraki, A.K., Nazarahari, M., Namin, S.G.: A multi-wavelet optimization approach using similarity measures for electrocardiogram signal classification. Biomed. Signal Process. Control **20**, 142–151 (2015)
15. Moody, G.B., Mark, R.G.: The impact of the MIT-BIH arrhythmia database. IEE Eng. Med. Biol. **20**, 45–50 (2001)
16. Niang, O., Thioune, A., Delechelle, E., Lemoine, J.: Spectral intrinsic decomposition method for adaptative signal representation. ISRN Signal Process. **9**, 3 (2012)
17. Kloft, M., Gornitz, N., Braun, M.: Hidden Markov anomaly detection
18. Pal, S., Mitra, M.: Empirical mode decomposition based on ECG enhencement and QRS detection. Comput. Biol. Med. **42**, 83–92 (2012)
19. Rodriguez, R., Mexicano, A., Bila, J., Cervantes, S., Ponce, R.: Feature extraction of electrocardiogram signals by aplying adaptative threshold and principal component analysis. J. Appl. Res. Technol. **13**, 261–269 (2015)
20. Slimane, Z.H., Nait Ali, A.: QRS complex detection using empirical mode decomposition. Digit. Signal Process. **20**, 1221–1228 (2010)
21. Purdy, S., Agha, Z., Ahmad, S., Lavin, A.: Unsupervised real-time anomaly detection for streaming data. Neurocomputing **262**, 134–147 (2017)
22. Zhang, H.: An improved QRS wave group detection algorithm and matlab implementation. Phys. Procedia **25**, 1010–1016 (2012)

Cyber-Healthcare Kiosks for Healthcare Support in Developing Countries

Mukuzo Fortunat Bagula[1], Herman Bagula[1], Munyaradzi Mandava[2],
Claude Kakoko Lubamba[2], and Antoine Bagula[2(✉)]

[1] School of Health, University of Cape Town, Cape Town, South Africa
[2] ISAT Laboratory, University of the Western Cape, Cape Town, South Africa
abagula@uwc.ac.za

Abstract. Cyber-healthcare can be described to be virtual medicine applied in reality. It involves the use of healthcare professionals consulting and treating patients via the internet and other modern communication platforms and using different techniques and devices of the Internet-of-Things (IoT) to automate manual processes. This paper aims to revisit cyber-healthcare and its applications in the health sector in the developing countries with the expectation of (i) assessing the field-readiness of emerging bio-sensor devices through a cross-sectional pilot study that benchmark the arduino sensors against manually captured vital signs using calibrated devices and (ii) comparing unsupervised and supervised machine learning techniques when used in Triage systems to prioritise patients.

Keywords: Cyber-healthcare · Internet-of-Things ·
Patient condition recognition · Disease identification ·
Patient prioritisation

1 Introduction

The internet of things consists of physical devices embedded with sensors, software and communication capabilities thus resulting in an ability for sensing the environment of the physical devices and enabling information exchange between devices (devices-to-devices (D-2-D) communication) and between human and devices (devices-to-human (D-2-H) communication). With technological advancements in the internet of things and healthcare, cyber-healthcare has become an interesting industry to combat various health care problems in developed and developing countries.

The application of cyber-healthcare would rely on the introduction of sensor networks for health data capture. These sensor networks would allow the monitoring and capturing of vital parameters which would then be processed and thereafter condition recognition would be performed using artificial intelligence techniques as suggested in [3]. Data capture using sensor networks can be non-invasive or invasive. It can also be based on different technologies such as using

G. Mendy et al. (Eds.): AFRICOMM 2018, LNICST 275, pp. 185–198, 2019.
https://doi.org/10.1007/978-3-030-16042-5_18

body sensor networks (BSN) or fixed sensors. While different protocols have been used for the dissemination of information, cyber-healthcare relies on specific protocols that have been engineered to meet healthcare data requirements. These include ZigBee, Bluetooth, WiFi [1] and many other emerging communication protocols.

By capturing patient vital signs, mapping of these signs as patient medical records can occur and patient prioritisation and disease identification can be performed as well as dissemination of these records to required parties through cloud infrastructure [4]. The focus of cyber-healthcare lies in the digitalisation of all clinical work, whether it be imaging, physical therapy, medical supply provision and more [3]. Although the clear advantage of cyber-healthcare includes addressing the supply-demand issue caused by an ever-increasing population, other important benefits of cyber-healthcare include its cost and time saving aspects. However, besides the ethical problems that may arise with information processing and interoperability, issues such as the field readiness of e-health bio-sensor devices used to monitor vital parameters exist. Furthermore, while many studies have been conducted to perform patient prioritisation, none of them have confirmed which is the best between supervised and unsupervised machine learning when performing patient condition recognition.

This paper revisits the application of cyber-healthcare for patient condition recognition as a service offered to citizens through healthcare kiosks located in the rural areas of the developing world. The objective of this paper is to assess the field-readiness the sensor devices used in these kiosks and compare different machine learning solutions to the issue of patient condition recognition. The rest of the paper will do so by focusing on the following sections: the Cyber-healthcare kiosk model in Sect. 2, a deployment scenario for rural areas and its validation in Sect. 3 and finally Sect. 4 contains our conclusions.

2   The Cyber Healthcare Kiosk Model

A network of wind/solar powered Cyber-healthcare Kiosks is presented in Fig. 1. It is designed to monitor patients' vital well-being through their vital signs, including blood pressure, blood oxygen levels, temperature, position, glucose levels, air flow, and heart rate. It allows medical tests to be scheduled and the results reported to a clinician without a traditional office visit. Furthermore, the collected results may be processed by a patient condition recognition that uses machine learning techniques to provide decision support to the healthcare professionals. As a community support tool, the Cyber-healthcare kiosk gives all citizens access to easy, convenient and affordable evaluations of their health on a regular or recurring basis. Some of its benefits include (i) providing tracks/reports trends daily, weekly, monthly which can be integrated into regional health information systems for planning and management (ii) providing quick, easy-to-read results with are free from errors resulting from manual data capture (iii) increasing communication and sending data remotely to enable information sharing and access to remote health expertise (iv) saving time and lowering health visit costs

(v) availing resources for multiple users/clinician sharing (vi) supporting early detection of health concerns and (vii) allowing integration with electronic health records.

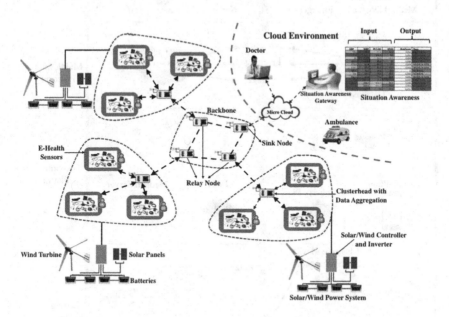

Fig. 1. Cyber-healthcare Kiosk network

2.1 The Cyber-Healthcare Framework

Figure 2 depicts a framework derived from the Cyber healthcare kiosk model in Fig. 1. It reveals a process transformation from vital signs collection to service delivery through different applications. The framework borrows from (i) the general Internet-of-Things (IoT) its multi-layer architecture with different layers describing the functionalities of different digital platforms and (ii) the four layer architectures in [4, 23, 24] but with focus on healthcare and using solar/wind powered Cyber-Healthcare kiosks. These include:

A sensing platform at the bottom of the architecture used to collect physiological signals as well as the voltage and currents collected by the solar/wind battery system. The environmental conditions where the solar/wind system is operating will also be accounted by including environmental parameters such as temperature, humidity and air pressure in the measurements.

A dissemination platform layered above the sensing platform to enable communication of the sensor yields to places where these readings are processed and further decisions are taken about the health system. Such platform may be developed using different technologies and protocols such as WiFi, ZigBee, Bluetooth, GSM and many others depending on the health system's communication requirements.

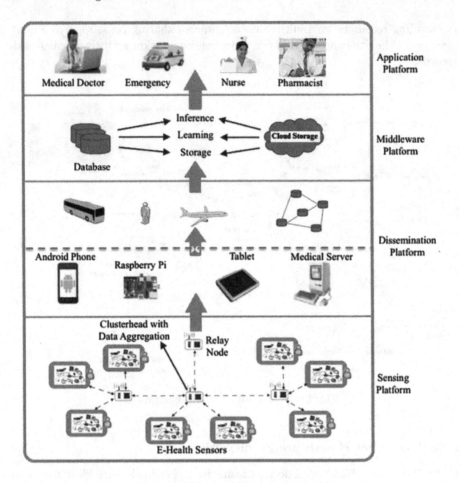

Fig. 2. Cyber-healthcare framework

A Middleware platform that serves as cement between the lower and higher layers of the framework and hides the complexity of the lower layers to the application layer. In that platform, situation recognition operations such as Triage and any form of medical support such as disease identification is carried out.

The application platform where different medical applications are integrated to the cyber-healthcare kiosk to provide different services to the users through different applications. These include pharmaceutical controls, hospital management and many others which are not necessarily directly connected to sensor networks.

The focus of this paper lies on the sensing platform where different bio-sensor devices are used to capture patients' vital signs and the middleware platform where machine learning algorithms are used to achieve patient prioritisation.

2.2 The Cyber-Healthcare Sensing Platform

Different bio-sensor devices are used to measure different vital signs. These include

The **pulse oximetry sensor** uses a noninvasive method of indicating the arterial oxygen saturation of functional haemoglobin. Oxygen saturation is defined as the measurement of the amount of oxygen dissolved in blood, based on the detection of Hemoglobin and Deoxyhemoglobin. It is useful in any setting where a patient's oxygenation is unstable.

The **nasal airflow sensor** is used to measure airflow rate to a patient in need of respiratory help.

The **patient position sensor (Accelerometer)** monitors five different patient positions: standing/sitting, supine, prone, left and right. In many cases, it is necessary to monitor a patient body's positions and movements because of their relationships to particular diseases (i.e., sleep apnea and restless legs syndrome).

The **glucometer sensor** is a medical device for determining the approximate concentration of glucose in the blood. A small drop of blood, obtained by pricking the skin with a lancet, is placed on a disposable test strip that the meter reads and uses to calculate the blood glucose level.

The **body temperature sensor** allows measurements of body temperature. It is important to measure body temperature since a number of diseases are accompanied by characteristic changes in body temperature. Likewise, the course of certain diseases can be monitored by measuring body temperature, and the efficiency of a treatment initiated can be evaluated by the physician.

The **electrocardiogram (ECG or EKG) sensor** is a diagnostic tool that is routinely used to assess the electrical and muscular functions of the heart. The electrocardiogram (ECG) has grown to be one of the most commonly used medical tests in modern medicine. Its utility in the diagnosis of a myriad of cardiac pathologies ranging from myocardial ischemia and infarction to syncope and palpitations has been invaluable to clinicians for decades.

The **skin conductance (Sweating) sensor** uses the galvanic skin response (GSR) method of measuring the electrical conductance of the skin, which varies with its moisture level. This is of interest because the sweat glands are controlled by the sympathetic nervous system, so moments of strong emotion, change the electrical resistance of the skin. Skin conductance is used as an indication of psychological or physiological arousal.

The **blood pressure sensor** measures the pressure of the blood in the arteries as it is pumped around the body by the heart. When the heart beats, it contracts and pushes blood through the arteries to the rest of the body. This force creates pressure on the arteries.

The **electromyogram (EMG) sensor** measures the electrical activity of muscles at rest and during contraction. EMG is used as a diagnosis tool for identifying neuromuscular diseases, assessing low-back pain, kinesiology, and disorders of motor control. EMG signals are also used as a control signal for prosthetic devices such as prosthetic hands, arms, and lower limbs.

2.3   The Cyber-Healthcare Middleware Platform

Patient' condition recognition involves the identification of patient's signs and symptoms. This allows a gain of insight into the patient's condition and allows patient prioritisation, an important healthcare factor targeted by cyber-healthcare. Healthcare professionals will be better aided by this "human-assisted-decision-making" system resulting in more efficient decision making and ultimately better patient care and health outcomes. The focus of this work lies on patient prioritisation. It is based on the traditional triage system, involves the analysis of patient's condition and prioritising urgent cases. The aim of the traditional triage system was to categorise patients into groups according to urgency of their medical condition in warfare situations [6]. Triage scores have evolved, however, and have become key players in emergency departments all over the world with various scores such as the Australian triage scale, the Manchester triage scale as well as Canadian triage scale being applied in their respective locations. In Southern Africa, the South African Triage Scale, founded in 2004, is used to assign triage early warning scores (TEWS) to infants, children and adults in emergency situations [3]. These scores which focus on observed physiological parameters have often resulted in a mis-triaging of patients due to various factors such lack of human resources to carry out the triage, lack of adequate triage training as well as human error [7]. Patient prioritisation with cyber-healthcare was proposed in [8] as a four components system including: (i) a database with storage of patient medical records as well as physiological parameters received from bio-sensors (ii) a scoring system adapted from WHO standardised table of vital parameter risk zones (iii) a server application allowing data analysis so that situation awareness is performed and (iv) a visualisation application which would provide an interface between cloud, the whole system and users. The process of patient prioritisation has been described in a paper by Bagula et al. and has included the following: Data capturing in various forms including crowd sourced data on mobile phones and bio-sensed data followed by local and/or remote processing of the collected information to allow data analysis, distribution and decision making [3]. The use of cyber-healthcare to bring about patient prioritisation may be a solution to the mis-triaging of patients as the elimination of human error due to various reasons will occur. Furthermore, a paper by Muhammed Mahtab Alam looking at various environments where sensors can be worn has shown that the sensor's ability to monitor physiological parameters (heart rate, stress level), body motion (posture, orientation) as well as surrounding environment (toxic gases, humidity), allows it to be used in settings that may lie outside of the normal hospital environment but where triaging is required [9]. These settings include rescue and emergency management where sensors can be used to better predict and manage life threatening situations as well as in mobile workforce safety and health management where construction workers fitted with sensors can be tracked and notified about possible health hazards such as carbon monoxide [9]. Therefore, although these sensors may be used to bring about patient prioritisation, they may also be used as preventative tools thereby decreasing the burden of healthcare on healthcare departments and the economy. Four patient prioritisation machine learning techniques were compared to evaluate their efficiency and time complexity. Their characteristics are described in Table 1.

Table 1. Machine learning characteristics

Characteristic	Multivariate linear regression	K-means clustering	Knowledge based	Support vector machine
Use of the algorithm	(i) Detecting patient deterioration (ii) Generates warnings when threshold values are reached and (iii) Generates priority list from all patient data in order to perform patient prioritisation	(i) Detecting patient deterioration and (ii) generates warnings when threshold values are reached	Generates priority list from all patient data in order to perform patient prioritisation	(i) Detecting patient deterioration (ii) Generates warnings when threshold values are reached and (iii) Generates priority list from all patient data in order to perform patient prioritisation
Scoring	(i) Uses the knowledge based system to score the training data before training (in other words it is an improved expert system knowledge based algorithm) and (ii) Algorithm learns from the data, calculates the weights for each variable or generates a linear hypothesis which it uses to score the vital parameters	A patient status index is calculated from the data provided; k clustering means are calculated from history data	Uses knowledge base to score the patients (the algorithm uses expert knowledge to score the patients)	(i) Uses the knowledge based system to score the data before training and (ii) Algorithm learns from the data, with input and output. From examples, the algorithm can predict output for any other input if given enough examples to train it

3   Deployment Scenario and Validation

Two set of experiments were conducted to complement the models proposed in [1,3,8] with (i) an additional assessment of the field readiness of the bio-sensor devices used in our study and (ii) a comparison of supervised and unsupervised machine learning techniques when performing patient prioritisation. The underlying deployment scenario consists of a smart village with bio-sensing devices used to collect patients' vital signs in Cyber-healthcare kiosks which are networked to transmit the vital signs to a situation awareness gateway/server where patient condition recognition is performed following the illustration of Fig. 1.

3.1   Sensors Field Readiness

The most common method used to test sensor-field readiness has been to perform experiments and comparing the results with other devices that have been declared field ready according to recognised standards. The experiments were conducted by looking at readings of bio-sensor devices to see whether results would be within normal ranges of such group of individuals. In cases where results were not within normal ranges, calibrations were performed to obtain realistic values, given that the sensors were prototype sensors. This research could have been improved largely by collecting vital signs of participants at various points of the day e.g. morning or after gym and analysing this information whilst taking into consideration the normal behaviour of the vital signs in each case [1]. This paper complements the work done in [1] by a cross sectional pilot study conducted on masters students at the university of Western Cape. Opportunity sampling was done to recruit participants due to the pilot nature of the study. Vital parameters were monitored by Arduino sensors as well as manually and data was compared to assess the field-readiness of the Arduino sensors. Data was analysed using Pearson's correlation coefficient. The experimental results are reported below:

Systolic Blood Pressure: As revealed by Fig. 3, the mean systolic blood pressure fell within the normal range for all participants except participant three who had a systolic blood pressure greater than 120 mmHg. The Pearson correlation coefficient is 0.984449.

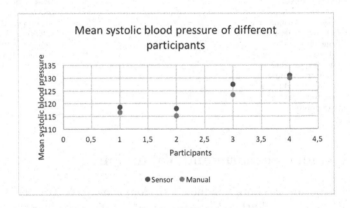

Fig. 3. Systolic blood pressure

Diastolic Blood Pressure: Figure 4 reveals that the mean diastolic blood pressure for all participants was normal. Pearson's correlation coefficient is 0.778418.

Oxygen Saturation: As shown in Fig. 5, the oxygen saturation for all participants fell within the normal range of 94–100% except those taken by the manual sats monitor for participants one and four. The Pearson correlation coefficient is 0.946335.

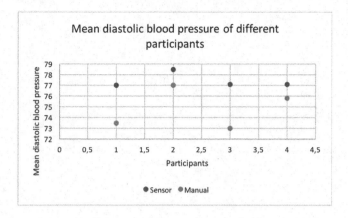

Fig. 4. Diastolic blood pressure

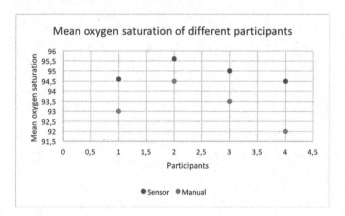

Fig. 5. Oxygen saturation

Heart Rate: The results displayed in Fig. 6 revealed that all heart rates fell within the normal range of 60–100. The Pearson correlation coefficient is 0.999676.

Temperature: The experiments conducted on temperature are reported in Fig. 7. They reveal that all temperature readings were within the normal range. The Pearson correlation coefficient is 0.46992.

A summary of results is presented below:

Blood Pressure Results Summary: The Pearson correlation coefficient for systolic and diastolic blood pressures of 0.984449 and 0.778418, respectively, revealed a strong correlation between the values received when using the Arduino sensors vs the manual sphygmomanometer. Therefore, the sensors ability to detect blood pressure may be described as similar to the manual sphygmomanometer. Studies looking at the accuracy of blood pressure readings in

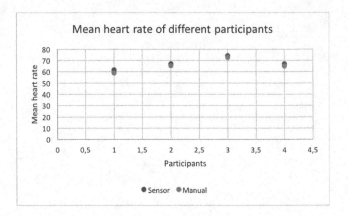

Fig. 6. Heart rate

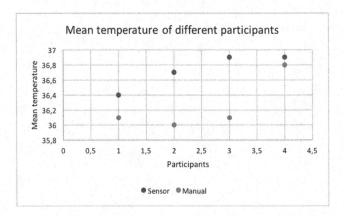

Fig. 7. Heart rate

sphygmomanometers vs digital devices have shown that using a stethoscope and sphygmomanometer produces more accurate results than when taken with digital devices18. Therefore, the strong correlation between the sensors and the manual sphygmomanometer show that the sensors are reliable.

Oxygen Saturation Results Summary: There was a strong correlation between the values received from the Arduino sensors and that of the pulse oximeters. A study by Milner and Matthews looking at the accuracy of pulse oximeters revealed that many pulse oximeters are inaccurate due to flaws with the mechanical electrical integrity or due to emission spectra inaccuracy. This study only examined a small proportion of pulse oximeters used in a few hospitals in the UK and may not necessarily be a true projection of the pulse oximeters used within this pilot study. Therefore, although the adequacy of the pulse oximeter used in the study may still be in question, it may be stated that the sensors, when compared to the pulse oximeter used in the study, produces similar results [17].

Heart Rate Results Summary: There was a very strong correlation between the heart rate taken by the sensors and that taken manually. Although manual palpation of heart rate may factor in human error, the palpation of heart rate for one full minute and ensuring supine position of participants, as mentioned in a study by Kobayashi, was done to decrease human error [18].

Temperature Results Summary: There is a moderately positive correlation between the values taken by the Arduino sensors and thermometer. This may be due to the type of thermometer used (auditory thermometer) as well as various other reasons such as an underlying ear infection, wax build up or the angle at which the thermometer was held.

3.2 Patient Prioritisation

The comparison of the four machine learning techniques described in Table 1 is reported in Table 2. Table 2 reveals through experimental results that the K-means clustering is slower than the other algorithms and through analysis that it presents issues of convergence. It should hence be less preferred compared to supervised learning techniques.

Table 2. Machine learning performance

	Multivariate linear regression	K-means clustering	Knowledge based	Support vector machine
Efficiency	(i) Not affected by amount of data and (ii) Algorithm is able to learn data patterns and generates a hypothesis	Affected by the amount of data, algorithm becomes slow if a large number of cluster centers are required, may also fail to converge (requires a lot of data to train without problems)	Not affected by amount of data	Algorithm is able to learn data patterns and predict a label
Time complexity	0.01425 min	0.237 min for 10 cluster centers	0.0034167 min	0.1701666 min

4   Conclusion and Future Work

A Cyber-healthcare kiosk model with its underlying multi-layer IoT-based framework has been presented in this paper and its relevance revealed through a study of the field readiness of the bio-sensor devices used by the model and the application of machine learning techniques complementing the model with patient prioritisation.

4.1   Summary of Results

Field Readiness. The field readiness study aimed at finding a correlation between vital parameters taken by Arduino sensors vs manual detection was assessed. The results revealed strong correlations between manually derived vital parameters and those taken by Arduino sensors. These results revealed that strong correlations existed for the measurements of blood pressure, heart rate and oxygen saturation whilst a moderately positive correlation existed for the temperature measurement. However, even though sensor reliability was displayed, the lack of condition variability testing and possible measurement bias may be factors that influenced results and should be looked at in future studies. Findings from this study indicate that with further testing these sensors could be used in public health facilities to provide accurate and reliable readings which may be used in medical decision making to bring about better health outcomes.

Machine Learning. Four different machine learning techniques were compared to assess the relevance of using the unsupervised learning (K-means clustering) technique compared to three supervised learning techniques: multi-linear regression, knowledge based and support vector machine. The analysis and results revealed that supervised learning techniques were faster in terms time complexity and were a better fit for patient prioritisation compared to the unsupervised learning technique.

4.2   Study Limitations

Some of the limitations of the work presented in this paper include:

Population: Due to the pilot nature of the study, a small sample was used to carry out the sensor readiness experiment. A larger sample would have increased reliability of the results. Lack of variability in population (various ages, different health statuses, various ethnicities) meant that there was very little variation in results.

Condition Variability Testing: Sensor operability in variable conditions was not tested. This would have provided greater knowledge about performance of the equipment in different conditions.

Human Error: Human error in the manual capturing of information must be considered as this may have affected the results received thereby decreasing reliability of results.

Measurement Bias: Measurement bias is a factor that may have come into play as vital parameters were taken manually and values may have been over- or underestimated.

4.3   Future Work

Future work will extend the work presented in this paper to cater for the limitations described above and consider traffic and network engineering aspects of the Cyber-Healthcare framework to enable efficient sharing of the health information among patients and medical practitioners.

Moving the traffic from the Cyber-healthcare kiosks to the local cloud where the situation recognition server performs patient condition recognition is a challenging aspect of the Cyber-healthcare model which can be solved by enhancing connection-oriented traditional traffic engineering techniques such as described in [19] to set traffic pipes between kiosks and cloud with the possibility of carrying both classic and IoT traffic and or emerging traffic engineering techniques such as in [20] and route discover mechanisms [21] to carry only IoT traffic from kiosks to the situation awareness server. Furthermore, the organisation of the network of Cyber-healthcare kiosks is another challenging issue that can be tackled by network engineering techniques borrowed from [22]. These techniques are an avenue for future research. Using drones for the transport of blood samples and data between Cyber-Healthcare kiosks is an effective way of adding value and enhancing the services provided to citizens in a smart village. The implementation of such services following the model and framework described in [25] is another direction for future work.

References

1. Participatory Healthcare systems (Sensing and Data Dissemination). Masters thesis. University of Western Cape (2014)
2. Buckland, D.: Future of healthcare. Raconteur (0396), 3–5 (2018)
3. Mandava, M., Lubamba, C., Ismail, A., Bagula, H., Bagula, A.: Cyber-healthcare for public healthcare in the developing world. In: Proceedings of the 2016 IEEE Symposium on Computers and Communication (ISCC), pp. 14–19. IEEE (2016)
4. Bagula, A., Mandava, M., Bagula, H.: A framework for healthcare support in rural and isolated areas. J. Netw. Commun. Appl. (JNCA) (2018)
5. Manthorpe, R.: Meet Olivia, the virtual nurse on duty. Raconteur (0396), 6–7 (2016)
6. Robertson-Steel, I.: Evolution of triage systems. Emerg. Med. J. **23**(2), 154–155 (2006). https://www.ncbi.nlm.nih.gov/pmc/articles/PMC2564046/. Accessed 2 Feb 2018
7. Goldstein, L., et al.: The accuracy of nurse performance of the triage process in a tertiary hospital emergency department in Gauteng Province, South Africa. S. Afr. Med. J. **107**(3), 243 (2017). https://pdfs.semanticscholar.org/2b1e/2bf934ba01207943b02001916ebb3ceed070.pdf. Accessed 2 Feb 2018
8. Bagula, A., Lubamba, C., Mandava, M., Bagula, H., Zennaro, M., Pietrosemoli, E.: Cloud based patient prioritization as service in public health care. In: Proceedings of the ITU Kaleidoscope 2016, Bangkok, Thailand, 14–16 November 2016. IEEE (2016)

9. Alam, M., Hamida, E.: Surveying wearable human assistive technology for life and safety critical applications: standards, challenges and opportunities. Sensors **14**(12), 9153–9209 (2014)
10. Pediatric Emergencies and Resuscitation [Internet]. Clinical Gate (2018). https:// clinicalgate.com/pediatric-emergencies-and-resuscitation/. Accessed 1 Feb 2018
11. Clinical assessment of patients suspected to have ischemic chest pain [Internet]. Cursoenarm.net (2011). http://cursoenarm.net/UPTODATE/contents/mobipreview.htm?15/40/16006. Accessed 1 Feb 2018
12. Mingle, D.R.: Machine learning techniques on microbiome-based diagnostics. Adv. Biotechnol. Microbiol. **6**(4) (2017)
13. Celesti, A., Fazio, M., Celesti, F., Sannino, G., Campo, S., Villari, M.: New trends in biotechnology: the point on NGS cloud computing solutions [Internet]. IEEE Computer Society (2016). https://www.computer.org/csdl/proceedings/iscc/2016/0679/00/07543751-abs.html. Accessed 2 Feb 2018
14. Hornby, A., Deuter, M.: Oxford Advanced Learner's Dictionary of Current English. Oxford University Press [u.a.], Oxford [u.a.] (2015)
15. Joglekar, P., Kulkarni, V.: Mobile crowd sensing for urban computing. Int. J. Latest Trends Eng. Technol. **7**(4), 344–351 (2016)
16. Shahbabu, B.: Which is more accurate in measuring the blood pressure? A digital or an aneroid sphygmomanometer. J. Clin. Diagn. Res. **10**(3), LC11–LC14 (2016)
17. Milner, Q., Mathews, G.: An assessment of the accuracy of pulse oximeters. Anaesthesia **67**(4), 396–401 (2012)
18. Kobayashi, H.: Effect of measurement duration on accuracy of pulse-counting. Ergonomics **56**(12), 1940–1944 (2013)
19. Bagula, A.: Hybrid traffic engineering: the least path interference algorithm. In: Proceedings of the 2004 Annual Research Conference of the South African Institute of Computer Scientists and Information Technologists on IT Research in Developing Countries (SAICSIT 2004), pp. 89–96 (2004)
20. Bagula, A., Djenouri, D., Karbab, E.: Ubiquitous sensor network management: the least interference beaconing model. In: Proceedings of the 24th IEEE Personal Indoor and Mobile Radio Communications (PIMRC) (2013)
21. Chavula, J., Feamster, N., Bagula, A., Suleman, H.: Quantifying the effects of circuitous routes on the latency of intra-Africa internet traffic: a study of research and education networks. In: Nungu, A., Pehrson, B., Sansa-Otim, J. (eds.) AFRICOMM 2014. LNICSSITE, vol. 147, pp. 64–73. Springer, Cham (2015). https://doi.org/10.1007/978-3-319-16886-9_7
22. Bagula, A., Abidoye, A.P., Zodi, G.L.: Service-aware clustering: an energy-efficient model for the Internet-of-Things. Sensors **16**(1), 9 (2016). https://doi.org/10.3390/s16010009
23. Masinde, M., Bagula, A.: A framework for predicting droughts in developing countries using sensor networks and mobile phones. In: Proceedings of the 2010 Annual Research Conference of the South African Institute of Computer Scientists and Information Technologists, pp. 390–393. ACM (2010)
24. Masinde, M., Bagula, A., Muthama, N.J.: The role of ICTs in downscaling and up-scaling integrated weather forecasts for farmers in sub-Saharan Africa. In: proceedings of ICTD 2012, pp. 122–129. ACM (2012)
25. Chiaraviglio, L., et al.: Bringing 5G into rural and low-income areas: is it feasible? IEEE Commun. Stand. Mag. **1**(3), 50–57 (2017)

Data Model for Cloud Computing Environment

Samson B. Akintoye[1](✉), Antoine B. Bagula[1], Omowumi E. Isafiade[1],
Yacine Djemaiel[2], and Noureddine Boudriga[2]

[1] University of the Western Cape, Cape Town, South Africa
3515640@myuwc.ac.za
[2] CNAS Lab, Cartage University, Tunis, Tunisia
ydjemaiel@gmail.com

Abstract. The emergence of cloud computing has reduced the cost of
deployment and storage dramatically, but only if data can be distributed
across multiple servers easily without disruption. In a complex SQL
database, this is difficult because many queries require multiple large
tables to be joined together to provide a response. Executing distributed
joins is a very complex problem in SQL databases. In addition, previous
studies have shown that NoSQL databases performance better than SQL
databases especially in the cloud computing environment where there is
occurrence of huge volume of data. In this paper, we presents a novel
data model for cloud services brokerage that supports the allocation,
control and management of virtual system based on brokering function
between cloud service providers (CSPs) and cloud users by integrating
and man- aging cloud resources in a heterogeneous cloud environment.
The model is implemented on a private lightweight cloud network using a
graph and document-oriented databases. The experimental results show
that a graph model has better performance than a document-oriented
model in terms of queries execution time.

Keywords: Cloud computing · Graph model ·
Document-oriented model · Cloud Services Brokerage

1 Introduction

Cloud computing has recently emerged as one of the most promising and challenging technologies. It is based on a computing paradigm where a large pool
of systems are connected in private, public or hybrid networks, to provide
dynamically scalable infrastructure for computing resources [19]. The computing
resources are available to the users via the internet [13]. The characteristics of
cloud computing include on-demand self service, broad network access, resource
pooling, rapid elasticity and measured service. On-demand self service means
that organizations can access and manage their own computing resources. Broad

© ICST Institute for Computer Sciences, Social Informatics and Telecommunications Engineering 2019
Published by Springer Nature Switzerland AG 2019. All Rights Reserved
G. Mendy et al. (Eds.): AFRICOMM 2018, LNICST 275, pp. 199–215, 2019.
https://doi.org/10.1007/978-3-030-16042-5_19

network access allows services to be offered over the Internet or private networks. Pooled resources mean that customers draw from a pool of computing resources. Services can be scaled larger or smaller; and use of a service is measured. The cloud computing service models are Software as a Service (SaaS), Platform as a Service (PaaS) and Infrastructure as a Service (IaaS) [10]. In Software as a Service model, consumer uses the provider's applications running on a cloud infrastructure. Example of SaaS is Salesforce [2]. In PaaS, an operating system, hardware, and network are provided, and the customer installs or develops its own software and applications. The most prominent key players of PaaS are Azure platform [8] and Google App Engine [5]. The IaaS model provides just the hardware and network; the customer installs or develops its own operating systems, software and applications. The examples of IaaS are Amazon EC2 service [1], GoGrid [4], Flexiscale [3], and Redplaid [7].

Cloud services are deployed as a private cloud, community cloud, public cloud or hybrid cloud [10]. In public cloud, services are offered over the Internet and are owned and operated by a cloud provider. In a private cloud, the cloud infrastructure is operated solely for a single organization, and is managed by the organization or a third party. In a community cloud, the service is shared by several organizations and made available only to those groups. The infrastructure may be owned and operated by the organizations or by a cloud service provider. A hybrid cloud is a combination of two or more cloud infrastructures (private, community, or public) that remain unique entities, but are bound together by standardized or proprietary technology that enables data and application portability. Virtualization technologies are usually used to access computing resource by the users. Users can specify required software stack such as operating systems, software libraries, and applications, then package them all together into virtual machines (VMs). VMs will be hosted in cloud service providers. Lightweight cloud computing infrastructures combine cloud and grid computing concept to provide a shared infrastructure over commodity hardware such as mobile phones, desktop, tablets, etc. As the cloud computing market expands and the number of users and cloud service providers increases, there is a need for a centralised system [22], called cloud services brokerage (CSB), to optimize resource allocation by managing and monitoring the activities of cloud users and cloud service providers. For the CSB to work efficiently, a reliable database management system needs to be implemented on the CSB site to keep and update the track of customer requests and cloud infrastructures status. Relational database management systems (RDBMS) otherwise known as SQL database cannot cope with the unprecedented scale factors that modern cloud-based applications have introduced. The cloud applications need to support large numbers of concurrent users and be able to handle unstructured and semi-structured data. To solve this problem, NoSQL (Not Only SQL) databases emerge to support large-scale application demands. In addition, previous studies have shown that NoSQL databases perform better than SQL databases especially in the cloud computing environment where there are occurrence of huge volume of data [27].

1.1   Contributions and Outline

In this paper, we present a data model for cloud computing environment to help the CSB support the allocation, control and management of virtual resources between CSPs and cloud users. We implement this model using the graph database (Neo4j) and document-oriented database (mongodb) on our private lightweight cloud testbed, using a syntactic of cypher language to store, update and retrieve the customer requests and cloud infrastructures status in the database. Building upon the free and open source OpenStack software platform for cloud computing, the model is intended to provide infrastructure-as-a-service (IaaS) in community sensor networks [29] for applications such as drought mitigation for small scale farming [30,31] and cyber healthcare [32,33] in the rural areas of the developing countries. Potential applications which might also benefit from this model include smart parking [34], pollution monitoring [35] and public safety [36] in the smart developing cities. The rest of this paper is organized as follows; In Sect. 2, we describe the concept of cloud service brokerage system. The next section presents previous studies related to the management of virtual resources information in data center and cloud computing. Section 4 describes proposed cloud computing environment model. The data model of cloud computing environment is presented in Sect. 5. Implementation of the models and experimental results are found in Sects. 6 and 7, and finally, we conclude the paper in Sect. 8.

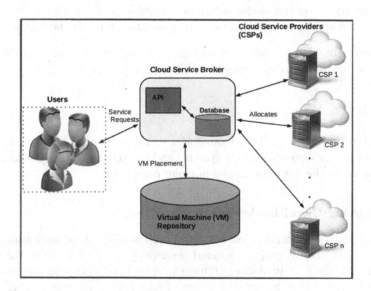

Fig. 1. Cloud computing environment

2   Cloud Services Brokerage

As depicted in Fig. 1, the cloud computing environment considered in this paper consists of user, virtual machine repository (VMR), and cloud services broker and CSP, which consists of physical machines (PM) and data center (DC). A cloud services broker is a third-party individual or business acting as a middle man between cloud service users and CSPs. Cloud service brokers rent different types of cloud resources from many cloud Service providers and sublet these resources to the requesting cloud users. The cloud service broker performs the following functions: (i) optimal placement of the virtual resource of a virtual infrastructure across multiple cloud service providers; (ii) management and monitoring of these virtual resources; and (iii) aggregation of multiple cloud services into one or more customer-tailored cloud services. OPTIMIS [6] identifies the requirement and capabilities that a cloud service broker needs to have in order to play the role of brokerage services:

- Effectively match the requirements of the cloud user with the service provided by the CSPs.
- Negotiate with CSPs and cloud users over service level agreements (SLA).
- Effectively deploy services of CSP onto the cloud users.
- Maintain performance check on these SLA's and take actions against SLA violations.
- Ensure data confidentiality and integrity of CSP's service.
- Enforce access control decisions uniformly across multiple CSPs.
- Securely map identity and access management systems of the CSPs.

However, an effective database management system needs to be included as one of the functional components of a CSB.

3   Related Work

This section presents two broad categories of related work. The first category discusses existing cloud brokerage systems and the second category presents the related work to the database model in cloud computing.

3.1   Existing Cloud Brokerage Systems

Many broker-based systems have been proposed to solve cloud computing problems. Heilig et al. [16] propose a cloud brokerage approach to solve the Cloud Resource Management Problem in multi-cloud environments with aim to reduce the monetary cost and the execution time of consumer applications using Infrastructure as a Service of multiple cloud providers. In [15], the authors propose a broker-based architecture and algorithm for placing and migrating virtual resources to physical machines. In [20], the authors propose a federated cloud computing environment in which a cloud broker has the ability to interface more than one cloud provider to support several users. These Users access cloud services via web interface. The cloud service broker pays the usage of the cloud resources to the cloud service provider, and charges the user for these resources. In [25], a solution to manage the information of a large number of cloud service providers via a unique indexing technique is proposed. STRATOS [21] proposes a cloud brokerage service that solves a Resource Acquisition Decision (RAD) problem in the selection of n resources from m cloud services. In [18] develops a cloud brokerage service for measuring the performance of a range of cloud services including; elastic compute clusters, persistent storage, intra-cloud networking and wide-area networking. [17] proposes a novel secure sharing mechanism for a secure cloud bursting and aggregation operation in which the cloud resources are shared in a confidential manner among different cloud environments.

3.2 Database Model in Cloud Computing

Goli-Malekabadi et al. [14] proposes an effective database model for storing and retrieving big health data in cloud computing. The study presents the model based on NoSQL databases for the storage of healthcare data and was implemented in the cloud environment for gaining access to the distribution properties. The experimental results of the model was evaluated with relational database model in terms of query execution time, data preparation, flexibility and extensibility parameter. The results show that the proposed model outperforms the relational database. In [28], the authors propose a novel protocol to enable secure and efficient database outsourcing. First, the authors propose a new cloud database model by introducing computation service providers which can accommodate the conventional DBaaS model and introduce a proposed database outsourcing protocol secureDBS which uses a secret sharing mechanism. The experiments conducted show that the proposed model is reliable, secure and efficient. In [12], the authors propose a novel management scheme that enables the representation and the retrieval of (structured or unstructured) big data using conceptual graphs and structured marks. Curino et al. [11] proposes relational database as-a-service for the cloud. This work describes the challenges and requirements of a large-scale, multi-node DBaaS and presents the design principles and implementation status of relational cloud. The advantage of this work is that it addresses three significant challenges, which are: (i) efficient multi-tenancy; (ii) elastic scalability; and (iii) database privacy.

However, none of these works have proposed a graph data model and its implementation using graph database as of the requirement for the effectively cloud brokerage services.

4   Cloud Computing Environment Model

In this section, we introduce the system model for our cloud computing environment. As depicted in Fig. 1, the cloud computing environment consists of User, Virtual Machine Repository (VMR), Cloud Service Provider (CSP), Physical Machines (PM), Data Center (DC) and Cloud Services Broker (CSB).

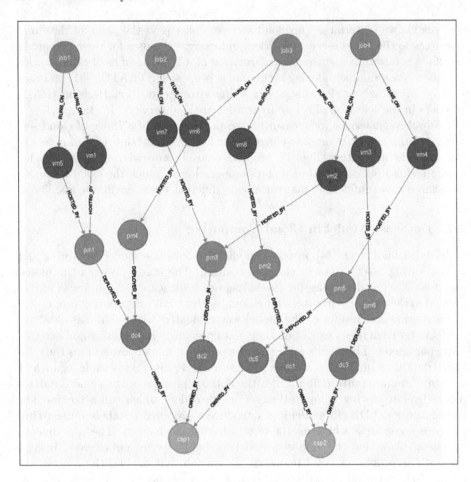

Fig. 2. Graph model for cloud computing environment

We consider a set CSP,

$$CSP = \{csp_1, csp_2....csp_n\} \tag{1}$$

where n is the number of CSPs managed by the CSB. Each CSP consists of DC,

$$DC = \{dc_1, dc_2....dc_m\} \tag{2}$$

where m is the number of DCs in a CSP and each DC contains a member of PMs,

$$PM = \{pm_1, pm_2....pm_q\} \tag{3}$$

where q is the number of PM in a DC and each PM hosts t number of VMs as expressed by the set

$$VM = \{vm_1, vm_2....vm_t\} \tag{4}$$

We consider that K jobs need to be allocated to CSPs. Each job k requires w_j number of virtual machines. The CSB allocation is expressed by the notation

$$k \longrightarrow vm_{w_j} \tag{5}$$

subject to $w_j = 1$ or $w_j \leq t$. Each vm is placed in one pm,

$$vm \longrightarrow pm \tag{6}$$

Each pm is hosted by one data center dc,

$$pm \longrightarrow dc \tag{7}$$

Finally, each data center is owned by one cloud service provider (csp),

$$dc \longrightarrow csp \tag{8}$$

5 Data Model of Cloud Computing Environment

There are many different NoSQL data models and each one of them has a different structure. In this section, we present the deployment of graph and document-oriented models for cloud computing environments.

5.1 Graph Model

Graph data models have emerged with the objective of modeling information whose structure is a graph [9]. It encodes entities and relationships between entities using directed graph structure [23]. It is a set of vertices and edges where vertices denote nodes and edges represent relationship between these Nodes. Graphs are data structures for storing data that is heterogeneously structured. Graphs can be directed or undirected. Undirected graphs can be traversed in both directions while directed graphs can be traversed only in one direction. The properties of a graph model includes the following [24];

- It contains nodes and relationships.
- Nodes contain properties (key-value pairs).
- Nodes can be labelled with one or more labels.
- Relationships are named and directed, and always have a start and end node.
- Relationships can also contain properties.

The graph model of cloud computing environment can be represented mathematically as a graph $G(V, E)$ where V is the set of resource nodes and E is the set of relationships between the nodes such that,

$$\{CSP, DC, PM, VM, K\} \subset V \tag{9}$$

Constrained by the notation:

$$|DC| \geq |CSP| \tag{10}$$

$$|VM| \geq |PM| \tag{11}$$

$$|K| \geq |VM| \tag{12}$$

The relationships between the nodes of the graph (V, E) are defined as follows:

- $csp \to dc$ represents the relationship between cloud service provider and data center.
- $dc \to pm$ represents the relationship between data center and physical machine.
- $pm \to vm$ represents the relationship between physical machine and virtual machine.
- $vm \to k$ represents the relationship between virtual machine and job.

Such that,

$$csp \to dc, dc \to pm, pm \to vm, vm \to k \subset E \tag{13}$$

The graph is illustrated by Fig. 2.

5.2   Document-Oriented Database

In a document-oriented model, data objects are stored as documents; each document stores data which can be updated or deleted. Instead of columns with names and data types, data is described in the document, and provide the value for that description. The difference between a relational model and a document-oriented model is as follows: in a relational model, data is added by modifying the database schema to include the additional columns and their data types while in document-based data, additional key-value pairs will be added into documents to represent the new fields. The document-oriented model for cloud computing environment is represented in Fig. 3.

6   Experiments

We conducted two different experiment in order to evaluate the both graph and document-oriented models on a proxy node of our private lightweight cloud testbed running on Openstack architecture. The proxy node is a Linux Machine with an Inter(R) core(TM) i5-4590, 3.30 Ghz CPU, 8 GB RAM and serves as a cloud brokerage system which initiate upload and download operations across multiple storage nodes. The CSB can update the cloud resources status in database either manually or through real-time process by building Application Protocol Interface (API) connecting cloud infrastructures to a database. We explore the suitability of two different databases in a cloud environment, the database are: (i) graph database: Neo4j; and document-oriented database: MongoDB respectively.

```
{
    "_id":ObjectId(),
    "job_id": "Job identity",
    "name": "name of job",
    "length": "length of the job",
    "file-size" : "size of the job",
    "VIRTUALMACHINE" : [
        {
            "vm_id" : "VM identity",
            "name" : "name of VM",
            "mips" : "value of mips",
            "ram" : "valus of ram"
            "PHYSICALMACHINE": [
                {
                    "pm_id": "PM identity",
                    "name" : "name of pm",
                    "storage" : "value of storage",
                    "ram" : "value of ram",
                    "mips" : "value of mips"
                    "DATACENTER": [
                        {
                            "center_id": "center identity",
                            "name" : "name of center",
                            "OS" : "OS",
                            "location" : "location",
                            "arch" : "Arch",
                            "time_zone" : "Time zone",
                            "CLOUDPROVIDER" : [
                                {
                                    "csp_id": "provider ID",
                                    "name": "provider name"
                                    "cost_per_BW": "value",
                                    "cost": "value"
                                }
                            ]
                        }
                    ]
                }
            ]
        }
    ]
}
```

Fig. 3. Document-oriented model for cloud computing environment

6.1   Implementation of Graph Database

Graph databases are databases that support graph model. One of the examples of graph database is Neo4j and it can be accessed using cypher query language. The graph database is implemented using Neo4j Community version 3.0.1.

The database contains nodes with labels, properties and relationship between them as follows:

- csp('CLOUDPROVIDER', cspid, name, cost, costPerMem, costPerStorage, costPerBw)
- dc('DATACENTER', name, centerid, location, arch, os, time_zone)
- pm('PHYSICALMACHINE', name, pmid, mips, ram, bw, storage)
- vm('VIRTUALMACHINE', name, vmid, mips, ram)
- job('JOB', job_id, name, length, filesize).

6.2   Cypher Query Language

Here, we discuss the Cypher syntax to create and retrieve nodes and relationships in graph database.

- Cypher syntax to create Nodes and relationship.
  - Create Datacenter, Cloud provider nodes and relationship between them.

    CREATE (dc1:DATACENTER{ name ='dc1', centerid =1, location ='Capetown', arch = "x86", os ="Linux", time-zone = 10.0 }) -[:OWNED-BY]-> (csp:CLOUDPROVIDER { name = 'csp1', cspid = 0, cost = 3.0, costPerMem = 0.05, costPerStorage = 0.001, costPerBw = 0.0 })

  - Create Datacenter, Physical Machine nodes and relationship between them.

    CREATE (pm:PHYSICALMACHINE{ name ='pm1', pmid = 0, mips = 1000, ram = 20148, bw = 1000, storage = 1000000 }) -[:DEPLOYED-IN]-> dc1:DATACENTER { name = 'dc1', centerid = 1, location = 'Capetown', arch = "x86", os = "Linux", time-zone = 10.0 })

  - Create Virtual Machine, Physical Machine nodes and relationship between them.

    CREATE (vm:VIRTUALMACHINE{ name = 'vm1', vmid = 0, mips = 250, ram = 20148 } -[:HOSTED-BY]-> dc1:DATACENTER { name = 'dc1', centerid = 1, location = 'Capetown', arch = "x86", os = "Linux", time-zone = 10.0 })

  - Create Virtual Machine, Job nodes and relationship between them.

    CREATE (job:JOB{ app_id = 0, name = 'job1', length = 4000, filesize = 24 -[:RUNS-ON]-> vm:VIRTUALMACHINE { name = 'vm1', vmid = 0, mips = 250, ram = 20148 }).

- Cypher queries to retrieve information from graph database.
  - *Query 1:* Find all Virtual Machines assigned to Jobs.

    MATCH (a)-[:RUNS_ON]->(b) RETURN a.name as JOB, b.name as VIRTUALMACHINE;

- *Query 2:* Find name of resources owned by Cloud Service Providers.

MATCH (b)-[:HOSTED_BY]->
(c)-[:DEPLOYED_IN]-> (d)-[:OWNED_BY]->
(e:CLOUDPROVIDER) RETURN b.name as VIRTUALMACHINE,
c.name as PHYSICALMACHINE,
d.name as DATACENTER, e.name as CLOUDPROVIDER;

- *Query 3:* Find all resources used by job 1.

MATCH   (a:JOB{name:'job1'})-[:RUNS_ON]->(b)-[:HOSTED_BY]-
>(c) -[:DEPLOYED_IN]->(d)-[:OWNED_BY]->(e) RETURN a as
JOB, b as VIRTUALMACHINE, c as PHYSICALMACHINE, d as DAT-
ACENTER, e as CLOUDPROVIDER;

6.3 Document-Oriented Database

Document-oriented databases are one of the NoSQL databases. A document-oriented database is designed for storing, retrieving, and managing document-oriented, or semi structured data. The main concept of a document-oriented database is the notion of a Document. MongoDB, CouchDB and Terrastore are examples of the Document-oriented databases. In this work, document-oriented database is implemented using MongoDB shell version: 2.4.9. Mongodb is very famous NoSQL databases in the data industry [26]. All the formats are loaded in JSON format. In MongoDB, data is grouped into sets that are called collections. Each collection has a unique name in the database, and can contain an unlimited number of documents. Collections are similar to tables in a relational database, except that they do not have any defined schema.

MongoDB Query Language. The Queries to create and retrieve collections in MongoDB re discussed below.

- Commands to create Collections. In MongoDB, there is no need to create collection. MongoDB creates collection automatically, when inserting document.
  - Create JOB collection

    db.JOB.insert({ job_id : 0, name : 'app1', length : 4000, file-size : 24,
    vm_id : 0 })
  - Create Virtual Machine collection

    db.VIRTUALMACHINE.insert({ vm_id : 0, job_id : 0, name : 'vmm1',
    mips : 250, ram : 20148, pm_id : 0 })
  - Create Physical Machine collection

    db.PHYSICALMACHINE.insert({ pm_id : 0, job_id : 0, name : 'pm1',
    mips : 1000, ram : 20148, storage : 10000, vm_id : 0, center_id : 0 })

- Create Data center collection

    db.DATACENTER.insert({ center_id : 0, pm_id : 0, name : 'dc1', OS : Linux, location : 'Durban', arch : 'x86', time_zone : 10, csp_id : 0 })
- Create Cloud Provider collection

    db.CLOUDPROVIDER.insert(csp_id : 0, center_id : 0, name : 'csp1', cost_per_BW : 0, cost_per_storage : 1, cost : 3 })
- Mongodb queries to retrieve information from relational database.
- *Query 1:* Find all Virtual Machines assigned to Jobs.

    db.VIRTUALMACHINE.find({ JOB: { vm_id: [0, 1, 2, 3, 4, 5, 6, 7, 8, 9, 10, 11, 12, 13, 14, 15, 16, 17, 18, 19, 20, 21, 22, 23] } })
- *Query 2:* Find name of resources owned by Cloud Service Providers.

```
db.CLOUDPROVIDER.aggregate([
  { $ match: { _id: ObjectId("5901a4c63541b7d5d3293766") } },
  {
   $ lookup:
   {
    from: "DATACENTER",
    localField: "center_id",
    foreignField: "center_id",
    as: "DATACENTER"
   },
  {
   $ lookup:
   {
    from: "PHYSICALMACHINE",
    localField: "pm_id",
    foreignField: "pm_id",
    as: "PHYSICALMACHINE"
   },
  {
   $ lookup:
   {
    from: "VIRTUALMACHINE",
    localField: "vm_id",
    foreignField: "vm_id",
    as: "VIRTUALMACHINE"
   }
])
```

- *Query 3:* Find all resources used by job 1.

```
db.JOB.aggregate([
  { $ match: { name: "job1") } },
  {
  $ lookup:
  {
   from: "VIRTUALMACHINE",
   localField: "vm_id",
   foreignField: "vm_id",
   as: "VIRTUALMACHINE"
  },
  {
  $ lookup:
  {
   from: "PHYSICALMACHINE",
   localField: "pm_id",
   foreignField: "pm_id",
   as: "PHYSICALMACHINE"
  },
  {
  $ lookup:
  {
   from: "DATACENTER",
   localField: "center_id",
   foreignField: "center_id",
   as: "DATACENTER"
  },
  {
  $ lookup:
  {
   from: "CLOUDPROVIDER",
   localField: "csp_id",
   foreignField: "csp_id",
   as: "CLOUDPROVIDER"
  }
```

Table 1. Cloud computing entities

	Case 1	Case 2
Number of Cloud Service Providers (CSP)	2	5
Number of Data Center (DC)	4	10
Number of Physical Machine (PM)	12	30
Number of Virtual Machine (VM)	24	60
Number of job	48	120

Table 2. Comparison of graph and document-oriented databases

Queries	Databases	Response times (ms)	
		Case 1	Case 2
1	Neo4j	7.1	9.6
	Mongodb	4.5	7.2
2	Neo4j	8.6	11.8
	Mongodb	5.6	9.8
3	Neo4j	6.3	8.4
	Mongodb	4.7	6.1

7   Experimental Results

We consider two cases as shown in Table 1. where the number of cloud infrastructures are varied. We run each query 5 times on each database for the two
cases, execution time are recorded and the average of the execution times are
calculated for each query. All times are measured in milliseconds. The result for
the queries on the databases are presented in Table 2.

It can be observed from the values in Table 2 that the times taken to process
queries for mongoDB are less when compared to that of Neo4j. For instance, in
case 1 and query 2, mongoDB takes 5.6 ms while Neo4j takes 8.6 ms. Further
analysis of the results show that the time taken to process case 1 and query 2
on MongoDB is less by 28% than that of Neo4j. It can also be deduced from
the results that as the number of cloud computing elements increases, the query
processing times gets increased manifoldly. More specifically, the time taken to
process queries for case 2 is higher than that of case 1 due to the varied increased
parameter in case 2 as opposed to lower parameter values in case 1.

8   Conclusion and Future Work

Cloud service brokerage system is a third party system that acts as a middleman
between users and cloud service providers. However, for cloud service brokers to
remain relevant in the cloud computing era, there is need to adopt an effective database model that can withstand the unprecedented demand from cloud
users and providers. Hence in this research, we present a novel data model and
explore the suitability of these database models in a cloud computing environment. The models are: (i) graph; and (ii) document-oriented models. We implement the models on our private cloud network testbed using Neo4j and MongoDB
databases respectively. We also present query syntax to retrieve information from
the databases. Finally, we compare the efficiency of the these database models in
terms of query processing time, and varied the experimental parameters in order
to establish the suitability of the models in a cloud computing environment. The
experiment results show that document-oriented model has better performance

in a cloud computing environment than graph modes, in terms of queries processing time. Ultimately, MongoDB emerges as the most suitable database model with respect to flexibility, elastic scalability, high performance, and availability [37–39].

In future, an optimization module can be developed on top of mongoDB database in cloud service brokerage system. The module will interface the system with cloud service providers and updating the status of cloud resources in the database.

References

1. Amazon Elastic Compute Cloud (amazon ec2). http://aws.amazon.com/ec2/
2. Crm-salesforce.com. http://www.salesforce.com/
3. Flexiscale. http://www.flexiscale.com
4. Gogrid. http://www.gogrid.com/
5. Google App Engine. http://code.google.com/appengine/
6. Optimis - Optimized Infrastructure Service. http://optimis-project.eu/
7. Redplaid Managed Hosting. http://www.redplaid.com
8. Windows Azure Platform. http://www.microsoft.com/windowsazure/
9. Angles, R., Gutierrez, C.: Survey of graph database models. J. ACM Comput. Surv. (CSUR) **40**(1), 1 (2008)
10. Badger, L., Grance, T., Comer, R.P., Voas, J.: Draft cloud computing synopsis and recommendations. Recommendations of National Institute of Standards and Technology (NIST), May 2012
11. Curino, C., et al.: Relational cloud: a database service for the cloud. In: CIDR, pp. 235–240 (2011)
12. Djemaiel, Y., Essaddi, N., Boudriga, N.: Optimizing big data management using conceptual graphs: a mark-based approach. In: The proceedings of the 17th International Conference on Business Information Systems (BIS 2014), Larnaca, Cyprus (2014)
13. Foster, I., Zhao, Y., Raicu, I., Lu, S.: Cloud computing and grid computing 360-degree compared. In: Proceedings of Grid Computing Environments Workshop (GCE) (2008)
14. Goli-Malekabadi, Z., Sargolzaei-Javan, M., Albari, M.K.: An effective model for store and retrieve big health data in cloud computing. J. Comput. Methods Programs Biomed. **132**, 75–82 (2016)
15. Grit, L., Irwin, D., Yumerefendi, A., Chase, J.: Virtual machine hosting for networked clusters: building the foundations for autonomic orchestration. In: Proceeding of IEEE International Workshop on Virtualization Technology in Distributed Computing (VTDC), November 2006
16. Heilig, L., Lalla-Ruiz, E., Voß, S.: Cloud brokerage approach for solving the resource management problem in multi-cloud environments. J. Comput. Ind. Eng. **95**, 16–26 (2016)
17. Jain, P., Rane, D., Patidar, S.: A novel cloud bursting brokerage and aggregation (CBBA) algorithm for multi cloud environment. In: Proceedings of IEEE Second International Conference on Advanced Computing and Communication Technologies, ACCT, pp. 383–387. IEEE (2012)

18. Li, A., Yang, X., Kandula, S., Zhang, M.: CloudCmp: comparing public cloud providers. In: Proceedings of the 10th ACM SIGCOMM Conference on Internet Measurement, IMC, New York, USA, pp. 1–14, June 2010
19. Mell, P., Grance, T.: The NIST definition of cloud computing. National Institute of Standards and Technology (2015). http://www.nist.gov/itl/cloud. Accessed 10 Feb 2015
20. Nair, S.K., Porwal, S., Dimitrakos, T., Rajarajan, M., Khan, A.U.: Towards secure cloud bursting, brokerage and aggregation. In: Proceeding of IEEE 8th European Conference on Web Services, ECOWS, pp. 18–196. IEEE (2010)
21. Pawluk, P., Simmons, B., Smit, M., Litoiu, M., Mankovski, S.: Introducing STRATOS: a cloud broker service. In: IEEE 5th International Conference Cloud Computing (CLOUD), pp. 891–898, June 2012
22. Perry, J., Ousterhout, A., Balakrishnan, H., Shah, D.: Fastpass: a centralized zero-queue datacenter network. In: ACM SIGCOMM 2014, August 2014
23. Angles, R., Gutierrez, C.: Survey of graph database models. J. ACM Comput. Surv. (CSUR) **40**(1), 1 (2008)
24. Robinson, I., Webber, J., Eifrem, E.: Graph Databases. O'Reilly Media Inc., Sebastopol (2015)
25. Sundareswaran, S., Squicciarini, A., Lin, D.: A brokerage-based approach for cloud service selection. In: Proceeding of IEEE 5th International Conference on Cloud Computing, CLOUD, pp. 558–565. IEEE (2012)
26. Chodorow, K., Dirolf, M.: MongoDB: The Definitive Guide, 1st edn., p. 216. O'Reilly Media, Sebastopol (2010)
27. Vicknair, C., Macias, M., Zhao, Z., Nan, X., Chen, Y., Wilkins, D.: A comparison of a graph database and a relational database: a data provenance perspective. In: ACM SE 2010 Proceedings of the 48th Annual Southeast Regional Conference, Oxford, Mississippi, April 2010
28. Xiang, T., Lib, X., Chenc, F., Guob, S., Yang, Y.: Processing secure, verifiable and efficient SQL over outsourced database. J. Inf. Sci. **348**, 163–178 (2016)
29. Zennaro, M., Pehrson, B., Bagula, A.B.: Wireless Sensor Networks: a great opportunity for researchers in Developing Countries. In: The Proceedings of WCITD 2008 Conference, Pretoria, South Africa, October 2008
30. Masinde, M., Bagula, A.: A framework for redirecting droughts in developing countries using sensor networks and mobile phones. In: Proceedings of the 2010 Annual Research Conference of the South African Institute of Computer Scientists and Information Technologists, pp. 390–393. ACM (2010)
31. Masinde, M., Bagula, A., Muthama, N.J.: The role of ICTs in downscaling and up-scaling integrated weather forecasts for farmers in sub-saharan Africa. In: Proceedings of the Fifth International Conference on Information and Communication Technologies and Development, pp. 122–129. ACM (2012)
32. Bagula, A., et al.: Cloud based patient prioritization as service in public health care. In: Proceedings of the ITU Kaleidoscope 2016, Bangkok, Thailand, 14–16 November 2016, pp. 122–129. IEEE (2016)
33. Mandava, M., et al.: Cyber-healthcare for public healthcare in the developing world. In: Proceedings of the 2016 IEEE Symposium on Computers and Communication (ISCC), Messina-Italy, 27–30 June 2016, pp. 14–19. ACM (2016)
34. Bagula, A., Castelli, L., Zennaro, M.: On the design of smart parking networks in the smart cities: an optimal sensor placement model. Sensors **15**, 15443–15467 (2015)

35. Bagula, A., Zennaro, M., Inggs, G., Scott, S., Gascon, D.: Ubiquitous sensor networking for development (usn4d): an application to pollution monitoring. Sensors **12**, 391–414 (2012)
36. Isafiade, O.E., Bagula, A.: Data Mining Trends and Applications in Criminal Science and Investigations. IGI Global, Hershey (2016)
37. Truica, C.O., Boicea, A., Trifan, I.: Crud operations in MongoDB. In: International Conference on Advanced Computer Science and Electronics Information (ICACSEI 2013) (2013)
38. Kanoje, S., Powar, V., Mukhopadhyay, D.: Using MongoDB for social networking website. In: IEEE Sponsored 2nd International Conference on Innovations in Information Embedded and Communication Systems, ICIIECS 2015 (2015)
39. Gyorodi, C., Olah, I.A., Gyorodi, R., Bandici, L.: A comparative study between the capabilities of MySQL vs. MongoDB as a back-end for an online platform. (IJACSA) Inter. J. Adv. Comput. Sci. Appl. **7**(11), 73–78 (2016)

The Quest for White Spaces
in the Democratic Republic of Congo

Isaac Kamiba[1](✉), Patrick Kasonga[1], Hope Mauwa[2], and Antoine Bagula[2]

[1] ESIS Salama, Lubumbashi, Democratic Republic of the Congo
isaac.kamiba@esisalama.org
[2] University of the Western Cape, Cape Town, South Africa
abagula@uwc.ac.za

Abstract. At a time when the opportunistic access to white spaces is a big opportunity for boosting innovation in broadband Internet services, many countries of the developing world are still lagging behind. In the Democratic Republic of Congo (DRC), for example, the TV White Space concept has not yet been tabulated in the operational plan of the national regulator, thus leaving a void in terms of white space discovery and usage. While many studies are still conducted to discover white spaces in several countries of the developing world, most developed countries such as the UK and USA have moved beyond the stage of testing and experimentation to embark on real white space deployments. This paper revisits the issue of spectrum sensing to identify white spaces in the UHF analog broadcast spectrum band ranging from 470 MHz to 862 MHz in the DRC. The experimental results collected from the cities of Lubumbashi and Kinshasa reveal significant white spaces in the frequency band. They provide a proof-of-concept that the national regulator could use as a starting point towards the migration to the digital terrestrial television. The experimental framework can also be used by different telecommunication operators and researchers as a guideline for white spaces identification.

Keywords: TVWS · White spaces · Opportunistic access's · Spectrum sensing

1 Introduction

Since 2006, many efforts have been made and resources invested in a project that targets the design and implementation of a fiber optic backbone to provide *Internet for all* in the Democratic Republic of Congo (DRC). The expectation is that such an IT infrastructure will benefit rural communities, many public and private institutions of education, the public administration, the health and safety sectors, and many others. However, since 2009, the project has stalled by many administrative, technical and economic issues. Furthermore, due to the country's geographic size, its demographic diversity and the lack of supporting

© ICST Institute for Computer Sciences, Social Informatics and Telecommunications Engineering 2019
Published by Springer Nature Switzerland AG 2019. All Rights Reserved
G. Mendy et al. (Eds.): AFRICOMM 2018, LNICST 275, pp. 216–227, 2019.
https://doi.org/10.1007/978-3-030-16042-5_20

infrastructure such as a stable electricity grid, capable of supporting the optical Internet backbone expansion, such a project has a low probability of meeting its goal. Wireless communication is a promising alternative to the battling optical backbone infrastructure of the country and white spaces implementation is a great opportunity for providing a new wireless access model, where the current wireless infrastructure is complemented by additional spectrum.

1.1   TV White Spaces Deployment

TV white spaces (TVWSs) are unused channels in the licensed TV spectrum, which either have been allocated but remained unused by the TV operator or can be availed by the spectrum owner for being used by the spectrum borrower on a temporary lease agreement. They fall within the category of unlicensed spectrum. When shared between a primary user (a TV provider) and the secondary user (a Wireless service provider (WSP)), white spaces can become a great opportunity for providing broadband connectivity, especially in the rural and low income areas of the developing world. For different countries of the world, they represent considerable wireless resources that can boost innovation through secondary usage. While the ubiquitous WiFi can not cross walls due to its high operating frequencies, TV white space (TVWS) networks offer the advantages of (i) longer range of more than 10 km; (ii) reaching well beyond certain obstacles (walls, hills, etc.), and; (iii) operating in the unlicensed frequency spectrum, thus enabling to build affordable internet for all networks.

Research in TVWSs identification has revealed significant amount of white spaces in many places worldwide [6,9,13]. The number of white space channels varies by region but the spectrum of exploration in terrestrial network transmission (TNT) lies in the 470–790 MHz range [1,7]. The transition from analog to digital television will enable new wireless architectures to be implemented and services delivered over wireless platforms operating in the white space frequency band. However, while many countries of the developing world are still lagging behind in terms of white space implementation, more developed countries such as the UK and USA have moved beyond the planning and testing stage to embark into real implementation of innovative projects using the TVWSs in view of the advantages they present. Several white space researches and practical experiments have already been conducted in different continents including Africa, Asia, Europe, South America and North America. In most cases, the application targets the provision of additional wireless capacity in rural areas, university campuses, government services support, education and health systems, and public administration systems [6,7]. The USA with Federal Communications Commission (FCC) and the UK with Ofcom [17] can serve as good examples of the use of TVWS. In Africa, Kenya, South Africa, Malawi, Mozambique, and Tanzania are examples of countries that have embarked into TVWS trials. For these countries, the investigation of white space use is a first step towards rational management of the spectrum [16].

1.2   Contributions and Outline

According to the International Telecommunication Union (ITU) recommandations of 2006 [16], the period of transition from analog to digital transition television was due to expire on 17 June 2015 for the UHF band ranging from 470–862 MHz to 470–690 MHz, and on June 17th, 2020 for the VHF band of 174–230 MHz for the countries of Region 1 and 3, of which the DRC is part. However, at both the regulation and research levels, white space identification is still a myth in the DRC.

The aim of the paper is to present a TVWS identification model using spectrum sensing as a first experimental study of white spaces in the DRC. Measurement experiments targeting the dynamic acquisition of TVWS data in the 470–862 MHz broadcast spectrum were conducted in two cities of the DRC: Lubumbashi, the economic capital, and Kinshasa, the political capital of the country. The objective was to acquire an overall view of the existence of the TVWSs in the country by building upon the experimental work conducted in the two cities. Base on the results of the experiments, the channels, which were found actually occupied from the measurements were mapped to the list of TV stations actually registered with the regulatory authority to discover their activity. The results collected from the experiments revealed significant TVWSs in the frequency band. The experimental setting presented in this paper is a proof-of-concept that the national regulator could use as a starting point towards white space quantification during its migration to the digital terrestrial television (DTT). As a contribution to research and practice in the emerging white space research field, the experimental framework proposed in this work can be adapted to be used by different national telecommunication operators and researchers as a guideline for white space identification and quantification. This work also contributes to bridging the gap that exists in many African countries in terms of experimental research leading to the discovery of TVWSs and also scientific literature targeting TVWS identification in these countries.

This paper comprises five sections. The first section introduces the research work while Sect. 2 presents a TVWS Identification Model. Section 3 shows the TVWS identification methodology used. Section 4 describes the experimental settings and results collected from two experiments carried out in the two cities. Section 5 presents conclusions and directions for future work.

2   TVWSs Identification Model

TVWSs can be identified and used based on their temporal, spatial and dynamic characteristics. As such, they provide access to dynamic spectrum (DSA) as described in [17], hence the importance of knowing their spatio-temporal availability and geo-localization in addition to their electromagnetic characteristics. The accurate identification of TVWSs in a given area depends on the way and method applied for its identification. Spectrum detection and geo-location database [8] are two of the methods, which are traditionally used to identify the TVWSs. A third method referred to as beacon transmission has also been investigated by different researchers [17].

Spectrum detection is based on the detection of the signal energy (amplitude) to determine the number of TVWS channels and occupied channels. This method was used for this research because of its flexibility and the possibility of using low cost off-the-shelf equipment that was available. The technique consists of measuring the lowest signal strength of a TV station (the lowest power received from the lowest TV signal also called Low Power Television (LPTV)) and comparing this signal strength to a threshold that is considered normal for a White Spaces Device (WSD). The FCC sets the lower limit of the threshold to $-114\,\text{dBm}$ [15], while the European Communications Commission (ECC) spectrum threshold ranges between $-91\,\text{dBm}$ and $-155\,\text{dBm}$. There is a great debate on the spectrum detection method with regards to the admissible threshold it uses to detect the presence of white spaces. It should be understood that such a level of sensitivity, according to FCC, corresponds to a noise whose power corresponds to almost $-100\,\text{dBm}$ and to a signal-to-noice ratio (SNR) of $-15\,\text{dB}$. The identification of the TVWSs will be found based on the measured direct values on one hand, and on the other hand, on the basis of a statistical analysis made. The mathematical identification scheme can be represented as follows:

Consider a frequency band, where it is possible to measure the probability of the existence of TVWSs at a given time, on a given channel and for a given place. Let us denote a TVWS by ws:

$$ws = \begin{cases} 1, & \text{one of the spectrum channels is occupied and busy} \\ 0, & \text{one of the spectrum channels is white space.} \end{cases} \quad (1)$$

The TVWS is determined by the average value of the signal strength of the channel in question with respect to a fixed threshold. This leads to the following series of equations.

$$ws = \begin{cases} 1 & \Longleftrightarrow \forall \frac{1}{n} \sum_{k=1}^{n} p_k - p_{th} \leq 0 \\ 0 & \Longleftrightarrow \forall \frac{1}{n} \sum_{k=1}^{n} p_k - p_{th} > 0 \end{cases} \quad (2)$$

where:

- n: the number of measurements performed per channel for a given period of time;
- p_k: discrete powers taken and recorded during the measurement;
- p_{th}: threshold set.

The number of white space channels are given by

$$n_{ws} = \sum_{i=1}^{j} n_{ws}(i) \quad (3)$$

For the DTT, the channel bandwidth is $8\,\text{MHz}$. Therefore, the number of channels located between channels i and j are given by

$$n_c = \frac{f_i - f_j}{\Delta f} \quad (4)$$

where, f_i is the starting frequency of channel i, f_j is the starting frequency of channel j and $\Delta f = 8\,\mathrm{MHz}$.

3   TVWS Identification Methodology

This section describes both the system and software architectures behind the TVWS identification methodology proposed in this paper. These architectures are expressed in terms of a TVWS identification system that describes the main hardware components used by the system and a TVWS identification process showing the different software components used.

3.1   TVWS Identification System

The device configuration for the TVWS identification used in this experiment is shown in shown in Fig. 1. It shows how the different elements were integrated into a white space identification system called RTfTrack. RfTrack is composed of the following key elements [14]:

- RF-Explorer, a low cost spectrum analyzer.
- An Android device (tablet or smart phone) equipped with GPS and running RfTracker [14], an application for logging management.
- Analysis server, accessible via the Web: receives data from measurement campaigns and generates spectrum measurements reports.

During the TVWSs tracking campaign, the RF-Explorer makes measurements and records TVWSs data continuously using the RFtracker [14]. Connected to mobile cellular Internet and equipped with an integrated Global Positioning System (GPS), the smart phone registers the GPS coordinates of the

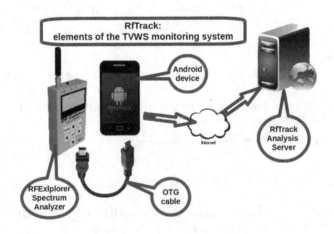

Fig. 1. White spaces tracking infrastructure

location of interest as well as the amplitude of the measured signal automatically. After acquisition, the data is stored either locally or uploaded by mail on the International Centre for Theoretical Physics (ICTP) (Trieste, Italy) platform located at the url http://wireless.ictp.it/tvws/ from where it can be accessed using various tools that the platform offers. During a measurement campaign, the battery life of the phone is an important parameter that determines the volume of data recorded.

In our experiments, the RFTracker was installed on a Galaxy A3 smart phone connected to the RF-Explorer. During the measurements, On the smart phone, an Orange 3G mobile Internet connection was used for the whole duration of the measurement campaign.

For each measurement campaign, we proceeded in the same manner by: (i) connecting the devices as shown in the diagram 1, (ii) having the mobile Internet connection on our smart phone set up, and (iii) then performing a dynamic acquisition of data while moving aboard a vehicle on the streets and avenues in most densely populated and urbanized areas of the two cities. According to satellite reports collected from the platform at the url http://wireless.ictp.it/ platform, we have travelled 53 km in Lubumbashi and 56.6 km in Kinshasa.

3.2 TVWS Identification Process

TVWS Identification methodology is summarized in Fig. 2, which shows the whole process from measurement to analysis of the results. The process include three main steps:

1. **Parameters setting.** This is done by setting the parameters to be used during a TVWS identification campain. These include parameters of the RFtracker software and RFexplorer spectrum sensing device and as well as activation parameters for the mobile phone to be used.
2. **Data acquisition and uploading.** This is done by using the RFexplorer to collect the energy in different channels along the route planned using Google Map.
3. **White space identification.** This step include the analysis of the data collected using a given threshold for differentiation between free and occupied channels and the analytical model expressed by the equations in Sect. 2.

4   Experimental Evaluation

Our experiments consisted of two main activities: (i) identification of white spaces channels in the UHF analog TV broadcasting band in Lubumbashi and Kinshasa in the DRC and (ii) association of the identified TVWS channels to the spectrum owners in order to find out how the spectrum is being used in the two cities.

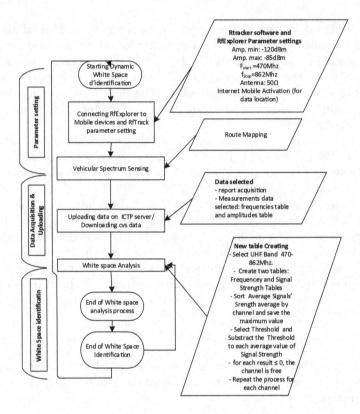

Fig. 2. The white spaces identification process.

4.1   City Wide TVWS Identification

Lubumbashi and Kinshasa are among the most developed and urbanized cities of the DRC but with prospect of migrating to DTT is still unknown. Kinshasa has about fifty TV stations whereas Lubumbashi has about twenty. The two cities are about 2000 km apart.

A statistical analysis was applied to the collected data based on the Eqs. 1, 2 and 3 to calculate the approximate number of TVWSs in the UHF TV band for each of the two cities. Taking into account the lower limit set by the FCC, the threshold values were chosen in the range −114 dBm to −85 dBm. The data was accessed from the ICTP Web site using SQLite Database. The database was consulted to extract the data to a Microsoft Excel spreadsheet using the SqlStudio tool. For the purposes of this paper, two tables from the whole SQLite Database were selected: a frequency measurement and the measurement of amplitude.

Eleven threshold values were used in the analysis from the range −114 to −85 dBm. Table 1 shows the total number of occupied channels and the corresponding number of total TVWSs detected by each of the thresholds used. The plots in Fig. 3 tell us more about the availability of whites spaces in the two cities at the moment. The spectral measurement results between the two cities

Table 1. Occupied and TVWSs channels detected by 11 threshold values

Threshold (dBm)	Kinshasa		Lubumbashi		Total
	Occupied	*TVWSs*	*Occupied*	*TVWSs*	
−85	2	47	3	46	49
−90	3	46	5	44	49
−95	8	41	8	45	49
−100	19	30	24	25	49
−105	40	9	43	6	49
−106	47	2	49	0	49
−107	49	0	49	0	49
−108	49	0	49	0	49
−109	49	0	49	0	49
−110	49	0	49	0	49
−114	49	0	49	0	49

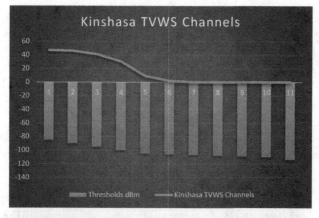

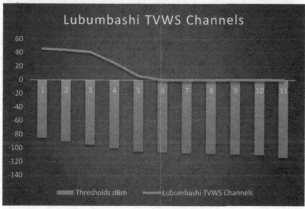

Fig. 3. Trend graphs of TVWS channels

reveal a certain similarity based on the results depicted in Table 1 and Fig. 3. At thresholds below −100 dBm, detection becomes rare and almost impossible.

4.2   White Spaces/Channel Owners Association

In order to discover how the television broadcasters of the two cities use their allocated channels and associate the TVWSs found with a detection threshold of −100 dBm to the TV broadcast owners as allocated by the regulator, the spectral measurements results were compared with the TV channel allocation to the TV broadcasters by the DRC telecommunications regulator. The results of the comparison between the TVWSs discovered and the TV channel allocation to the broadcasters are reported in Table 2. They reveal that: (i) many of the allocated channels are unused by their owners, (ii) Lubumbashi has a small number of TV providers owning to several consecutive channel allocation to same broadcaster and Kinshasa has many TV broadcasters.

Table 2. Channels/Broadcasters Association: Lubumbashi- and Kinshasa

Channel	Lubumbashi		Kinshasa		Channel	Lubumbashi		Kinshasa	
	Owner	Status	Owner	Status		Owner	Status	Owner	Status
1	La V. Berger	Free	Ant. A	Free	26	La V. Kat.	Occ	CEBS	Free
2	-	Free	CMB	Occ	27	Mapendo	Free	Fond. P. E.	Free
3	-	Occ.	Retalki	Occ.	28	-	Free	CCTV	Free
4	-	Free	TV5	Occ.	29	TV5	Occ.	B-One	Free
5	-	Free	RTMV	Free	30	heritage	Occ.	Hope TV	Occ.
6	-	Free	tropicana	Free	31	-	Occ.	Africa TV	Occ.
7	RTIV.	Free	Mirador TV	Free	32	-	Occ.	Global TV	Free
8	Malaika	Free	Raga TV	Free	33	-	Occ.	Digital	Occ.
9	-	Free	C. Num. TV	Free	34	-	Occ.	Ant. V	Free
10	-	Free	Amen TV	Free	35	-	Occ.	RTDV	Occ.
11	Kyondo	Free	Canal5	Free	36	-	Free	RTACK	Occ.
12	-	Occ.	KTM	Free	37	-	Free	RTVA	Free
13	-	Free	Horiz.33	Free	38	-	Occ.	RTC	Free
14	Nyota	Free	Euro News	Occ.	39	Tele50	Occ.	DRTV	Occ.
15	Wantanshi	Occ.	Nzondo	Occ.	40	-	Free	Alpha-Om.	Occ.
16	Jua	Occ.	CMC	Occ.	41	-	Free	Numerica	Free
17	Tam Tam	Occ.	RTNC2	Occ.	42	-	Free	2 AS TV	Occ.
18	-	Occ.	RTK	Free	43	Molière	Occ.	RTVS1	Free
19	-	Free	CVV	Free	44	-	Occ.	RLTV	Free
20	-	Free	DRTV	Free	45	-	Free	-	Occ.
21	Canal de V.	Occ.	Congo Web	Free	46	-	Occ.	-	Free
22	Digital	Occ.	Canal Futur	Free	48	-	Occ.	Brazzaville	Occ.
23	-	Free	SSM TV	Free	48	-	Occ.	Brazzaville	Occ.
24	-	Free	RTAE	Free	49	-	Occ.	RTC Elikya	Occ.
25	-	Occ.	RTGA	Free					

From the experimental results presented Table 1 and the association results in Table 2, it looks like a threshold of −100 dBm is a good fit for the white space identification as it gives results close to reality. Note that the number of TVWSs identified through spectrum sensing and the numbers of channels identified as unused through the TV channel owner association as allocated by the DRC telecommunication regulator are similar as revealed by Table 3. It is important to point out that in both cities, there are channels that are theoretically occupied but are no longer functional or active, as the television broadcasting service in those channels was closed by government.

Table 3. Correlation between spectrum sensing and channel association

City	Spectrum sensing	Channel association
Lubumbashi	25	33
Kinshasa	30	2

Following the current regulator plan, Kinshasa has a total of 392 MHz spread along about 49 analog TV registered channels in the UHF band without counting those reaching the city from the neighbouring country of Congo/Brazaville. Lubumbashi has 176 MHz, totalling 22 channels registered in the UHF band, making half of the quantify found in Kinshasa.

5   Conclusion and Future Work

This paper has addressed the issue of TVWS with the objective of finding if there are TVWSs in the DRC. To address this issue, spectrum sensing measurements were carried out using three parameters: location, frequency, and time. The experiments were conducted with the aim of not only assessing the availability but also discovering the quantity of TVWSs at various locations and at different times of the day. Overall, our experimental goal was to demonstrate the possibilities of reusing licensed frequency channels by detecting unused licensed channels in the UHF analog TV frequency band from 470 MHz to 862 MHz in DRC. The experimental results revealed the existence of TVWSs in both DRC cities, even though the TV broadcasting technology in DRC is still analog. Licensed spectrum encourages investment and guarantees interference avoidance among the users. However, freeing unused spectrum is open to innovation. Studies in [10] have shown that 95% of the licensed spectrum, only 20% is used in general. Innovations are therefore possible in white spaces and we believe that the DRC should invest in these frequencies to boost innovations.

The availability of white space in the DRC is a great opportunity for complementing the capacity of the existing mobile networks with wireless mesh networks used to expand broadband availability. For a country like the DRC, routing and route identification models such as proposed in [2,4] can be redesigned to implement time-of-the-day traffic engineering depending on the temporal variations of white spaces. It is also expected that the findings presented in this paper will lead to broadband access boost and create an opportunity for the design of novel data dissemination techniques in rural applications such as proposed in [11,12] and urban applications such as presented in [3,10] to provide additional spectrum for specific applications. The identification and quantification of white spaces could also be piggy-backed on the techniques and architectures proposed in [5] by mounting the RF devices on UAV/Drones. The design of such novel white space identification and quantification techniques is an avenue for future work.

References

1. ETSI EN 301 598: White Space Devices (WSD); Wirless access system operating in the 470 MHz to 790 MHz TV broacasting band (2014)
2. Bagula, A.: Hybrid traffic engineering: the least path interference algorithm. In: Proceedings of the SAICSIT 2004, pp. 89–96. ACM, October 2004. ISBN 1-58113-982-9
3. Bagula, A., Abidoye, A.P., Lusilao Zodi, G.-A.: Service-aware clustering: an energy-efficient model for the internet-of-things. Sensors 16(1), 9 (2016)
4. Chavula, J., Feamster, N., Bagula, A., Suleman, H.: Quantifying the effects of circuitous routes on the latency of intra-Africa internet traffic: a study of research and education networks. In: Nungu, A., Pehrson, B., Sansa-Otim, J. (eds.) AFRICOMM 2014. LNICSSITE, vol. 147, pp. 64–73. Springer, Cham (2015). https://doi.org/10.1007/978-3-319-16886-9_7
5. Chiaraviglio, L., et al.: Bringing 5G in rural and low-income areas: is it feasible? IEEE Commun. Stand. Mag. 1(3), 50–57 (2017)
6. Dynamic Spectrum Alliance (DSA): Règles de modèles des espaces blancs (2015). http://dynamicspectrumalliance.org
7. Gilpin, L.: White Space, the Next Internet Disruption: 10 Things to Know (2014). http://www.techrepublic.com
8. Han, Y., Ekici, E., Kremo, H., Altintas, O.: A survey of MAC issues for TV white space access. Ad Hoc Netw. 27, 195–218 (2015)
9. Holland, O., Bogucka, H., Medeisis, A.: Opportunistic Spectrum Sharing and White Space Access: The Practical Reality. Wiley, Hoboken (2015)
10. Karbab, E.M., Djenouri, D., Boulkaboul, S., Bagula, A.: Car park management with networked wireless sensors and active RFID. In: The Proceedings of the IEEE International Conference on Electro/Information Technology. IEEE (2015)
11. Masinde, M., Bagula, A.: Framework for predicting droughts in developing countries using sensor networks and mobile phones. In: Proceedings of SAICSIT 2010. ACM, October 2010
12. Masinde, M., Bagula, A., Muthama, N.J.: The role of ICTs in downscaling and up-scaling integrated weather forecasts for farmers in sub-Saharan Africa. In: Proceedings of ICTD 2012, Atlanta, GA, USA, 12–15 March 2012, pp. 122–129. ACM (2012)
13. Oh, S.W., Ma, Y., Tao, M.-H., Peh, E.: TV White Space: The First Step Towards Better Utilization of Frequency Spectrum. IEEE (2016)
14. Rainone, M., Zennaro, M., Pietrosemoli, E.: RFTrack: a tool for efficient spectrum usage advocacy in developing countries. In: Proceedings of the Eighth International Conference on Information and Communication Technologies and Development, p. 34. ACM (2016)

15. Shellhammer, S.J., Sadek, A.K., Zhang,W.: Technical challenges for cognitive radio in the TV white space spectrum. In: Information Theory and Applications Workshop, pp. 323–333. IEEE (2009)
16. UIT: Actes finals dee la Conférence régionale des radiocommunications chargée de planifier le service de radiodiffusion numérique de Terre dans certaines parties des Régions 1 et 3, dans les bandes de fréquences 174–230 MHz et 470–862 MHz (CRR-06), Genève (2006)
17. Webb, W.: Dynamic "White Space" Spectrum Access. New methods to access radio spectrum using dynamic sharing (2013)

QoS Strategies for Wireless Multimedia Sensor Networks in the Context of IoT

Muwonge S. Bernard[1,2], Tingrui Pei[1,4(✉)], Zhetao Li[1], and Keqin Li[3]

[1] College of Information Engineering,
Xiangtan University, Xiangtan, Hunan 411105, China
peitingrui@xtu.edu.cn

[2] Department of Networks, College of Computing and Information Sciences,
Makerere University, Kampala, Uganda

[3] Department of Computer Science, State University of New York,
New Paltz, NY 12561, USA

[4] Key Laboratory of Hunan Province for Internet of Things
and Information Security, Xiangtan, China

Abstract. Wireless multimedia sensor network (WMSN) can collect not only scalar sensor data, but also multi-dimensional sensor data. It is regarded as the foundation of IoT (Internet of Things). A lot of Quality of Service (QoS) indicators (e.g. energy-efficiency, real-time, reliability and so on) are used to evaluate data collection. This paper presents different QoS strategies for WMSNs in the Context of IoT from the network layer, transport layer and cross-layer. As for QoS Strategies at the network layer, many routing protocols are introduced, and their characteristics are compared. This paper also discusses congestion control protocols, error recovery protocols and priority-based protocols at transport layer. Cross-layer QoS strategies play an important role for system optimization. Three cross-layer strategies are discussed. For each layer's strategies, the challenges and opportunities are compared. Finally, the potential future directions of QoS strategies are discussed for research and application.

Keywords: Wireless multimedia sensor networks · Internet of Things · Internet of Multimedia Things · Media access control · Quality of service · Cross-layer · Time division multiple access · Code division multiple access

1 Introduction

As the monitoring environment of Wireless Sensor Networks (WSNs) becomes more complex, scalar data such as temperature, location, pressure, cannot cope with the demand for accurate environmental monitoring which necessitates support for multimedia, so as to improve information gathering and environmental monitoring. Hardware items such as cameras, microphones, S.D cards, memory cards, smart phones, have significantly reduced in cost due to the recent development in technology making them drastically increase in application; wireless communication capabilities have also increased due to the improvement in bandwidth capabilities [1]. Subsequently, WSNs are evolving into WMSNs which have capacity to transmit instantaneously, store, compare and combine data that originates out of heterogenous origins.

© ICST Institute for Computer Sciences, Social Informatics and Telecommunications Engineering 2019
Published by Springer Nature Switzerland AG 2019. All Rights Reserved
G. Mendy et al. (Eds.): AFRICOMM 2018, LNICST 275, pp. 228–253, 2019.
https://doi.org/10.1007/978-3-030-16042-5_21

WMSNs are networks for wireless embedded devices which can enable users to retrieve multimedia info out of their surroundings [2]. A WMSN may interact with its physical environment through observation using multiple media and performance of internet content editing [2]. WMSNs have drawn attention from many researchers and scholars because of the high number of low-cost smart phones, cheap imaging sensors, digital cameras, microphones, among other gadgets, which can be used to capture multimedia content from the fields with ease coupled with the enormous available devices for storage including Hard discs, memory cards, S.D cards, DVDs, CD-ROMs among others. The WMSNs have a number of applications including but not limited to usage in surveillance and environmental monitoring systems, traffic monitoring and target tracking, intrusion detection systems, telemedicine for advanced health care.

Advantages of WMSNs include [3]: (i) Enlargement of the scenery making it better if many cameras are used, (ii) Enhancement of the view through provision of an enormous Field of View in watching an event (iii) Provision of many points of view of a similar incident. The FOV for a fixed camera limits coverage. But despite the above advantages, there is a problem of too much network traffic that subsequently consumes more energy of the network.

1.1 Architecture of WMSN

The WMSN architecture is divided into three categories depending on application characteristics:

(a) single-tier flat architecture – comprising homogeneous multimedia nodes that can carry out any function to the sink using multihop route;
(b) single-tier clustered architecture – nodes are heterogeneous passing sensed information to the cluster head for processing; and
(c) a multi-tier architecture – also heterogeneous and does object sensing, target capturing and target tracking.

Figure 1 is a typical example of a WMSN architecture.

WMSNs have been widely deployed to provide infrastructural support and sensor accessibility making them handy for IoMT transmission [4]. Most of the applications in IoMT e.g., wearable devices make use of the WMSN technology.

1.2 The Internet of Things (IoT)

IoT envisages a scenario where all smart objects are linked to one network – the Internet. The IoT has today gained more popularity and recognition than ever before. Most of the recent applications that are rapidly evolving are in the IoMT category with at least four distinct features namely [5]: (i) video-oriented apps with incoming streams (ii) video-oriented apps with outbound streams; (iii) speedy mobile sensors, e.g., sensors on automobiles, aero planes, etc.; and, (iv) many distributed endpoints having the above three features, e.g., stationary traffic monitoring/security cameras in a city, high-density ring-of-steel surveillance applications [5]. IoMT has however not yet got a lot of momentum in the research fraternity leaving a lot yet to be done.

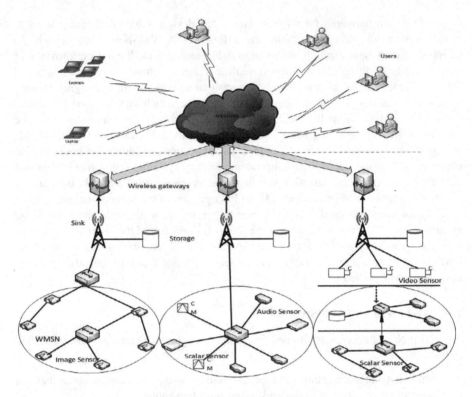

Fig. 1. Architecture of a WMSN

Many applications based on IoTs and IoMTs are recently emerging and have attracted a lot of attention [5]. They include among others, Smart Cities, Smart vehicles, homes, factories, (Fig. 2), GPS tracker devices, [5, 6] attracting a number of innovations in the Americas, Asia, Europe and elsewhere.

Figure 2 is a typical architecture of the IoT that can be enabled by RFID, optical tags and QR codes, Bluetooth low energy, Wi-Fi direct, LTE-Advanced, etc. A number of researchers on IoT focus on better efficiency on how to handle enormous real-time info but hardly address the issues with multimedia communication [7, 8]. The desire to make smart devices able to observe, sense and understand the world through multimedia data efficiently, moves the research direction from traditional IoT to multimedia-based IoT [9, 10] hence emerging of the field of Internet of Multimedia Things (IoMT).

IoMT is *"the IoT-based paradigm that enables objects to connect and exchange structured and unstructured data with one another to enable multimedia-based services and applications"* [3]. To attain a favorable QoS during transmission of multimedia data, the devices need high processing power and memory as well as a high amount of bandwidth compared to scalar data transmission in a typical IoT environment. A number of commercial and military applications come up due to introduction of multimedia objects in transmission of data such as remote patient monitoring in tele-health and telemedicine, traffic management systems enhanced by smart video cameras,

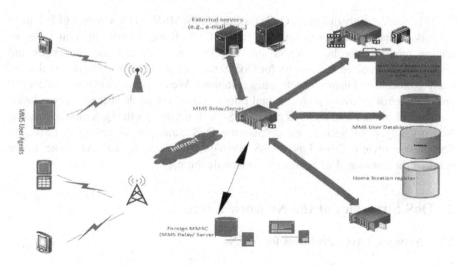

Fig. 2. Example of multimedia service architecture in the context of IoT.

among others [4]. This thus calls for an upgrade in functionality of IoT systems to IoMT. IoT compares with IoMT in some ways including [7]:

  i. IoT has standardized communication protocols whereas IoMT's protocols are non-standardized.
 ii. In terms of QoS, IoT requires low bandwidth whereas IoMT requires higher bandwidth.
iii. IoMT transmits heterogenous multimedia data whereas IoT data transmitted has limited heterogeneity.
 iv. IoT sensor nodes consume less energy than IoMT sensor nodes.
  v. IoT devices are deployed in application-dependent RFID tags but IoMT are in video and audio sensors.
 vi. In terms of service composition, IoMT has no available specialized middleware whereas IoT has specialized Service Oriented Architecture-based and event-based middleware.

We discuss a number of strategies for QoS in WSNs and WMSNs in IoT context. **Quality of service (QoS)** may refer to the capacity of a network to achieve maximum bandwidth for the end-users and manage the performance metrics of a network such as delay, bit rate, jitter, throughput, uptime, etc. To ensure a high QoS in IoMT applications, high level multimedia supported routing is becoming significant among researchers in the field of WMSNs on routing protocols, algorithms and techniques basing on network architectures and other application requirements to ensure best-effort services and energy efficiency. For high QoS and a reliable route, transmission of multimedia traffic in WMSNs will depend on the routing protocol employed [1]. The resource efficiency includes both effective bandwidth utilization, and lowest energy consumption possible hence requiring many special considerations when developing routing protocols.

This paper mainly discusses QoS strategies for WMSNs in the Context of IoT from network, transport and cross-layer in each of which we discuss different types of routing protocols for both WSNs and WMSNs and thereafter the challenges and opportunities involved therein. As for QoS Strategies at the network layer, we discuss many protocols and their characteristics compared. We also discuss congestion control protocols, error recovery protocols and priority-based protocols at the transport layer.

The rest of the paper flows as given: In Sect. 2, we discuss the QoS Strategies at the Network Layer. In Sect. 3, we discuss the QoS Strategies at Transport Layer. In Sect. 4, we review Cross-Layer QoS Strategies, in Sect. 5, we give some future research directions and in Sect. 6, we conclude the paper.

2   QoS Strategies at the Network Layer

2.1   Network Layer Protocols for WSNs

Data Centric Routing Protocols
Since nodes do not have global identification numbers, they employ DCRPs to control data redundancy. Unlike traditional address-centric protocols, in data centric routing, a sink requests for data from the nearest node which subsequently sends the requested data if available. So, data is from the source node to sink [11].

SPIN (Sensor Protocol for Information via Negotiation)
This protocol is appropriate for small and medium size WSNs making it more effective with increased energy in a particular environment. SPIN performs better than other protocols for energy and bandwidth consumption [12]. It exchanges its metadata among sensors using an advanced advertisement mechanism in which nodes advertise to neighbors newly available data and those that need it send a request for the same. The messages used include: **ADV message** which allows sensor nodes publicize certain data; **REQ message:** for requesting particular data; **DATA message:** for carrying real data [13]. SPIN is advantageous over others in that a node needs to only know the next-hop neighbors, and no useless info passing making it highly efficient [11].

SPIN-1
This "*is a data centric, flat routing, source initiated and data aggregation protocol*" according to [14] that uses the three-way handshake to establish a connection with the following assumptions [11]:

  i. Nodes have the same initial energy with symmetrical link;
 ii. Other nodes do not interfere when two nodes are communicating,
iii. No power constraints and nodes remain stationary;
 iv. Signals use the same amount of energy,
  v. Nodes are strategically located on path to sink to receive packets transmitted.

SPIN and SPIN-1 differ in the sense that in SPIN, if a node already had data, it makes no further response.

M-SPIN (Modified - SPIN)

This protocol transmits information only to the sink node other than the entire network. Fewer packets are transmitted thus saving a lot of energy. Energy is consumed during data sensing, processing, transmission and reception of the packets from neighboring nodes, hence these should be controlled to save energy [11]. This protocol is a good choice therefore in emergency response apps like security and telemedicine responses.

Flooding and Gossiping

These mechanisms don't use routing algorithms and topology maintenance during data transmission as discussed:

Flooding: Before they reach the destination, the sensor node continues to send packets to all its neighbors. It can easily be implemented though it's affected by implosion due to replica messages. In addition to that, there also exists the overlap problem whereby **multiple** nodes sense an event as a result of overlapping of different coverage regions leading to energy wastage and reduced network lifetime due to the many redundant transmissions [12].

Gossiping: A random neighbor receives a packet from a node that selects other neighbors to whom it sends the data. It avoids implosion though this delays data transmission among nodes [15].

Directed Diffusion

Data is transmitted using a data-naming scheme. Any node will seek the information it needs from its neighbors by using broadcast messages to all. Attribute pairs are used by on-demand basis to query the sensor using queries that are created by use of attribute value pairs like object name, interval, duration, geographical area etc. Matching data to queries requires extra overhead hence the protocol is not good for rapid response applications [12]. Other Data-centric routing protocols include Energy-aware routing, Rumor routing, constrained anisotropic diffusion routing, etc.

Hierarchical Routing Protocols

Hierarchical Routing

This is built on hierarchical addressing whereby routers are hierarchically arranged e.g., in a corporate intranet. In this architecture, high-energy nodes may process and forward information whereas those with lower energy can sense near target. Hierarchical routing can efficiently reduce the energy consumed in a cluster and reduce the messages transmitted to Base Station through data aggregation [16]. We discuss some hierarchical routing protocols.

Low Energy Adaptive Clustering Hierarchy Protocol (LEACH)

To communicate between nodes, it uses adaptive clustering and for timeline operation, it uses TDMA scheme to reduce collisions. Some nodes are randomly selected to act as Cluster Heads (CH), which role is rotational so as to manage the energy load in participating sensor nodes. This is done in order to makes use of local CHs as routers to the sink and to form clusters depending on the received signal strength. LEACH operates in 2 phases [16]; setup phase and steady state phase. Clusters in the setup phase, are arranged to randomly select the CHs according to Eq. 1 below:

$$T(n) = \begin{cases} \frac{p}{1-p\left(r mod \frac{1}{p}\right)}, & if\ n \in G \\ 0 & otherwise \end{cases} \tag{1}$$

where $T(n)$ = threshold value, P = probability that a given node is selected as CH, r = current round number, n = given node, and G = set of nodes that haven't acted as CHs in previous $1/P$ rounds.

A node randomly picks a digit from 0 to 1, which in case it's below $T(n)$, it becomes CH, i.e., the node with the highest energy becomes CH, invites nodes in its cluster to join and then assigns TDMA scheme to those that send acknowledgements [16, 17]. Common nodes receive information from all nodes and wait for a message from the CH to which it sends a joining request. After joining the cluster, all nodes wait for TDMA slots from the CH. The process becomes steady for one round. Some characteristics and drawbacks of LEACH include [16, 18]:

Characteristics:

  i. It randomly rotates the cluster heads for stable consumption of energy,
  ii. Sensors are designed with synchronized clocks for determining the new cycle beginning,
  iii. Sensors need not know the info about location.

Drawbacks:

  i. It's not applicable in big networks because it makes use of single-hop routing.
  ii. Dynamic clustering leads to additional overhead, reducing gain in energy.
  iii. Since CHs are elected randomly, they may all be concentrated in the same area.

Power-Efficient Gathering in Sensor Information Systems (PEGASIS)

This protocol is an improved version of LEACH. Nodes are assembled in form of a chain as opposed to a cluster in LEACH. The farthest node sends its data via its neighbor forming a chain in which the last node is the leading node that transmits the information to the BS (Fig. 3) which saves energy since each station only communicates with its neighboring station and thus improves the lifetime of the network. In this protocol, nodes use signal strength in measuring the distance to the neighboring nodes to locate the nearest one, alters signal strength such that 1 node only is heard [16]. The protocol uses two ways to conserve energy [16]:

  i. The head node at most receives two data messages.
  ii. The data is transmitted to the next-hop neighbor in a very short distance meaning that energy is conserved in this protocol and the head node has few data messages.

Significant features of PEGASIS:

i. It employs only one node for transmission to the BS thereby avoiding cluster formation.

ii. Using collaboration, it enhances the lifetime for the participating nodes.

iii. It minimizes energy for data transmission by uniformly distributing the power draining across the nodes.

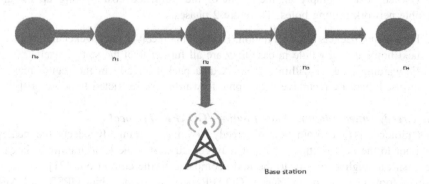

Fig. 3. Chaining in PEGASIS protocol.

Hierarchical-PEGASIS

This was developed to reduce the delay in packets during transmission to BS.

Other protocols here include Hybrid, Energy-Efficient Distributed Clustering (HEED) [16], Energy-aware routing protocol for cluster-based sensor networks (EARP) [16], Threshold-Sensitive Energy Efficient Sensor Network Protocol (TEEN): [19], Adaptive Threshold Sensitive Energy Efficient Sensor Network Protocol (APTEEN) [19].

Location-Based Routing Protocols

Here we refer to sensor nodes basing on location and use signal strength for incoming signal to estimate distance between adjacent nodes.

Geographic Adaptive Fidelity (GAF)

This is an energy-aware routing protocol adopted for Wireless Networks having been originally developed for MANETs. GAF saves energy by turning off redundant nodes in the network while at the same time preserving routing fidelity. A virtual grid is formed and the network is subdivided into fixed zones with each having one node awake for purposes of monitoring the network and reporting to the BS while others are in sleep mode to save energy [19]. Nodes are connected to the virtual-grid points through GPS-indicated location information. GAF comprises three states namely; (i) active state, (ii) sleeping state and (iii) discovery state. In sleeping state, energy is saved by the sensor turning off its radio; then in discovery state, each sensor determines its neighbors in its grid; and in active state, the sensor reflects participation in routing [19]. The time spent in each state depends on needs and sensor mobility. Much as this protocol is location-based, it may also be categorized hierarchical [20].

Geographic and Energy Aware Routing (GEAR) Protocol [19]

This protocol employs an energy-based geographical neighbor selection to direct the packets to the destination. It only sends interests to a certain region of the whole network so as to limit the interests in directed diffusion implying more efficient utilization of power. For nodes to reach the destination, they go thru the neighbors and have got to keep both estimated and learning costs of doing so. The estimated cost is comprised of residual energy as well as the distance from source to destination whereas the learned cost is simply an increment of the estimated cost making up for any possible network routing holes. There are 2 phases:

  i. Forwarding packets to target region: Here station receives data packet and looks for next hop creating a hole in case they are all further than the station itself.
 ii. Forwarding packets within region: A data packet already in the region may be diffused there by recursive geographic forwarding or restricted flooding [19].

The Greedy Other Adaptive Face Routing (GOAFR) Protocol

This protocol is a combination of greedy and face routing. It selects the nearest neighbor to the next routing node but may get stuck at some local minimum in case there isn't a neighbor nearer to the node compared to the current one [21]. Average-case performance can be enhanced. GOAFR performs better than GPSR and AFR algorithms [19].

Other location-based routing protocols include: Coordination of Power Saving with Routing, Trajectory-Based Forwarding (TBF), Bounded Voronoi Greedy Forwarding (BVGF), Geographic Random Forwarding (GeRaF), Minimum Energy Communication Network (MECN), Small Minimum-Energy Communication Network (SMECN) [20]. Table 1 summarizes some protocols with their advantages and disadvantages.

Table 1. Some advantages & disadvantages of location based routing protocols.

S. No	Protocol	Advantage(s)	Disadvantage(s)
1	Geographic Adaptive Fidelity (GAF)	Optimizes WSN performance Good scalability Maximizes network lifetime Conserves energy	Limited mobility Limited power management Ignores data transmission QoS
2	Geographic and Energy Aware Routing (GEAR)	Reduces energy consumption Increases the network lifetime	Not so scalable and mobile Power management issues High overhead and no QoS
3	Coordination of Power Saving with Routing	Less overhead Supports data aggregation Low node energy consumption	No QoS Limited scalability
4	Trajectory Based Forwarding (TBF)	Increases reliability and security Increases network management	High overhead

Negotiation-Based Routing Protocols
They remove idle data transmission by negotiation using data descriptors and communication decisions can be made based on accessible resources [19]. The SPIN family of routing protocols are one major example of such protocols since they are made to disseminate data from sensor to sensor being potential Base Stations. Other negotiation-based, SPIN protocols are discussed:

SPIN-PP
Uses a 3-way handshake (ADV–REQ–DATA) and is designed point-to-point transmission media networks where two stations can directly communicate without interfering with other stations. A node advertises new data to be transmitted through an ADV message sent to the neighbors (ADV stage). If the contacted node has not received the data, it sends REQ message to sender requesting for missing data (REQ stage). The protocol ends with the initiator responding by sending the missing data (DATA stage) [13].

SPIN-EC
This too uses a three-stage handshake but only when the energy is enough to complete the process, otherwise it doesn't take part in protocol [13]. It thus adds an energy-conservation heuristic to SPIN-PP.

SPIN-BC
It also uses a three-way handshake. Designed for broadcast media, network nodes share one single channel for communication, so all nodes will receive any packet broadcast over the channel and will first listen to ensure the channel is free before transmitting [13].

SPIN-RL [13]
This a more reliable version of SPIN-BC designed for efficient data dissemination through a broadcast network, though it may suffer data losses. It includes some adjustments to SPIN-BC to achieve reliability.

Multipath-Based Routing Protocols
Developed to protect against route failure by providing alternative paths in case the primary route fails. During route rediscovery, fault tolerance and reduction of routing frequency can be done via alternate path routing [22].

Sensor-Disjoint Multipath Routing
A simple technique in which a few alternate paths are constructed from node to sink to be used if primary path fails whereby, the sink and sensor nodes determine the best neighboring node where there is less delay and this goes on until the primary path is established after which the process is repeated by the sink which sends out the reinforcement path to the next preferable sensor node [23]. The technique provides fault tolerance by identifying alternate disjoint paths. However, the alternate paths are less efficient in terms of energy since they are longer.

REAR: Reliable Energy Aware Routing Protocol

When establishing routes, this multi-path routing protocol considers sensor nodes' residual energy capacity and also supports the DATA-ACK oriented packet transmission thus enabling sensor nodes to confirm if data transmission to other sensor nodes was successful [24].

Braided Multipath Routing

Alternate routes to the primary path are constructed but may not be disjoint. It begins with computation of the primary path and on all its nodes the most optimal path from sensor to sink is computed. Alternative paths are on or close to this path saving more energy compared to other mutually disjoint paths. But the method lowers the fault-tolerance since there may be a single point of failure for nodes that are shared by many paths [23].

Multi-constrained QoS Multipath Routing (MCMP)

Delivers packets to sink nodes by using intertwined routes. This is done in terms of reliability and delay [22]. MCMP aims at utilizing the multiple paths to enhance network performance at low energy cost. But information is routed over the shortest path to satisfy QoS, leading to more energy consumption at times [25].

N-to-1 Multipath Discovery

It uses flooding to discover many node-disjoint routes from the sensor to sink [26]. It has a mechanism that comprises two phases, i.e., branch aware flooding and multipath extension of flooding in both of which it broadcasts the same messages flooded in the network with this message format {mtype, mid, nid, bid, cst, path}, whereby mtype = message type, mid = sequence number of the current routing update, nid = Sender ID, bid = branch ID, path = sequence of node visited by this message, and cst = cost of the path. When a node gets this message, it appends its ID to the path, updating its cost and then broadcasts to its neighbors an update of the message. The protocol generates multiple node-disjoint paths for all sensors [23] but disregards node-energy level.

Other protocols include: Reliable Information Forwarding using Multiple Paths in Sensor Networks, HDMRP; An Efficient Fault-Tolerant Multipath Routing, Multipath Multispeed Protocol (MMSPEED), Energy-Efficient and QoS-based Multipath Routing Protocol (EQSR), Delay-Constrained High-Throughput Protocol for Multipath Transmission (DCHT).

Mobility-Based Routing Protocols

Data Mules (Mobile Ubiquitous LAN Extensions)

MULES has a 3-layer architecture [27] with the bottom layer having stationary WSN nodes for sensing the environment, middle layer having mobile units (MULEs) moving around the sensor field to collect information from the nodes to nearby access points; the upper layer has got units connected to the Internet and connects to the central data warehouse via the network access points which subsequently synchronizes the collected data, identifies redundant data and acknowledges data sent by MULEs for transmission reliability [28]. It achieves affordable connectivity in small WSNs, saves power due to short-range data transfer and requires less infrastructure. But it has a high latency, and limited mobility due to change in terrain which might cause unexpected failures [27].

Scalable Energy-Efficient Asynchronous Dissemination (SEAD)

This is a location aware protocol suitable for saving energy and minimizing delay. It mainly has three steps, namely: (i) dissemination tree construction (ii) data dissemination (iii) link maintenance to mobile sink nodes. The working assumption here is that sensor nodes know their physical positions [27]. It operates at a low cost yet distributes most of its data successfully though there is a problem of delay in delivering packets to the sink [28].

Tree-Based Efficient Data Dissemination Protocol

It creates a tree with a root node in the network that has a relay node for data transfer between 2 nearby nodes and a unidirectional non-relay node both of which can work as gateways. This gateway changes when the sink is out of range [27]. The protocol gives very high throughput and low overhead for control packets. Nevertheless, tree construction and node organization require a lot of memory.

Mobility Based Clustering Protocol (MBC)

MBC threshold is changed to include residual energy and mobility factor (Eq. 2) and a new threshold is as given

$$T(n)_{new} = \frac{p}{1 - p\left(r \bmod \frac{1}{p}\right)} * \left(\frac{En_{current}}{E_{max}}\right)\left(\frac{v_{max} - vn_{current}}{v_{max}}\right), \forall n \in G \qquad (2)$$

where $En_{current}$ is the current energy, E_{max} is the initial energy, $v_{n_{current}}$ is the current speed and v_{max} is the maximum node speed. This protocol supports longer lifetime for the network and is efficient in energy consumption. Packets are also well delivered at a relatively high frequency and the stability of the connection is reliable. For this protocol, the following are assumed [29]:

i. A symmetric model of the receiver.
ii. All WSNs are standardized and synchronized with time.
iii. Each WSN is aware of its position and speed.
iv. The Base Station is static.
v. Packet transmission time for each WSN can be approximated.

2.2   Network Layer Protocols for WMSNs

Ant-Based Service-Aware Routing Algorithm (ASAR)

ASAR is a QoS-based routing protocol designed for WMSNs. It has a cluster-head that is responsible for moving different data classes as well as the sink node [30]. For network optimization and algorithmic speedy convergence in ASAR, the sink's pheromone values are quantified decreasing the control message sending frequency. In most metrics, ASAR is significantly more advantageous over Dijkstra and Directional Diffusion (DD) though it has a higher delay and packet loss rate [31].

Two-Phase Greedy Forwarding (TPGF)

This geographic routing protocol is designed for WMSNs to support multipath broadcast. This it does by executing the algorithm several times so as to discover the remaining on-demand routes available in the network for resource maximization when many more routes are discovered [32]. Nodes are assumed to know their position co-ordinates and those of the base station. Discovery of the route happens in phase one of the protocol through greedy forwarding and/or step back and mark steps, while route optimization of the discovered route happens in phase two through label-based optimization method [31]. TPGF attains a more optimal (shorter) average path length than GPSR [33].

Multimedia Enabled Improved Adaptive Routing (M-IAR) Protocol

This protocol is designed to handle multimedia content by regulating delay and jitter [34]. It assumes nodes know their locations and those of the close neighbors and sink and can thus discover the shortest path with fewer nodes from source to sink, thus exploiting the physical position of WSN nodes, the reason it's called a flat multi-hop routing protocol [31]. The protocol employs the forward ant for source node and backward ant for the sink [34].

Multimedia-aware Multipath Multi-speed (Multimedia-aware MMSPEED)

It's a newer version of MMSPEED protocol where the closest optimal route is ear-marked for I-packets whereas the marginal routes are for P-frames [31]. MMSPEED [36], also an extension for SPEED protocol [37] was developed for WSN and is handy for video transmissions though MMSPEED is not good for multimedia traffic like advanced video frame rate and packet's information reliance [35].

2.3   Challenges and Opportunities

Some of the challenges include [29]:

i. There is a decline in quality of the connection leading to more possible dropped packets and subsequently increasing packet retransmission rate.
ii. Flexibility brings regular variations in the routes, resulting in considerable delay in the delivery of packets.
iii. A mobile node on joining a network takes some time to begin data transmission since its neighbors need to first discover its presence before deciding on collaboration with it, which requires some time.

In light of these challenges, Khan et al. [38] have proposed two protocols – power controlled routing (PCR) and enhanced power controlled routing (EPCR) that work for mobile and static WSNs with a mechanism for recovering lost packets although it only supports homogenous networks. Ali et al. [39] have also proposed a distributed grid based robust clustering protocol for mobile sensor networks that sends aggregated data to neighbor CH with the help of guard nodes thereby decreasing packet loss during inter-cluster communication, though it only supports homogeneous networks.

3   QoS Strategies at the Transport Layer

3.1   General Transport Layer Protocols

The traditional Internet transport layer protocols include UDP and TCP which nevertheless can't be directly applied in WSNs and WMSNs [40] due to the distinctive characteristics of these networks and the many applications with specific requirements [31].

Congestion Control Protocols
In communication networks and queuing theory, network congestion occurs when too much data is transmitted over a given link node causing its QoS to deteriorate leading to queuing delay, packet loss or blocked connections. Here we discuss some of the available Congestion Control Protocols.

Datagram Congestion Control Protocol (DCCP)
This protocol is designed for apps that may require running a session as well as congestion control and are tolerant to unreliable communication without retransmission. These may have a tradeoff between delay and in-order delivery [41] like streaming audio and on-line gaming. It can control datagram congestion and provide an excellent procedure to stop internet failure due to congestion. DCCP is different from UDP, since it encompasses a way of controlling congestion and also differs from TCP, since it doesn't guarantee reliability. It implements bidirectional connections between two hosts, either of which can initiate the connection comprising two unidirectional connections, called half-connection [42]. DCCP provides primitive support for multi-homing and mobility via connection endpoint transfer between addresses. Although DCCP doesn't guarantee cryptographic security, highly security sensitive applications can use IPsec or any end-to-end security. It can however protect against some attacks like session hijacking [42].

XCP (eXplicit Control Protocol)
This protocol has high scalability, stability and efficiency when deployed in higher bandwidth-delay product routes in routers. It further has superior performance in satellite IP networks although it exhibits lower performance when subjected to high-link error rate circumstances though this is addressed with the emergence of P-XCP. So, it's a good option for congestion control over IP [43].

Variable-Structure Congestion Control Protocol (VCP)
VCP possesses TCP characteristics like sliding window though it applies a different window management mechanism [44]. It has 3 congestion levels: low-load, high-load, and overload for encoding into IP packet headers. VCP enabled routers usually calculate Load Factor (LF) mapping it to a congestion level [45]. The router's upstream link congestion level is examined when the packets are delivered and if down-stream

link is more congested, ECN bits are updated. The receiver will then notify the sender of the link congestion status using ACK packets and thus the sender responds with 3 strategies of congestion control namely: the low-load region's Multiplicative Increase, high-load region's Additive Increase, and the overload region's Multiplicative Decrease. It has a low rate of packet loss and low persistent queue length and is highly utilized for homogeneous networks making it very practical for deployment despite less feedback delivery to end nodes [44].

TCP-Tahoe
This protocol uses 'Additive Increase Multiplicative Decrease' (AIMD) for congestion control and any packets lost will be considered as congestion. With half the current window as the threshold, it sets cwnd = 1 and by slow start, it increments linearly after reaching the threshold until packet loss occurs for it to slowly increase the window before reaching bandwidth capacity. The protocol is costly since it takes a lot of time to detect packet losses [43].

TCP-RENO
Here there is early detection of lost packets and always pipeline retains some packets even after a loss. In the 'Fast Re-Transmit' algorithm, receiving 3 duplicate ACK's signals loss of the segment, so the segment is retransmitted before timeout. Reno performs far better than TCP in limited packet losses. Under multiple packet losses in one window, RENO performs almost like Tahoe [43].

TEAR (TCP Emulation at Receivers)
This comprises window-based and rate-based congestion control making it a hybrid. The source node will thus change its transmission speed. TEAR calculates TCP sending rate other than using the congestion window (cwnd) [43].

3.2 Error Recovery Protocols

Stop-and-wait ARQ
It ensures that information sent between two devices is not lost due to dropped packets and that packets get delivered in correct order [40]. The source node sends one frame at a time with transmit window size = 1 and receive window size more than one. After sending each frame, no further frames are sent before acknowledgement is got, and if ACK doesn't come before the timeout, the frame is retransmitted.

Go-Back-N ARQ
The source node sends many frames according to window size, before receiving ACK packets from the receiver and N frames can be transmitted before an ACK is sent. The receiver keeps track of next frame's sequence number, which it sends with every ACK it sends; and discards any frame that does not have the expected sequence number and also resend an ACK for the last correct in-order frame [46]. When all frames are sent, it returns to the last received ACK's sequence number and fills its window starting with that frame and repeats the process. Since it doesn't wait for each packet's ACK, this protocol uses the connection more efficiently than Stop-And-Wait ARQ.

Hybrid Automatic Repeat-Request (HARQ)

This protocol is a combination of both ARQ and FEC. No retransmission is necessary to fix small errors but major ones are corrected by retransmission [40]. A system that incorporates this protocol change the coding scheme to adapt to conditions of the channel. This protocol consumes a lot of energy and is suitable in delay-tolerant applications. Other protocols in this category include Forward Error Correction (FEC), Selective Repeat ARQ/Selective Reject ARQ [47].

3.3   Transport Layer Protocols for WSNs

Priority-Based Protocols

Pump Slowly Fetch Quickly (PSFQ)

This protocol is designed for WSNs. It addresses some issues such as point-to-multipoint reliability. It can be employed both in multicast and unicast applications. It's a hop by hop protocol where there is data reconstruction over each node and so doesn't guarantee reliable connection [48]. It is useful in transmitting messages, recovering errors and selective status reporting which three functionalities are referred to as pump, fetch and report operations respectively. This protocol was developed for applications that need reliable packet delivery and transmits binary images but is inefficient for multipoint-to-point sensor transmissions [49]. For Loss Detection, PSFQ uses NACK-based quick fetch mechanism to achieve reliability and gap detection to detect losses. It assumes light traffic in a WSN and so detecting and controlling congestion is not a very big issue here and it employs TTL field in the header to sort this [49].

Reliable Multi-segment Transport (RMST)

This protocol is designed for WSNs and does fragmentation and segment reassembly and reliable delivery of messages [50, 51]. It is selective NACK-based extension of directed diffusion applicable to a sensor node and configurable with no need to recompile. It can be configured at run-time to enable end-to-end recovery, guaranteed delivery, fragmentation and reassembly to some applications and can detect packet loss at the sink. Congestion control arises from use of directed diffusion, for reliability, a timer-driven NACK is sent to the previous node for missing packets using hop-by-hop method. End-to-end retransmissions are reduced through storage of unacknowledged packets in caches and it uses ARQ for lost packet retransmission [49].

Improved Pump Slowly Fetch Quickly (IPSFQ)

It's designed to deal with the shortcomings of PSFQ to enable it perform better via error tolerance and mean latency [48].

Event to Sink Reliable Transport (ESRT)

It enables reliable event detection from source to sink and permits the course description for an event but doesn't provide details making it inapplicable to apps requiring full message delivery. The essential features of this protocol include congestion control, energy awareness, self-configuration, biased implementation and collective identification. It has a loss detection mechanism that depends on the congestion control and doesn't provide guaranteed delivery or loss prevention for messages but determines the right frequency, f for message delivery [49].

Priority-Based Congestion Control Protocol (PCCP)

In this protocol, the usefulness of sensor nodes is reflected by the node priority index [52]. The degree of congestion is computed as the ratio of packet inter-arrival time to packet service time and it's on this basis that it exploits cross-layer optimization and does congestion control using hop-by-hop mechanism and flexible weighted fairness for single and multipath routing is achieved. This brings about increase in energy efficiency and better QoS in terms of packet loss rate and delay. Other priority-based protocols include **DB-MAC;** a contention-based scheduling protocol in which packets from a node close to the source are more highly prioritized; **GTS (Guaranteed Time Slot)** in which prioritization is done using a toning signal, **RAP** whereby with higher requested velocity, a packet is assigned a higher priority, etc.

3.4   Transport Layer Protocols for WMSNs

Queue-Based Congestion Control protocol with Priority Support (QCCP-PS)

This protocol utilizes the length of the queue to indicate the degree of congestion [53] which subsequently together with the priority index determines the assignment rate to each traffic source. It achieves highly when it comes to congestion detection and priority and is efficient for WMSNs multimedia traffic. With fewer packet losses and retransmissions, a lot of energy at nodes is saved [56]. It focuses on transport layer congestion control since WMSN supports different applications [31]. The mode of congestion control here has 3 units based on hop-by-hop approach and are congestion detection, congestion notification, and rate adjustment unit. Congestion is detected using the length of the queue indicating congestion degree. Input packets from each child node and that source traffic from the receiving node are stored in separate queues. Nodes are assumed to have different priorities which together with the congestion degree determines the sending rate of a given node.

Multipath Multi-stream Distributed Reliability (MMDR)

This is designed for WMSNs for video transmission and exploits multi-stream coding of video and multipath routing. Source coding methods like Layered Coding, Multiple Description Coding, Distributed Video Coding [54] are used to partition the source-encoded video data into many streams. To do channel coding of the many video streams to cover up for errors in some wireless links, the protocol employs Low Density Parity Check codes. Bit errors are recovered using progressive error recovery algorithm (D-PERA). Other protocols here include Load Repartition based Congestion Control (LRCC), Reliable Synchronous Transport Protocol (RSTP), etc....

3.5   Challenges and Opportunities

i. Performance and Robustness: There should be trade-offs in congestion control, e.g., high link utilizations and fair resource sharing should be allowed and algorithms be robust enough. Routers may improve performance, though may cause more complexity and control loops which requires careful algorithmic design to ensure stability and avoid oscillations. Excessive congestion may further delay feedback signals and so, robust congestion control mechanisms with significant benefits with less additional risks should be designed.

ii. Congestion control mechanisms usually interpret packet loss to be due to congestion whereas for wireless networks, dropped packets may be due to corruption. For corrupted packets, most congestion control mechanisms will react as if there are no dropped packets. There is need to design mechanisms that can be able to detect corruption though this is not easy especially for cross-layer interactions.

iii. Most data in multimedia streaming belongs to control traffic. Minor packet congestion control mechanisms should be enhanced, tightly coordinated and controlled over WANs.

iv. Additional router processing is a challenge for scalability of the internet and may increase end-to-end latency. This should be further investigated as no known full solution that does not require per-flow processing. Without affecting Internet scalability, there should be some realizable granularity for router processing.

v. We need to define the protocol layer at which feed-back signaling occurs and the optimal feedback frequency.

4 Cross-Layer QoS Strategies

4.1 Cross-Layer MAC Protocols

Adaptive Cross-Layer Forward Error Correction (ACFEC)
This is realized in Access Point (AP) that adaptively adds FEC to video data, in infrastructure mode. Nodes exchange data packets with each other via the access point [55]. Video data is encapsulated by the streaming server in RTP packets via the wireless AP to the receiver node. The packet header is retrieved from UDP by the adaptive FEC controller that will detect the packet type from the RTP header [56]. The block's source packet number determines the number of error correction packets generated by the Packet-level FEC encoder. Adaptive FEC controller monitors video data transmission results by snatching up MAC layer failure information and the controller's failure counter will be incremented by one in case the transmission flops. When a block is transmitted, the controller adjusts number of generated redundant FEC packets using the failure counter. When packet losses are detected, redundancy rates are adjusted, more packets generated to compensate for lost packets and meet receiver needs [55].

MAC-PHY Cross-Layer Protocol
The authors in [57] propose a cooperative cross-layer protocol for cooperation at physical layer in next generation WSNs and provision of full MAC layer algorithm supporting the PHY-MAC layer cooperative structure. The scheme used is similar to CoopMAC's which depends on an intermediate node for inter-node communication.

Modification of the MAC layer protocol has enabled it to take control of the Physical layer communication. By the new scheme, the destination node can get two copies of the original packet, from source and helper for decoding [57].

Cross-Layer Cooperative MAC (Coop-MAC)
Here a source node uses the two-way handshake (RTS/CTS) to establish a link with the destination node after a random back off. On getting the CTS packet and the short inter-frame space (SIFS), the source will directly send the packets to destination node in case the cooperation is not beneficial, and when there is a cooperation opportunity, the source and the destination first establish, using a Helper Indication signal, whether there is a helper to confirm the feasibility of a cooperative transmission. In case there's a signal, a cooperative communication is initiated, otherwise, direct transmission is triggered. Since there is an RTS/CTS exchange, the helper-initiated cooperation is preferred in a distributed wireless system [58]. Spatial diversity between the 3 nodes (faster two-hop "alternative path" via the helper compared to direct path) puts this protocol at an advantage [57]. Other protocols here include EC-MAC Protocol in which besides the 3 control frames (RTS, CTS and ACK) supported in IEEE 802.11MAC, 3 new frames (Cooperative Request-to-Send, Helper-to-Send – HTS, and Cooperative Clear-to-Send – CCTS frame) are introduced in [54].

4.2   Cross-Layer Network Layer Protocols

Cross-Layer and Multipath based Video Transmission (CMVT)
This is designed as a collaboration between the application and network layer. In the application layer, the protocol encodes video streams into video data frames (I-frame, P-frame and B-frame) by using MPEG-4 encoding scheme. The core of the protocol is the network layer design where route discovery and data transmission take place. Under route discovery, many paths from the source node to the sink node are found through two schemes namely: greedy forwarding and rollback [59]. A given node i uses Eq. 3 to compute the evaluation of its neighboring node j

$$f_{ij} = (1 - \alpha)\frac{d^2(j, D) - d_{min}^2(i)}{d_{max}^2(i) - d_{min}^2(i)} + \alpha\frac{e_{init}(j) - e_{res}(j)}{e_{init}(j)} \tag{3}$$

where, f_{ij} = evaluation value of node i to node j, $d^2(j, D)$ = distance from node j to destination node D, $d_{min}^2(i)$ is minimum distance for neighbors of node i to D, $d_{max}^2(i)$ is maximum distance for neighbors of node i to D, $e_{init}(j)$ is initial energy of node j, $e_{res}(j)$ = current residual energy of node j, and α is energy coefficient, given by:

$$\alpha = \frac{e_{max}(i) - e_{min}(i)}{e_{max}(i)} \tag{4}$$

where, $e_{max}(i)$ = maximum remaining energy of all neighbors of node i, $e_{min}(i)$ = minimum remaining energy of all neighbors of node i. The network layer also sends video data whereby CMVT does status evaluation to select a suitable transmission path for the given type of packets and the QoS guarantee level of a path i is computed using Eq. 5:

$$f_i = (1 - \omega) \frac{h_i}{\sum h_i} + \omega \frac{n_i}{\sum n_i}, \tag{5}$$

where, f_i = path i evaluation value, h_i are the hops for path i, n_i = sum of packets sent via i, Σn_i = sum of packets sent by sources, and ω = energy consumption factor.

Network Layer QoS Support Enforced by a Cross-Layer Controller

It enables packet-level service differentiation as a function of throughput, end-to-end packet error rate and delay [60] (Fig. 4).

This improves QoS at the network layer. It has a cross-layer control unit (XLCU) to configure and control networking functions at physical, MAC, and network layer basing on a unified logic which decides for application layer requirements and status of functional blocks that implement networking functions thus, cross-layer interactions can be controlled with no compromise on the upgradeability, modularity, and ease of system design [60].

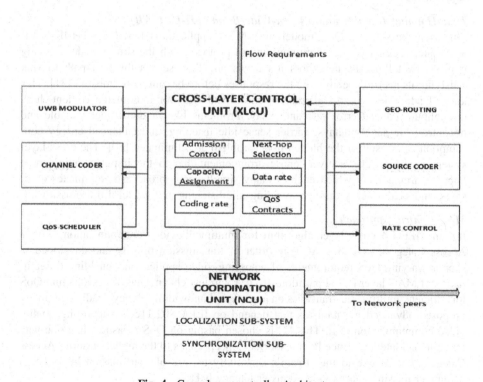

Fig. 4. Cross-layer controller Architecture.

4.3   Cross-Layer Protocols for WMSNs

Multi-path Multi-priority (MPMP) Transmission Scheme
A context-aware cross-layer optimized scheme that employs multipath routing in routing layer and multipath selection in transport layer [32]. To discover the highest number of sensors of node-disjoint routing paths, we use Two-Phase geographic Greedy Forwarding (TPGF) routing protocol and to select the number of optimal paths for data delivery to the sink, Context-Aware Multipath Selection (CAMS) algorithm is employed which further guarantees node-to-node transmission delay [31]. Depending on the multimedia content to be transmitted, end-to-end transmission delay-based priority for real-time video, CAMS will choose the right path for routing the WMSN data. To do data gathering in WMSNs, we use a CLD whereby RRA scheme that is adaptive alters dynamically the radius of transmission as well as the data generation rate adjustment. The RRA scheme's cross-layer framework takes place in four steps name: (i) the optimal transmission radius at physical layer is chosen for the nodes, (ii) use of multipath routing protocols such as TPGF to construct numerous routing paths, (iii) do path selection at the transport layer from among the discovered paths by the routing protocol (iv) for source nodes at physical layer, their data generation rate is adjusted [31].

Time-Hopping Impulse Radio Ultra-Wide-Band (TH-IR-UWB)
This is a cross layer, QoS model in WMSN applications based on TH-IR-UWB technique. It employs the admission control protocol with the source node initiating requests by telling the neighbors it's needs and then selects the best path to sink satisfying its needs depending on the responses before beginning to transmit [31]. This kind of admission control guarantees end-to-end QoS for multimedia content, high throughput, reduced error rate and delay. Problems like random timer variable and uncontrollable access delays, carrier sense idle listening, and enhanced energy consumption as a result of the hidden node problem are eliminated [60]. The cross-layer system further offers receiver-centric arrangement due to the impulse radio's time hopping arrangement which enables many simultaneous broadcasts, eliminates collisions, and saves energy through avoiding idle listening and wasteful transmissions.

MAC Centric Approach
It's an MPEG-4 cross layer algorithm for multimedia/video communication, with 4 Access Categories (AC3 – AC0) in order of transmission priority and developed to support varying QoS requirements of emerging video applications, enabling differentiation of MAC layer H.264 partitions [61]. A wireless channel has issues affecting QoS for efficient multimedia transmission e.g., low bandwidth, latency leading to many proposed advanced mechanisms that depend on IEEE 802.11e in supporting quality video communication [55]. The AC is chosen basing on QoS measures like one-way loss rate and latency, hence Parameter Set Concept maps to the highest-priority Access Category (AC3) due to the stream's sensitivity to loss of transmission bits since a parameter missing causes video transfer latency [61].

Minimum Hop Disjoint Multipath Routing Algorithm with Time Slice Load Balancing Congestion Control Scheme

MHDM routing algorithm is divided into 2 phases: (i) path build up phase, (ii) path acknowledgment phase with 3 disjoint paths built up per source since there are multiple sources. The paths are primary path, alternate path and backup path. Considering the 2 phases, in the path build-up phase, when the source sensor node is activated, it sends requests to build up a path to the smallest hop count neighbor compared to sender node [62]. (a) The first step in path build-up phase is that when a source is activated, it sends a request package for path build up to the neighbor node which upon receipt of it adds its node number and timestamp before forwarding it to its smaller hop count neighbor until it reaches the lowest time latency sink with primary route info to build up the primary route [63]. (b) The second step under this phase is such that on arrival of a new package from another route, the route is extracted and compared to primary route and package discarded in case of a shared node, or an alternate path is found. Then a back-up path is found by further comparing the previous two paths. Under the second phase of path acknowledgement, (c) the third step after path build-up is that the sink sends back to the source an acknowledgement message (ACK) comprising the path info that includes the nodes and the related time info calculated from the timestamp by the sink. MHDMwTS protocol reduces the end to end delay and controls and prevents congestion [62].

4.4   Challenges and Opportunities of the Cross-Layer Design (CLD)

i. The physical layer plays a major part in CLD which is highly invaluable. Functions like rate adaptation, channel allocation are provided at the physical layer through signal processing. CLD bases on physical layer features for improved QoS. Variations in wireless medium affect end-to-end performance if network layer protocol functionality is affected. CLD offers solution for power conservation, ..., making it an opportunity for designers to consider other layers. There is also need to determine CLDs that affect performance of network and get closer attention.

ii. Coexistence of different CLD Solutions: Major concern is if CLD solutions meant for a similar challenge can be independently applied, e.g., if there are common mechanisms to use by different CLD approaches.

iii. Standardizing interfaces for CLD: CLD architecture needs to provide functionality for its modules though there is a question on potential interfaces between modules which interfaces will be determined by the need to exchange and share info between non-adjacent protocol layers. Technical challenges include developing, designing, and standardizing of cross-layer interfaces and algorithms that meet cross-layer optimization requirements.

5 Future Research Directions

i. QoS and Energy efficiency are important aspects in WMSN mostly real-time applications needing guaranteed bandwidth and throughput during network lifetime. Many protocols don't consider Base Station and multimedia sensor nodes' mobility. Applications like traffic management, telemedicine, battlefield surveillance need node or Base Station mobility hence need for designing dynamic routing protocols that can be adaptable in such conditions. For CLD, we need to investigate how different CLD proposals will coexist.

ii. Security of information carried on WMSNs, e.g., patients' data, data in military surveillance, e-commerce, etc. is paramount with QoS and energy efficiency and so requires more attention by the research community.

iii. We need to investigate, specify, develop, and standardize cross-layer algorithms that will meet cross-layer optimization standards.

iv. There is need to develop energy efficient MAC protocols since power management and saving schemes have challenges of throughput, protocol overhead, and prone to channel errors.

6 Conclusion

We have reviewed the different QoS strategies for WMSN in the Context of IoT from the network layer, transport layer and cross-layer paradigm. For network layer, we have discussed many protocols with their characteristics including general network layer protocols, protocols suitable for WSNs and WMSNs. We reviewed data centric, Hierarchical, Location-based, Negotiation-based, Multipath-based, and Mobility-based Protocols. We have then discussed transport layer protocols like congestion control, error recovery and priority-based protocols. For these we reviewed general, WSN and WMSN protocols. For system optimization, Cross-layer QoS strategies are important. We have seen three cross-layer strategies for each of which challenges and opportunities were compared. These are: Cross-Layer MAC, Cross-Layer Network Layer and Cross-Layer Transport Layer Protocols. Finally, some possible future directions of QoS strategies have been discussed for research and application.

Acknowledgement. This work was funded by The National Natural Science Foundation of China (No. 61672447, No. 61711540306).

The authors hereby declare no conflict of interest as regards the publication of this work.

References

1. Shen, H., Bai, G.: Routing in wireless multimedia sensor networks: a survey and challenges ahead. J. Netw. Comput. Appl. **71**, 30–49 (2016)
2. Akyildiz, B.I.F., Melodia, T., Chowdhury, K.R.: Wireless multimedia sensor networks: applications and testbeds. Proc. IEEE **96**(10), 1588–1605 (2008)
3. Ang, L., Seng, K.P., Chew, L.W., Yeong, L.S., Chia, W.C.: Wireless Multimedia Sensor Networks on Reconfigurable Hardware. Springer, Heidelberg (2013). https://doi.org/10.1007/978-3-642-38203-1
4. Alvi, S.A., Afzal, B., Shah, G.A., Atzori, L., Mahmood, W.: Internet of multimedia things: Vision and challenges. Ad Hoc Netw. **33**, 87–111 (2015)
5. Wang, Q., et al.: Multimedia IoT systems and applications, no. 2 (2017)
6. Madani, S.A., Hassan, Q.F., Khan, A.U.R. (eds.): Internet of Things: Challenges, Advances, and Applications. CRC Press Taylor & Francis Group: A Chapman & Hall Group, Boca Raton (2018)
7. Curry, E.: Towards a generalized approach for deep neural network based event processing for the internet of multimedia things. IEEE Access **6**, 25573–25587 (2018)
8. Jridi, M., Chapel, T., Dorez, V., Bougeant, L., Le Botlan, A.: SoC-based edge computing gateway in the context of the internet of multimedia things: experimental platform. J. Low Power Electron. Appl. **8**, 1 (2018)
9. Noura, H., Chehab, A., Sleem, L., Rapha, M.N.: One round cipher algorithm for multimedia IoT devices. Multimed. Tools Appl. **77**, 18383–18413 (2018)
10. Balan, T., Robu, D., Sandu, F.: Multihoming for mobile internet of multimedia things. Mob. Inf. Syst. **2017**, 16 (2017)
11. Dhand, G., Tyagi, S.S.: Survey on data-centric protocols of WSN. Int. J. Appl. Innov. Eng. Manage. (IJAIEM) **2**(2), 279–284 (2013)
12. Karthikeyan, K., Kavitha, M.: comparative analysis of data centric routing protocols for wireless sensor networks. Int. J. Sci. Res. Publ. **3**(1), 1–6 (2013)
13. Kulik, J., Heinzelman, W., Balakrishnan, H.: Negotiation-based protocols for disseminating information in wireless sensor networks. Wirel. Netw. **8**(2–3), 169–185 (2002)
14. Akyildiz, I.F., Su, W., Sankarasubramaniam, Y., Cayirci, E.: Wireless sensor networks: a survey. Comput. Netw. **38**(4), 393–422 (2002)
15. Akkaya, K., Younis, M.: An energy-aware QoS routing protocol for wireless sensor networks. In: Proceedings of the International Conference on Distributed Computing Systems Workshops 2003, pp. 710–715 (2003)
16. Waware, S., Sarwade, N., Gangurde, P.: A review of power efficient hierarchical routing protocols in wireless sensor networks. Int. J. Eng. Res. Appl. (IJERA) **2**(2), 1096–1102 (2012)
17. Ram, D.B., Shah, G.S.: Analysis of different hierarchical routing protocols of wireless sensor network. IJRET **3**(2), 616–620 (2014)
18. Kaur, P., Katiyar, M.: The energy-efficient hierarchical routing protocols for WSN: a review. Int. J. Adv. Res. Comput. Sci. Softw. Eng. **2**(11), 194–199 (2012)
19. Al-Karaki, J.N., Kamal, A.E.: Wireless sensor networks routing techniques in wireless sensor networks: a survey. IEEE Wirel. Commun. **11**, 6–28 (2004)
20. Rama, G.V., Srikanth, L.V.: Location-based routing protocol in wireless sensor network-a survey. Int. J. Adv. Res. Comput. Sci. Softw. Eng. **5**(4), 663–667 (2015)
21. Kuhn, F., Wattenhofer, R., Zollinger, A.: Worst-case optimal and average-case efficient geometric ad-hoc routing. In: Proceedings of the 4th ACM International Symposium on Mobile Ad Hoc Networking & Computing - MobiHoc 2003, pp. 267–278 (2003)
22. Masdari, M., Tanabi, M.: Multipath routing protocols in wireless sensor networks: a survey and analysis. Int. J. Futur. Gener. Commun. Netw. **6**(6), 181–192 (2013)

23. Chaudhari, P., Rathod, H., Budhhadev, B.: Comparative Study of multipath-based routing techniques for wireless sensor network. In: Proceedings published by International Journal of Computer Applications®(IJCA) International Conference on Computer Communication and Networks CSI-COMNET-2011, pp. 50–53 (2011)

24. Shin, K.-Y., Song, J., Kim, J., Yu, M., Mah, P.S.: REAR: reliable energy aware routing protocol for wireless sensor networks. In: The 9th International Conference on Advanced Communication Technology, pp. 525–530 (2007)

25. Ben-Othman, J., Yahya, B.: Energy efficient and QoS based routing protocol for wireless sensor networks. J. Parallel Distrib. Comput. 70(8), 849–857 (2010)

26. Lou, W.: An efficient N-to-1 multipath routing protocol in wireless sensor networks. Computer Engineering, pp. 665–672 (2005)

27. Krishna, K.K., Augustine, R.: A survey on mobility based routing protocols in wireless sensor networks. Int. J. Comput. Appl. 135(5), 434–438 (2016)

28. Yadav, R., Kumar, A., Kumar, R.: a survey - heterogenity and mobility based routing protocol in WSN, pp. 320–328 (2015)

29. Lofty, S., Padmavati: A survey on mobility based protocols in WSNs. In: Proceedings of the International Conference on Computer Communication Manufacturing, pp. 12–15 (2014)

30. Sun, Y., Ma, H., Liu, L., Zheng, Y.: ASAR: an ant-based service-aware routing algorithm for multimedia sensor networks. Front. Electr. Electron. Eng. China 3(1), 25–33 (2008)

31. Almalkawi, I.T., Zapata, M.G., Al-Karaki, J.N., Morillo-Pozo, J.: Wireless multimedia sensor networks: current trends and future directions. Sensors 10(7), 6662–6717 (2010)

32. Shu, L., Zhang, Y., Yang, L.T., Wang, Y., Hauswirth, M., Xiong, N.: TPGF: geographic routing in wireless multimedia sensor networks. Telecommun. Syst. 44(1–2), 79–95 (2010)

33. Karp, B., Kung, H.: GPSR: greedy perimeter stateless routing for wireless networks. In: ACM MobiCom, pp. 243–254 (2000)

34. Rahman, M.A., GhasemAghaei, R., El Saddik, A., Gueaieb, W.: M-IAR: biologically inspired routing protocol for wireless multimedia sensor networks. In: 2008 IEEE Instrumentation and Measurement Technology Conference, pp. 1823–1827 (2008)

35. Darabi, S., Yazdani, N., Fatemi, O.: Multimedia-aware MMSPEED: a routing solution for video transmission in WMSN. In: 2008 2nd International Symposium on Advanced Networks and Telecommunication Systems, ANTS 2008, October 2014 (2008)

36. Felemban, E., Lee, C.G., Ekici, E.: MMSPEED: multipath Multi-SPEED protocol for QoS guarantee of reliability and timeliness in wireless sensor networks. IEEE Trans. Mob. Comput. 5(6), 738–753 (2006)

37. He, T., Stankovic, J.A., Lu, C., Abdelzaher, T.F.: A spatiotemporal communication protocol for wireless sensor networks, pp. 1–13 (2005)

38. Khan, A.U.R., Madani, S.A., Hayat, K., Khan, S.U.: Clustering-based power-controlled routing for mobile wireless sensor networks. Int. J. Commun Syst 25, 529–542 (2011)

39. Madani, S., Ali, S.: Distributed Grid based Robust Clustering Protocol for Mobile Sensor Networks. Int. Arab J. Inf. Technol. 8(3), 414–421 (2011)

40. Wang, C., Sohraby, K., Li, B., Daneshmand, M., Hu, Y.: A survey of transport protocols for wireless sensor networks. IEEE Netw. 20(3), 34–40 (2006)

41. Chowdhury, I.S., Lahiry, J., Hasan, S.F.: Performance analysis of datagram congestion control protocol (DCCP). In: 12th International Conference on Computers and Information Technology, ICCIT 2009, vol. 3, no. 5, pp. 454–459 (2009)

42. Kohler, E., Floyd, S.: Datagram congestion control protocol (DCCP) overview, pp. 1–9, July 2003. http://www.icir.org/kohler/dcp/summary.pdf

43. Bhujbal, P., Nagaraj, U.: Study of various congestion-control protocols in network. Int. Res. J. Eng. Technol. (IRJET) 5(3), 3890–3894 (2014)

44. Xia, Y., Subramanian, L., Stoica, I., Kalyanaraman, S.: One more bit is enough. IEEE/ACM Trans. Netw. **16**(6), 1281–1294 (2005). Sigcomm
45. Li, X., Yousefi'zadeh, H.: MPCP: multi packet congestion-control protocol. ACM SIGCOMM Comput. Commun. Rev. **39**(5), 5–11 (2009)
46. Kurose, J.F., Ross, K.W.: Computer Networking A Top-Down Approach Featuring the Internet, vol. 1, p. 712. Pearson Education, India (2005)
47. Agarwal, R., Popovici, E., De Feo, O., O'Flynn, B.: Energy driven choice of error recovery protocols in embedded sensor network systems. In: Proceedings of the 2007 International Conference on Sensor Technologies and Applications, SENSORCOMM 2007, pp. 560–565 (2007)
48. Wan, C.-Y., Campbell, A.T., Krishnamurthy, L.: PSFQ: a reliable transport protocol for wireless sensor networks. In: Proceedings of the 1st ACM International Workshop on Wireless Sensor Networks and Applications, WSNA 2002 (2002)
49. Jones, J., Atiquzzaman, M.: Transport protocols for wireless sensor networks: state-of-the-art and future directions. Int. J. Distrib. Sens. Netw. **3**(1), 119–133 (2007)
50. Stann, F., Heidemann, J.: RMST: reliable data transport in sensor networks. In: Proceedings of the 1st IEEE International Workshop on Sensor Network Protocols and Applications, SNPA 2003, pp. 102–112 (2003)
51. Intanagonwiwat, C., Govindan, R., Estrin, D.: Directed diffusion : a scalable and robust communication. In: Proceedings of the 6th Annual International Conference on Mobile Computing and Networking (MobiCom 2000), pp. 56–67 (2000)
52. Wang, C., Li, B., Sohraby, K., Daneshmand, M., Hu, Y.: Upstream congestion control in wireless sensor networks through cross-layer optimization. IEEE J. Sel. Areas Commun. **25**(4), 786–795 (2007)
53. Yaghmaee, M.H., Adjeroh, D.: A new priority based congestion control protocol for wireless multimedia sensor networks. In: IEEE International Symposium on a World of Wireless, Mobile and Multimedia Networks (2008)
54. Zhang, X., Guo, L.: An energy-balanced cooperative MAC protocol in MANETs. In: 2011 International Conference on Advanced Information Technology, vol. 20, pp. 44–49 (2011)
55. Rao, S., Shama, K.: Cross layer protocol for multimedia transmission in wireless network. Int. J. Comput. Sci. Eng. Surv. **3**(3), 15–28 (2012)
56. Han, L., Park, S., Kang, S., In, H.P.: An adaptive cross-layer FEC mechanism for video transmission over 802.11 WLANs. In: KSII International Conference on Internet, pp. 209–215, December 2009
57. Liu, F., Korakis, T., Tao, Z., Panwar, S.: A MAC-PHY cross-layer protocol for wireless ad-hoc networks, pp. 1792–1797 (2008)
58. Shan, H., Cheng, H.T., Zhuang, W.: Cross-layer cooperative MAC protocol in distributed wireless networks. IEEE Trans. Wirel. Commun. **10**(8), 2603–2615 (2011)
59. Guo, J., Sun, L., Wang, R.: A Cross-layer and multipath based video transmission scheme for wireless multimedia sensor networks. J. Netw. **7**(9), 1334–1340 (2012)
60. Melodia, T., Akyildiz, I.F.: Cross-layer QoS-aware communication for ultra wide band wireless multimedia sensor networks. IEEE J. Sel. Areas Commun. **28**(5), 653–663 (2010)
61. Ksentini, A., Naimi, M., Guéroui, A.: Toward an improvement of H.264 video transmission over IEEE 802.11e through a cross-layer architecture. IEEE Commun. Mag. **44**(1), 107–114 (2006)
62. AlAmri, A., Abdullah, M.: Cross-layer quality of service protocols for wireless multimedia sensor networks. In: Proceedings of the International Conference on Communication, Management and Information Technology, ICCMIT 2016, pp. 649–658 (2017)
63. Sun, G., Qi, J., Zang, Z., Xu, Q.: A reliable multipath routing algorithm with related congestion control scheme in wireless multimedia sensor networks. In: 2011 3rd International Conference on Computer Research and Development, vol. 4, pp. 229–233 (2011)

A User-Centered Approach to the Development of E-Health Systems: A Case of Uganda

Aminah Zawedde[1]([⊠]), Bernard Engotoit[1], Osbert Osamai Omeja[2], and Peter Kahiigi[2]

[1] School of Computing and IT, Makerere University, Kampala, Uganda
sazawedde@gmail.com, bengot4ms@gmail.com
[2] National Information and Technology Authority of Uganda, Kampala, Uganda
omeja4ever@gmail.com, Kahiigi@gmail.com

Abstract. Over the years the quality of health service delivery has drastically improved through deliberate efforts that have been made to implement e-health systems in developing economies. In Uganda particularly, e-health systems have been introduced and implemented in both government and private-owned healthcare units. However, due to lack of a structured mechanism to guide the development of usable e-health systems there have been growing concerns related to usability challenges with the e-health systems. The challenges that include complexity of system user interfaces, limited interactivity of e-health systems, security and confidentiality concerns are attributed to ad-hoc design of system interfaces, limited involvement of users in the design process and misalignment of e-health interventions with user needs. In this research we examine the challenges of usability of e-health systems in Uganda. The research process was guided by the design science methodology that is premised on systems analysis, surveys and interactions with medical personnel and IT practitioners working with the health sector in the country. The overall goal was to identify the niches for the development of a user-centered approach to guide the development of e-health systems for enhanced and sustainable health services delivery in Uganda. The developed user-centered approach was evaluated by experts to ensure that it was fit for the development of usable e-health systems in Uganda.

Keywords: User-centered · E-health systems · Developing economies

1 Introduction

Over the years the quality of health service delivery and governance has drastically improved in developing economies through embracing internet and other technologies (Lau and Kuziemsky 2016; Pankomera and Greunen 2018). Deliberate efforts have been made to implement e-health systems that have the ability to greatly impact positively on health service efficiency in developing economies and also potentially reduce on treatment costs (Bedeley and Palvia 2014; Pankomera and Greunen 2018). In Uganda particularly, e-health systems have been introduced and implemented in both government and privately-owned healthcare units. The government systems have been implemented by the Ministry of Health with support from Development Partners

G. Mendy et al. (Eds.): AFRICOMM 2018, LNICST 275, pp. 254–264, 2019.
https://doi.org/10.1007/978-3-030-16042-5_22

(DPs) and donors and these include the electronic Health Management Information System (e-HMIS), Integrated Diseases Surveillance and Response System (IDSR), the open Medical Records System (open MRS), patient records management systems, and the drug monitoring and control systems used in numerous healthcare units (Namakula and Kituyi 2014; Ministry of Health 2016). Other initiatives implemented include EMR system at Reach out Mbuya clinic, m-Health initiatives such as u-reporting which is an SMS- based platform, and the mTrac SMS-based health management information tool (Kiberu et al. 2017).

Although various e-health initiatives have been implemented and reported (Fanta et al. 2016; Namakula and Kituyi 2014), there have been growing concerns related to usability challenges with e-health systems in developing economies (Nahurira et al. 2016). The challenges include complexity of system user interfaces, limited interactivity of e-Health systems, security and confidentiality concerns (Kubbo et al. 2016). Vélez et al. (2014) argue that the usability challenges are attributed to poor design interfaces of the systems, limited involvement of users in the design process and misalignment of e-heath interventions with user needs. In many cases this has resulted in e-health system failures and unsustainable systems in the long run yet significant resources are being invested in e-health development at all levels (Nahurira et al. 2016). A preliminary investigation and extensive literature review were done that revealed no evidence of a structured mechanism to guide the development of usable e-health systems in developing economies (Bogale et al. 2015). This motivated the researchers to examine the challenges of usability of e-health systems and determine an appropriate approach to guide the development of usable e-health systems in Uganda.

The rest of the paper is structured as follows: Sect. 2 provides an overview of the usability concepts and highlights the gaps of the existing approaches used to guide the development of systems; Sect. 3 is a discussion of the research methodology that guided the research; Sect. 4 discusses the results of the research that include field findings on the state of usability of e-health systems in Uganda, the efficacy of usable e-health systems for Uganda and the proposed approach for the development of usable e-health systems in Uganda; and Sect. 5 concludes the paper and points to further research directions.

2 Related Works

Usability, defined in terms of its attributes as the degree to which a system is easy to learn and use together with its safety, effectiveness and efficiency, is a technical factor that is fundamental in the sustainable development of e-health systems in developing countries (Goldberg et al. 2011). The ISO standard (ISO 9241-210, 2010) provided the most ideal and state of the art guidelines for user interface design for both hardware and software. For usability to be achieved, the ISO standard's definition includes three aspects namely; effectiveness, efficiency and user satisfaction (Vitanen 2009).

Abran et al. (2003) also describe learnability, memorability and low error rate and security as aspects of usability that are described below:

User satisfaction: is the extent to which users' expectations of the information system meet their informational requirements (Zawedde 2016).

Effectiveness: the ability of an e-Health system to enable users to accomplish certain goals with high accuracy and completeness and its measure is in terms of *error rates* (Mumford 2014).

Efficiency: the measure of how many clicks it will take to progress through the various steps so as to have a task completed and its measure is in terms of *task completion time* and *learning time* (Mumford 2014).

Learnability: is the potential of a system to enable ease of learning by its intended users so that they can rapidly get work done (Harrison et al. 2013).

Memorability: is the ability of a user to retain how to use an application effectively (Harrison et al. 2013).

Error: are actions that prevent a user from accomplishing the desired goal and its unit of measure are the *number of errors* made by a user during the standard user test (Zawedde 2016).

Security: is a set of software attributes that prevent unauthorized access to programs and data (Abran et al. 2003).

A critique of the existing usability approaches discloses that while some approaches were successfully implemented in the developed economies, they were not adaptable in the context of the developing economies. Table 1 presents a summary of the gap analysis of some of the approaches that were reviewed.

Table 1. Gap analysis of existing usability frameworks

Framework	Strengths	Weaknesses
• A usability framework for electronic health records in Nigerian healthcare sector (Taiwo et al. 2016)	• Designed for developing economies • Has parameter indicators for usability measurement	• Focuses on one domain of e-health (i.e. Electronic Health Records) • Context of use analysis is ignored • Missing guidelines for the design of e-health systems • No evaluation of designed system
• The ISO 9241-11 model (Bevan 2009; Scandurra et al. 2013)	• Analyses context of usage, design and evaluation of usability as well as usability measures/attributes	• Leaves out other important usability measures • No emphasis engagement of users in systems design
• A user-centered model for web site design: needs assessment, user interface design, and rapid prototyping (Kinzie et al. 2002)	• Articulates the steps involved in development of usable health related websites • Based on the UCD process which is argued to successfully guide the development of usable systems	• Designed for developed countries particularly USA • Does not emphasize the evaluation of the designed website • Training users of the developed website is not key • Collaboration among the key stakeholders of e-health systems is not emphasized

Given the relative strengths and deficiencies in the usability approaches, to successfully guide the development process of e-health systems in Uganda, an appropriate approach was developed guided by the methodology described in Sect. 3.

3 The Design Science Research Methodology

This research was guided by the design science research methodology (Peffers et al. 2007) to achieve the objectives of the research. Table 2 illustrates the alignment of the objectives and activities with the phases of the methodology.

Table 2. Alignment of the objectives with the methodology

Methodology	Objectives	Methods, techniques, & tools	Outcomes
1. Problem identification	To examine the challenges facing usability of e-health systems in developing economies	• Primary & secondary data collection • Surveys & desk reviews	Usability challenges and possible solutions
2. Defining the Objectives for a solution	To determine the requirements for achieving usability of e-health systems in developing economies	• Data analysis and reporting using SPSS tool	Requirements and corresponding design decisions for the user-centered framework
3. Design and development	To design a user centered framework in line with the requirements that will guide the development of e-health systems in developing economies	• Review of ISO model (Scandurra et al. 2013) on usability and user centered model for Web Site Design (Kinzie et al. 2002). • MS Visio 2016 for framework design	User-centered framework
4. Evaluation	To evaluate the designed framework in order to determine whether it fulfills the requirements for developing usable e-health systems in developing economies	• Analytical evaluation by IT experts and the potential end users • Structured walk-throughs	Revised user-centered framework based on evaluation

4 Results

4.1 State of Usability of E-Health Systems in Uganda

A survey was conducted to determine the state of usability of e-health systems in Uganda. Given the non-existent data on healthcare units using e-health systems in

Uganda, Cochran's (1963) formula was used to determine the sample size. The survey was carried out in Wakiso and Kampala which are some of the central districts of Uganda. The sample size was determined using non-probability purposive sampling. Validity and reliability tests of the research instruments were also conducted. Out of the 136 questionnaires distributed to the selected respondents in 68 sampled healthcare units, 127 valid responses were obtained from 65 IT practitioners and 62 medical personnel. This constituted a valid response rate of 93% which is an excellent representation of the actual situation (Mundy 2002). Analysis of the two categories of data collected (IT practitioners and medical personnel) was processed using SPSS to obtain an understanding of the results on all the study variables.

Respondents reported on the usability attributes of e-health systems in their healthcare units. From the findings, 70% of the respondents agreed that their e-health systems are memorable given that they recalled how to use the e-health system. However, 70.2% of the respondents argued that the e-health systems were not efficient and effective given that they accomplish their tasks with much effort and more time. Furthermore, 82.2% of the respondents argued that the e-health systems in their healthcare units were not learnable, had high error rates (68%), limited and weak security measures (74.2%) and were not satisfactory (67.1%). These results confirmed the challenges of usability of e-heath system for healthcare service delivery in Uganda.

4.2   Efficacy of Usable E-Health Systems for Uganda

To address the challenges identified from literature and the field studies, requirements were determined for the appropriate approach that should guide the development of usable e-health systems in Uganda. The findings from the field data informed the choice of usability requirements and the corresponding design decisions for the proposed approach as summarized in Table 3.

Table 3. Challenges facing usability vs. requirements vs. design decisions

Usability challenges	Usability requirements	Framework design decisions
• Complexity of user interfaces (UI)	– Consider needs of a broad spectrum of users, including general public, specialized audiences, people with disabilities, those without access to advanced technologies, and those with limited English proficiency and ICT skills – Localization of UIs and online help	– UI design favourable to a range of audiences such as persons with disabilities, low technology users, and those with limited ICT skills – Localized UIs and online help at key stages

(*continued*)

Table 3. (*continued*)

Usability challenges	Usability requirements	Framework design decisions
• System limitations	– Need to engage users in systems design – Undertake business process analysis/re-engineering to assess system value to the business	– Engage users throughout the design of the e-health system
• Resistance to change from traditional paper-based systems	– Engage users in systems design and communicate the benefits of the system to user roles	– Engage users throughout the design of the e-health system and indicate system benefits
• System delays in task execution	– Funds for acquisition of computer hardware and reliable connectivity for faster execution of e-health system tasks – Use efficient design patterns and architecture for faster execution	– Avail funds for acquisition of state of the art computer infrastructure and reliable connectivity
• Poor security measures	– Implement stronger e-health systems security measures to enhance user confidence – Design and conduct security awareness programs for staff	– Identify and select appropriate security and privacy measures – Security awareness training in line with security requirements and application security components
• Poor system design and display	– Need to design e-health systems within the context of use analysis and usability performance objectives	– Conduct context based use analysis of e-health systems and determine usability performance objectives
• Uncoordinated stakeholder collaboration in e-health systems development	– Government, IT practitioners, Development Partners/donors, academia and private health service providers to co-operate and champion the development of usable e-health systems	– Collaboration between government policy makers, IT practitioners, Development Partners/donors, academia and private healthcare service providers
• Multiple data entry in related systems	– Integration of processes, data and applications	– Integrated systems

4.3 Proposed Framework for Development of Usable E-Health Systems in Uganda

Guided by the design phases from the sustainable architecture model (Kim and Rigdon 1998), the design decisions in Table 3 were adapted into the frameworks of the

ISO 9241-11 model on usability (Scandurra et al. 2013; Bevan 2009) and the user centered model for Web Site Design (Kinzie et al. 2002). The developed user-centered approach in this study is therefore an improvement of the selected frameworks aimed at overcoming the usability challenges of e-health systems in developing economies like Uganda.

The framework that advocates for engagement of users throughout the entire process of e-health systems development, is iterative and constitutes three phases: the pre-design, design and post design phases as illustrated in Fig. 1. At each one of the phases, there are various actors with roles to play and activities to execute with an aim of following a structured approach to developing a usable e-health system for developing economies. In the **pre-design phase**, financial support is solicited by top management of healthcare units and the responsible sectors of the Government to fund the development of usable e-health systems. A context of use analysis is also done to establish the requirements of the system. In the **design phase**, the design and testing of the e-heath system prototype is done while engaging all users to ensure that the designed system meets the user requirements and the set usability performance objectives. This requirement is derived from Kinzie et al. (2002) model. In the **post design phase**, testing and evaluating of the designed e-health system is done to ensure that the system is secure, memorable, learnable, efficient, effective and has lower error rates.

Table 4. Evaluation results of the developed user-centered approach

Functionality	Mean	Std. Deviation
Outlines key usability attributes required of an e-health system	4.55	.522
Addresses key challenges of usability of e-health systems	4.27	.647
Simplifies the process of developing usable e-health systems by providing guidelines	4.55	.688
Applicable in guiding development of usable e-health systems	4.45	.522
Ease of use	Mean	Std. Deviation
The framework is easy to learn and understand	4.27	.467
The framework requires little or no training to be used	4.09	.302
The phases in the framework are logically arranged	4.27	.467
The various components of the framework are well explained	4.27	.647
Traceability	Mean	Std. Deviation
The framework phases are interdependent with each other	4.09	.831
The framework components are interdependent with each other	3.82	.982
The guidelines/principles of the framework are interrelated	3.82	.874
The guidelines/principles in the framework are interdependent.	3.82	.874
No of respondents	11	

The designed framework was tested and evaluated to determine the efficacy of the research and to ascertain that the framework achieves the purpose for which it was developed (Peffers et al. 2012). Evaluation of the framework was conducted based on the parameters of functionality, ease of use and traceability of the designed user-centered approach (Hevner et al. 2008). The structured walkthroughs method (Buon-odono 2014) was used in evaluation of the designed framework. The procedure for the method included first determining the purpose of the walkthrough, secondly, deter-mining the inputs of the walkthrough (the designed framework and the evaluation questionnaire); thirdly, selecting participants in the walkthrough (eleven (11) skilled IT experts); and finally, outputs of the structured walkthrough (in form of feedback related to the designed framework).

Pre-testing of the evaluation questionnaire was conducted using validity (content validity index (CVI)) and reliability (Cronbach alfa coefficient (CAC)) tests. Results from pre-testing confirmed that the evaluation questionnaire was valid with a CVI = 0.80 and reliable with CAC = 0.75 (Polit et al. 2007; George 2011). From the results, we conclude that the experts are in agreement with the usefulness and appli-cability of the approach in guiding the development of usable e-health systems in Uganda. This conclusion was based on the assumption that a mean statistic in the range of 3.5 to 5 is a representation of positive perception (George 2011). The results in Table 4 indicate a positive perception of the respondents regarding the functionality, ease of use and traceability of the framework.

The experts also made recommendations for improvement on the developed approach. In order of their importance, these include the need:

- To clearly state the high-level roles of Government, IT practitioners/vendors and the healthcare units in development of usable e-health systems,
- To enact e-health inter-operability policies and standards during the design of e-health systems, so as to achieve integrated & interoperable systems and
- To engage all categories of users such as the visually impaired persons, users with limited skills.
- To involve top management of healthcare units as champions of e-health systems usability.
- To include change management in addition to training of healthcare staff as one of the components/guidelines in the post design phase of e-health systems,
- To conduct business process analysis during the design and development of e-health systems.
- To review software architecture and measure execution times as per business requirements.
- To design Localized User interfaces (UIs) and online help at key stages.

The researchers revised the approach based on the concerns raised by the experts and the final designed approach is illustrated in Fig. 1.

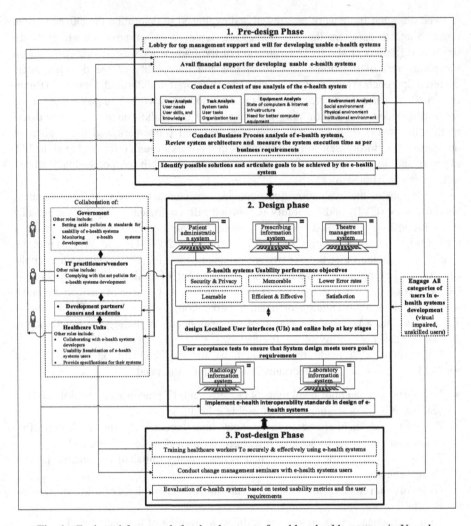

Fig. 1. Evaluated framework for development of usable e-health systems in Uganda

5   Conclusion and Future Work

This study examined the concept of usability of e-health systems and how it can be attained based on the paradigm of user-centered design so as to ensure that usable e-health systems are developed for staff of healthcare units in developing economies. To this end a framework was developed to guide the development of usable e-health systems in Uganda. The findings of the study indicated that there are a number of challenges hindering usability of e-health systems in Uganda. The challenges identified informed the requirements for the framework. The framework was evaluated by selected IT experts in the field of e-health, e-health policy experts and the end users of e-health systems in selected healthcare units.

Although the framework was found fit for the purpose of guiding the development of usable e-health systems in Uganda, further research can be done to explore the generalizability of the framework to healthcare units in developing economies Uganda that could have differences in e-health usability requirements.

References

Abran, A., Khelifi, A., Suryn, W., Seffah, A.: Consolidating the ISO usability models. In: Proceedings of 11th International Software Quality Management Conference, vol. 2003, pp. 23–25, April 2003

Fanta, G.B., Pretorius, L., Erasmus, L.D.: An evaluation of eHealth systems implementation frameworks for sustainability in resource constrained environments: a literature review. In: IAMOT 2015 Conference Proceedings, Cape Town Google Scholar (2015)

Bevan, N.: International standards for usability should be more widely used. J. Usability Stud. 4(3), 106–113 (2009)

Bedeley, R.T., Palvia, P.: A study of the issues of e-health care in developing countries: the case of Ghana. In: Twentieth Americas Conference on Information Systems, Savannah (2014)

Bogale, G.F., Pretorius, L., Erasmus, L.: An evaluation of e-health systems implementation frameworks for sustainability in resource constrained environments: a literature review. In: International Association for Management of Technology IAMOT 2015 Conference Proceedings (2015)

Buonodono, D.: Structured walkthrough process guide (2014)

Goldberg, L., et al.: Usability and accessibility in consumer health informatics: current trends and future challenges. Am. J. Prev. Med. 40(5), S187–S197 (2011)

George, D.: SPSS for Windows Step by Step: A Simple Study Guide and Reference, 17.0 Update, 10/e. Pearson Education India, Delhi (2011)

Harrison, R., Flood, D., Duce, D.: Usability of mobile applications: literature review and rationale for a new usability model. J. Interact. Sci. 1(1), 1 (2013)

Hevner, A.R., March, S.T., Park, J., Ram, S.: Design science in information systems research. Manag. Inf. Syst. Q. 28(1), 6 (2008)

Kubbo, M., Jayabalan, M., Rana, M.E.: Privacy and security challenges in cloud based electronic health record: towards access control model. In: The Third International Conference on Digital Security and Forensics (DigitalSec 2016), p. 113, September 2016

Kiberu, V.M., Mars, M., Scott, R.E.: Barriers and opportunities to implementation of sustainable e-Health programmes in Uganda: a literature review. Afr. J. Prim. Health Care Fam. Med. 9(1), 1–10 (2017)

Kim, J., Rigdon, B.: Sustainable architecture module: introduction to sustainable design. National Pollution Prevention Center for Higher Education (1998). http://www.umich.edu/~nppcpub. Accessed June 2015

Kinzie, M.B., Cohn, W.F., Julian, M.F., Knaus, W.A.: A user-centered model for web site design: needs assessment, user interface design, and rapid prototyping. J. Am. Med. Inform. Assoc. 9(4), 320–330 (2002)

Lau, F., Kuziemsky, C.: Handbook of eHealth Evaluation: An Evidence-Based Approach. University of Victoria, Victoria (2016)

Ministry of Health: The Annual Health Sector Performance Report 2016/17 (2016). http://www.health.go.ug/publications/reports?page=1

Mumford, C.: Five measures of software usability that impact user buy-in (2014). https://www. ifma.org/publications/blog-fmj/article/blog-fmj/2014/04/30/five-measures-of-software-usability-that-impact-user-buy-in. Accessed 5 Sept 2016

Mundy, D.: A question of response rate. Sci. Editor **25**(1), 25 (2002)

Nahurira, E., Businge, J., Nakato, R.: A framework for assessing information systems adoption and utilization in the healthcare. Int. J. Comput. Trends Technol. **39**(2), 89–99 (2016)

Namakula, S., Kituyi, G.M.: Examining health information systems success factors in Uganda's healthcare system. J. Glob. Health Care Syst. **4**(1), 1–16 (2014)

Pankomera, R., van Greunen, D.: A model for implementing sustainable mHealth applications in a resource constrained setting: a case of Malawi. Electron. J. Inf. Syst. Developing Countries **84**(2), e12019 (2018)

Peffers, K., Rothenberger, M., Tuunanen, T., Vaezi, R.: Design science research evaluation. In: Peffers, K., Rothenberger, M., Kuechler, B. (eds.) Design Science Research in Information Systems. Advances in Theory and Practice, DESRIST 2012. LNCS, vol. 7286, pp. 398–410. Springer, Heidelberg (2012). https://doi.org/10.1007/978-3-642-29863-9_29

Peffers, K., Tuunanen, T., Rothenberger, M.A., Chatterjee, S.: A design science research methodology for information systems research. J. Manag. Inf. Syst. **24**(3), 45–77 (2007)

Polit, D.F., Beck, C.T., Owen, S.V.: Is the CVI an acceptable indicator of content validity? Appraisal and recommendations. Res. Nurs. Health **30**(4), 459–467 (2007)

Scandurra, I., Åhlfeldt, R.M., Persson, A., Hägglund, M.: Building usability into national eHealth strategies, an action research approach. In: The 4th Infrastructure Workshop on Infrastructures for Healthcare: Action Research, Interventions, and Participatory Design, Tromsö, Norway, June 2013

Taiwo, O.O., Awodele, O., Kuyoro, S.O.: A usability framework for electronic health records in Nigerian healthcare sector. Int. J. Comput. Sci. Eng. (IJCSE) **5**(01), 16–20 (2016)

Vélez, O., Okyere, P.B., Kanter, A.S., Bakken, S.: A usability study of a mobile health application for rural Ghanaian midwives. J. Midwifery Women's Health **59**(2), 184–191 (2014)

Viitanen, J.: A user-centred approach to healthcare ICT development. Licentiate's Thesis, Espoo, 18 May 2009

Zawedde, A.: Modeling the dynamics of requirements process improvement. Technische Universiteit Eindhoven (2016)

Community Tools for Digital Inclusion

Elsa Oliveira, Eduardo Pereira, Pedro Madureira[✉],
Pedro Almeida, and Waldir Moreira

Fraunhofer Portugal AICOS,
Rua Alfredo Allen, 455/461, 4200-135 Porto, Portugal
{elsa.oliveira,eduardo.pereira,pedro.madureira,
pedro.almeida,waldir.junior}@fraunhofer.pt

Abstract. Involving the citizens in their community dynamics and giving them an active role in tackling their main needs and reaching their expectations can be a successful recipe for a well-functioning society. In developing countries, this community strategy is even more important since these societies suffer from a lack of means that may compromise the effectiveness of their public services. Intended also to encourage the access to digital solutions and therefore to digital inclusion, our Community Tools solution proposes two participatory and collaborative governance digital applications: IZIDoc, a solution that allows the user to request official documents to the related administrative institution; and OurMoz, an application that enables the citizen to report community occurrences, concerning the public services. Both applications have been co-created, designed, tested and validated with the help of target users to facilitate adoption of the proposed solutions in Mozambique.

Keywords: Community tools · Digital inclusion · Governance · Citizens · Developing countries

1 Introduction

In social interactions, citizenship, political awareness or public services, the use of Information and Communication Technologies (ICT) solutions to facilitate the communication and spread of information may play an important role in the development of a given community. Gathering people around one topic or gathering the necessary information about a city, being it about a community problem, market prices, health or other public services, may strongly contribute to human development. Still, access to ICT is not available for all citizens, with the problem being further aggravated in developing countries [1].

Despite of ICT increasing popularity (e.g., mobile broadband access is cheaper; half of world population is online; 7 out of 10 youngsters are connected), there is much to do in what concerns to Internet access (Percentage of disconnected are: 33% in developing countries; 70% in least developed countries; 90% of non-connected youngsters are in Africa or Asia and the Pacific; women access is 25% lower than men in Africa) [2].

© ICST Institute for Computer Sciences, Social Informatics and Telecommunications Engineering 2019
Published by Springer Nature Switzerland AG 2019. All Rights Reserved
G. Mendy et al. (Eds.): AFRICOMM 2018, LNICST 275, pp. 265–274, 2019.
https://doi.org/10.1007/978-3-030-16042-5_23

Upon this, the development of community tools should promote social and digital inclusion of these citizens located in underserved communities. These tools are expected to combine the use of new technologies and digital education, bringing the interactivity, innovation, and inclusivity for underserved groups, which are still put aside due to the digital divide.

In this paper, we present IZIDoc and OurMoz. A pair of community tools, developed to improve the quality of life of the citizens. Based in a scalable and widely used framework - i.e., Material Design [3] from Google – these tools aims to reduce the gap between the western interface design pattern and the purposed solution, which was created, designed, tested, and validated with users from a community with different levels of digital literacy, namely in Mozambique.

The paper is structured as follows. Section 2 describes the context in which the community tools shall be used, considering the profile of the Mozambican citizens, the areas they live in, and the technology they have access to. Section 3 presents the user-centric design process used in the development. Section 4 details the validation tests and obtained results from the testing methods used. Section 5 describes the relevant redesign work carried out after the validations tests. Finally, Sect. 7 concludes the work, providing insights on the future next steps.

2   Contextual Description

The context in which IZIDoc and OurMoz applications could be applied considers the profile of the Mozambican citizens, the areas they live in, and the technology they have access to. As aforementioned, we reduced the scope of the work to Mozambique, but at a later stage we want to further consider other countries and validate the tools with the respective users as further explained in Sect. 7.

Since Mozambique comprises different provinces and municipalities, we built the profile of the citizens of Maputo city and its surrounding, based either on accounts from the citizens or on field visits to Mozambique, as described next.

2.1   Setting

The most common settings of Maputo and surrounding areas where citizens find themselves can be divided into urban and suburban areas.

Urban areas are parts of the city with better conditions such as pavement roads, tall buildings, better availability of services and overall better quality of life; Internet connectivity is available by subscription at homes, and for free at universities.

Suburban areas tend to be more humble, often with large numbers of people living in small houses built with little planning and bad materials, precarious sanitation, difficult access by car to some parts due to narrow pathways that do not accommodate cars, no pavement on the roads, creating a mix that results in overall worst quality of life; Internet may be available at Internet cafés in these areas, but users may resort to their mobile data plans, which can be less costly.

2.2   Users

Regarding the users, we observed that the community tools should consider different characteristics from which we highlight in Table 1, considering different aspects.

Table 1. Observed aspects and characteristics of the target user.

Observed aspects	Users
Types	Are regular citizens (youngster, adults, workers, students, …)
Living area	May live in the urban centre or surrounding suburban areas;
Age	Are of different age groups
Employment	Self-employed, employees of private and governmental entities, informal jobs, and unemployed
Education	Have different literacy levels, from a minimum literacy level to fully educated
Technology	Most likely are technologically challenged, although some are proficient with tech devices
	May own up to two mobile phones, with most having at least one device
	May or may not know how to use mobile apps, including how to discover and install them
	May have access to a desktop computer at home/work, even though it is not widely common
	Rely on basic and feature phones, which are enough for everyday use (e.g., most banks offer USSD-based access to some of their services, which require the simplest of phones)
Communication	Use social media, but most of utilization refers to SMS and voice
	Access the internet mostly through their cell phones, by buying mobile data plans
	Might access the internet through home subscriptions, or for free at universities and offices
	Have limited internet access or bad quality internet connection even in urban areas
	Find internet data plans to be expensive, and are very careful about spending data
	May have cellular coverage in the villages where they live

It is worth noting that the list is not meant to be exhaustive, and we may have left out aspects/characteristics that can be as relevant as the aforementioned ones. However, our main goal is to understand the community and respective users to meet their needs and expectations throughout the development of the proposed solutions.

3 Proposed Community Tools

The community tool IZIDoc aims at improving the process of requesting a document from an official entity, e.g., requesting a new ID card from the registry office.

Often citizens find themselves losing significant amount of time in long queues to perform tasks that could be easily simplified, using a smartphone. IZIDoc was designed to reduce the time spent in those queues, allowing the user to request a document or provide information about all the process and needs to acquire such document.

For documents that have been requested and are yet to be issue, the user is able to check the status of the request and details about the document in case. Once the document is issued, the application notifies the user of its readiness and the user shall proceed to collect the document in the near service point. Saving time of both citizens and entities, since the application overcomes the need of requesting documents in person.

Regarding OurMoz, the citizen is expected to have a more proactive behaviour within society. This proactiveness relates to the fact that the user will have the possibility to report on any issue (e.g., a broken pipe, an unattended garbage bin) that may affect his/her community's quality of life. Upon an issue (e.g., broken pipe), the user may add it to the city's repository, and once the issue reaches (i.e., it is posted to) the authorities (e.g., Water department), they will send a team to fix what has been reported. Location, small description, and picture can also be added to the reported issues, which can be used by authorities to assess such issues and even prioritize the order of work to resolve them. Keeping the process of reporting as simple as possible, in order to encourage users to participate in the process of improving their communities. The user can also search for specific issues or items related to issues of interest (i.e., to find out for instance if there are any other reports on the same issue).

3.1 Design Approach

Based on the context and profile of the target community, we followed a user-centric design approach while developing the IZIDoc and OurMoz applications. An iterative methodology, which began earlier by analysing and understanding the context of the user, followed by the specification of user requirements, creating personas and scenarios that are suitable for users' needs and expectations.

We prototyped possible solutions using storyboards and mockups allowing us to quickly design, discuss and redesign ideas, considering the user, its context, and its tasks within a framework that ensured a present-day user interface [3].

However, the validation tests have proved the need of several adaptations in the user interface as further detailed next (cf., Sect. 4).

4 Validation Tests

The process of designing suitable solutions for the context of the target user considers the evaluation of the designed prototypes, in order to discover if there are usability problems in the user interface regarding IZIDoc and OurMoz applications.

Both applications were submitted to two validation phases, considering Human-Computer Interaction experts and potential users, respectively. Our goal with these two validation methods was to gather feedback from experts and potential users, using quick and effective tools to evaluate the user experience of both applications, and to further improve both applications upon those issues.

4.1   Heuristic Evaluation

For the first validation phase, we used heuristic evaluation for mobile computing [4] to help development team members to identify and estimate the impact of each issue found during the development process, and a severity rating scale [5], a well-known method that allows to allocate the resources to fix the main problems and provides an estimate effort for additional usability resolutions.

Heuristic evaluation was carried out by three researchers with a wide working experience in user testing. However, we ensure that two of them had no contact with the project, in order to ensure an independent and unbiased evaluation for comparing purposes. The results were recorded as written reports, summarizing all issues from the evaluators. As for the severity rating, the evaluators were asked to estimate each usability issue found, in order to understand their impact in the user experience.

Gathering the results from the researchers, we analysed and discovered a total of twenty-seven reported issues in IZIDoc (nine issues with severity level 1; eight issues with severity level 2; and ten issues with severity level 3), from which the most relevant are summarized in Table 2, along with the proposed solutions.

Table 2. Reported issues and implemented solutions for IZIDoc.

Identified issues	Implemented solutions
How to identify a document with processing issues	Added a warning sign to identify a document with processing issues
Confusing app entrance point and hierarchy structure	Changed the designation of the menu items in order to highlight the main action and clarify the content
Labels and buttons look the same	Moved the labels to the left, on buttons' opposite side
Notification after request document almost imperceptible	Increased the notification time informing the request creation

As for OurMoz, the researchers identified twenty-one issues (two issues with severity level 1; fourteen issues with severity level 2; and five issues with severity level 3). Table 3 presents those issues that required more attention and respective solutions.

Regarding this analysis and its importance to the development cycle, these were the most relevant issues and that led to meaningful changes to the user interface (UI). It is worth noting that, independently of the severity level, all the reported issues were considered during the UI improvement process for IZIDoc and OurMoz.

Table 3. Reported issues and implemented solutions for OurMoz.

Identified issues	Implemented solutions
If Filter is active, show selected options	A new view was designed in order to accommodate new visual elements
'Clear' filter button	Redesigned filter view
The 'Refresh' button is hidden, within a menu with a single item	Added SwipeRefreshLayout and kept the menu option
After add location, button should change to 'Change location'	Button label changed after a location is assigned
'Save' button in navbar should use same component as other main action buttons	Save button became sticky on the bottom of the viewport

4.2 Field Tests

On a second validation phase, we followed the usability test protocol [6], which uses three usability metrics: (i) effectiveness, expressed in terms of unassisted and assisted completion rate, number of errors, and number of assists; (ii) efficiency, measured in terms of task execution time, i.e., time taken to successfully complete a task; and (iii) satisfaction, expressed in terms of a usability score, obtained by a System Usability Scale [7] questionnaire which all participants completed after each test session.

This validation phase was performed in Mozambique and driven by two native administrators, which recorded all tests for later analysis. These tests (cf., Fig. 1. Field tests regarding IZIDoc (on the left) and OurMoz (on the right). Fig. 1) considered 21 users (IZIDoc: 10; OurMoz: 11), where 6 were women and 15 were men.

Fig. 1. Field tests regarding IZIDoc (on the left) and OurMoz (on the right).

The target user population was broad in terms of age and gender, aged between 18 and 41, and one of the inclusion criteria for the test was that they were required to know how to use a smartphone. Each user performed 4 tasks for both IZIDoc and OurMoz (cf., Table 4). The overall system usability score, for both applications, was between 77 and 87, which is above the suggested reference value [7] regarding applications that meet the minimum usability requirements.

Table 4. Tasks performed by users with IZIDoc and OurMoz.

IZIDoc		OurMoz	
Tasks	Description	Tasks	Description
A	Change profile settings	E	Change profile settings
B	Request document	F	Add occurrence
C	Update list "A processar"	G	Update list
D	Check if the requested document is ready	H	Filter occurrences

During the tests with the IZIDoc application, the users had no issues with Task A. Regarding Task B, the users were uncomfortable with the scrollable tabs, which hid part of the document categories and that most of the users did not realize it was a scrollable component display.

In Task C the users have difficulty on finding the refresh action to update the current list which was hidden in a menu in the action bar, and, lastly, in Task D many of the users did not notice the notifications regarding the status of the requested documents. Regarding OurMoz application, the administrators identified the following events: the users had no issues related with the Task E; in Task F, the floating button (plus icon) which provided the main action of the application - Adding an occurrence – appeared obfuscated due to the background images, and, even so, the plus icon was too abstract to be related with activation of the main action.

As for Task G, the results were apparently better than those from the IZIDoc's Task C. This was due to the fact that some of the users had already participated on the similar task on the IZIDoc's application usability test, or they discovered the functionality of the button during their attempts on the OurMoz's Task F.

Finally, in Task H, it was noted that many times users shifted the right order for the fields corresponding to 'De' and 'Até'. In other words, they selected the actual date for the field 'De' (from) and the previous date for the field 'Até' (To).

5 Redesign Approach

After the validation tests, we analysed its outcomes and, considering the common findings on the two applications, the redesign team proposed the following.

In order to overcome the difficulty in updating the documents status list (Task C) and the occurrences list (Task G) which involved finding the 'Refresh' action, we incorporated a direct icon placed in the action bar (Fig. 2a) instead of having the refresh action within a hidden menu. We also decided to highlight the search bar when activated by adding a lighter background colour to the text input field in order to focus the search intention (Fig. 2b).

Secondary actions and its 'text buttons' needed to be emphasized and distinguished from the normal text, for that purpose we added a light background colour as if the button was focused (Fig. 3a). Another relevant resolution was about the layouts' update throughout the app, providing a continuous data actualization and that is crucial for this type of tool, which relies on the updates by the server side.

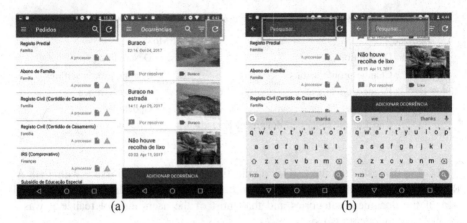

Fig. 2. (a) Update/refresh icon placed in the action bar (left: IZIDoc; right: OurMoz); (b) Search form emphasized (left: IZIDoc; right: OurMoz).

One of the main improvements was enabling the user to request documents or report occurrences being offline (as connectivity may be intermittent) with requests and reports being sent automatically when connectivity is restored.

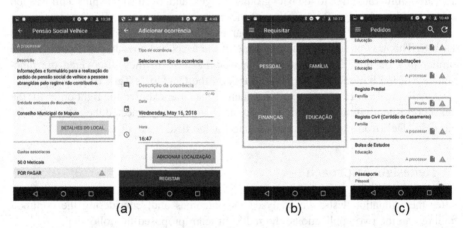

Fig. 3. (a) Emphasised 'Text buttons' (left: IZIDoc; right: OurMoz); (b) IZIDoc: Tile navigation with documents' categories; (c) IZIDoc: List navigation with the requested documents status.

Regarding IZIDoc's specificities and the usability issues pointed out in the validation tests, the redesign solution aimed to tackle the following constraint, seeking improved alternatives. Concerning the users' difficulty on using the scrolling navigation tabs, which organized the documents by category, we solved by suggesting a new display screen to navigate through the documents' categories with tiles (Fig. 3b), avoiding hidden tabs/categories.

To ensure consistency along the interface, the navigation through two fixed tabs which organized the documents by its status ('A processar' and 'Pronto'), was also replaced by a full list of documents organized by request order. The document status and a related icon were placed beside each listed document (Fig. 3c).

Considering OurMoz's findings, we started by improving the obfuscation of the application main action, replacing the floating button component '+' by a persistent footer button entitled 'Adicionar Ocorrência' (Fig. 4a).

To provide a straightforward interface related with the image picker, we opted for a 'call to action' display by adding the sentence 'Adicione uma foto' followed by the two options: adding a photo taken by the phone camera or a photo stored at the photo gallery (Fig. 4b).

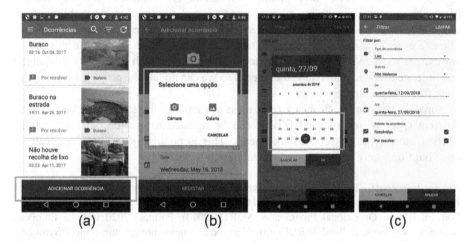

Fig. 4. (a) A 'Persistent footer button' for the main action instead of the floating button component; (b) Image picker with a straightforward interface; (c) Dates older than the one selected on the 'De' field are disabled for the 'Até' field.

Then, to better guide and simplify users' date input, using restrictions, the allowable dates for the 'Até' field are now newer than the one selected on the 'De' field.

Finally, we also included a map view with (i) pending occurrences enabling a different experience on the perception of the issues per area; and (ii) with location of a specific occurrence helping the user on better understand the mentioned location.

6   Discussion

The validation tests proved that a widely used user interface design framework [3] may still entail usability constraints depending on the users' level of digital literacy. Some of the proposed components may not be easily recognized by the users in their associated action. Thus, they require a level of abstraction that may trigger a rejection during the initial contact with both applications.

We followed with a redesign work, as described in the Sect. 5, avoiding abstract and unfamiliar concepts in order to provide a straightforward user interface, still considering the Material Design guidelines from Google.

7 Conclusions and Future Work

This paper presented two solutions – IZIDoc and Ourmoz – to users from underserved communities, identifying their main characteristics, settings and commonly used technology. Following a user-centric design methodology, requirements, user tasks, personas, and scenarios were identified, allowing the development of prototypes that were tested iteratively, throughout several usability tests – heuristic evaluation and field trials. This process allowed us to identify multiple usability improvements in both applications, leading us to a stable version of both community tools.

As future work, we have planned to extend the validation test beyond the Mozambican context, including other countries, in order to increase the usability of the tools. Moreover, we want to make both systems more inclusive by allowing (digitally) illiterate users to perform the proposed tasks. At the time of the writing of this paper, our experts were on a field trip to Mozambique interacting with technically challenged and illiterate users, to understand their needs so we can update the proposed community tools from this perspective.

Finally, we want to further extend these community tools: OurMoz can include different types of reports; and IZIDoc can be updated to include other institutions offering other types of services/documents. This is possible since both applications were built on top of a flexible and modular architecture.

Acknowledgments. The authors would like to acknowledge the support from Universidade Eduardo Mondlane during the field work and tests, and the financial support obtained from North Portugal Region Operational Programme (NORTE 2020), Portugal 2020 and the European Regional Development Fund (ERDF) from European Union through the project Symbiotic technology for societal efficiency gains: Deus ex Machina (DEM), NORTE-01-0145-FEDER-000026, and project Collective Transfer FhP, NORTE-01-0246-FEDER-000029.

References

1. Pereira, A., Madureira, P., Resende, C., Almeida, P., Moreira, W.: SV4D architecture: building sustainable villages for developing countries. In: Proceedings of the 9th EAI International Conference on e-Infrastructure and e-Services for Developing Countries (AFRICOMM) (2017)
2. International Telecommunication Union (ITU): ICT Facts and Figures 2017 (2017)
3. Material Design. https://material.io/design/. Accessed 15 June 2018
4. Bertini, E., Catarci, T., Dix, A., Gabrielli, S., Kimani, S., Santucci, G.: Appropriating heuristic evaluation for mobile computing. Int. J. Mob. Hum. Comput. Interact. (IJMHCI) **1**(1), 20–41 (2009)
5. Nielsen, J.: Severity Ratings for Usability Problems. https://www.nngroup.com/articles/how-to-rate-the-severity-of-usability-problems/. Accessed 15 June 2018
6. ISO/IEC 25062: Software Engineering - Software product Quality Requirements and Evaluation (SQuaRE) - Common Industry Format (CIF) for Usability test Reports (2006)
7. Sauro, J.: Measuring Usability with the System Usability Scale (SUS) (2011). Retrieved from MeasuringU: https://measuringu.com/sus/

Comm4Dev: Communication Infrastructure for Development

António Sousa, Carlos Resende, André Pereira,
and Waldir Moreira[✉]

Fraunhofer Portugal AICOS,
Rua Alfredo Allen, 455/461, 4200-135 Porto, Portugal
{antonio.sousa, carlos.resende, andre.pereira,
waldir.junior}@fraunhofer.pt

Abstract. One of the main reasons for the still observed digital divide is the lack of communication infrastructure in regions away from urban centres. As these regions are normally spread over long distances and have small populations (i.e., prospective users), operators see little business opportunities and refrain from large investments to reach these areas. Upon this scenario, our Communication Infrastructure for Development (Comm4Dev) solution was built to offer a low-cost backhaul infrastructure, providing these underserved communities with broadband access. As to allow a wider range of application scenarios (e.g., precision agriculture, industrial production support), our Comm4Dev solution has been updated not only to further promote digital inclusion, but also to allow the development of communities that are in remote areas. To illustrate the potential of our Comm4Dev solution, we validated it in an indoor hydroponic farming testbed.

Keywords: Broadband access · Low-cost backhaul infrastructure ·
Communication for development · Digital inclusion

1 Introduction

Broadband access in remote areas is not a priority for operators due to the high deployment costs: providing fibre infrastructure and/or broadband cells is expensive and the return of investment in such regions is very low (and even inexistent) given the low number of users and their power of purchase. Moreover, these regions are characterized for being rather disruptive, which means that users in these communities might be completely disconnected, with eventual periods of connectivity. This consequently contributes to the digital divide we witness today [1].

However, off-the-shelf solutions can be considered to provide these underserved communities with a communication for development (Comm4Dev) network, aiming at an easy-to-deploy solution that can be used to improve the lives of the people in isolated areas.

Our Comm4Dev network infrastructure [2] presents a hardware and software solution to address this digital divide challenge. And working on top of such solution, we currently focused on the reduction of its off-grid installation complexity and cost, as

G. Mendy et al. (Eds.): AFRICOMM 2018, LNICST 275, pp. 275–283, 2019.
https://doi.org/10.1007/978-3-030-16042-5_24

well as on the inclusion of more high power backhaul interfaces and the integration with Bluetooth Low Energy (BLE) [3, 4] and Global Positioning System (GPS) to allow the inclusion of more demanding scenarios, that is, where (i) energy may not be available; (ii) more links are required (i.e., star topology); (iii) there is the need to interoperate with other communication technologies (e.g., data exchange with temperature/humidity sensors deployed in farm); and (iv) location information is important to pinpoint maintenance needs.

Thus, the capabilities of the wireless backhaul (WiBACK) node evolved into a ready to deploy off-grid module, capable of building multiple backhaul links and easily interface with BLE-enabled devices or networks.

This paper documents such evolution and its validation, and is structured as follows. Section 2 presents the new challenges imposed to WiBACK node, and how its new features and capabilities answer the needs of new envisioned application scenarios. Section 3 presents the validation performed considering the particular case for precision agriculture, where the WiBACK node shall serve as gateway for BLE sensors in an indoor hydroponic farming testbed. And finally Sect. 4 presents conclusions and future work.

2   WiBACK and New Challenges Addressed

Comm4Dev's first version [2] addresses the goal of connecting people in isolated areas by proposing a low-cost and easy-to-deploy hardware and software solution. On the hardware side, the WiBACK technology with its QoS-provisioning, auto-configuration, self-management, self-healing and "Plug & Play" characteristics allows for easy, hassle-free deployment.

However, the installation of WiBACK nodes in off-grid scenarios is still a challenge: considering the use of renewable energy on such locations, the selection and installation of the components to harvest (e.g., solar panels, wind turbines, etc.), manage (e.g., DC/DC converters, MQTT controllers, battery charging and battery protection circuits, etc.) and store (e.g., batteries selection and dimensioning) the energy are complex tasks that still require highly skilled technicians to perform them.

Additionally, Comm4Dev's first version considers an earlier version of the WiBACK node that has only two high power backhaul interfaces. Consequently, in topologies requiring multiple links (e.g., star), different WiBACK nodes would be required to cover different locations. Thus, having one WiBACK node capable of providing multiple links is desired and shall reduce the installation cost and complexity.

As different communication technologies may exist, and upon the need to offer an IoT-compliant solution, a Bluetooth Low Energy (BLE) interface should be considered, as this technology is expected to be the one with the biggest market share [5]. In fact, the choice for the BLE interface is related to the penetration of this technology on the smartphones, sensors, actuators and gateways. Such penetration eases the expansion of the backhaul links by: connecting the WiBACK to multiple manufacturer devices, which can be connected with each other through a BLE mesh network; or by connecting it to smartphones, or other mobile apparatus, equipped with a BLE interface, which in turn can serve as data relays. These scenarios enable the IoT concept to be applied in the Comm4Dev installations.

Finally, GPS capability is desired to enable the node not only to perform GPS tagging on the data being generated at the sites, but also to help in pinpointing those sites that may require maintenance. These are value added features that should be considered.

With such challenges in mind, the WiBACK N4C was developed by Fraunhofer FIT/DeFuTech in partnership with Fraunhofer Portugal AICOS, and includes power management components for off-grid installations, more high power backhaul radios for the creation of multiple links, and BLE and GPS interfaces to broaden the range of application scenarios (e.g., precision agriculture, industry-related solutions).

Regarding the power management unit, WiBACK N4C integrates components that safely and efficiently control the energy harvested, which is then stored on a Lithium Iron Phosphate (LiFePo) battery that can be integrated inside the device's enclosure. With this approach, the installation technician only needs to consider the dimensioning of the harvester (e.g., solar panels power, orientation/positioning) and battery capacity for the location of the site as the N4C comes with a simpler and more compact energy solution for off-grid operation.

In what concerns the multiple links challenge, WiBACK N4C is equipped with 4 high-power 5 GHz radio interfaces, which, using a WiFi based communication protocol, provide the possibility of establishing more links per site with a single node. This improvement provides not only more flexibility to the network design process, but also a reduction on the cost and on the energy footprint, since a single node is now able to have the double amount of links when compared to its predecessor.

The BLE interface is added using a BLE module with Bluetooth SIG mesh [6, 7] capabilities, allowing the connection to BLE devices or networks, opening the possibility to use Comm4Dev solution on IoT-like scenarios, or to use the BLE as a configuration interface for the WiBACK N4C node.

The GPS interface is an added-value feature allowing not only to get the location of the deployment sites which aid in the detection of problematic nodes and fast maintenance, but also geotagging of produced data for more localized understanding of specific sites.

Figure 1 illustrates a Comm4Dev installation where the WiBACK N4C is being used to address these new features in a set of illustrative application scenarios. Node A is an off-grid and multilink node, powered by solar energy and using its 4 backhaul radios operating at its maximum capacity to relay the incoming traffic, linking several sites to the central location (Node B) that connects to the WiBACK controller.

On the edge of the network, the N4C nodes may also be solar powered or directly connected to power grid, and in some situations they may still be serving as a relay to multiple locations. An example is Node E which is in the District administration that locally offers Internet access to citizens through the installed access point (AP) and further extends the internet connectivity to villages 1, 2, and 3.

Moreover, the N4C nodes may be used as a gateway to BLE sensors and actuators on remote monitoring applications, integrating the IoT concepts into the Comm4Dev installation: for instance, Node C is being directly connected to BLE sensors/actuators on small remote monitoring/control scenario (e.g., precision agriculture), while Node D makes use of the BLE mesh network to allow the remote monitoring/control of large installations (e.g., in an industry setting overseeing production lines).

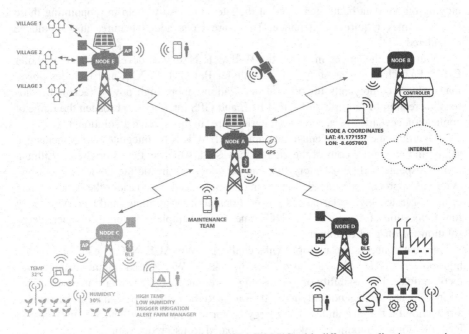

Fig. 1. A Comm4Dev installation based on WiBACK N4C with different application scenarios.

Finally, all the monitored information may be geotagged by the GPS module of the WiBACK N4C, a feature that can also be used in the maintenance process of non-working WiBACK nodes and/or of the site where the nodes are deployed.

3 Sample Application Scenario and Performed Evaluation

Out of the aforementioned application scenarios, we focused on the remote monitored agriculture. This section starts by presenting our indoor hydroponic farming testbed as a sample application scenario considering the BLE capabilities of the WiBACK N4C node. Then, the section details the tests carried out concerning a potential BLE mesh network that can extend the communication capabilities of our Comm4Dev solution.

3.1 Sample Application Scenario

In order to understand the BLE capabilities of the WiBACK N4C, we updated our Comm4Dev Porto network [2]. Figure 2 presents a BLE device (a) that monitors the water temperature, water pH, water electro conductivity, ambient temperature, relative humidity, atmospheric pressure and sensor battery level in an indoor hydroponic farming testbed. The monitored data is transmitted over BLE to the WiBACK N4C (b), which in turn sends it to a remote server for storage and visualization through a web-portal.

Fig. 2. WiBACK N4C as a gateway for an indoor hydroponic farming testbed.

On the described installation, the mesh feature of the WiBACK N4C is tested by connecting its BLE interface through a simple one-hop link towards the aforementioned BLE device (e.g., PANDLETS equipped with more sensors – PANDLETS Sensing+ [8]). However, a more complex mesh of BLE devices may be easily integrated to further extend the communication range of the Comm4Dev solution. For this extended scenario, the BLE devices communicate with each other under the Bluetooth SIG mesh specification [6, 7] to reach the central gateway, that is, the WiBACK N4C, and through it connect to the Internet as it already happens in the illustrated scenario.

This sample scenario helps us illustrate the applicability of WiBACK N4C in a precision agriculture setting, where our Comm4Dev solution can be used to further develop underserved communities. Next, we present a performance evaluation on the potential BLE mesh network that can further extend the communication range of our Comm4Dev solution in such applications.

3.2   Performed Evaluation

We studied the BLE mesh capabilities in order to characterize and validate the applicability of this feature to the aforementioned scenario, and also to assess the limits of the network and the possibility of applying it to more demanding applications. To accomplish this, we assessed the minimum time between events considering a couple of Nordic Thingy:52 devices [9], mimicking a BLE mesh network. The choice to test this parameter is based on the need to understand if the BLE mesh network supports the reception of events at a rate that is suitable for the devices that are monitoring and actuating on the described application scenarios (cf., Sect. 2), and if so, understand the limits to which the BLE mesh network can be applied to.

Minimum Time Between Events. For the sake of simplicity, an event is defined as sending a Request message that expects a Response message. This evaluation focused on determining the rate at which a new event could take place without having information loss. The size of the Request/Response messages includes the BLE and Mesh headers with a payload of at most 8 bytes.

Figure 3 depicts the test setup with a two-node Bluetooth mesh network and a computer, where Node 1 sends a Request message, and Node 2 sends a Response message back (i.e., an event). The computer is connected to Node 1 setting the frequency at which Request messages are sent, and keeps track of the minimum time period between events that do not cause information loss.

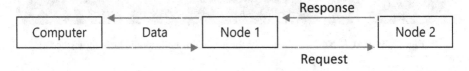

Fig. 3. Laboratory test setup.

Considering this setup, the computer configured Node 1 to send 200 Request messages (i.e., perform a test with 200 events) with an initial time period between events of ∼457.5 ms to Node 2. At the end of each test, the computer checks if all the Request messages received the corresponding Response, i.e., if all the events (pair of Request-Response messages) successfully happened over the network. If successful, a new test cycle with a shorter (more demanding) time period is tested. Otherwise, a higher (less demanding) time period is tested. This process continues with new test cycles until the computer discovers the shortest possible time period between events that do not cause information loss, i.e., all the Request messages received the corresponding Response.

Figure 4 presents the results of this performance evaluation test, where the "Test #" refers to a new test cycle composed of 200 events, and "Event period" is the time period between events considered for each test. The light grey dots represent test cycles at which information was lost (at least 1 of the 200 events failed, i.e., either the Request or Response message was lost during the transmission due to network overload), and the black dots represent test cycles with no information loss.

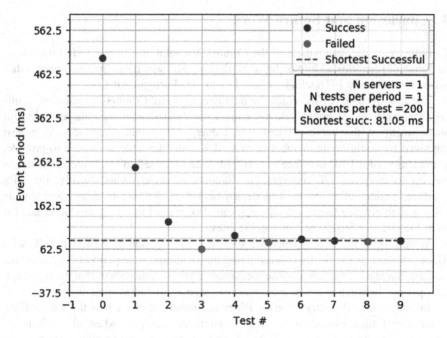

Fig. 4. Test results for the minimum time between events.

It can be seen in Fig. 4 that the minimum time period between events is ∼81 ms, achieved on test cycle 9, i.e., Node 1 is able to send a new Request message (i.e., start a new event) every ∼81 ms and neither the Request message or the Response is lost.

As more nodes are added to the network, the minimum time period will tend to increase, due to the nodes having to deal with bidirectional message transmission. Nevertheless, such limitation may not be critical in certain application scenarios where real time message exchange is not mandatory, or in scenarios where monitoring does not demand high sampling frequencies, which consequently increases the time period between Request messages.

Agricultural and some industrial applications are some of those scenarios, where temperature, soil characteristics (e.g., humidity, nutrient level, etc.), machine degradation status, among others, are variables that vary slowly in time, and/or the variation does not require an immediate reaction, so sampling frequencies (i.e., time period between data requests) may be above the milliseconds mark. In fact, even scenarios with high sampling rate sensors, or a mixture of high and slow sampling rate sensors, can be considered, as long as the dimensioning of the monitoring solution takes into consideration the observed network limitations, and the inherent energy consumption associated with the amount of data travelling in the network.

4 Conclusion and Future Work

To further ease the deployment of the Comm4Dev solution [2], and to further extend the range of scenarios addressed by it, WiBACK N4C was developed in a partnership between Fraunhofer FIT/DeFuTech and Fraunhofer Portugal AICOS.

The new WiBACK N4C eases the deployment of the Comm4Dev solution in off-grid scenarios by integrating all the complexity related with the safe and efficient management of the harvested and stored energy. The radio interfaces were also improved by doubling the number of WiBACK links the node is capable to provide. The addition of a BLE interface is two-fold: it can be used to configure the node, as well as to integrate IoT concepts on Comm4Dev deployments. Finally, the GPS interface, besides allowing to map deployment sites, helping to detect problematic nodes and to provide fast maintenance, it can also be used to geotag produced data for more localized understanding of specific sites.

Within the scope of this paper, we studied the integration of WiBACK N4C with Bluetooth mesh networks by characterizing the minimum time period between events (i.e., exchange of Request/Response messages). The test results show that the minimum time periods between every new Request message is limited to ~ 81 ms.

In conclusion, the integration of Bluetooth mesh networks into the Comm4Dev solution to further extend its range is feasible for scenarios where the volume of information to be transmitted is reduced, and where real-time communication is not mandatory. The presented indoor hydroponic farming testbed is one of such scenarios.

Fully integrating the WiBACK N4C in the Porto testbed to test all the new features of the WiBACK node is one of the ongoing next steps, as well as the fully integration of the WiBACK N4C with mesh networks. For that, we plan to extend the Porto testbed by adding more WiBACK N4C nodes powered by solar energy to simulate a multiple-link, off-grid installations.

Moreover, we intend to increase the number of BLE nodes within the mesh to prove the system concept in the field. This is expected to help us further understand the behaviour concerning the minimum time period between every new Request message as well as test other network performance parameters. More knowledge on these parameters will drive the performance improvement of the BLE mesh network, allowing the Comm4Dev solution to answer the technical needs of new specific application scenarios.

Acknowledgments. The authors would like to acknowledge the financial support obtained from North Portugal Region Operational Programme (NORTE 2020), Portugal 2020 and the European Regional Development Fund (ERDF) from European Union through the project Symbiotic technology for societal efficiency gains: Deus ex Machina (DEM), NORTE-01-0145-FEDER-000026, and project Collective Transfer FhP, NORTE-01-0246-FEDER-000029.

References

1. ITU: ICTs, LDCs and the SDGs-achieving universal and affordable Internet in the least developed countries. International Telecommunication Union, Geneva (2018)
2. Pereira, A., Madureira, P., Resende, C., Almeida, P., Moreira, W.: SV4D architecture: building sustainable villages for developing countries. In: Proceedings of the 9th EAI International Conference on e-Infrastructure and e-Services for Developing Countries (AFRICOMM 2017) (2017)
3. Bluetooth SIG: Bluetooth Core Specification v5.0. https://www.bluetooth.com/specifications/bluetooth-core-specification. Accessed 19 June 2018
4. Heydon, R.: Bluetooth Low Energy: The Developer's Handbook. Prentice Hall, Upper Saddle River (2013)
5. Grand View Research, Inc.: Connected Retail Market Analysis by Solution (Hardware, Software), Technology (ZigBee, Wi-Fi, Bluetooth LE, Near-Field Communication), Service (Managed Services, Professional Services, Remote Device Management Service) and Segment Forecasts to 2022, Grand View Research, Inc. (2016)
6. Bluetooth SIG: Mesh Networking Specifications. https://www.bluetooth.com/specifications/mesh-specifications. Accessed 19 June 2018
7. Bluetooth SIG: Radio Versions. https://www.bluetooth.com/bluetooth-technology/radio-versions. Accessed 19 June 2018
8. Fraunhofer Portugal: Pandlets – Personal Area Dots: Letting Everything Sense. http://www.fraunhofer.pt/en/fraunhofer_aicos/projects/internal_research/pandlets.html. Accessed 19 June 2018
9. Nordic Semiconductor Nordic Thingy:52 - IoT Sensor Kit. https://www.nordicsemi.com/eng/Products/Nordic-Thingy-52. Accessed 19 June 2018

Adaptability of Learning Games Based on Learner Profiles in the Context of Autonomous Training

Maho Wielfrid Morie$^{(\boxtimes)}$ ⓘ and Bi Tra Goore

Institut National Polytechnique Felix Houphouët-Boigny,
Yamoussoukro, Côte d'Ivoire
maho.morie@inphb.ci, goore@inphb.edu.ci

Abstract. Learning games are widely used as teaching resources, because of their capacity to help learners' increase their knowledge in conditions of autonomous learning, especially in domains for which training is expensive. However, to get the best productivity of these learning games, they should be adapted to the learners' profile. To propose content in an application that satisfies the uniqueness of each learner is difficult. We therefore want to provide learners with learning games that meet their profiles and improve the proposal by tacking their new skills into account, so that they are always in the presence of games adapted to their needs. The idea of this paper is to propose a model, that provides a training plan based on learning games, adapted to the learners' profile. The ALGP (Adaptive Learning Games Provider) model defines the learning profiles of individuals, then characterizes learning games to make a mapping between the profiles and characteristics of the games. But, to meet the needs of learners throughout the lessons, monitoring data are added, to dynamically adapt the content according to their progress. An evaluation of the model through learner follow-up in two separate classes, a first class assisted by the ALGP model and a second class with the traditional system without assistance of the model were carried out, and the results obtained show that the learners in the assisted class, are more motivated and more involved than in the non-assisted class, which increases their productivity.

Keywords: Learning games · Adaptive learning · Classification · Learner profile

1 Introduction

The quality of training has always been a central concern to the academic world. Recent research on Learning Games (LGs) have proven their effectiveness, for training. It is important to note that their success factors are numerous and have been widely demonstrated in several scientific publications [1]. The development of technology and design platforms have contributed to the spread of LGs in the marketplace. Thus, thousands of LGs are now available for learning basic to academic skills [2]. However, the major problem that presents itself, is to provide appropriate LGs to learners, so that their attractiveness remain maximal [3]. In practice the problem to be solved is to adapt

G. Mendy et al. (Eds.): AFRICOMM 2018, LNICST 275, pp. 284–293, 2019.
https://doi.org/10.1007/978-3-030-16042-5_25

the selection of games provided in a training course considering the learner's learning specificities. This problem cannot be solved by adaptation one game, by changing its content according to the learner's profile. In fact, adapting to the game level, would be expensive and is limited in the use of new games that can be useful. The aim of this paper is to propose a model of adaptability that is not only associated with the game and the perception of the player. The ALGP (Adaptive Learning Games Provider) model first studies the learner's learning profile and player profiles, then a classification of available games is realized using metadata indexing [4, 5]. In addition, the analysis of the learner's acquired experience and level of knowledge to make a matching with the prerequisites of the training. All these are analyzed to provide the game adapted to each learner to the nearest of his profile. Finally, the cycle is repeated for another analysis. To evaluate the model, an experiment was realized in two first-grade computer science classes on a group of 28 learning games, and the results obtained provide information on the effectiveness of the ALGP model, compared to an autonomous training based on learning games without assistance.

This paper is structured as follows:

The state of the art presents previous work related to the topic. We then present the ALGP model. The third part of this paper presents the experimentation that was set up to evaluate the model. Finally, we discuss the results and perspectives to our work.

2   Purpose of the Work

To satisfy the growing training demand, a large variety of free online resources, such as training LGs, are now available. However, the use of LGs in a free learning process without considering the profiles of learners, does not generate real motivation. Thus, the objective of this paper is to propose a model that will provide a list of LGs, that are adapted to the learner's profile, and that will consider the new knowledge they acquire, in order to maintain their motivation, and hence increase their knowledge acquisition.

3   Related Work

In previous work, much research has been led to provide models that improve learners' understanding of educational content. A classification of learners on how they learn is often determined to offer the same type of content per learner segment. However, this requires prior knowledge of the different learner profiles before providing them with training content.

The difficulty, in using the LGs, lies in the correlation between the concepts of the game and the training objectives. The transfer of knowledge of the chosen game activity to defined teaching cases is not always obvious and it is up to the teacher to find the subject to be taught. An alternative proposed is the modification of existing games to adapt them to the realities of teaching, with *Type of dead* for example, we have a historic zombie game attacking the player who must hurry to exterminate them, the modification to make on the weapons to use, which are the letters of the keyboard in order to improve the mastery of the keyboard in the learner. These types of game modifications are common to provide a learning environment to which the learner can be accustomed, such as *Prog & Play* and *Zombie Division*. But these modifications, even if they are interesting, bring the knowledge deficiencies that can traditionally be found in his games. An obvious solution is to create games directly based on the training objectives, so in some jobs there are games specially created for specific types of training. In [6], we find a game created to stimulate cow rearing among agricultural students, the skill is directly derived from the learning notions of the field, with practical cases. But as tools used for training, the acquisition of knowledge diffused by LGs depends strongly on the learner's profile, i.e. the learner's preferred means of acquiring, retaining and processing information [7], in specific how he perceives and understands what is being taught [8]. The learning profile considers the individual's ability to adapt to his or her learning environment, to transpose what he learns into real-world activities and to use his new and old knowledge to propose new solutions to problems [9]. But since it is above all a question of the play, it is necessary to consider not only the learner's profile in terms of comprehension but also the learner's profile as a player. Thus, to propose games that adapt to the learner's profile in an assisted training, work has proposed game designs that change in the aspects of the scenario according to the interaction with the learner. In [10], an adaptation of learning is defined according to the learner's profile, but we always remain in the same game with the same types of action and the same playability. Obviously, it is difficult for a game to cover all aspects of training, and if it were possible it would be difficult to develop, so in assisted learning, several games will be used. We want to have a training adaptability model with the learner's profile that will not depend on the learning game but where any game can be inserted. For the ALGP model, we start by analyzing the student's learning profile with an analysis of the student's player profile and then match it with the classification that would be made of the games.

4 Adaptive Model Design

4.1 Learning Profile

There are many learning profile theories and definitions because it's difficult to delimit. So, in *Learning Styles And Pedagogy In Post-16 Learning, Coffield* has determined 71 different learning profiles with 60 profiles that have their own measurement tools [11]. Among these, Felder-Silverman's learning model is widely used in game-based learning as opposed to other learning profile models. This model classifies the profiles into five dimensions of ten opposing elements, two by two, in the relationship of personalities by showing from the outset the nonconformity of learner type. The most important aspect of this model is the correspondence that it made between the learning profile and the learning concept.

- Sensitive/intuitive: this dimension calls for perception.
- Visual/verbal: this dimension uses training elements.
- Induction/deduction: this dimension deals with the organization of things.
- Active/reflective: this is a bit of a sensitive and intuitive sequence, here we talk about processes.

– Sequential/global: this dimension characterizes the learner's faculties in terms of learning approach, it is the understanding of things. Sequential is best in step-by-step learning where training is presented from the simplest to the most complicated [9].

So, in characterizing learners, the *Felder-Silverman learning style model* (FSLSM) give good tools to classify the learner in learning based on LGs.

4.2 Playing Profile

The other aspect to be considered when using LGs, is the learner's player profile because, in addition to the way of learning, the learner's preferences in terms of game types, content and scenario are important if we want to create motivation and increase their knowledge.

Early work on defining personality models focused on aspects of motivation, such as achievement, social and immersion [12]. However, most of the work on the player profile is done on specific types of games, the games in their different specificities are analyzed to bring out a few determinants to rely on to define player profiles. What is needed is a global representation of the player profile that can fit into the mold of most LGs. The most recent model that considers this is the *BrainHex* classification [13], which divides players into seven categories:

– The Achiever is objective oriented, motivated by long-term rewards and likes to act.
– The Conqueror is driven by challenges, tends to start games with the difficult or expert level and is captured by the desire to win everything.
– The Daredevil likes risk and prefers to play games where victory is not obvious.
– The Mastermind likes reflection, calculation, strategies, and solving enigmas.
– The Seeker is always looking for discovery and will prefer games where there are frequent changes of scenery.
– The Socializer likes interactions with other players and, prefers games where we go to meet other players either as a team or as an opponent.
– The Survivor likes fear and enjoys games where there is a lot of negative experience.

This classification in addition to not being dependent on a particular of game, is based on a neurological study with a questionnaire widely (+60 000 times) used to illustrate the approach [14] and conduct other types of classification.

Now that we have defined the classifications for the two aspects of learners' profile (learning and playing), it is also necessary to define a way of classifying LGs to match this profile.

4.3 Game Classification

The classification of LGs is important in proposing specific training content for learners' profiles. Most LGs indexing methods are based on metadata representation. But this metadata, although effective for describing content, is not sufficient to classify LGs appropriately. Indeed, to attain our objective, the type of classification to adopt must imply the playability, the level of required implication, the technicality of the game... in this sense the Gameplay, Purpose, Scope (G/P/S) model [15] proposes to classify LGs, but which can be extended by add the specific characteristics of LGs. It is on this model that we will build to classify LGs based on indexing by metadata standards.

The classification models will start from a prior description of the games by the LOM (Learning Object Metadata) [5, 16] standard which includes 9 categories of 68 elements, however, not all fields need to be described representing a LG. Then an extension of the G/P/S model is made to provide a classification that can match the learning profile (Fig. 1).

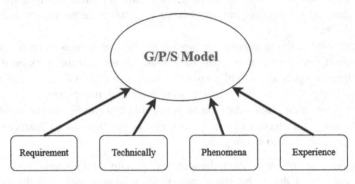

Fig. 1. G/P/S model extended

The extensions we add to the G/P/S model allow us to get as close as possible to the learning profile.

- The requirement will be able to, an entry questionnaire to define the type of games of the learner's beginning.
- The phenomena already give a glimpse of the actions that may intervene in the game.
- The experience goes as you learn to help you tell when to change games and which game to play next.
- The technicality will make it possible to define the concepts of handling of the game.

These new combinations will also enrich the concepts of this model, for example the gameplay will be more evocative with the consideration of the technicality and the phenomena defined in the game. It is these grids of representations that will be used by the game adaptability model according to the learner profile, to offer pedagogical content that is always like the type of learner, however, LGs adapted to the learning profile cannot be proposed without the consideration of the user experience.

There are many works on the adaptability of LGs, but they are oriented towards methods so that a single game which could be adapted according to player's behavior during the execution of the game. Thus, the learner's techniques are analyzed to extract data to be interpreted to add new actions as the game progresses, move to a specific step, lead the player differently [10].

4.4   Adaptive Learning Games Model

Indeed, in the process of learning, learners go from a state X to state Y. This new state means acquiring new knowledge and new techniques, understanding the phenomenon of the LGs they are playing. So, we will have to update their profile to offer another game that fits and redefine their learning characteristics. For example, if we are facing intuitive learners making them repeatedly play the same game may result in a drop in the motivation because they will already have apprehended this game and therefore will get tired of playing. What we propose in this paper is to provide, from a list of LGs analyzed, the game that would be closest to the learners' aspirations at that specific moment, considering their change of state.

- As input, a survey is carried out to define an initial learner profile.
- An indexing of the LGs based on the metadata makes it possible to describe them to have a general knowledge of the LGs.
- A classification is made to categorize the games that will constitute the catalog list.
- We take the objectives to achieve defined in the proposed training.
- An analysis of the objectives is carried out with the learner's knowledge and skills in order not to offer them what they already know.

A matching between the learner profile, the training objectives defined by the teacher and the LGs are done through a scoring system assigned to the game profiles and characteristics using the *BrainHex* model platform http://survey.ihobo.com/BrainHex/ [13]. Next, LGs that stand out are proposed to the learner (Fig. 2).

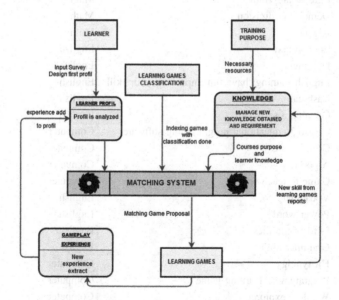

Fig. 2. Adaptive Learning Games Proposal model cycle

After playing, the learner's playing experience is extracted to be used as data in the composition of the learner's profile. In addition, the lessons transmitted in the learning game played increase the knowledge and give new skills to the learner, this is used with the objectives of the training to serve a content that will deal with the lessons coming just after this newly acquired knowledge and that will serve as a prerequisite. Each time the process is repeated to enrich the model and serve new LG in the learner's training.

5 Experimentation

The experimentation of the model was carried out on two classes of twenty-five first grade students in computer science, from the Virtual University of Côte d'Ivoire in self-learning. The LG catalogue includes 28 LGs in the areas of math, English language and

Table 1. Learning games catalogue for experiments.

Learning games	Fields
Maxtrax	Math
Luminosity: chalkboard challenge	Math
Cisco binary game	Math
Zombie division	Math
Prog & play	Math, computer
A.I wars: the insect mind	Math
Lure of labyrinth	Math
Demolition division	Math
Algebot	Math
English taxi	English
Duolingo	English
English training: have fun improving your skills	English
Cash cab	English
Opening a sales call	English
CeeBot3 educational programming software	Computer
Cisco aspire	Computer
Algo-bot	Computer
Game to teach sql	Computer
Vocabulary.co.il	English
Power words	English
Lord of the files	English
Grammar ninja	English
Hit typing	Computer
Programming learning game	Computer
Wireless explorer	Computer
Iscen	Computer
Computer quiz	Computer
Typing of dead	Computer

computer science with programming and network teaching. The experiments took place in two stages (Table 1).

The students were divided into two classes homogeneously according to their learning profiles, in the first class named "free class" the game catalog was provided without assistance, the games were classified by teaching subjects, so it was up to them to choose themselves the ones they want to play to get the knowledge required by the training. On the other hand, the second class called "assisted class" was assisted by the model to suggest the LG that should played, according to the learner's profile and their learning objectives.

The experiment took place over six weeks, and a satisfaction survey was conducted to collect the learners' motivation [17, 18] level each week. At the end, a questionnaire was produced to determine the level of learners' involvement in these training sessions.

6 Results and Discussions

The surveys were carried out on the following criteria; motivation, knowledge acquired, and level of engagement observed. It is by a qualitative measurement of the factors that we proceeded. A percentage is generated to serve as a result at the motivation level and scores are assigned for the other factors (Figs. 3 and 4).

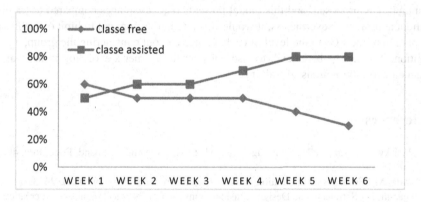

Fig. 3. Motivation evolution graph in %, generated from the evaluation score

The observation that we make on these results is striking, about motivation, after the excitement of the first week the level of the free class decreases constantly while that of the assisted class increases. This is due to the fact that, the games offered are adapted to the learning profiles of each student. As the proposals are based on the preferences of the learners, motivation continues to grow. For acquired knowledge, the level follows the same logic as that of motivation, in fact the level of knowledge obtained from a game is linked to the level of motivation [19].

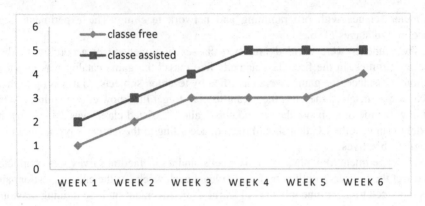

Fig. 4. Knowledge level score graph

7 Conclusion

The use of LGs to support learner training is widespread, especially in the case of self-directed learning. The success of learners in training based on LGs depends a lot on their level of involvement, their motivation to learn, and the experience that results to generate better knowledge of the concepts addressed. For this a model of game adaptability is proposed, and this model presents real advantages compared to training without assistance. Nevertheless, it would be more interesting, not to limit oneself to an adaptation of the LGs to the level of each learner without considering the group, and in addition, it would be beneficial, to also consider the learner's evolution in his way of understanding the notions of training.

References

1. Prensky, M.: "Engage Me or Enrage Me": what today's learners demand. Educ. Rev. **40**, 60 (2005)
2. Zyda, M.: From visual simulation to virtual reality to games. Computer **38**, 25–32 (2005)
3. Djaouti, D.: Serious Game Design: considérations théoriques et techniques sur la création de jeux vidéo à vocation utilitaire (2011)
4. Hernandez, N., Mothe, J., Ramamonjisoa, A.B.O., Ralalason, B., Stolf, P.: Indexation multi-facettes des ressources pédagogiques pour faciliter leur ré-utilisation, p. 10. Institut de Recherche en Informatique de Toulouse (2009). ftp://ftp.irit.fr/IRIT/SIG/2008_RNTI_HMRRS.pdf
5. Marfisi-Schottman, I., George, S., Tarpin-Bernard, F.: Un profil d'application de LOM pour les Serious Games. In: Environnements Informatiques pour l'Apprentissage Humain, Conférence EIAH 2011, pp. 81–94. Editions de l'UMONS, Mons 2011, Belgium (2011)
6. Michel, H., Kreziak, D., Héraud, J.-M.: Évaluation de la performance des Serious Games pour l'apprentissage: Analyse du transfert de comportement des éleveurs virtuels de Vacheland. Systèmes d'information & management **14**, 71–86 (2009)
7. Felder, R.M., Silverman, L.K.: Learning and teaching styles in engineering education. Eng. Educ. **78**, 674–681 (1988)

8. James, W.B., Gardner, D.L.: Learning styles: implications for distance learning. New Dir. Adult Contin. Educ. **1995**, 19–31 (1995)
9. Khenissi, M.A., Essalmi, F., Jemni, M., Kinshuk, Graf, S., Chen, N.-S.: Relationship between learning styles and genres of games. Comput. Educ. **101**, 1–14 (2016)
10. Pinto, T., Vale, Z.: Adaptive learning in games: defining profiles of competitor players. In: Omatu, S., Neves, J., Rodriguez, J.M.C., Paz Santana, J.F., Gonzalez, S.R. (eds.) Distributed Computing and Artificial Intelligence. AISC, vol. 217, pp. 351–359. Springer, Cham (2013). https://doi.org/10.1007/978-3-319-00551-5_43
11. Coffield, F., Moseley, D., Hall, E., Ecclestone, K.: Learning Styles and Pedagogy in Post-16 Learning: A Systematic and Critical Review. Learning and Skills Research Centre, London (2004)
12. Yee, N.: Motivations for play in online games. Cyberpsychol. Behav. Impact Internet Multimedia Virtual Reality Behav. Soc. **9**, 772–775 (2007)
13. Nacke, L.E., Bateman, C., Mandryk, R.L.: BrainHex: a neurobiological gamer typology survey. Entertain. Comput. **5**, 55–62 (2014)
14. Monterrat, B., Lavoué, E., George, S., Desmarais, M.: Les effets d'une ludification adaptative sur l'engagement des apprenants, vol. 24. STICEF (2017)
15. Djaouti, D., Alvarez, J., Jessel, J.-P.: Classifying serious games: the G/P/S model. In: Handbook of Research on Improving Learning and Motivation Through Educational Games: Multidisciplinary Approaches (2011)
16. Neven, F., Duval, E.: Reusable learning objects: a survey of LOM-based repositories. In: Proceedings of the Tenth ACM International Conference on Multimedia, pp. 291–294. ACM, New York (2002)
17. Badri, M., Nuaimi, A.A., Guang, Y., Rashedi, A.A.: School performance, social networking effects, and learning of school children: evidence of reciprocal relationships in Abu Dhabi. Telematics Inform. **34**, 1433–1444 (2017)
18. Dunn, R.S., Griggs, S.A. (eds.): Practical Approaches to Using Learning Styles in Higher Education. Bergin & Garvey, Westport (2000)
19. Mayer, I.: Towards a comprehensive methodology for the research and evaluation of serious games. Procedia Comput. Sci. **15**, 233–247 (2012)

Multi Agent-Based Addresses Geocoding for More Efficient Home Delivery Service in Developing Countries

Al Mansour Kebe[1]([⊠]), Roger M. Faye[2], and Claude Lishou[1]

[1] Ecole Superieure Polytechnique, Universite Cheikh Anta Diop, Dakar, Senegal
manskebe@gmail.com
[2] Université Amadou Mahtar MBOW, Diamniadio, Senegal

Abstract. In this study, we present an original method that enhance geocoding system in poorly mapped areas thanks to multi-agent system. In contrast with industrialized countries, many developing countries lack formal postal address systems assignments and usage, making the operation of translating text-based addresses to absolute spatial coordinates, known as geocoding, a big challenge. We recreated a standard of address as it is perceived and used by local people, a kind of non-official national address standard since there is no official one in these areas. Then, we designed a multi agent system in which agents are assigned different tasks of geocoding process and can perform negotiation to achieve global objective: find the best possible match or approximation of a location based on current knowledge. A verification of the usefulness of the proposed approach is made in comparison with Google geocoding API which shows that the proposed approach has great potential to geocode addresses considering local context semantic issues.

Keywords: Geocoding · Multi agent · Text mining · Knowledge discovery · Address standard

1 Introduction

From standard service delivery to emergency system dispatching, addresses are the most common and convenient way to locate people. Addresses are easily comprehensible to people, but not directly suitable for use in an IT environment. Translating text based addresses to absolute spatial coordinates is known as geocoding. However geocoding technology is very common on commercial Geographical Information Systems (GIS) products, it's usually limited to fully standardized structures with a respect of elements order as well as writing style.

In contrast with industrialized countries, many address systems in developing countries lack standards, making the addressing system ambiguous, incomplete or imprecise. The prompt provision of a precise location from unstructured or even vague addressing data provided by people is critically important, especially in emergency situations, and have a socio-economic impact in day-to-day life.

Furthermore, with the rapid development of e-commerce and internet, products and services delivery to customers is a challenge for companies, therefore increasing the

G. Mendy et al. (Eds.): AFRICOMM 2018, LNICST 275, pp. 294–304, 2019.
https://doi.org/10.1007/978-3-030-16042-5_26

need for appropriate geocoding tools in poorly mapped area. In fact, even if online mapping system is widely used, many developing countries suffer from good addressing and geocoding system, even internet connectivity.

Due to the essential life services they provide, water, energy and garbage collection utility companies have mastered addressing and geocoding systems for years now. Through their day-to-day interaction with customers to quickly troubleshoot water supply breakdowns or electricity distribution failures, these utility companies need to have a good knowledge of the field they operate in. To deal with this permanent challenge, these companies have to create their own geolocation systems that become over the years an important source of geographical and customers' addresses data.

Hence, we investigate ten years of addresses data collected by Senegal power company through customer's trouble calls. On any power outage, verbal description of their location is given by customer to callcenter officers without any account references. This collected data is characterized by its vagueness and full of misspelling or unknown places from common mapping facilities.

To express these challenges, we first needed to produce an address standard by text mining historical data and creating a reference dataset before being able to achieve the matching operations.

Afterwards, we designed a multi agent system in which agents are assigned different tasks of geocoding process and can perform negotiation to achieve global objective: find the best possible match or approximation of a location based on current knowledge.

The rest of the paper is organised as follow: Sect. 2 presents the background of the study including geocoding process and literature review. In Sect. 3, the model of the proposed system is set out with a definition of a standard address format from data and description of the proposed multi agent system with its implementation. In Sect. 4, experiments to measure the accurateness of the proposed approach is carried out in comparison to the results of Google Maps Geocoding API against a set of local addresses for which we have verified latitude-longitude and we discuss results.

2   Background

2.1   The Process of Geocoding and Its Challenge

As well documented in the literature [1–3], within classical approach, the geocoding process is divided in three main phases: address normalization, address matching and address locating (Fig. 1).

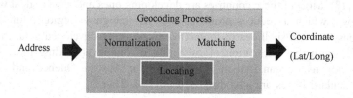

Fig. 1. The process of geocoding

The normalization phase transforms the address to a standardized form which allows to accomplish the comparison with reference data. Because addresses are not free from errors, they must be cleaned and standardized to get the same format as the reference data. The cleaning process involves solving issues such as case variation, abbreviation and punctuation. Standardization is accomplished by tokenizing the address string and assigning meaning to each token from different address element types.

Matching phase is the attempts to link the normalized address to a corresponding record from the reference data set. The performance of this stage depends on the completeness of the reference data. If exact matching cannot be obtained, approximation is made to get the best available adjacent area in the data set.

Locating process allow to return a geocode, thanks to geographic coordinate assigned to matched address in reference data. The geographic coordinate goes from polygons representing locality (which have a coordinate assigned to his centroid) through line segment representing street (coordinate assigned to his mid-point) to point representing single address.

From this brief description of geocoding process, we can notice that we face two big challenges when attempting to geocode address in poorly mapped area:

- Input address must be converted to a standardized format but there is no standard address in many developing countries (as reported in [4]).
- Standardized address should be compared to a reference data set but since these areas are poorly mapped, incomplete database with unknown places are very common from all mapping facilities.

2.2   Related Work

Geocoding is a well-studied question with plenty of contributions that have been proposed to expand the process specially in the domain of classical geocoding [1] but less in what we can call intelligent geocoding which deal with geocoding difficult address by using control and knowledge improvements [3, 5] to depart from simply matching and table lookups approaches.

Since addressing systems vary largely between countries, as addresses have a strong cultural bias, one main part of studies revolve around some issues introduced by the natural language in the process of geocoding such as in Chinese [6–8] or Croatian [9] and more specifically on twitter [10].

Another part of the current geocoding literature deals with geocoding application and issues solving in an explicit geographic area such as in Croatia [11], Turkish [12], Brazil [13], China [6–8], Australia [14], South Africa [15], Morocco [16], Cuba [17] and India [18]. Most of these countries are developing ones and have to deal with rapid urban growth which introduces problems such as ambiguous region boundaries and lack of convention in spellings of toponyms. Concerning developed area, the studies deal mainly with the verification of suitability of online geocoding tools [2] for a specific region as we can find in [11, 19, 20] for Austria, Quebec and Germany. Address Standard issues are also discussed in [1, 4, 21–23].

This literature survey shows a strong dynamic in geocoding process from regional and cultural point of view. Thus, to improve the geocoding course, knowledge need to be added in the process to take into consideration lack of standard, semantic issues and complicated logic existing in many countries. Therefore, Multi Agents System (MAS) which utilizes theories and concepts from many areas such as computer science, artificial intelligence, distributed systems, social sciences, economics, organization and else is a good candidate for this purpose.

In this tendency, in [5] Wei et al. present a knowledge-based agent prototype for Chinese address geocoding. Toward the statement that Chinese address geocoding is a difficult problem to deal with due to intrinsic complexities in Chinese address systems including Chinese language and civil history and a lack of standards in address assignments and usages, the authors propose a spatial knowledge-based agent proto-type to improve existing address geocoding algorithm. To construct this agent, they first introduce a knowledge base consisting of a basic ontology for Chinese address validation domain and an internal fact database. An inference rule set is integrated into this agent to deduce the spatial accuracy of these potential matches. However, this approach is limited to some inferential ability to help matching process and had to be improved to solve issue like geocoding addresses containing two or more geographical classes of the same kind.

In [24] Hutchinson and Veenendaal present an agent-based framework for intelli-gent geocoding. Having noted that despite progress in the field of geocoding, there remain a sizable proportion of addresses that are difficult to geocode due to missing information and wrong addresses, they explore how agent-based processing, which utilizes the belief, desire, intention (BDI) model, can add intelligence to the geocoding process. The goal of the system is to correct address element allowing to find them in reference data set and every agent pursues its own intention to this goal. Nevertheless, this study is confined to geocoding matching process assuming that, it will take longer but complex sites and rural sites will have reliable geocode data.

Our work extends those of Hutchinson and al which is conducted in context of a developed country with a comprehensive geocode data updated every three months (the Australia G-NAF files). In contrast with Hutchinson we are in a poorly mapped area [25] which conduct to include more dynamics in all geocoding process (data nor-malisation, data set acquisition and cleaning).

3   Proposed Approach

3.1   Definition of an Address Standard

To define an address standard, an ontology for this domain is constructed as the basic vocabulary to represent spatial knowledge in the address geocoding domain. Hence we analysed ten years of addresses data collected by Senegal public energy utility through customer's trouble calls. This collected data is characterized by its sketchiness and full of misspelling and unknown places from common online mapping. This basic ontology includes geographical classes such as city, county, road, house number, community, building number, points of interest (POI) and other concepts needed for comparing and evaluating address matches.

Example of address data from the trouble call data corpus:

- Guediawaye Cite des Enseignants Villa N° D/10
- Yeumbeul Ben Barack Darou Salam 4/C Qrt Elhadj Ablaye Diop
- Ngor Diongoran Qrt Pape Moustapha Ba
- Yeumbeul Cite Comico 4 Villa N°129/D

Thanks to the determination of most often used terms we have identified the terminology used to describe an address.

Words like "villa" (house), "qrt" (abbreviation of French word quartier which mean neighbourhood), 'rue' (street) are in focus.

Many mistakes and spellings are encountered in the data due to typos and abbreviations knowing that they are collected verbally by phone from call center.

In order to reunite the various spelling of frequent words, language processing algorithms have been used such as Levenshtein distance and Jaro-Winkler distance combined with TF-IDF (Term Frequency-Inverse Document Frequency) [26].

We classify these address concepts in family and settle a hierarchy between them. Considering the current national administrative division of the country including Administrative district and Municipality we get the Fig. 2 with the main families in focus: property, subdivision, administrative division, space for circulation, municipality and administrative district.

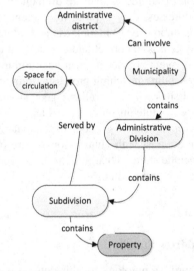

Fig. 2. Simplified addressing concept hierarchy

The developed version of the addressing concept is presented in Fig. 3 with a detail of words used frequently in each family of concept giving an ontology of how address is nowadays expressed by Senegalese People.

This ontology is an input used by the multi agent system to accomplish the goal of the LOGEMAS system.

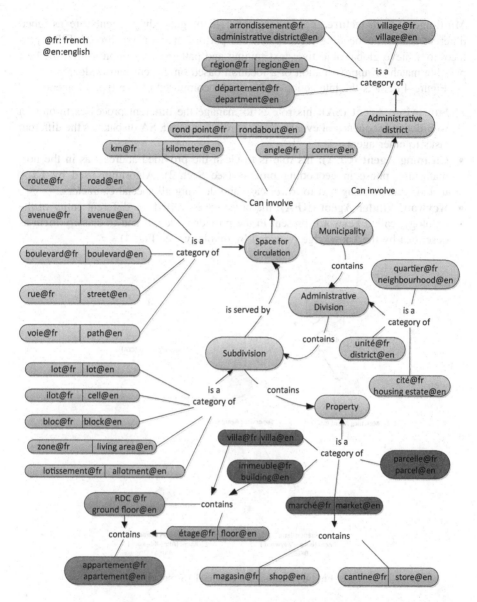

Fig. 3. Ontology of urban geography in Senegal

3.2 LOGEMAS-Location Geocoding with Multi Agent System

In this section, we present the LoGeMAS (Location Geocoding with Multi Agent System) architecture in which the various geocoding tasks are delegated to different agents.

Multi-agent Architecture. To achieve the task of geocoding, agents are assigned different tasks of geocoding process and can perform negotiation through FIPA protocol to achieve global objective: text mining and pattern recognition to find the best possible match or approximation of a location based on current knowledge.

Figure 4 depicts the interaction in the model composed of five type of agents.

- **Supervisor Agent (SA):** his role is to manage the different processes through a well-defined sequence of events. As a coordinator agent, **SA** dispatches the different tasks to other agents.
- **Cleaning Agent (CLA):** his role is to clean the provided address, as in the normalization phase in geocoding process (see Sect. 2). Algorithm used by **CLA** include transforming text to lower case and deleting all special characters.
- **Keyword Finder Agent (KFA):** his objective is to find the different entity of the ontology, called keyword, present in the provided address and to classify them as described by the knowledge provided by ontology (see Fig. 4).

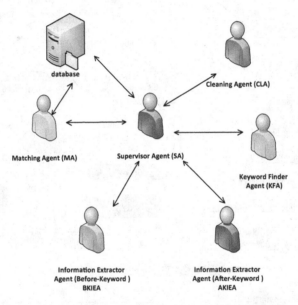

Fig. 4. Multi agent LOGEMAS model

- **Before Keyword Information Extractor Agent (BKIEA):** as his name shows, this is an information extractor agent specialised on information appearing before a keyword. Example in the address:

    "Guediawaye **Cite** des Enseignants **Villa** N° D/10"

    BKIEA will retrieve the couple ['Guediawaye', 'des Enseignants']
- **After Keyword Information Extractor Agent (AKIEA):** as his name show, this is an information extractor agent specialised on information appearing after a keyword. Example in the address:

"Guediawaye **Cite** des Enseignants **Villa** N° D/10"

AKIEA will retrieve the couple ['des Enseignants', 'N° D/10']

- **Matching Agent (MA):** The Matching Agent role is to do the matching action by finding geocode corresponding to address as described in geocoding process in Sect. 2. From each found keyword completed with his proprieties, information are looked in the database and the process is completed with heuristics rules that allow to define the accuracy.

3.3 Data Set Acquisition

To track crew performance during outage recovery, Senelec utility has introduced a vehicle tracking system in 2015. The data collected during breakdown reparation combined with these captured tracking data gives a potential of learning new regions and landmarks by reverse geocoding concerned customer address.

3.4 The Multi-agent System Design and Implementation

To implement a multi-agent system, there are several open-source agent platforms available in the literature that helps developers to build a complex agent system in a simplified manner. The GAMA platform [27, 28] was chosen to implement our system. This platform which is a new trend in multi agent developing, enables multi agent development through an intuitive interface and programing language GAML. GAMA has the advantage to implement many features like FIPA compliance, Geographical Information System (SIG) and the ability to build spatially explicit multi-agent simulation which is one characteristic of geocoding system.

4 Experiment Result and Discussion

To challenge our approach and demonstrate its capability, a case study in Dakar City Senegal is carried out with text mining and pattern recognition.

First we measure the ability of the system to geocode up to different levels of precision from the proposed address standard including property, subdivision, administrative division, space for circulation, municipality and administrative district. To achieve this test, we run the LOGEMAS process through one month of trouble call data containing 6321 addresses (June 2015 data). The test is compliant since only 23 addresses were not recognised. The Fig. 5 shows an example of the results provided by LOGEMAS system.

```
Address : 'HLM 5 VILLA 2209 angle 2'
hlm5 is :['quartier', 'unite','cite']**Familly: administrative district
2209 is villa **Familly: property
2 is angle **Familly: space for circulation
```

Fig. 5. Sample of address recognition through LOGEMAS process

When analysing the address that was not well recognized we found that they had in common the fact of containing natural language part of speech like in 'Yarakh Hann Pecheur ne connait pas le nom du Chef de qrt' (meaning Yarakh Hann Pecheur doesn't know the name of the head of district!!!).

Finally, a comparison of LOGEMAS results with those of Google's geocoding service against a set of addresses verified latitude-longitude coordinates was conducted and we arrive at these conclusion:

- Google Maps was not able to consider semantic issue while LOGEMAS well recognised standard address as expressed by local people;
- Google geocoding service is limited to street name, municipality and completed Point of Interest (POI) and LOGEMAS try to give a level of precision from its known database.

We can conclude that the architecture we are developing has great potential to geocode addresses considering local context issues with integration of semantic question (Fig. 6).

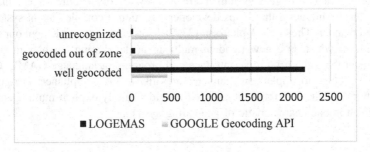

Fig. 6. Comparison between LOGEMAS and Google Maps Api geocoding process results

5   Conclusion and Future Work

In this paper, we presented a system called LOGEMAS - Location Geocoding with Multi Agent System. We investigated ten years of addresses data collected by Senegal public energy utility through customer's trouble calls. We recreated a standard of address as it is perceived and used by people. Afterwards, we designed a multi agent system in which agents are assigned different tasks of geocoding process and can perform negotiation to achieve global objective: find the best possible match or approximation of a location based on current knowledge. A verification of the usefulness of the proposed approach is made in comparison with Google geocoding API which shows that the proposed approach has great potential to geocode addresses considering local context semantic issues and can contribute to more efficient home delivery service in developing countries. In future work the tool will be enhanced with more semantic skills and propose an application to outage management in power companies.

References

1. Goldberg, D.W.: A Geocoding Best Practices Guide. North American Association of Central Cancer Registries (2008)
2. Karimi, H.A., Sharker, M.H., Roongpiboonsopit, D.: Geocoding recommender: an algorithm to recommend optimal online geocoding services for applications. Trans. GIS 15(6), 869 (2011)
3. Hutchinson, M.J.: Developing an agent-based framework for intelligent geocoding. Curtin University of Technology (2010)
4. Coetzee, S., et al.: Towards an international address standard. In: 10th International Conference for Spatial Data Infrastructure (2008)
5. Wei, R., Zhang, X., Ding, L., Ma, H., Li, Q.: A knowledge-based agent prototype for Chinese address geocoding. In: Geoinformatics 2008 and Joint Conference on GIS and Built Environment: Advanced Spatial Data Models and Analyses, p. 71,461D. International Society for Optics and Photonics (2009)
6. Tian, Q., Ren, F., Hu, T., Liu, J., Li, R., Du, Q.: Using an optimized Chinese address matching method to develop a geocoding service: a case study of Shenzhen. ISPRS Int. J. Geo Inf. 5(5), 65 (2016)
7. Gao, D., Li, Q.: Preliminary results of a Chinese address segmentation algorithm based on self-organizing neural network. In: Geoinformatics 2007, p. 67,530U. International Society for Optics and Photonics (2007)
8. Fang, L., Yu, Z.Y., Zhao, X.: The design of a unified addressing schema and the matching mode of China. In: 2010 IEEE International Geoscience and Remote Sensing Symposium (IGARSS), pp. 3987–3990. IEEE (2010)
9. Ugrina, I., Zigo, M.: Searching for semantically correct postal addresses on the Croatian web. In: Central European Conference on Information and Intelligent Systems, p. 276. Faculty of Organization and Informatics Varazdin (2014)
10. Zhang, W., Gelernter, J.: Geocoding location expressions in twitter messages: a preference learning method. J. Spat. Inf. Sci. 2014(9), 37 (2014)
11. Cetl, V., Kliment, T., Jogun, T.: A comparison of address geocoding techniques–case study of the city of Zagreb. Surv. Rev., 1–10 (2016)
12. Yildirim, V., Yomralioglu, T., Nisanci, R., Inan, H.: Turkish street addressing system and geocoding challenges. Proc. Inst. Civ. Eng. 167(2), 99 (2014)
13. Davis Jr., C.A., de Alencar, R.O.: Evaluation of the quality of an online geocoding resource in the context of a large Brazilian city. Trans. GIS 15(6), 851 (2011)
14. Christen, P., Churches, T., Willmore, A., et al.: A probabilistic geocoding system based on a national address file. In: Proceedings of the 3rd Australasian Data Mining Conference, Cairns (2004)
15. Coetzee, S., Cooper, A.K.: What is an address in South Africa? S. Afr. J. Sci. 103(11–12), 449 (2007)
16. Malaainine, M.E.I., Rhinane, H., Baidder, L., Lechgar, H.: Omt-g modeling and cloud implementation of a reference database of addressing in Morocco. J. Geogr. Inf. Syst. (2013)
17. de Armas Garcia, C.J., Gutierrez, A.A.C.: Deployment of a national geocoding service: Cuban experience. URISA J. 25(1), 53 (2013)
18. Chatterjee, A., Anjaria, J., Roy, S., Ganguli, A., Seal, K.: SAGEL: smart address geocoding engine for supply-chain logistics. In: Proceedings of the 24th ACM SIGSPATIAL International Conference on Advances in Geographic Information Systems, p. 42. ACM (2016)

19. Burns, S., Miranda-Moreno, L., Stipancic, J., Saunier, N., Ismail, K.: Accessible and practical geocoding method for traffic collision record mapping: Quebec, Canada, case study. Transp. Res. Rec. J. Transp. Res. Board **2460**, 39 (2014)
20. Ahlers, D., Boll, S.: On the accuracy of online geocoders. Geoinformatik 2009 (2009)
21. Davis, C.A., Fonseca, F.T.: Assessing the certainty of locations produced by an address geocoding system. Geoinformatica **11**(1), 103 (2007)
22. Karimipour, F., Alinaghi, N., Weiser, P., Frank, A.U.: Cognitive engineering for spatial information processes: from user interfaces to model-driven design (2015)
23. Coetzee, S., Rademeyer, M.: Testing the spatial adjacency match of the Intiendo address matching tool for geocoding of addresses with misleading suburb or place names. In: Proceedings International Cartography Conference, pp. 15–21 (2009)
24. Hutchinson, M.J., Veenendaal, B.: An agent-based framework for intelligent geocoding. Appl. Geomat. **5**(1), 33 (2013)
25. Irwin, M.: Mapping missing maps (2014). https://www.mapbox.com/blog/mapping-missing-maps/, Accessed 20 Jan 2017
26. Graham, S.A.: String Searching Algorithms. World Scientific Publishing Co. Pte Ltd. (1994)
27. Kravari, K., Bassiliades, N.: A survey of agent platforms. J. Artif. Soc. Soc. Simul. **18**(1), 11 (2015)
28. Documentation sur la plateforme GAMA (2016). https://github.com/gama-platform/gama/wiki, Accessed 4 Dec 2016

The Contribution of LMS to the Learning Environment: Views from the State University of Zanzibar

Mwanajuma Suleiman Mgeni[1(✉)], Maryam Jaffar Ismail[2],
Said Ali Yunus[2], and Haji Ali Haji[1(✉)]

[1] Department of Computer Science and Information Technology,
The State University of Zanzibar, Zanzibar, Tanzania
{m.mgeni,haji.haji}@suza.ac.tz
[2] Department of Education, The State University of Zanzibar,
Zanzibar, Tanzania

Abstract. Learning Management Systems (LMS) have become a common feature in contemporary higher education institutions globally. In recent years, LMS have been adopted in some higher education institutions in sub-Saharan Africa including Tanzania, however, there are limited research in this area, which could hinder future developments. Therefore, this study investigates the adoption and usage of LMS as pedagogical tool among students and instructors at the State University of Zanzibar (SUZA). The methodology used in this study included the review of the literature, focus group discussions and semi-structured interviews. The study was conducted in Zanzibar from March 2016 to March 2017. A total of 431 students and 10 instructors participated in this study. The participants were selected based on the courses that have been involved in the pilot study. Microsoft Excel was used to present the findings in figures and tables. The findings reveal that 70% of instructors and 44.4% of students showed preferences to LMS system as a tools to be used in teaching and learning and 26.1% of students were neither agree nor disagree. However, there are various challenges influencing the level of use of LMS including, internet connections, access to computers, unfamiliar with Moodle and integration of LMS with others university systems. Overall, the study provided an insight into the environment surrounding the early adoption phases of LMS in SUZA, which offers a better understanding of the phenomenon. Subsequently, this will help enhance the adoption process in current contexts and assist in future utilization of LMS systems.

Keywords: Learning management systems · Higher learning institution · e-Learning · Blended learning · Zanzibar

1 Introduction

This paper discusses the contribution of Learning Management System (LMS) to the learning environment from the academia perspective of the State University of Zanzibar (SUZA). The paper is organized as follows: Sect. 1 introduces the topic, including

G. Mendy et al. (Eds.): AFRICOMM 2018, LNICST 275, pp. 305–314, 2019.
https://doi.org/10.1007/978-3-030-16042-5_27

theoretical background of the study, Sect. 2 describes the methodology of the study. Followed by the presentation of the results and discussion of the study in Sect. 3, and finally the conclusion and recommendations in Sect. 4.

1.1 Theoretical Background

Learning Management Systems (LMS) have been adopted in most higher education institutions in sub-Saharan Africa. These web-based LMS are intended to support teaching and learning activities in a traditional classroom. LMS consists of various features that enable university instructors to share learning materials as well as providing interaction with their students both synchronously and asynchronously. Currently, there are various LMS available worldwide, and common LMSs be largely grouped into two groups: first, Open-source LMS, such as Moodle, Sakai and Segue, and second, Commercial systems, like WebCT, Blackboard and Desire2Learn [1]. The most widely adopted LMS in sub Saharan Africa are Blackboard, Sakai, and Moodle [1].

LMS is a collaborative platform used to manage online learning courses. LMS is a software environment that enables the management and delivery of learning content and resources to students. It provides an opportunity to maintain interaction between the instructor and students and to assess the students by providing immediate feedback on the online quizzes [2]. LMS presents an overview of common motivations for e-learning. E-learning is organized and managed within an integrated system. Different tools are integrated in a single system, which offers all necessary tools to run and manage an e-learning course. All learning activities and materials in a course are organized and managed by and within the system. LMS typically offer various activities including discussion forums, management of assignments, file sharing, chats, and syllabus [3].

In traditional lectures, an instructor stands before a class take a centre stage, recite a paper or read part of the book that contains all that is considered important for the students to know, and may resort to use chalkboard [4]. As technology grows, the model changed to using presentation cues in Microsoft Power Point slides visible to all students rather than in notes used only by the instructor. However, the most important mode of verbally exposing information to the students remained. This model has been criticized because of its assumption that dissemination of content is the primary purpose of a classroom. It has been argued that, instead, such content is better learnt on an individual basis and the classroom sessions are better utilized for discussion and active engagement with the content [5, 6]. This in turn could lead to higher levels of understanding than if classrooms are used purely for presentation of the content to students.

In this regards, LMS usability, flexibility, and accessibility for use in 24/7 are the most significant characteristics that have attracted both students and instructors [2]. LMS allow communication and interaction between teachers and students in virtual spaces. However, the literature indicates that there are gaps in research, especially in the management of platform and its associated opportunities and challenges. Consequently, the aim of this study is to assess the perceptions of using LMS as pedagogical tool among students and instructors at SUZA, specifically the study looks at LMS features used by students for learning and its challenges.

SUZA recognizes the pedagogical role of Information and Communication Technology (ICT) in improving the quality of the learning environment. Several initiatives emerged at SUZA through Centre for ICT services to boost ICT capacity and effective utilization in teaching and learning. The centre for ICT services engaged in several initiatives including building and maintaining a robust infrastructure to support student learning. Among the recent measures that took place at university include the increase internet bandwidth, equipping computer labs, establishment of e-library, LMS (Moodle), and ICT policy.

In 2014, SUZA with support from Build Stronger University (BSU) II project through work package 3 (ICT in Education) embarked on an activity "Pilot Implementation of e-modules through LMS for selected courses". The courses selected in this implementation are shown in Sect. 3.1. The participants of this activity were students enrolled in the courses and instructors who are teaching the courses. However due to various infrastructural challenges not all students were accessing the developed e-modules. Thus, this pilot study involved the students who were using the e-module in academic year 2016/2017 in different semesters.

2 Methodology

The main aim of this research is to investigate the perceptions of using LMS as pedagogical tool among students and instructors at SUZA, with a specific focus on teaching practice as manifest when using systems. Focus group discussions and semi-structured interviews were used as data collection tool for this study. The interviews contained both open and closed-ended questions. Later, the participants were interviewed to gather their perceptions on using LMS for their teaching and learning activities.

2.1 Sample and Sampling Techniques

Currently, SUZA has seven campuses in Unguja and Pemba islands. The study was conducted between March 2016 to March 2017 in three SUZA campuses Tunguu, Vuga and Nkrumah before the merging of other institutions. Random sample technique was used to select a number of students and instructors at university. Eight courses were selected as indicated in Sect. 3.1. Instructors were trained on how to upload course materials to the LMS platform. They then trained students on how to use the Moodle such as downloading materials, participating in online discussions, and quizzes. A total of 10 instructors and 431 Diploma and Bachelor degree students participated in the survey. The questionnaires were designed and integrated into each course to assess levels of students and instructors' satisfaction with the LMS.

3 Results and Discussion

3.1 Profile of the Participants

Table 1 shows the demographic information of students' participants. A total of 431 Diploma and Bachelor students (first year, second year and third year) participated. More than half (50.3%) of the participants were male and 49.7% female. The participants were of different ages. The majority of them, (66.1%) were aged between 21 to 25 years. Most of the participants, were the second year students (79.1%), followed by first year students (13%), and third year students comprised 7.9% of the participants. The participants were selected from nine programme as shown in Table 1.

Table 1. Demographic information of student participants (n = 431)

Parameter	n (%)
Gender	
Male	217 (50.5)
Female	214 (49.7)
Age	
16–20	7 (1.6)
21–25	285 (66.1)
26–30	85 (19.7)
31–35	37 (8.6)
36–40	15 (3.5)
40+	2 (0.5)
Year of Study	
First Year	56 (13)
Second Year	341 (79.1)
Third Year	34 (7.9)
Study Programme	
Bachelor of Science in Education (BSE)	64 (14.8)
Bachelor of Art in Education (BAE)	161 (37.4)
Bachelor of Art in Kiswahili and English (BAKE)	23 (5.3)
Bachelor of Medicine (MD)	62 (14.4)
Bachelor of Science in Computer Science (BSc. SC)	10 (2.3)
Diploma in Information Technology (DIT)	54 (12.5)
Diploma in Computer Science (DCS)	6 (1.4)
Bachelor of Information Technology with Education (BITED)	14 (3.2)
Bachelor of Science in Environmental Health (BSc. EH)	37 (8.6)
Campus	
Tunguu	262 (60.8)
Nkurumah	105 (24.4)
Vuga	64 (14.8)

Table 2 shows the demographic information of instructor participants. Ten (10) instructors participated in this study, where 70% were males and 30% females. The Instructor participants were of four different groups of age, between 36–40 (30%), age greater than 40 (30%), between 31–35 (20%) and age between 26–30 (20%). Furthermore, the instructors were taught different level of education as shown in Table 2.

Table 2. Demographic information of instructor participants (n = 10)

Parameter	n (%)
Gender	
Male	7 (70)
Female	3 (30)
Age	
26–30	2 (20)
31–35	2 (20)
36–40	3 (30)
40+	3 (30)
Department	
Education	4 (40)
Science	1 (10)
Computer and IT	4 (40)
Social science	1 (10)
Level taught	
Degree	5 (50)
Diploma	2 (20)
Both	3 (30)

Students from different programmes were allocated to various courses which they are registered for pilot implementation. There were eight courses involved in the study of the LMS and number of students participated in the bracket as follows: DS 1101-Development Studies (47), CL 1101 Communication Skills (38), ED 1201-Educational Psychology (5), ED 2103-Educational Resources, Media and Technology (262), CS 0119-Interactive Website Development (60), CS 3106-Distributed System (10), EH 1204-Sociology of Health and Illness (17), and EH 2111-Waste and Waste Management (18).

3.2 Frequently Utilized LMS Features

LMS Moodle contained different features such as quiz, forum, file and video uploader, multiple media, resources, enabling alternative technologies, and presenting information in an organized manner to fulfill its main purpose, which is the construction of learning through interaction.

Figures 1 and 2 show various activities performed by participants while accessing the Moodle. Figure 1 shows activities performed by students which depict that downloading of Power point lecture materials was a major activity when students interacted with the Moodle. This is because downloading materials was convenient for the majority of them since they do not have internet access at their homes.

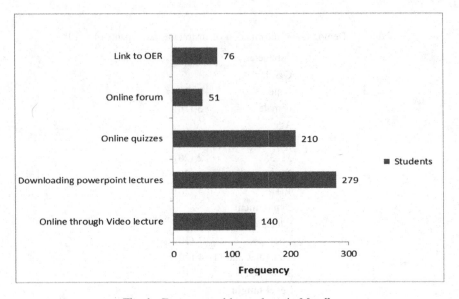

Fig. 1. Features used by students in Moodle

Figure 2 shows activities performed by instructors. On the hand, it is revealed that most of the instructors used the LMS for uploading Power point lectures, uploading online video lectures and post online assignments, as indicated in Fig. 2.

The data in Figs. 1 and 2 further reveal that 'share simulation' and 'uploading Power point with speak' were the activities that performed less by instructors while link to external online quiz found no one was using among instructors. Additionally, both figures show that instructors applied many features compared to students this is because the instructors are major actors of the module who create learning activities to students.

3.3   Perceptions on the Use of LMS Platform

The participants were given several LMS aspects to identify their perceptions as shown in the Table 3. Some of these aspects were directed to both students and instructors and others were directed to either students or instructors. The results indicated that 70% of instructors and 44.4% of students indicated that they preferred the LMS to the tradi-tional way of teaching and learning. However, 30.4% of student neither agree nor disagree. This finding therefore show that students learning is better supported by LMS indicating interest in digital learning. Concerning the availability of LMS, 55.5% of instructors and 46.8% of students agreed that the LMS was available. Regarding

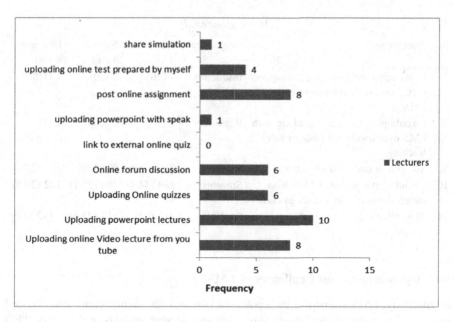

Fig. 2. Features used by instructors in Moodle

accessibility of LMS in ICT devices (laptop, smartphone), 90% of instructors and 47.3% of students' report that it was accessible. Moreover, 70% of students and 37.7% of instructors responded that they had adequately technical support during the use of LMS. Other aspects are illustrated in Table 3.

Table 3. Instructors' and students' perceptions on the use of LMS for teaching and learning

No	Perceptions	Respondents	Agree n (%)	Neutral n (%)	Disagree n (%)
1.	I have adequately technical support during the use LMS	Instructors	7 (70)	2 (20)	1 (10)
		Students	157 (37.5)	135 (30.4)	125 (30)
2.	The Learning Management System was accessible through any ICT device (Desktop, laptop, tablet)	Instructors	9 (90)	1 (10)	0 (0)
		Students	195 (47.3)	90 (21.6)	130 (31.2)
3.	Availability of learning materials in the LMS was 24/7	Instructors	5 (55.5)	2 (22.2)	2 (22.2)
		Students	194 (46.8)	139 (33.5)	82 (19.8)
4.	LMS is too complicated for teaching and learning	Instructors	1 (10)	1 (10)	8 (80)
		Students	134 (32.2)	133 (32)	148 (35.7)
5.	The learning materials delivered through LMS were relevant to this course	Instructors	10 (100)	0 (0)	0 (0)
		Students	143 (34.4)	244 (58.7)	29 (6.5)
6.	The participation of students in my course was very low in LMS than in the classroom	Instructors	2 (20)	4 (40)	4 (40)

(continued)

Table 3. (*continued*)

No	Perceptions	Respondents	Agree n (%)	Neutral n (%)	Disagree n (%)
7.	I have adequately pedagogical support during course development within LMS	Instructors	7 (70)	2 (20)	1 (10)
8.	I would prefer blended teaching with LMS over traditional (face to face) teaching	Instructors	7 (70)	2 (20)	1 (10)
9.	The course had clear objectives	Students	274 (65.4)	92 (22)	53 (12.7)
10.	I would have preferred LMS than taking down my own notes in class	Students	184 (44.4)	108 (26.1)	122 (29.4)
11.	The online quiz and assignments were graded fairly	Students	215 (52)	114 (27.6)	84 (20.3)

3.4   Opportunities and Challenges of LMS

In this study, LMS seemed to be a potential platform for strengthening teaching and learning. For example, the finding show that second year students in the course "ED 2103" participated well in the LMS to perform learning activities. Therefore, the results indicated that when the instructor committed to use LMS consequently the students will be engaged to frequently use online learning activities. On the hand, several challenges were reported by both students and instructors while using the LMS. These include challenges related to both software and hardware. The most challenge reported was internet connection, including slowness on internet, network failure, unavailability of WiFi in some days and poor internet access at the campuses.

Internet Connectivity at Campus. For example, student A1 stated that "*Sometimes make hard time for us to interact with LMS because of network*". And instructor B1 stated that "*Lack of resources such as internet lead student to not accessing LMS*".

Cost Effectiveness. Another challenge reported by participants was cost effective. This incurs the cost of downloading the materials from LMS. This challenge particularly reported by students, they said that always they need internet connection while at home to perform activities related to LMS such downloading any task posted by instructor. The majority of them said that they don't afford to buy data bundle for the internet services.

Devices. Inadequate number of ICT devices like computers or laptops was also mentioned as challenge faced participants while using the LMS. This is supported by the following statement from instructor B2 "*The big problem of implementing LMS is infrastructure in terms of networking, shortage of lab as well as shortage of learning devices such as computer, ipad, etc.*".

Time Consuming. Move over, some of students mentioned that LMS is time consuming. They claim that they had limited time to access computer labs for LMS system whilst the most of them had no laptop computers or smartphone that support LMS.

For example, student A2 stated that *"This e-learning system seems good for us and helpful, but the challenge is that some of us don't have smart phone or laptop and labs are always full"*.

Integration of LMS vs Students' Information System. Integration of LMS and other University's system such as students' information system (zalongwa) was another challenge mentioned faced the LMS systems. The participants raised that after register to the zalongwa they have to register again in LMS in order to get access to services.

Limited Availability of Technical Support. Another challenge raised by both instructors and students was technical support. The participants mentioned that they get minimal technical support on the using LMS. For example, one of the students, student A3 stated that *"The system produce error on php to the students when using after sometime"*. Thus, most of participants suggested that long time training is needed on how to use the LMS features before it deployment.

3.5 Participants Views, Opinions and Recommendations

The participants shared their views on improving the use of LMS for teaching and learning at SUZA. Their responses were directly related to LMS and ICT infrastructures that support the implementation of the LMS. These include availability of the internet and supportive staff. The participants suggested that the internet connection should be available at all time and with high speed, and the University should allocate staff who specifically available for providing support to LMS.

Another suggestion was about a number of computers available at University. The participants suggested that the computers are not adequate to be used for all students at University, thus the University should increase a number of computers to be available for LMS system. Once the computers adequately settled, training on how to use the Moodle and LMS in general should be provided to all instructors and students.

The integration of zalongwa and LMS was also suggestion provided by the participants in order to improve the LMS system. They recommended that once student registered to zalongwa system, it should then automatically grant the access to LMS system without ask students to register again.

Literature suggests that students are increasing using different forms of digital technologies to support their learning [2, 3, 6], however in many developing countries there are a number of challenges associated with perceptions, adoption, and technical infrastructure.

4 Conclusion

Learning management systems (LMS) have been widely used in higher education for enhancing traditional classroom teaching. This study found number of opportunities and challenges associated with the implementation of LMS at SUZA as one of the university in developing countries. Although, SUZA is in the process of deploying the LMS to entire University, the findings of this study indicated that there is need to integrate the Moodle into every course provided by the University in order to easily support pedagogical activities. However, to do this successfully, the University has to strengthen ICT infrastructure. The findings clear show that almost half of the participants have keen interest and are willing and believe in the power of the LMS to effectively support their teaching and learning. Although the students who participated in this study showed their willingness to use the Moodle, the findings demonstrated that the overall participation of students was low compared to the total number of students who registered a particular course. The participants proposed that strengthening the ICT infrastructures like computers lab with internet connections, stable power supply and reliable internet will afford them the opportunity to utilize LMS in teaching and learning effectively. Both students and instructors believe that once infrastructural challenges were taken care of, the Moodle can be easily integrated into all programmes and courses at SUZA as a results it will raise student's performance.

The main contribution of this paper is related to the administration of e-learning platform. In order to successful LMS operate, needs dedicated administrator and technical support. The implementation of LMS necessitates reliable internet and enough computers especially when you have large number of students. It is also worthy for remote learning environment.

The findings of this study indicate some research opportunities that can be developed, seeking to fill the gaps identified by this study. The implications for the LMS in pedagogy cannot be weighted unless there is a research agenda.

Acknowledgement. We would like to express our sincere appreciation to the DANIDA through BSU II project for funding this pilot study and all participants from the State University of Zanzibar who contributed in one way or another to the work embodied in this project.

References

1. Mtebe, J.S.: Learning management system success: increasing learning management system usage in higher education in sub-Saharan. Afr. Int. J. Educ. Dev. Inf. Commun. Technol. (IJEDICT) **11**(2), 51–64 (2015)
2. Bernard, R.M., et al.: A meta-analysis of three interaction treatments in distance education. Rev. Educ. Res. **79**(3), 1243–1289 (2009)
3. Black, E.W., et al.: The other side of the LMS: considering implementation and use in the adoption of an LMS in online and blended learning environments. TechTrends **51**(2), 35–41 (2007)
4. Suleman, H.: Flipping a course on computer architecture. In: Gruner, S. (ed.) SACLA 2016. CCIS, vol. 642, pp. 83–94. Springer, Cham (2016). https://doi.org/10.1007/978-3-319-47680-3_8
5. Becker, W.E., Watts, M.: Chalk and talk: a national survey on teaching undergraduate economics. Am. Econ. Rev. **86**(2), 448–453 (1996). http://www.jstor.org/stable/2118168
6. Lage, M.J., Platt, G.J., Treglia, M.: Inverting the classroom: a gateway to creating an inclusive learning environment. J. Econ. Educ. **31**(1), 30–43 (2000). https://doi.org/10.2307/1183338

Secure Exchanges Activity in Function of Event Detection with the SDN

Salim Mahamat Charfadine[(✉)], Olivier Flauzac, Florent Nolot,
Cyril Rabat, and Carlos Gonzalez

Université de Reims Champagne-Ardenne, Laboratoire CReSTIC, Reims, France
{salim.mahamat-charfadine,
carlos.gonzalez-santamaria}@etudiant.univ-reims.fr,
{olivier.flauzac,florent.nolot,cyril.rabat}@univ-reims.fr

Abstract. With the exponential evolution of the Internet of Things (IoT), ensuring network security has become a big challenge for network administrators. Network security is based on multiple independent devices such as firewall, IDS/IPS, NAC where the main role is to monitor the information exchanged between the inside and outside perimeters of the enterprises networks. However, the administration of these network devices can be complex and tedious if it is performed independently on each of them. In recent years, with the introduction of the Software Defined Networking concept (SDN) offers many opportunities by providing a centralized and programmable administration. In this article, we propose a distributed SDN architecture for IoT with a coupled controllers/IDS, by using APIs to dynamically analyze, detect and delete malicious flows. The management of network security is therefore simplified, dynamic and scalable with this approach. We also present the deployment of a real network to test our solution.

Keywords: IoT · SDN · Security · OpenFlow · Firewall · IPS/IDS · NAC

1 Introduction

With the emergence of a large variety of internet-connected devices which are used in many areas of everyday life, such as health, education, economy, transport and military, it raises new challenges related to the network security management and monitoring a high network traffic of end-users communication.

Nowadays, the most networks security systems are commonly based on traditional techniques such as firewall, intrusion detection system (IDS), intrusion prevention system (IPS) and network access control (NAC). These mechanisms are difficult to manage and need to evolve toward the next network generation architectures [1].

To simplify the management and to secure network traffic exchanges, the new concept of SDN was introduced in 2011. This technology has many and varied

G. Mendy et al. (Eds.): AFRICOMM 2018, LNICST 275, pp. 315–324, 2019.
https://doi.org/10.1007/978-3-030-16042-5_28

advantages presented in [2]. The SDN is a new approach for network architecture which consists in decoupling the control plane from the data plane[1,2], allowing the centralization of all control functions on an external node which is called SDN controller. The controller implements forwarding flow rules and it may be installed on one machine or several physical or virtual machines. It exists several types of SDN controllers such as ONOS[3], OpenDayLight[4], POX[5], RYU[6] and so on. Their fundamental differences are related to the programming language and the southbound supported protocol. For example, the OpenDayLight (ODL) controller that we use in our testbed platform, is designed in Java and Python including REST services.

OpenFlow is a standard protocol[7] that allows the communication between the SDN controller and network devices (switches, routers, etc.). The message exchanges are encrypted by the SSL protocol. OpenFlow protocol has the ability over the SDN controller to access and manipulate [3] forwarding rules of packets installed on an OpenFlow switch. ODL supports the OpenFlow version 1.3.

The enthusiasm of the principal technology companies such as Google and Microsoft [4,5] in the deployment of SDN at their datacenters create many opportunities for this new concept which can become a reality. Moreover, it has become an open solution and is begin to be generalized in small infrastructures.

However, IoT involves new challenges. The number of devices is greater, resulting in an increase of flows rules, security menaces and the overload on the controller. Classical architectures must therefore be adapted to take those issues into account. In this article, we propose a decentralized solution based on SDN controllers coupled with IDS. In a domain that we call a cluster, each network OpenFlow device is connected to a SDN controller. The IDS allows to monitor the flow of a cluster and, by communicating with the controller via the REST API, to block the malicious flows. In this case, it reduces the overload of the controller.

In order to analyze our solution, we deployed an architecture in a real test environment based on virtual machines. Thus, instead of using simulators or emulators, we can analyze our solution in a real case of use and highlight monitor OpenFlow messages exchanged.

In the next section, we present a state of the art on network security with SDN. Then, we propose our security approach that allows to detect and isolate a flow of malicious packets dynamically with the SDN concept. Finally we conclude by including some ideas for our perspectives of future works.

---

[1] https://www.opennetworking.org/sdn-resources/sdn-definition.

[2] https://www.opennetworking.org/sdn-resources/openflow.

[3] http://www.onosproject.org.

[4] https://www.opendaylight.org/.

[5] https://openflow.stanford.edu/display/ONL/POX+Wiki.

[6] https://osrg.github.io/ryu/.

[7] https://www.opennetworking.org/sdn-resources/openflow.

2   State of the Art

To secure a network, we have two main directions: The first option includes the use of the traditional solution based on specific security components (like firewall, IPS, IDS, etc.) and the second one uses the SDN architecture. Previously, we describe that the SDN simplifies the network management with a centralized global view allowing to program the security thanks to the different APIs provided by the controllers.

Software Defined Networking (SDN). To illustrate the operational principle of SDN, we propose a simple network with two hosts h1 and h2 connected through a switch managed by an ODL controller. Figure 1 shows the different phases of an ICMP packet exchanged between h1 and h2. First, the ICMP packet is sent to the switch (1) and it is transmitted to the controller (2). The controller analyses the ICMP packet and installs the flow on the switch (3). h2 receives the ICMP packet (4). Finally, the flow is installed and h1 can exchange ICMP packets with h2 (5).

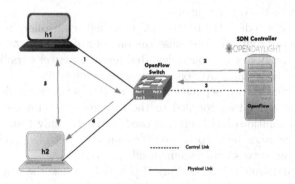

Fig. 1. Flow exchange in an OpenFlow network

When a flow rule is installed on the switch, the controller will not be contacted again to install the same flow. In this case if h1 or h2 are compromised, all the network security become vulnerable.

SDN and the Networks Security. In [6], the authors propose a level 2 centralized firewall based on MAC address filter and the SDN POX controller. But, the network attacks are more and more sophisticated, this kind of detection is not suitable. The authors in [7] describe a firewall application based on layers 2 to 4. They analyze network traffic and compare the packets headers received according to predefined rules. If the application detect a threat the packet is deleted, otherwise it is transferred to its destination. In these two works, the SDN controller is central point of detection. However, the centralization with only one controller is a critical point failure: if the controller is attacked and if an attacker takes its control, the security of the whole network is compromised.

In addition, if there are a large volume of traffic the controller will have an over-load resources. The controller is no longer enough available to perform security and the analysis of network traffic.

In this context, in [8], the authors propose to deploy an SDN infrastructure with a single controller. The study overview the impacts of OpenFlow related to flow processing on communications latency. Using the Mininet network simulator and implementing ICMP traffic, they can verify that the filtered rules of the firewall reach the controller. Even though, the latency can increase due to a bottleneck using a single controller. The use of Mininet reflects only a part of the variability of a real network traffic which involve a large number of OpenFlow rules.

To improve this fact, Flauzac *et al.* propose in [9] a solution based on several controllers with the possibility to organize them into domains. The aim is to distribute the control network in multiple controllers. An other solution based on this architecture is described in [10]. The authors propose the use of several NOX controllers coupled to Hyperflow. Hyperflow is an application that allows the propagation of events detected by a controller to the neighbors controllers. Also, the proposed solution helps the management of a controller failure, redirecting the flows traffic to the other controllers.

Theses solutions reduce the bottleneck on a single controller, but the division into domains is not dynamical because the number of components increase and reduces the efficiency of each controller. Redirect the network traffic impacts on the network and controllers overload, increasing the latency.

A solution consists on separate a part of the network traffic analysis by using another security tool coupled to the controller: for instance, an IDS or an IPS. Several solutions has been proposed in [11–13] only tested on Mininet. Furthermore, the rules need to be specified on the controller and on the IDS which difficult the network management effectively.

To improve dynamicity, the authors of [14] and [15] use the machine learning and deep learning concepts coupled to the IDS. The neural network as well as known datasets, they show that their solution could have good performances in most of the environment test. However, a global architecture based on alerts detection linked to the SDN controller has not been proposed. Also, it may be difficult to adapt with several neural networks.

SDN and IoT. The authors in [16], provides a current status overview of the IoT networks as well as the security challenges such as object identification, privacy, integrity, authentication, authorization, and malicious software threats. Also, they propose a security architecture with an SDN-based security mechanism where an IoT controller exchanges messages with the IoT agents. The IoT controller is responsible for the transfer decisions based on information received from the IoT agents and then send the network policies rules through the SDN controller. Upon receiving the connection request from an IoT agent, the IoT controller establish the forwarding rules based on network protocols and communicate these rules to the SDN controller.

Bull *et al.* [17] provides a method to detect and mitigate the suspicious activity of a connected devices from an SDN-based IoT gateway. The IoT gateway has flows entries pre-installed to allow flow traffic analysis, detecting any suspicious behavior and it can associate to many actions. Three types of action have been defined: block, transfer or apply QoS rules. The issue of this proposed solution is the static configuration of the rules on the IoT gateway.

In [18], the authors propose a distributed security architecture for IoT by using the SDN architecture. Their solution secure the traffic monitoring of the entire network and the high availability with several SDN controllers synchronized and organized into domains. They also propose a multi-domain routing protocol in an SDN framework to secure the integrity of messages exchanges between the controllers with the different domains. Although, this solution has the advantage of a tested virtual environment. However, it does not have an intrusion detection system. Threats from inside/outside perimeter of the network could compromise the security management.

3   Collaborative Solution for Securing Network Exchanges

Our solution is inspired by the concept of grid of security [1] and the smart firewall approach [19] to improve security in a traditional network and extend these proposed solutions to IoT. In this approach, we propose a collaborative security solution with a distributed controller architecture coupled with an IDS as shown on Fig. 2. We divide the network into clusters. A cluster is a SDN-domain that use OpenFlow protocol for communication between the networking devices with the SDN controller, and an IDS to manage the security on domain which we call the trusted zone.

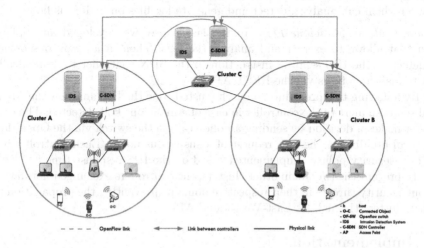

Fig. 2. Our SDN distributed cluster-based architecture

As we described previously, once a flow request is installed on an Openflow switch, the controller do not receives another request for the same forwarding rules which exposes the network to threats in case of compromise devices. Figure 3 shown how to proceed in three phases to solve this problem.

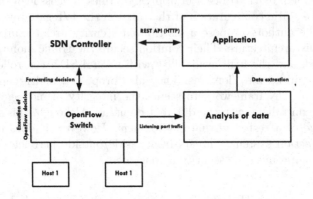

Fig. 3. Theoretical model of the approach

Network Data Collection. During this first phase, we collect the data to be analyzed and find a mechanism to take control over all of the data. For this, we use the port mirroring technique to track all network traffic flow through a particular port which is constantly analyzed.

Analysis, Detection and Generation of Alerts in Case of Threat. The second phase consists of analysis and detection of a threat, followed by generation of an alert in a directory of files logs. To realize this step, we use an intrusion detector system which can analyze, detect and generate log files on malicious flow.

Removal of the Malicious Flow. In the last phase, we developed an application that allows to extract and analyze the logs. Then, if a suspicious device is detected, the IDS send an instruction to the SDN controller to dynamically delete malicious flows via the REST API.

By following this procedure, on each trusted zone the IDS analyzes the traffic and sends an alert to the controller in case of a malicious flow detected. The controller makes a decision by sending a policy rule to the switch via the OpenFlow protocol prohibiting the flow request of a suspicious nodes. Each controller has its own security policies implemented based on the IDS response time.

To prevent the threats in other clusters, the controllers exchange information about security threats in their respective domains preventing the propagation to other clusters through its East-Westbound API.

4   Implementation

In this part, we explain the implementation of a network management by an OpenDaylight controller and a Snort IDS.

Installation of OpenDayLight. The OpenDayLight Controller is an open source network operating system developed in Java and supported by the Linux Foundation. It is based on a modular architecture and can be programmed via applications using the SDN northbound APIs. OpendayLight communicates with network devices using southbound APIs. The most common southbound protocol used in SDN environment is OpenFlow.

To make forwarding decision at the level 2/3 of the OSI model, the OpenDayLight controller knows the network topology as well as the identity of each devices connected with their IP and MAC addresses. The flow on the OVS switch are set up with OpenFlow 1.3 version in order to manage and update the entire network.

For test purpose we have installed a virtual machine on a VMware platform with 2 CPU, 16 GB of RAM and the OS Ubuntu 16.04. The SDN controller installed on this machine is the OpenDayLight Beryllium-SR4.

Architecture Implementation. In the literature many tested solution uses the mininet network simulator. We use virtualization in a production environment with VMvare platform in order to test real case of use.

To realize our virtual network architecture, a second virtual machine is set up with Ubuntu 16.04 OS, 2 virtual CPUs and 16 GB of RAM. On this machine, we installed an OpenFlow 1.3 compatible virtual switch (OVS version 2.6.0) and Qemu, an open source virtual machine emulator for x86 architecture.

The OVS is an open source software implementation of an Ethernet switch with a multilayered and distributed system. It is designed to support level 2/3 of the OSI model switch in virtual environments including different protocols and standards. In our work, it allows the communication between the end-point devices. Qemu is used to emulate the end-point devices with an Alpine Linux OS, a lightweight Linux distribution with 48 MB of RAM.

A bash script is developed to launch several virtual end-point devices with the ability to remotely manage each one of them. The same script is used to launch the OVS interconnecting Alpine Linux virtual machines with each other. This allows us to create the link between the OpenFlow switch and the OpenDaylight controller allowing the control of whole network with OpenFlow protocol. Also, a dynamic IPv4 address assignment with DHCP is perform by the same code to each device. On our set up OpenFlow network we have the ability to scale the number of nodes and the OVS dynamically.

Snort Setting Up. In order to detect the threats, we used a Snort IDS. It's an open source network intrusion detection software that allows to analyze IP network traffic in real time and to detect a wide variety of attacks (e.g. port scan) with the ability to analyze protocols and search the content of matching rules.

In this study, we used Snort in NIDS mode, suitable for monitoring multiple network interfaces. In this mode, Snort acts as a network intrusion detector by analyzing network traffic and comparing this traffic with rules set up by the network administrator.

To deploy Snort, we use a centralized architecture with an IDS which monitors the network traffic on a particular port. Then with a mirroring port technique all the ports traffic of the network is forward to a particular port that is constantly analyzed. This centralized architecture with Snort presents the advantage of a simple implementation, but the disadvantage is bottlenecks in the event to perform scalable networks.

The integration of snort 2.9.11 into the our network platform, a third virtual machine is set up with an Ubuntu 16.04 OS, 2 virtual CPU and 16 GB of RAM. Figure 2 shows the integration of snort in our testbed platform.

After setting up Snort, we defined some non-exhaustive rules for generating logs for any ICMP request queries such as echo request and echo reply, port scan and source or MAC IP address spoofing. The alert data generated by Snort are saved in a log file.

To simulate an attack and evaluate the Snort detection, we installed the Nmap tool on one of the client virtual machine device. Then, we launch many successive denial of service attacks, port scans and an IP address spoofing from the attacker machine. The simulated attack scenarios to observe the reaction of our solution are described as follow:

Service Denial. At this step the aim is to detect and block attempts to saturate a target machine with DDoS attacks with the ICMP protocol. We proceeded by sending ICMP requests to a target machine in our network and determine if Snort reacted by detecting malicious flows.

Port Scan. In this case, the IDS detects any port scan attempts on the TCP or UDP protocols and it can block these requests from the source machine. If an attacker launches a scan to identify open ports and available services on the network, the snort IDS can detected this attack attempt.

IP or MAC Address Spoofing. With this kind of attack an attacker attempts to spoof a legitimate MAC or IP address in order to send packets to the network. A replication of MAC or IP address the systems believe that the source address is trustworthy.

We notice that Snort detected all kind of attacks performed and saved the information into logs files. This procedure can be extended to other types of threats more complex and intelligent.

Linking Snort with OpenDayLight. After setting up the network managed by an OpenDaylight controller and then integrate snort to monitor the network, we developed an application that allows the extraction and the analysis of information on logs generated by Snort. Then, it sends via the REST API a security rule to the OpenDaylight controller in order to uninstall a the malicious flow. REST API is used by the most SDN controllers to exchange network information with applications. To support the REST API, we added the *odl-restconf* feature at the start up of the OpenDaylight controller.

Our developed application exchanges information with the OpenDaylight controller through the REST API to isolate the source machine by executing a shutdown on the port at the origin of the threat.

Figure 4 shows the integration of snort and the OpenDaylight controller on an SDN network.

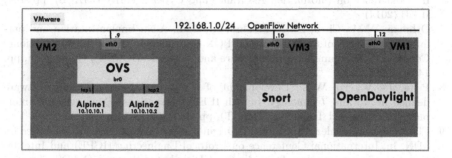

Fig. 4. Snort and OpenDaylight integration model

5 Conclusion

Traditional network security techniques based on independent network devices such as firewall, IPS/IDS and NAC are no longer enough to secure the needs of future networks architecture, especially the IoT. For this reason, we propose a new distributed security solution based on an automated threat analysis, detection and removal managed by the SDN concept. The SDN-based solution and the threat detection system provides the ability to manage security of a network based on events detection.

Nowadays, our solution is tested to secure traditional networks and future works it would be extended to verify the real behaviours performance of IoT devices. In perspective, the set up of a scalable network with several end-point devices will allow us to analysis the reaction time of our proposed solution. Finally, we focus experiments on a single cluster. We plain to monitor the communication between clusters and if it can be achieved by using the controller integrating SDN features.

References

1. Flauzac, O., Nolot, F., Rabat, C., Steffenel, L.A.: Grid of security: a new approach of the network security. In: 3rd International Conference on Network and System Security (NSS 2009), October 2009, Gold Coast, Australia, pp. 67–72 (2009)
2. Sezer, S., et al.: Are we ready for SDN? implementation challenges for software-defined networks. IEEE Commun. Mag. **51**(7), 36–43 (2013)
3. Lara, A., Kolasani, A., Ramamurthy, B.: Network innovation using OpenFlow: a survey. IEEE Commun. Surv. **16**, 493–512 (2014)
4. Wang, S., Li, D., Xia, S.: The problems and solutions of network update in SDN: a survey. In: IEEE Conference on Computer Communications Workshops (INFO-COM WKSHPS), pp. 474–479 (2015)

5. Hu, F., Hao, Q., Bao, K.: A survey on software-defined network and OpenFlow: from concept to implementation. IEEE Commun. Surv. **16**, 2181–2206 (2014)

6. Javid, T., Riaz, T., Rasheed, A.: A layer2 firewall for software defined network. In: Conference on Information Assurance and Cyber Security (CIACS), pp. 1–4. IEEE (2014)

7. Othman, W.M., Chen, H., Al-Moalmi, A., Hadi, A.N.: Implementation and performance analysis of SDN firewall on POX controller. In: IEEE 9th International Conference on Communication Software and Networks (ICCSN), Guangzhou, pp. 1461–1466 (2017)

8. Pena, J.G.V., Yu, W.E.: Development of a distributed firewall using software defined networking technology. In: 4th IEEE International Conference on Information Science and Technology (ICIST), pp. 449–452 (2014)

9. Flauzac, O., Gonzalez, C., Nolot, F.: Original secure architecture for IoT based on SDN. In: International Conference on Protocol Engineering (ICPE) and International Conference on New Technologies of Distributed Systems (NTDS), pp. 1–6 (2015)

10. Tootoonchian, A., Ganjali, Y.: HyperFlow: a distributed control plane for Open-Flow. In: Proceedings of the 2010 Internet Network Management Conference on Research on Enterprise Networking, vol. 103, pp. 3–3 (2010)

11. Jeong, C., Ha, T., Narantuya, J., Lim, H., Kim, J.: Scalable network intrusion detection on virtual SDN environment. In: IEEE 3rd International Conference on Cloud Networking (CloudNet), pp. 264–265 (2014)

12. Sayeed, M.A., Sayeed, M.A., Saxena, S.: Intrusion detection system based on Software Defined Network firewall. In: 1st International Conference on Next Generation Computing Technologies (NGCT), pp. 379–382 (2015)

13. Chen, P.J., Chen, Y.W.: Implementation of SDN based network intrusion detection and prevention system. In: International Carnahan Conference on Security Technology (ICCST), pp 141–146 (2015)

14. Abubakar, A., Pranggono, B.: Machine learning based intrusion detection system for software defined networks. In: Seventh International Conference on Emerging Security Technologies (EST), pp. 138–143 (2017)

15. Tang, T.A., Mhamdi, L., McLernon, D., Zaidi, S.A.R., Ghogho, M.: Deep learning approach for Network Intrusion Detection in Software Defined Networking. In: International Conference on Wireless Networks and Mobile Communications (WINCOM), Fez, pp. 258–263 (2016)

16. Vandana, C.P.: Security improvement in IoT based on Software defined networking. Int. J. Sci. Eng. Technol. Res. (IJSETR) **5**(1), 2327–4662 (2016)

17. Bull, P., Austin, R., Popov, E., Sharma, M., Watson, R.: Flow based security for IoT devices using an SDN gateway. In: IEEE 4th International Conference on Future Internet of Things and Cloud (FiCloud), Vienna, pp. 157–163 (2016)

18. Gonzalez, C., Flauzac, O., Nolot, F., Jara, A.: A novel distributed SDN-secured architecture for the IoT. In: International Conference on Distributed Computing in Sensor Systems (DCOSS), Washington, DC, pp. 244–249 (2016)

19. Gonzalez, C., Charfadine, S.M., Flauzac, O., Nolot, F.: SDN-based security framework for the IoT in distributed grid. In: International Multidisciplinary Conference on Computer and Energy Science (SpliTech), Split, pp. 1–5 (2016)

Author Index